Certified Wireless Security Professional
Official Study Guide

(CWSP-205)
Second Edition

Certified Wireless Network Professional

Second printing December 2016

ISBN: 978-0-9971607-2-7

Technical Editors

Tom Carpenter

Daniel Koczwara

Copy Editors

CWNP Staff

Production Supervisor

Josie Miller

Authors

Lee Badman

Robert Bartz

Project Manager

Brad Crump

Blog Contributors

Dale Rapp

Lee Badman

Devin Akin

Andrew von Nagy

Rasika Navanajith

Sam Clements

Jake Snyder

Chris Lyttle

Introduction

Security is important for the simple reason that information is valuable. If information shared on networks had no value, you could leave all networks open and never give a second thought to security. However, in the world we live in hardly a week goes by without some significant network breach and theft of information headlined in the media. Information is an important asset for both individual and business users.

As a security professional you must protect information at levels appropriate to the value of the asset. A fundamental principle in information security is that the cost of protection should not be greater than the value of the protected asset, and that the value of the asset must be determined as a lifetime value and not an acquisition value. However, in most cases, over time we tend to spend less to protect an asset than its actual lifetime value. This is because we must consider risk in the equation.

The good news for wireless administrators is that 802.11 WLANs can be secured at costs far below the value of the informational assets that we are typically protecting. Implementing the most secure WLAN solutions is typically accomplished for less than five to ten dollars per node, and the benefits of this security greatly exceed the costs. At the same time, wireless networks when compared to traditional wired networks face unique security challenges and require specialized knowledge and skill to properly secure them. In this book we will examine what makes wireless security unique and how wireless security fits in with overall network security.

This book is a study guide for the CWNP® certification of Certified Wireless Security Professional (CWSP®), and covers the topics addressed in exam CWSP-205.

The purpose of the CWSP exam is to prove your knowledge and real-world, critical-thinking skills related to security in 802.11 networks. As a professional-level exam on the CWNP certification path, CWSP requires that you also pass the CWNA® exam. After passing both exams, you will be a CWNA and CWSP-certified professional with documented proof that you possess important skills for administering and securing modern wireless networks.

CWSP-205 Exam Objectives

The CWSP-205 exam is organized into four knowledge domains as follows:

- Wireless Network Attacks and Threat Assessment—20%
- Security Policy—5%
- Wireless LAN Security Design and Architecture—50%
- Monitoring and Management—25%

This breakdown means that 20% of the questions on the exam are in the first knowledge domain, 5% in the second and so on. This means that the largest pool of questions come from the Wireless LAN Security Design and Architecture knowledge domain.

The following detailed objectives list should be used as your guide during exam preparation. All exam questions are written to the objectives.

CWSP-205 Objectives

1.0 Wireless Network Attacks and Threat Assessment—20%

1.1   Describe general network attacks common to wired and wireless networks, including DoS, phishing, protocol weaknesses, and configuration error exploits.

1.2   Recognize common attacks and describe their impact on WLANs, including PHY and MAC DoS, hijacking, unauthorized protocol analysis and eavesdropping, social engineering, man-in-the-middle, authentication and encryption cracks, and rogue hardware.

1.3   Execute the preventative measures required for common vulnerabilities on wireless infrastructure devices, including weak/default passwords on wireless infrastructure equipment and misconfiguration of wireless infrastructure devices by administrative staff.

1.4   Describe and perform risk analysis and risk mitigation procedures, including asset management, risk ratings, loss expectancy calculations, and risk management planning.

1.5   Explain and demonstrate the security vulnerabilities associated with public access or other unsecured wireless networks, including the use of a WLAN for spam transmission, malware injection, information theft, peer-to-peer attacks, and Internet attacks.

2.0 Security Policy—5%

2.1   Explain the purpose and goals of security policies, including password policies, acceptable use policies, WLAN access policies, personal device policies, device management (APs, infrastructure devices, and clients), and security awareness training for users and administrators.

2.2   Summarize the security policy criteria related to wireless public access network use, including user risks related to unsecured access and provider liability.

2.3   Describe how devices and technology used from outside an organization can impact the security of the corporate network, including topics like BYOD, social networking, and general MDM practices.

3.0 Wireless LAN Security Design and Architecture—50%

3.1   Describe how wireless network security solutions may vary for different wireless network implementations, including small businesses, home offices, large enterprises, public networks, and remote access.

3.2   Understand and explain 802.11 Authentication and Key Management (AKM) components and processes, including encryption keys, handshakes, and pre-shared key management.

3.3   Define and differentiate among the 802.11-defined secure networks, including pre-RSNA security, Transition Security Networks (TSN), and Robust Security Networks (RSN) and explain the relationship of these networks to terms including RSNA, WPA, and WPA2.

3.4   Identify the purpose and characteristics of IEEE 802.1X and EAP and the processes used, including EAP types (PEAP, EAP-TLS, EAP-TTLS, EAP-FAST and EAP-SIM), AAA servers (RADIUS), and certificate management.

3.5 Recognize and understand the common uses of VPNs in wireless networks, including remote access points, VPN client access, WLAN controllers, and cloud architectures.

3.6 Describe, demonstrate, and configure centrally managed client-side security applications, including VPN client software and policies, personal firewall software, mobile device management (MDM), and wireless client utility software.

3.7 Describe and demonstrate the use of secure infrastructure management protocols, including HTTPS, SNMP, secure FTP protocols, SCP, and SSH.

3.8 Explain the role, importance, and limiting factors of VLANs and network segmentation in an 802.11 WLAN infrastructure.

3.9 Understand additional security features in WLAN infrastructure and access devices, including management frame protection, Role-Based Access Control (RBAC), Fast BSS transition (pre-authentication and OKC), physical security methods, and Network Access Control (NAC).

3.10 Explain the purpose, methodology, features, and configuration of guest access networks and BYOD support, including segmentation, guest management, captive portal authentication, and device management

4.0 Monitoring, Management, and Tracking—25%

4.1 Explain the importance of ongoing WLAN monitoring and the necessary tools and processes used, as well as the importance of WLAN security audits, and compliance reports.

4.2 Understand how to use protocol and spectrum analyzers to effectively evaluate secure wireless networks, including 802.1X authentication troubleshooting, location of rogue security devices, and identification of noncompliant devices.

4.3 Understand the command features and components of Wireless Intrusion Prevention Systems (WIPS) and how they are used in relation to performance, protocol, spectrum, and security analysis.

4.4　Describe the different types of WLAN management systems and their features, including network discovery, configuration management, firmware management, audit management, policy enforcement, rogue detection, network monitoring, user monitoring, event alarms, and event notifications.

4.5　Describe and implement compliance monitoring, enforcement, and reporting. Topics include industry requirements, such as PCI-DSS and HIPAA, and general government regulations.

Target Audience

As an important note, this book is written for those preparing for the CWSP certification exam, and not as a general guide to all topics related to wireless networking. Collectively, the study of designing, securing, and supporting WLAN environments is far too wide-ranging to effectively cover in one book or with a single certification exam. This book is intended for the individual who already understands wireless networking from a functional perspective equivalent to the Certified Wireless Network Administrator (CWNA) certification. There is no in-depth review of basic 802.11 fundamentals in this text. If you are CWNA certified, then you are ready to begin exploring this book with the prerequisite background required for progressing towards CWSP. However, if you are not CWNA certified, you should have an equivalent knowledge of wireless networks before venturing further.

 Note:　Throughout this book, the term "802.11" is used to reference Institute of Electrical and Electronics Engineers (IEEE) 802.11. The acronym IEEE is not used each time to allow for faster reading.

Acknowledgements for Content

Finally, we at CWNP would like to thank the following individuals for assisting us in the production of this resource. They provided valuable content that greatly improved the book to help CWSP students and security professionals everywhere.

Major Content Contributors

Lee Badman contributed significant content and provided editing expertise for the most recent version of this book. As a long-time wireless network professional, classroom instructor, and technical writer, his work can be seen in the networks he has designed and currently supports at dozens of sites internationally, and in the hundreds of articles he has published for several online periodicals. A number of current industry professionals have participated as students in his network classes at the private university where Lee is an adjunct faculty member. Learn more about his professional activities at wirednot.net.

Robert Bartz, of Eight-O-Two Technology Solutions, assisted in the creation and editing of a significant portion of this material. His years of experience in teaching CWSP classes and real-world experience brought a wealth of knowledge and insight to the project. To learn more about Robert and his training and consulting services, which are continually rated among the highest in the industry, visit his website at eightotwo.com.

Tom Carpenter provided the technical editing efforts for the book and significant content as well. Tom is the author of several books on wireless networking, server administration, converged networking, and other IT topics. He is the CTO at CWNP, and provides direction and guidance in the development of new certifications and updates to existing certifications. Learn more about Tom's thoughts at tomcarpenter.net.

Daniel Koczwara is a Senior Field Application Engineer at EnGenius Technologies where he has done technical writing and technical training, product testing and development, as well as pre-sales network design and post-sales troubleshooting for hundreds of 900MHz cordless telephony and 2.4 GHz / 5 GHz Wi-Fi networks. He has over 20 years' experience in communications and is active in Amateur Radio. He also has a General Radio Operators License (GROL), and numerous CompTIA certifications and is currently applying for CWNE®.

Bloggers

The following authors provided one or more blog submissions, and their blogs are well worth visiting on a regular basis:

- Dale Rapp—dalewifisec.wordpress.com—Chapters 1 and 2
- Lee Badman—wirednot.wordpress.com—Chapter 3
- Andrew von Nagy—www.revolutionwifi.net—Chapter 4
- Rasika Nayanajith—mrncciew.com—Chapter 5
- Sam Clements—sc-wifi.com—Chapter 6
- Jake Snyder—transmitfailure.blogspot.com—Chapter 7
- Chris Lyttle—www.wifikiwi.com—Chapter 8
- Devin Akin——Chapter 9

x

Table of Contents

Chapter 1:

Security Fundamentals

Objectives

3.1   Describe how wireless network security solutions may vary for different wireless network implementations, including small businesses, home offices, large enterprises, public networks, and remote access.

When a student studies security, it is essential to start with a good foundation. In this chapter, you will examine the foundational CWSP material at a high level, adding depth to it in subsequent chapters. Please realize that many topics in this book are purposefully repetitive as they are introduced early in the text and then expanded on as we get deeper into the various concepts that use those topics. As with the CWNA material, few CWSP topics stand alone, suitable to discuss once and then put aside. The interdependencies of wireless security require us to revisit the same fundamental principles often as we continue to tie them all together throughout the text to build the full breadth of modern Wireless Local Area Network (WLAN) security concerns and options.

In the process of studying CWSP, you will explore security basics and briefly review the security knowledge gained from CWNA to refresh that material. Then you will continue with focus on organizations that shape the WLAN landscape, important terminology, and some of the more common vulnerabilities associated with 802.11 networks. Our first chapter introduces a range of topics and serves as a preview of the rest of the book.

A Brief History of Wireless Security

Any WLAN implementation should be designed with a secure foundation that provides Confidentiality, Integrity, and Availability. You can easily remember these functional pieces from the acronym CIA. Maintaining secure network communications is a very important part of wireless networking, just as it is with any other type of computer networking or information technology. In the early days of standards-based wireless networking, the need for strong security was not immediately recognized, and the only option to secure WLAN communications was Wired Equivalent Privacy (WEP). A 40-bit key was used to protect the wireless network from casual eavesdropping. In addition to the key, WEP used a 24-bit initialization vector (IV) as part of the encryption and decryption process. This 24-bit IV was relatively short, cryptographically speaking, allowing the IV to be reused with the same key and therefore causing WEP to be vulnerable to intrusion if enough frames with unique IVs were captured. You will often see the 40-bit key and the

24-bit IV together referred to as the 64-bit WEP key. Though optional, some manufacturers allowed for the use of a 104-bit key. Again, the 24-bit IV was used, and it was common to see the two components referred to as the 128-bit WEP key.

The evolution of standards-based WLAN security led to the adoption of the 802.11i amendment to the standard, which has since been rolled into 802.11-2012. This amendment provided the still-current concept of the robust security network association (RSNA). An RSNA is defined as an association between a pair of stations (STAs), which includes a 4-way handshake between the STAs. As per the 802.11 standard, a STA is defined as a "logical entity that is a singly addressable instance of a medium access control (MAC) and physical layer (PHY) interface to the wireless medium (WM)." The STA designator includes stations that are either APs or client devices, which is an important point to remember. An RSNA does not allow the use of 802.11 Shared Key Authentication and only allows devices to connect to the network using 802.11 Open System Authentication. We will talk about both of these concepts and what else is needed for RSNA later in the book.

Eventually, the 802.11i security amendment also introduced a new term: Pre-RSNA. It is important to note that the Pre-RSNA networks allow use of the legacy WEP cipher suite, using the Rivest Cipher 4 (RC4) algorithm, for data confidentiality, 802.11 Open System or Shared Key authentication methods and a single, weak Integrity Check Value (ICV) algorithm. Again, we have already established that WEP was weak, therefore Pre-RSNA is also weak.

With the advent of the 802.11-2012 standard, two classes of security algorithms used with standards based 802.11 wireless networking were defined:

1. **Robust Security Networks (RSNs)**—which allow only RSNAs and do not allow WEP.
2. **Pre-RSNA Networks**—which do allow WEP.

You might wonder why WEP was carried forward to Pre-RSNA and why Pre-RSNA was kept around as an option after RSNA was introduced. Recall from your CWNA studies that the notion of backward compatibility is prevalent in 802.11. This reality is very much the case when it comes to wireless security as well. Even though WEP has long-since been cracked, it is still a selectable (though ill-advised) option in many of the newest WLAN systems.

 Note: **The 802.11-2012 standard allows STAs to operate simultaneously with pre-RSNA and RSNA algorithms, but RSNA forbids the use of Shared Key 802.11 authentication, which Pre-RSNA allows. For RSNA, only the Open System Authentication mechanism can be used.**

The 802.11-2012 standard RSNA defines a number of security features in addition to those of pre-RSNA networks, including:

- Enhanced authentication mechanisms for STAs
- Key management (generation and distribution) algorithms
- Strong cryptographic key establishment
- Enhanced cipher suite solution in Counter Mode with Cipher-Block Chaining Message Authentication Code Protocol (CCMP) with the use of Advanced Encryption Standard (AES)
- An optional, transitional cipher suite, Temporal Key Integrity Protocol (TKIP) with the use of RC4
- Fast BSS transition (FT) mechanisms
- Enhanced cryptographic encapsulation mechanisms for robust management frames

Transitional security networks (TSNs) allow for both RSNA-level security and Pre-RSNA-level security. A TSN is identified by the indication in the Robust Security Network information element (RSN-IE or RSNE) of Beacon frames, in which the group cipher suite in use is Wired Equivalent Privacy (WEP). Yes, this is a lot to grasp, but do not get discouraged. All of this information is explored in more depth as you continue reading in later chapters.

Radio Frequency (RF) Does Not Respect Boundaries

Unlike the paradigm of data traversing a bounded wired network infrastructure such as Ethernet, wireless networks use radio frequency (RF) for communications. Because RF is an unbounded medium used to send and receive data, we find wireless networking has distinct security challenges. Like other types of radio-based communications, 802.11 wireless signals can easily pass through many types of obstacles and various construction materials. This often allows the signals to propagate beyond their intended target spaces and into unsecured areas where eavesdroppers and intruders may be present and monitoring the air for valuable information. WLAN designers, administrators, and users must all take their own special precautions to ensure that transmitted data remains private because physical RF security is not easily achieved. Furthermore, in modern WLAN implementations, the goal is often pervasive coverage that purposefully stretches the notion of keeping signal away from "outsiders." This effect makes strong wireless security that much more important.

Wireless professionals have to deal with the reality that someone monitoring the air with easily obtainable software utilities would likely never be noticed or seen as he or she eavesdrops on wireless networks. Keep in mind that, for WLAN communications to be successful, devices must be able to "hear" or receive each other's transmissions. However, with the proper free or low-cost tools and equipment, an intruder may be able to monitor RF communications from a surprising distance. While likely going unnoticed, the intruder is able to leverage the information harvested from the unbounded medium. Just because the wireless network is not logically aware of the intruder, it does not mean that they are not able to gather and use the information that is exchanged between legitimate wireless network devices. The software utilities needed for this type of eavesdropping are generally available from the Internet (and often include training videos). Someone with a limited skill set is able to easily and clandestinely gather valuable information from a wireless network that is lacking an adequate security solution. The advent of wireless networking was unfortunately paralleled by the advent of the notion of listening to wireless networks by genuine hackers and those who aspire to become proficient in hacking.

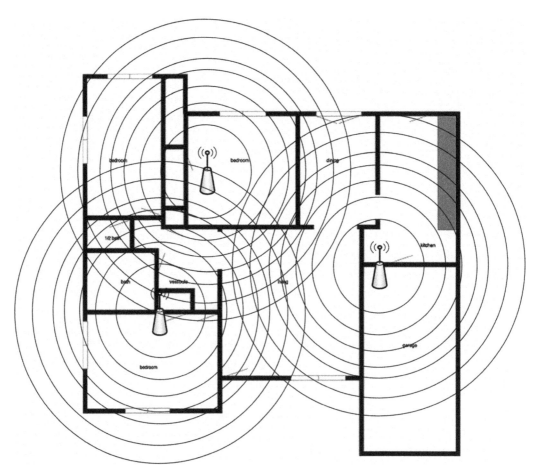

Figure 1-1: Unbounded Signals are Easily Seen by Attackers

Usage Threat Assessment

Relying on legacy 802.11 and weak security mechanisms carries significant risk, and can be equated with putting up a low fence to keep intruders off of your property. There can be no expectation of real security, as these mechanisms at best present a hurdle to network entry and not a barrier. Legacy solutions are those that are deprecated over time by the 802.11 standard because they were never very good security solutions in the first place. Yes, many of these options are still available because of the strong emphasis on backwards compatibility that pervades the 802.11 framework, but the security-minded WLAN administrator recognizes that using legacy security methods is not a good strategy.

 Note: The current 802.11 standard, as amended, has deprecated both WEP and TKIP as security solutions. Newly installed systems should no longer use these systems. TKIP is roughly equivalent to WPA.

It is important to understand the various wireless vulnerabilities that exist for the different types of WLAN deployments. Whether the WLAN is a home, small office, or an enterprise installation, all WLANs have their share of vulnerabilities for personal and business uses. Some vulnerabilities are common across all use cases (like malicious jamming), while others are more specific to individual types of environments. We will address personal and small business wireless environments first.

Considerations for Personal Network Usage Threat Assessment

- Anonymous intruders may perform illegal computer activities through open wireless networks.
- Intruders may compromise a home user's privacy.
- Intruders may learn financial and personal information for use in identity theft.
- Intruders may tamper with a home user's files and information.

- Intruders may insert malware, viruses, root kits, or backdoors onto the home user's network.
- Intruders could camp on the personal network and use so much bandwidth that the rightful owner's performance suffers.

Considerations for Home/Small Business Usage Threat Assessment

- Intruders may gather financial details of home-based businesses.
- Intruders may eavesdrop on business communications of employees working from home.
- Intruders may hijack logins to corporate accounts.
- Intruders may insert malware, viruses, root kits, or backdoors onto corporate network through remote connections.
- Intruders might leverage the WLAN to compromise or disrupt wired network devices.

Network Extension

Now let us consider larger environments. Due to the diverse set of network topologies, each with its own unique security concerns and requirements, it is important that a wireless security designer take into account the entire scope of the wireless deployment and how it fits into the overall network paradigm. Keep in mind that early wireless networks were more of an extension to an existing wired network infrastructure with a limited number of APs and a small number of users.

These early wireless networks allowed users to access network resources, but were usually limited in privilege. As wireless technology evolved to be the access method of choice in a growing number of environments, so has the need for access to more of the same network resources that are reachable from the wired network. With the growing acceptance of wireless, the need for stronger, more robust security solutions became necessary because the wireless network is now considered a primary part of the overall network and no longer just an extension with limited use.

Because most wireless installations occur at the edge of a wired infrastructure, any weaknesses in the wireless segments can lead to the exploitation of vulnerabilities on the wired segments as well. WLANs have become a tightly integrated network access resource, often with the same privileges as the wired LAN. The implication here is that a breach of the wireless network may well provide an ingress point to critical business resources that typically reside on the wired LAN.

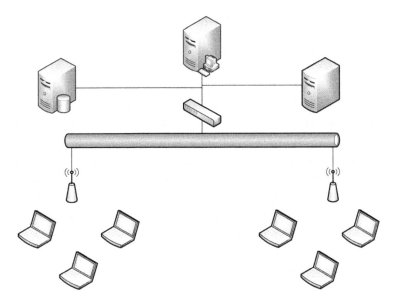

Figure1-2: Access WLANs are Client Access Networks

Network targets for intruders may include:

- Databases
- Application Servers
- Management Devices
- File Servers
- Client devices
- Other infrastructure devices
- Unpermitted network access

CWNA Security Review

The following is a review of WLAN security concepts that you may have learned in your CWNA studies, from equivalent wireless training or from personal experience.

IEEE 802.11 Open System Authentication

Open System Authentication is a required component for 802.11 devices to connect to a WLAN and is considered a null authentication algorithm. Open System authentication consists of two 802.11 management frames. These frames are not a request and response but merely identified as Authentication. For the most part this authentication is always successful from the device's perspective. In other words, a device says "I would like to communicate with you," and the other device says, "and I would like to talk with you as well." Though the mechanism is called Authentication, it is more or less guaranteed and there is no credential checking or other vetting used.

Without any additional authentication mechanisms, Open System Authentication allows all information sent across the air to be in clear text or plaintext and, therefore, remain vulnerable to eavesdropping. Most wireless hotspots use only Open System Authentication (to provide ease of connection), and users have to supply additional authentication methods or encryption solutions such as a virtual private networks (VPNs) to secure their wireless transmissions.

WEP

As mentioned earlier in the chapter, WEP was intended as an early way to protect information on a wireless network from casual eavesdropping using a 40-bit key and a 24-bit IV. When wireless networking was just gaining traction, robust security was not really considered. Unfortunately, it was discovered early on that WEP was functionally weak and was soon compromised as a result of the way the IV was used in conjunction with the 40-bit encryption key. Although it does not provide adequate wireless security and should not be employed as a rule, WEP may still be in use within some wireless networks due to the continued use of legacy equipment. Rather than continue to use WEP because older or poorly built client devices require this dated option, it is highly recommended to upgrade to newer devices that support a more secure solution such as CCMP/AES (roughly equivalent to WPA2).

From the perspective of "best practices," WEP, TKIP, and Shared Key authentication are all mechanisms deemed to be outdated and ineffective for securing 802.11 networks. They are considered to be deprecated as of the latest 802.11-2012 standard. When something is "deprecated" in networking or programming, it means that you are strongly encouraged to find other ways of accomplishing what the deprecated feature does because it has been proven to be faulty in some significant way or will soon be replaced and removed. Organizations should be moving quickly toward using only CCMP/AES and abandoning all deprecated security solutions as soon as possible. You cannot remove the actual options of using WEP and TKIP from wireless hardware, but you can and should avoid their use and select stronger options in every possible use case.

802.11 Shared Key Authentication

This wireless authentication method was defined in the original 802.11 standard in 1997 as a way to provide both 802.11 authentication and data encryption which was accomplished through the use of WEP. Because WEP has been proven to be vulnerable to eavesdropping and is not an adequate security solution, this authentication method adds no value to 802.11 WLAN technology. Unlike Open System authentication which uses two 802.11 management frames, Shared Key authentication requires four 802.11 management frames. With a challenge string sent in plain or clear text in the second frame, Shared Key authentication can easily be exploited, allowing unauthorized users to authenticate to the wireless network and view user data that should be secured. Though named similarly, it is important to avoid confusing legacy Shared Key Authentication with Wi-Fi Protected Access (WPA) or WPA2 pre-shared key.

Wi-Fi Protected Access (WPA) and WPA2

Given that the original 802.11 standards-based wireless security methods turned out to be weak, the Wi-Fi Alliance created a pre-802.11i certification known as Wi-Fi

Protected Access (WPA). WPA was introduced as a stop-gap measure while 802.11i was being developed. It takes time for amendments to the 802.11 standard to be written and adopted, and the Wi-Fi Alliance did well to bridge the gap between poor security and the more robust mechanisms that would eventually follow when it created the WPA certification. This certification was intended to provide wireless device manufacturers with the operational framework to build new equipment or to provide firmware updates that gave legitimate security options.

The WPA interoperability certification was based on the fact that Temporal Key Integrity Protocol (TKIP) provided an enhancement to WEP on pre-RSNA equipment and allowed the protection of 802.11 data frames. Equipment that supported legacy WEP and was capable of TKIP (usually determined by the components with which it was built) could be upgraded through firmware. Once the 802.11i amendment was ratified (in 2004), and due to the success of WPA certification in bringing a new level of security awareness the WLAN market, the Wi-Fi Alliance created a post-802.11i certification known as WPA2. Based on the 802.11i amendment to the standard, the WPA2 certification requires support for CCMP/AES and optionally allows TKIP/RC4 for backward compatibility. It is important to note that some very old devices may require firmware upgrades to support CCMP/AES or replacement if they cannot be updated in firmware for WPA2.

Wi-Fi Protected Access Personal Mode (WPA-Personal)

WPA personal mode (WPA-Personal) was created to provide individual users with an easy, but stronger way to secure their 802.11 wireless networks. Greater security was accomplished by entering a passphrase (used to create a pre-shared key) on all wireless devices that would be part of the same BSS. A passphrase can be a maximum of 63 ASCII characters in length. From the passphrase that is entered into the device, an algorithm is used to create a 256-bit pre-shared key (PSK). Although this key is secure, using a weak passphrase can make the wireless network vulnerable to intrusion. It is very common for users to pick a short and easily guessed passphrase, the dangers (of which are explained later in the book). A WPA network uses TKIP/RC4 as the cipher suite and encryption method. WPA-Personal mode is also called WPA

Pre-Shared Key (WPA-PSK) based on the use of a single key for all 4-way handshakes (also explained later in the book).

Wi-Fi Protected Access 2 (WPA2) Personal Mode

WPA2-Personal was created based on the ratification of the 802.11i amendment. This new amendment provided the capability of using an even stronger method to secure 802.11 wireless networks. A WPA2 network can use CCMP/AES as the cipher suite and encryption method for securing wireless communications but allows for TKIP/RC4 for backward compatibility for older devices. A WPA2 passphrase uses the same concepts as WPA but allows for stronger security. As noted earlier, 802.11 associations for devices that are capable of CCMP/AES are classified as a RSNAs. WPA2-Personal is currently the general standard mechanism for securing home and many small-business wireless network environments as well as many high-roaming scenarios with mobile devices that do not support fast roaming methods.

Wi-Fi Protected Access (WPA) and WPA2 Enterprise

WPA and WPA2-Enterprise modes (WPA- and WPA2-Enterprise) are far more robust methods of securing enterprise wireless networks. Compared to WPA-Personal, these modes use a much more sophisticated process to secure 802.11 wireless communications. Enterprise mode relies on another IEEE standard, 802.1X, which provides port-based access control and uses Extensible Authentication Protocol (EAP), which is an Internet Engineering Task Force (IETF) standard. It is important to note that 802.1X is not a wireless-specific standard, and it has great usefulness in the security of many network types. WPA/WPA2-Enterprise provides user-based access control and a much better authentication process for large wireless networks. The same cipher suites and encryption methods, TKIP/RC4 and CCMP/AES, are used as in WPA-Personal; however, the enhanced key generation and implementation process makes the two modes different.

Note: **You will learn much more about WPA and WPA2 in later chapters. Remember, this chapter is giving you a broad overview of security issues and technologies used in WLANs.**

Industry Organizations

Standardization and certification are as important to network security as they are to the basic operations of wireless networks. While proprietary solutions may provide some security advantages due to their secrecy, standardized security mechanisms are central to modern WLANs and the development of widely deployed wireless products.

Several different organizations play a role in standards-based WLAN technology, with each contributing various aspects to wireless technology and security. Their individual influences are combined and codified, with wide industry dissemination, having the ultimate goal of compatibility. This facilitates the ability of manufacturers to design and build equipment that operate together in a mixed environment regardless of which company produced the devices. A non-proprietary approach helps to grow the wireless technology and therefore makes it more affordable and supportable for homes, small offices, and enterprise companies. Given that modern client devices may be used in all three environments in the same day, wide-scale adoption of standards that much more important. The three main industry organizations responsible for the standards-based approach that has become the hallmark of the wireless industry are discussed here: IEEE, Wi-Fi Alliance, and IETF.

Institute of Electrical and Electronics Engineers (IEEE)

The IEEE is a nonprofit organization responsible for generating a variety of technology standards, including those related to information technology. The IEEE is the world's largest technical professional society. Since 1997 the IEEE has released a series of standards related to WLANs. Most important of these to the CWSP is the 802.11 standard. The IEEE has also given us the 802.3 Ethernet standard and the

802.1X Network Access Control standard. Both of these are very important to the wireless professional.

Wi-Fi Alliance

The Wi-Fi Alliance was created to both promote wireless networking technology and to provide interoperability testing of WLAN equipment. The Wi-Fi Alliance is responsible for many WLAN interoperability certifications, and has been instrumental in the growth and mass adoption of wireless as a network access method. The WPA and WPA2 certifications helped to move the industry forward by providing secure WLAN communications through interoperability testing, and removing a major barrier to business use of Wi-Fi.

Internet Engineering Task Force (IETF)

The IETF is responsible for creating Internet standards and promoting Internet technology and usage through the adoption of Request for Comment (RFC) documents. An RFC is a document created by engineers and scientists to define innovation and technology that works with the Internet. If an RFC is approved by the IETF, it will eventually become an Internet standard. The IETF has provided several important RFCs that aid in securing wireless networks. These RFCs include Remote Authentication Dial-In User Service (RADIUS), EAP, and Internet Protocol Security (IPSec). As with the IEEE, the IETF has interests far beyond wireless, but many of its initiatives end up being widely used in LAN, WLAN, and WAN applications.

Wi-Fi Alliance Compliance

Recall that the IEEE creates standards which manufacturers use to design the WLAN equipment that are used in our wireless networks. The IEEE does not perform any compliance or interoperability testing, leaving that up to the individual manufacturers. To promote interoperability across WLAN devices, the Wi-Fi Alliance maintains many certification programs to verify device compliance with generally specified interoperability parameters. This testing provides some basic assurance that equipment from different manufacturers work together when used within the same environment. It is important to consider the role of compatibility testing when selecting products and security solutions.

The security certifications of the Wi-Fi Alliance include WPA-Personal, WPA-Enterprise, WPA2-Personal, WPA2-Enterprise, Wi-Fi Protected Setup (WPS), and many different EAP types. In addition to these, the Voice-Enterprise certification addresses fast secure transition and is intended for larger wireless networks that support fast transitions between APs. This certification defines the requirements for voice quality, mobility, power save mechanisms (which helps to prolong battery life), and, of course, wireless security. Given that the wireless industry continues to evolve, we should expect future certifications from the Wi-Fi Alliance as needs arise.

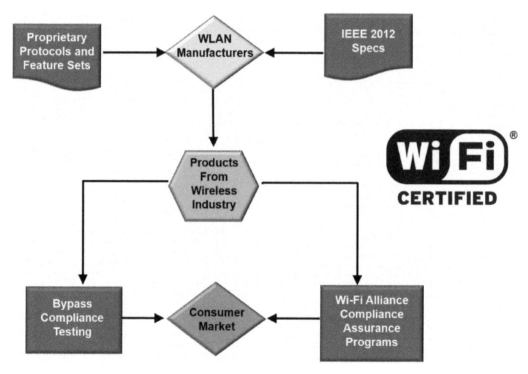

Figure 1-3: Wi-Fi Alliance Certification Process

Product Certificates

Product certificates provide a quick and easy reference to determine which security certifications a device has received from the Wi-Fi Alliance. Unless a proprietary solution is intentionally selected for added security (not uncommon in government applications), it is always recommended to use equipment that is Wi-Fi Certified. Using devices that are certified by the Wi-Fi Alliance help ensure interoperability between manufacturers and provide a higher quality user experience along with easier support.

To search for Wi-Fi certified devices, enter the following link into your web browser: http://www.wi-fi.org/product-finder. From this web page you can search by certificate ID, device model number, keyword, company, category, and other criteria. The Wi-Fi Alliance currently includes testing for several different EAP types (eight in total currently. We will discuss how EAP is used with 802.1X later.

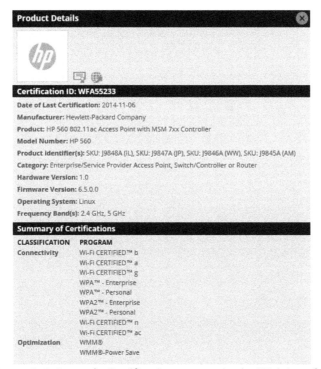

Figure 1-4: Example Certification as seen in the Web Interface

Search the certificates by following the steps below.

1) Open your Web Browser.
2) Navigate to http://www.wi-fi.org/product-finder.
3) Search for *IAP-224*.
4) On the results page, click the PDF icon in the lower left corner of the Aruba Instant Access Point IAP-224 result.
5) Open the PDF in your PDF viewer application.
6) On the first page, note the certifications awarded:
   a. Wi-Fi CERTIFIED™ a, b, g, n, ac
   b. WPA™—Enterprise, Personal
   c. WPA2™—Enterprise, Personal
   d. WMM®
   e. WMM®-Power Save
7) On the second page, note that
   a. all eight current testable EAP types are certified with this AP, and
   b. you can see the number of tested spatial streams. For this device, it supports three spatial streams in both 2.4 and 5 GHz.

Terminology Review

Use the following terms / basic definitions to enhance the learning process throughout this book:

AAA (Authentication, Authorization, and Accounting): A set of separate security functions performed on WLANs to identify and validate a user identity (Authentication), apply specific policies and privileges to his/her network access (Authorization), and monitor the actions performed while this user is associated to the network (Accounting).

Access Control—The prevention of unauthorized use of resources; a generic networking term referring to the mechanisms by which access to network resources is controlled.

Authentication—The service that identifies a STA as a member of a group of STAs authorized to join or associate with another STA. Authentication validates user identity to determine permission.

Cipher Suite—A set of one or more algorithms designed to provide data confidentiality, data authenticity or integrity, and/or replay protection.

Encryption—The alteration of a data stream using a secret code or algorithm so as to be unintelligible to unauthorized parties.

RADIUS (Remote Authentication Dial-In User Service)—An authentication protocol used to provide centralized AAA services for a network.

RSN (Robust Security Network)—A network that allows only robust security network associations (RSNAs) by exclusion of WEP.

802.1X/EAP—An enterprise authentication mechanism in which port-based access control (802.1X) is employed with a form of the Extensible Authentication Protocol (EAP) to authenticate STAs.

WPA-Personal—Security certification specified by the Wi-Fi Alliance in which passphrase-based authentication is paired with the TKIP cipher suite for encryption.

WPA-Enterprise—Enterprise security certification specified by the Wi-Fi Alliance in which 802.1X/EAP authentication is paired with the TKIP cipher suite for encryption.

WPA2-Personal—Security certification specified by the Wi-Fi Alliance in which passphrase-based authentication is paired with the AES-CCMP cipher suite for encryption, with optional TKIP support.

WPA2-Enterprise—Enterprise security certification specified by the Wi-Fi Alliance in which 802.1X/EAP authentication is paired with the AES-CCMP cipher suite for encryption, with optional TKIP support.

Home Office Security

The wireless security solution that you ultimately choose depends on several factors, including the number of APs, number and type of client devices, and the intended use of the wireless network. Home and home office installations typically consist of one wireless AP and a limited number of devices that associate to the network. For modest wireless networks like this, WPA2 passphrase is adequate. Indeed, this is currently far and away the most common way to secure home networks.

Using a strong passphrase and following general wireless security best practices usually suffice for this type of network. Manufacturers of home based WLAN equipment sometimes try to ease the process of securing wireless home routers by providing default security mechanisms including pre-supplied passphrases. Depending on how it is implemented, this could be a security risk. As a best practice, reconfigure the WLAN AP or router to use a strong passphrase with more than fifteen characters and mixed characters. In addition to this best practice, consider the following important list:

- Change all default settings including the SSID, passphrase, and device logon credentials.
- Do not use WEP.
- Upgrade to client devices that support WPA2.
- Use only CCMP/AES and avoid TKIP/RC4 if possible.
- Always use strong passphrases and change them often.
- Change your passphrase if you lose a client device.
- Be mindful of how family members share your passphrase with visitors.
- Disable Wi-Fi Protected Setup (WPS) features as many implementations introduce vulnerabilities.
- Periodically upgrade devices to the latest firmware versions that are available.

Small Business Security

Small business wireless may require more than one AP. Depending on the number of APs and connected wireless devices, apply the same security best practices as applied to home office security. Small business Wi-Fi may be controller-based or cloud-based (among others), which provide the opportunity to use stronger security mechanisms such as 802.1X/EAP.

In addition to the home office security best practices, small business security should consider using only WPA2 for CCMP/AES and not TKIP/RC4. Most client devices used in these environments support WPA2.

Many small businesses cannot justify a dedicated information technology professional, so using enterprise level security solutions such as 802.1X/EAP may be a challenge as configuring advanced security is usually beyond the skillset of non-IT employees. In these cases, an employee may need to get the proper training to support the advanced security requirements. Alternatively, outside consultants can be hired to assist with advanced security solutions based on specific business needs.

Large Enterprise Security

Large enterprise wireless networks require careful planning in order to ensure successful deployment, and wireless security plays a major role in that planning. At this scale, security needs are much more policy-driven and granular than in small networks, and the CWSP must be intimately acquainted with the particulars of enterprise wireless security, which are covered in great detail throughout this book.

802.1X addresses port-based access control and helps to provide a secure, scalable, and manageable security solution for enterprise wireless networks. To the uninitiated, the notion that port-based security is relevant in wireless where there are no obvious physical ports can be confusing. We will talk more about what port-based really means in the context of wireless security later in the book; for now, know that virtual ports are used within the AP for these processes.

802.1X works in conjunction with an appropriate EAP method to allow for user-based security. User-based security allows an administrator to restrict access to a WLAN and its resources by creating users in a centralized database or accessing a, typically, X.500 compliant server (a server storing and providing access to credentials according to the X.500 directory services standard) with an existing user database. Anyone trying to join the network is required to authenticate as one of the users by supplying a valid username and password or other valid credentials. After successful authentication, the user is able to gain access to resources to which they have been assigned appropriate permissions.

Wireless devices that use 802.1X technology are identified using different terminology than that used in 802.11 standards-based wireless networking. This terminology is used frequently by the wireless professional in their daily work and includes three key terms:

- **Supplicant**—the wireless client device or the device requesting authentication.
- **Authenticator**—the wireless AP, WLAN controller, or the device/system providing access to the network.
- **Authentication server**—the device or system providing the actual authentication, commonly a RADIUS server.

We will later explore how the supplicant and authentication server need to be configured with matching EAP types for 802.1X to function.

When implementing security for any business (small, medium, large, or even home office), it is essential that the network resources themselves are properly secured, as they are common targets of network attacks. That is, you should not rely on the WPA2-Personal or Enterprise authentication and encryption provided by the WLAN as your only security. Security should be properly implemented throughout the network. This is often called defense-in-depth or layered security.

Public Network Security

One common wireless network implementation is the publicly available Wi-Fi hotspot. This type of network is usually available at airports, hotels, restaurants, coffee shops, retail stores, on airplanes, and at countless public settings. In many cases these wireless networks are available for free as a value-added service to the patrons of the establishment that provides goods or services. Occasionally, the hotspot provider charges a fee for wireless network access.

The hotspot model typically involves users connecting their devices to an unsecured wireless AP in order to use Internet resources, or even to access corporate network resources across the Internet. The hotspot framework usually prioritizes ease-of-use over providing wireless security. As a result, this kind of wireless network can be a haven for hackers working to get a variety of data using various intrusion techniques. These techniques play on most people's ignorance of wireless security and include direct peer-to-peer attacks or connecting to another wireless station through the AP. Although it can be a hard message to get across, it is critical that devices connecting to a public wireless hotspot use appropriate and adequate security controls to minimize or eliminate potential security threats.

Here are common best practices for devices that connect to public wireless networks:

- Use a Virtual Private Network (VPN) connection whenever possible.
- Secure all login accounts with strong passwords.
- Ensure firewall software is installed, enabled, properly configured, and up-to-date.
- Ensure anti-virus software is installed, enabled, and up-to-date.
- Ensure that security vulnerabilities in the device operating system are patched and all service packs are installed.
- Secure any open file system shares that may be enabled.
- Disable file and print sharing features if not needed or used.
- Be aware of people who seem a little too close to you physically, who may be watching what you type.

Remote Access Security

As wireless technology availability and use continues to grow, so does the need for remote connectivity. Many organizations allow employees to work from remote locations such as home, satellite offices, and hotels part or full time. In some instances, there may not be a physical office to go to, and all employees work remotely. When someone connects remotely to a company network, that network for the most part is now extended to the remote location. Ensuring that the remote connection is secure is of utmost importance, and corporate security policy must address remote access security.

While working from a remote location, it is important for the user to follow all corporate security procedures to ensure the remotely accessed network remains secure. Given that the remote user has more freedom and is not in a controlled environment, this can be more of a challenge.

Proper training programs should be in place as part of the corporate security policy to address remote access and remote security solutions. One common way to ensure remote connections are secure is to use a VPN solution. A VPN provides users with the capability to create secure private communications over a public network such as the Internet, even if you connect from an open Wi-Fi hotspot.

> **Exam Moment:** Security policies should identify acceptable use and training requirements for users and support staff.

Security and the OSI Model

Security techniques work at various levels of the Open System Interconnection (OSI) model from the lowest, the Physical layer, to the highest, the Application layer. Let us look at some of the security concerns and solutions for the most commonly discussed layers of the OSI Model.

Note: **The OSI Model is fundamental to wired and wireless networking, and is covered in more detail in both the CWNA and CWTS® Official Study Guides. If you are unfamiliar with this model, consider using those resources to learn more. Additionally, the book, *The TCP/IP Guide*, by Charles Kozierok or the website (bit.ly/1xk2kjG) includes an excellent overview of the OSI Model.**

The Application Layer

The Application layer is considered the interface to the user, and is frequently referred to as Layer 7. This is where the protocols for common applications such as email, Internet web browsers, and file transfer programs reside. Some common Application layer protocols include Hypertext Transfer Protocol (HTTP), File Transfer Protocol (FTP), Post Office Protocol (POP), and Simple Network Management Protocol (SNMP), among others. These protocols provide no significant stand-alone security, and many transfer information in plain or clear text.

Clear text transmissions create serious concerns for WLAN communications when you consider that they are sent through the air using RF. Many Application layer protocols can use the Secure Sockets Layer (SSL) protocol alongside the Application layer protocols to provide for secure network communications using Internet Protocol (IP), but whether they do or not can be hit-or-miss, depending on the way the application was written. Because so many of these applications transmit in the clear, using encryption on the WLAN is essential in modern business. With wired networking and switch ports, it is far more challenging today to promiscuously sniff data on the wired network than it is on an open WLAN. The administrator should not leave the business wireless network open for such easy attack, and using TKIP or CCMP thwarts the would-be eavesdropper who is hoping to leverage weak Layer 7 protocols.

Some organizations are now using Application layer firewalls to help control the traffic at Layer 7. It is important to note that these firewalls do not typically assist with WLAN security. This is because they control ingress and egress on the wired network borders, but do not control what passes within the network itself. Eavesdroppers could still capture information passing within the wireless network because of the typical range of propagation with RF. For this reason, again, TKIP or better yet, CCMP should be used to protect the WLAN.

Below the Application layer, we have the Presentation, Session, and Transport layers. Though each plays an important role in networking, they are not tremendously relevant to our discussion of wireless security. We will not discuss them individually here.

The Network Layer

Although WLAN technology operates at the Physical and Data Link layers, the Network layer still plays a role with respect to wireless security because of the networking protocols that reside at this layer. This layer is often referred to as Layer 3. The Network layer provides the very important Internet Protocol (IP), which is responsible for the addressing and routing of computer data. When used with the Transport Control Protocol (TCP), a Layer 4 protocol, TCP/IP allows for communication across the Internet. TCP/IP itself is not a secure protocol stack and requires additional technology to ensure secure communications. One common way to secure data at the Network layer is through the use of a VPN. There are various VPN technologies available, of which some are more secure than others.

Two common examples of VPN protocols are:

- Point-to-Point Tunneling Protocol (PPTP)
- Layer 2 Tunneling Protocol (L2TP)

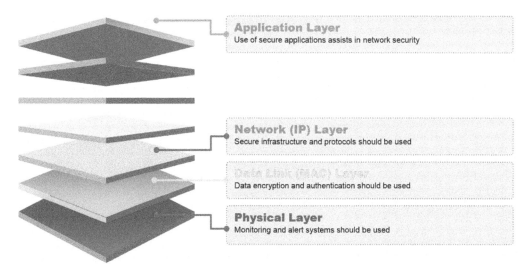

Figure 1-5: Security and the OSI Model

It is important to note that PPTP is considered a weaker legacy VPN technology that can introduce security vulnerabilities when used with wireless networking and improper configuration. L2TP itself provides only a tunneling mechanism; it gets its security from integration with an encryption protocol. With L2TP, the most common choice of encryption is IPSec, which provides authentication and encryption for each IP packet in the data stream.

The Data Link Layer

Layer 2 plays a key role with WLAN communications. The Data Link layer is actually made up of two sub-layers: Media Access Control (MAC) and Logical Link Control (LLC). Our discussion here focuses on the MAC sub-layer, but know that the LLC also exists. The MAC sub-layer is where bit-level communication is accomplished through MAC addressing and framing. The MAC sub-layer adds the MAC header and allows for various WLAN security mechanisms. The header information cannot be encrypted regardless of the 802.11 encryption method employed, which is a very important point of reference. For secure wireless communications, encryption must occur within the data payload of the data frames that traverse the air. Layer 2 security types include WEP, TKIP/RC4, CCMP/AES, and 802.1X/EAP. Using legacy or unsecured Layer

2 security mechanisms can cause many WLAN security related issues.

 Note: **802.11w-2009 (now part of 802.11-2012) introduced management frame protection. However, this does not encrypt the MAC headers of frames, and it only applies to certain management frames. The only frames protected are deauthentication, disassociation, and robust action frames. Data frames do not include this protection.**

The Physical Layer

Layer 1 provides physical connections to the network between devices using various methods. For Ethernet, this is the realm of patch cables and station wiring. For the wireless side of 802.11 networks, the Physical layer is RF. Since open air is the operating domain used with wireless communications, WLAN Layer 1 security concerns are vastly different than those of wired networks. Potential vulnerabilities include eavesdropping on unsecured communications and intentional RF interference (known as jamming). Jamming can be an attack unto itself, resulting in denial of service, or can be part of more sophisticated attacks as we will see later in the book.

In addition to the risks associated with Wi-Fi's unbounded medium, the wired network infrastructure at Layer 1 can be a security concern for wireless networking. This includes unsecured physical layer wired ports that connect to Layer 2 switches and that can be used to introduce rogue (not authorized) APs into the networking environment. Good practice includes securing unused switch ports through a variety of methods.

Security Analysis Basics

Threats include the individuals or groups who wish to attack your network and the systems they use to perform the attacks. Vulnerabilities are the points where your system is weak and could be penetrated. You must consider both to implement an effective wireless solution, understanding that both concepts evolve over the life of your WLAN. Several terms and concepts should be understood, which makes you a more effective security analyst. Much of the following applies to all networks, not just wireless. The first concept you must understand is the concept of the attack surface.

Attack Surface

The attack surface is inclusive of all areas that can potentially be attacked. Even small networks can have a sizeable attack surface, depending on network topology and services in use. For large network environments with sizable LAN, WLAN, and WAN components, it can take a fair amount of time and analysis to fully realize your attack surface. Additionally, just as threats change over time, so does your attack surface. Security is not a one-time thing on any network. Failure to realize the notion that your attack surface needs ongoing review can lead to catastrophic breaches.

Attack surface reduction is a security best practice and is the process of reducing the number of areas where your system can be attacked. This process is in line with the principle of security-as-a-process, because attack surface reduction acknowledges that a system cannot have an attack surface reduced to zero and still provide a functional benefit to the organization. Put another way: you can never be without some degree of risk.

Attack surface reduction is about reducing the likelihood of attack by reducing the number of attack points. You can sum it up like this: *If you do not need a particular technology or capability for some beneficial business purpose, do not use it or leave it in place for others to use.* Think of it like the booth at the fair where you throw the darts at the balloons. The smaller balloons warrant a bigger prize (the gigantic Elmo for a four-year-old) because they are harder to hit due to the reduced surface area. In the same way, your network is harder to penetrate when you reduce the attack surface. So go ahead and let the air out of your network's balloon by disabling unneeded services.

There are two general wireless device points of entry to consider when contemplating attack surface reduction: wireless entry and wired entry. Let us pause for a moment and remember that wireless networking is not without wires and that 802.11 infrastructure devices have 802.3 Ethernet interfaces along with their radio interfaces.

The wireless attack surface includes all access points, wireless routers, wireless bridges, and other wireless devices. You need to ensure that proper security mechanisms are in place to help prevent unauthorized access through these RF entry points. One common attack method is the rogue (self-installed or unauthorized) AP or wireless router. Even well-meaning users can install a rogue when they want wireless access or a different kind of wireless access in their work area. They may not mean to harm the network, but the default configurations and some having strong output power make them an easy target (not to mention the interference that comes with them).

To prevent wireless attacks, you should implement best practices for wireless security. Best practices include user training, using strong encryption, and securing the administrative interfaces of all network devices. In more advanced implementations, consider the use of 802.1X and EAP for authentication and encryption on the wired ports, which generally involves a centralized authentication, authorization, and accounting server (RADIUS).

The wired entry point is often overlooked when configuring wireless networks. Again, the typical wireless AP has at least one RJ-45 Ethernet uplink port providing Layer 1 and Layer 2 connectivity into the network environment. To understand the potential impact of ignoring the wired side of wireless networking, consider that the Ethernet port can be used to access the AP for a number of nefarious purposes. An attacker could modify configuration settings, harvest network information, and possibly exploit the underlying operating system on the AP for more sophisticated attacks. The bottom line is that the wired and wireless networks are not mutually exclusive in providing an easy attack surface for an attacker.

Imagine that an individual posing as a copy machine repair person or tradesman slips into a conference room or side office in your small business. This individual pulls out a small-footprint tablet or laptop PC and connects it to the Ethernet port in the office. Immediately, the attacker notices the LED lights indicating that the port is most likely active. The attacker then opens a command prompt and types the command ipconfig /renew to see if a DHCP server is available on the network. An IP configuration set comes down to the tablet PC and the results now displayed on the screen. The attacker now has an IP address on your network, along with additional information like gateway (router), subnet mask, and DNS servers in use.

The next step for this intruder might be to begin looking for devices to access on the network. After a brief scan with a scanning utility (like nmap), the attacker detects more than 30 active devices. The attacker runs a script that tries to connect to port 80 using HTTP on all the discovered devices (this port is the one used by most web servers). Two of the IP addresses respond positively to the script. The attacker can reasonably assume that these might be infrastructure devices like switches or APs, which could potentially be configured through a web interface on printers, or that they are actual web servers.

For our discussion, let us say that one of the two IP addresses that responded positively to the script was 192.168.0.250. The attacker opens the web browser and directs it to the IP address, only to see a screen asking for a username and password. Noticing the *Linksys* name in the dialog, the attacker remembers that the default logon for this device is no username and the password of *admin*. Even if he did not know the default credentials, the intruder could easily look them up online where many lists of network default information are openly shared among the hacker community. The attacker attempts a logon and in a moment is looking at the configuration interface for the wireless router. From here, he can maliciously reconfigure the router or do a number of other undesirable actions.

This security attack was made worse because the default administrative logon for the wireless router had not been changed. If the principles of attack surface reduction had been employed, the attacker would not have been able to reach the wireless router in the first place. Attack surface reduction, applied to this scenario, demands that the Ethernet port in the spare office be disabled until it is needed. With the port disabled, the attacker could not have used the port to obtain an IP address and then reach the wireless router to reconfigure it. Beyond the open Ethernet port being problematic, the router using a default credential set and even the standard HTTP port are weaknesses here.

Follow the steps below to perform a scan on a network where you are authorized to do so.

1. Start up a Kali Linux VM (as described in the appendix).
2. Logon as root with the password of toor.
3. Perform the following procedure:
   a. Navigate to Application > Kali Linux > Vulnerability Analysis > Misc Scanners > zenmap.
   b. In zenmap (which is a GUI front end for nmap), enter the IP subnet you wish to scan into the target field, for example 192.168.10.1-254.
   c. Under Profile, choose the scan type you desire.
   d. Click Scan and wait until the results are displayed.

      Result: You should see an image similar to the one in figure 1-6 below .

 Note: The different scan types can take different lengths of time to complete. Some scans take several minutes to scan just a single computer. When selecting a scan type, know that the Quick Scan Plus method is fast and returns open ports, which is a primary auditing tool for security analysts.

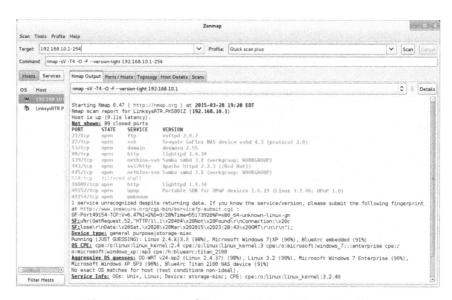

Figure 1-6: Image of Zenmap Network Scan Results

Data Flow

Data flow analysis is the scrutiny of data as it enters, traverses, and removed from your network. You are not generally concerned with the departure point from the network in most wireless implementations, though that is an important concern for your overall network security strategy.

For wireless networking security, the focus is on the flow of data from these four perspectives:

1) The data entry point.
2) The network traversal.
3) The live storage points.
4) The backup storage points.

The data entry point is where data starts its network journey, usually entered by a user on a laptop computer, a desktop computer, or even a web-based interface operating across the Internet. Regardless of which type of device serves as the entry point, you must focus on how that device connects to the network. If a wireless connection is in use, you must consider how to secure this data as it traverses the air.

Before we discuss the network traversal component of data flow, let us consider the types of data that are typically present on a wireless network and what we need to keep in mind about each. As a reminder, the level of security needed depends on the type of data in play. If you only use the wireless computer for general Internet access, you might not need advanced security techniques like VPNs and 802.1X/EAP authentication. Access to secure web sites should already be encrypted with native SSL, and insecure sites should not need encryption beyond that provided by WPA or WPA2 (more on these later).

You might categorize your data into three basic levels of data sensitivity:

- Public
- Private, and
- Highly private.

Public data is that which anyone can see and access. You might want to limit the ability of users to modify the data, but viewing the data is not a concern (and is usually made public for mass consumption). If a client uses only public data, you do not need to be as concerned about the security of the connection and common-sense wireless security practices should suffice, including WPA or WPA2.

Private data should be seen only by authorized organizational employees and members, such as human resource information, non-sensitive trade secrets, and other data not appropriate for sharing with the public. Here you generally combine common-sense wireless security measures with non-wireless network controls to keep "inside" data inside.

Highly-private data is described as information that only a select few should see. This data almost always requires advanced security mechanisms, such as VPNs for all wireless connections carrying the data, and possibly the use of certificates and a PKI (public key infrastructure).

Again, how data gets protected is driven by the sensitivity and value of the data. This is a fundamental tenet of wireless security and of IT security in general. Think of it like this: you would not spend $100 to protect a common modern penny, and you would not spend thousands on security equipment and software to protect data that is worth very little. At the same time, the headlines are full of nightmare examples of security incidents at companies who did not spend enough on resources and skills to protect high-value data. Ideally, as a CWSP you can help your employer or customers avoid these predicaments.

We just discussed entry points for data, as well as typical data types and their implications. Now we will examine the paradigm of data moving from Point A to Point B on a network, along with associated security concerns.

Once the data leaves the point of entry (the input device), it traverses the network and passes through many devices along the way. During this data flow, travel can be intercepted with the potential for data being viewed by an attacker if the traversal points are not secured properly. Part of data flow analysis is investigating these connection points, as well as the medium between them, for ease of access to those who might do harm.

Exam Moment: Data flow analysis results in information that is used to identify traffic patterns and areas of sensitivity that exist during network traversal.

As we talk about network traversal here, the main concern is with the wireless medium. Generally, wired network paths benefit from being hidden in walls or behind locked doors. Consider the network represented in the following image. Assume that the user enters data in the wireless laptop client and that data is then transferred to the database server on the network.

Two wireless traversal points are included in this example.

- The first is between the wireless laptop client and the AP connected to the wired network.
- The second is between the two wireless bridges connecting the two wired networks.

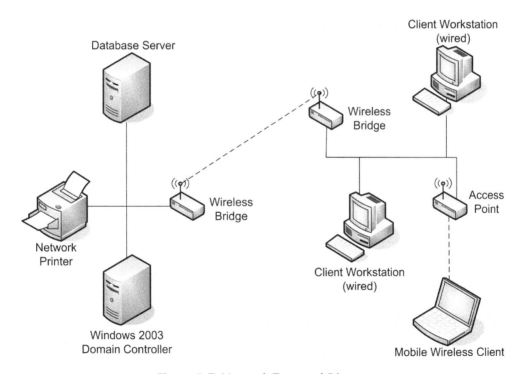

Figure 1-7: Network Traversal Diagram

Both of these wireless connections need to be secured to provide complete security to the data flow (the assumption here is that the wired path is secure). If you enable WPA2-Personal on the AP but do nothing to secure the wireless bridges, you have only addressed one wireless security concern. Bridges usually have a narrow RF propagation pattern, but this characteristic is not considered a security feature as an attacker can still position his device between the two bridges and sniff the traffic from the air.

The concept of "sniffing" the traffic means to pull the packets into your device even though they might not be intended for you. Sniffing packets is used on wired and wireless networks alike for both legitimate support and for hacking. There are many wireless network sniffers (more formally known as network monitors, packet analyzers, or protocol analyzers) available for free. There are powerful commercial tools available. Do not assume that attackers cannot acquire the powerful commercial tools because of the high cost, as attackers often get their tools through newsgroups, IRC chat, peer networks, or other sources of warez, which is the cracker term often used for pirated software. If the data being targeted by a professional hacker has high enough value, the legitimate purchase of high-end wireless packet capture tools may be a small price to pay versus the payoff of a successful breach.

The main purpose of network traversal analysis is to ensure that eavesdroppers cannot gain useful access to your data easily. You must encrypt the data because you cannot prevent the attacker from pulling the data packets from the unbounded RF medium. By encrypting the packets, you ensure that, even though attackers can acquire the packets, they cannot view the internal data. This precaution helps secure data in transit, and does not protect against data theft during storage, which is discussed next.

After the data has traveled the network to its final destination, it is processed in some way. In many cases, the data is stored in live storage. Live storage means that data is hosted in a location that can be accessed instantly by authorized users. There are, at minimum, two points of access where this data must be secured:

1) The network, and
2) The storage device itself.

When you encrypt the communications between a client device and an access point, you ensure that eavesdroppers cannot view the data easily. If attackers discover the configuration parameters needed to associate and authenticate with the AP, they can access the network. While discovering these parameters does not give attackers immediate access to the data, other wireless clients are transferring with RF technology, it might allow them to view the data as it enters the wired network or, as is the concern here, give them the ability to access the data in live storage.

 To protect against the scenario where attackers discover a method for associating and authenticating with your wireless network (in other words, they have breached the network access portion of your security), you should use secure authorization at the point of live storage on the storage device. Create users and groups, as supported by your network operating system or storage device, and assign proper permissions to those users and groups. Because the attackers are not members of one of these groups and/or are not one of these individuals, they should not be able to access the data.

To truly secure against attacks on live storage, you need to understand in depth the security mechanisms of your chosen network operating system or device. You do not need to know how to do this for the CWSP exam because it is beyond the scope of Wi-Fi security, but you must learn to do it for your production implementations. This understanding is critical to providing complete security to your network because skilled attackers often escalate their privileges once they gain access to the network—this means they become one of those users accessing the data "on the inside." You can see by now that "security" is not one step, and requires a broad view of what is going on with the entire network and the host devices attached to it.

The final point of attack is the storage media you use for data backup. Many organizations use physical backup devices that are connected directly to the live storage device. Sometimes organizations transfer the data across the network to an external backup device. In these scenarios, just as when securing the wireless laptop client connections earlier, you must ensure that the traversal path is secure by securing all wireless links in the path (if there are any).

This section was not intended to serve as a complete tutorial on data sensitivity analysis. Rather, you learned that there are many factors to consider depending on the construct of the network, and you should contemplate all the ways in which your data is used in order to provide proper security mechanisms. In a large organization, wireless security is one component of overall organizational security.

📝 From the Blogs

IT Security Skills Anyone Can and Should Learn

URL: dalewifisec.wordpress.com/2015/02/07/it-security-skills-anyone-can-and-should-learn
Author: Dale Rapp
Blog: DALESWIFISEC—dalewifisec.wordpress.com

I've been teaching IT security awareness for several years and I try to get those in attendance of the classes to learn some basic IT security skills. These basic skills build on each other and there is some cross over, but ultimately this blended set of security skills can help anyone stay safe online. As with any sport you always start by learning the fundamentals, and while no one skill can get you into the game or keep you safe online, they can definitely make you ready for either.

1) Physical Security

With free Wi-Fi available in coffee shops and many fast food restaurants I constantly see people leaving their devices unattended and this lapse can allow someone to walk off with the device unnoticed. Think about your device and the amount of data it may contain. The device may have your whole world stored on it! If someone takes your laptop, tablet, or phone, it is so much more than having the device stolen, but the data it contains. In addition to this Wi-Fi example, other times when you must pay attention to your device is when going through airport security or leaving the device in plain sight while stored in the car. These situations can also expose the device to being stolen, so physical security is a great starting point and a must have skill for overall IT Security.

2) Do Not Accept the Defaults

One of the most basic rules of security, but at the same time one of the most abused, is not changing settings from the vendor defaults. The excitement of

39

getting a new device and wanting to use it as soon as possible can cause people to rush through the setup and accept defaults with the promise to return later to change the settings. Unfortunately, the promise to return and change the settings never happens and beginning to use the device before setting it up properly has created a security risk.

For example, just plugging in a wireless router with its default settings is like forgetting to lock the door when you leave the house. Many wireless router administrative guides can be downloaded from the manufacturer's web site and these guides include default settings for the admin password or encryption key settings.

Another problem related to accepting the default settings is not checking for or applying updates. Whether during the initialization phase or during the life of the device, not applying these updates can render the device vulnerable to the security holes the updates were meant to patch. Many devices are insecure out of the box so take the time to secure them.

3) Sense of Urgency

When I teach email security awareness, a common theme with scams is the sense of urgency being portrayed in the emails. Many of these "don't think just click" type scams also show up in social media sites and text-based scams. The sense of urgency scams will try to get people to click or react without thinking about what they are doing. Some scams will have an emotional pull, such as someone you care about being in trouble, or losing access to your bank account, or even to let you know that you've won a prize. Before you know it, your judgment is clouded and you clicked and responded. There was a great awareness campaign started a few years ago called STOP THINK CLICK and those three words can make a big difference when responding or better yet not responding to these types of scams.

4) It Won't Happen To Me

I hear "it won't happen to me" or "I would not fall for that trick" all the time, and I have even said those same statements myself! Online scams are always evolving and new scams show up all the time, so always be alert and never let your guard down. If something seems out of place, start asking yourself some questions; does this person typically send this to me, why does my bank need me to verify my password, should I be logging into my email on unsecure Wi-Fi, why does this app need access to text messages and phone calls? After asking some questions you can make an informed decision, and if something just doesn't feel right trust your gut that it isn't right!

5) Social Networks

There is no such thing as private on social networks and anything you post your friends can share with the world!

Conclusion

It is not required that everyone be IT security experts to be safe online, but knowing some basic skills and practicing the skills can help anyone protect themselves. So after learning and practicing your IT security skills go outside and practice throwing, fielding, and hitting because the Yankees are looking for a new short!

Chapter Review

In this chapter, you learned about the foundational security concepts that are essential to understanding the remaining chapters of the book. You explored the importance of security and the terminology commonly used in relation to Wi-Fi security. You also reviewed the different types of networks and the security requirements they may have. Finally, you explored the relationship of the OSI Model to security.

Facts to Remember

Be sure to remember the following facts as you prepare for the CWSP certification, and be sure that you can explain the details related to them:

- All wireless security designs should include assurance of confidentiality, integrity, and availability (CIA).
- RF boundaries do not end at the walls of your facility. Consideration of the reach of your WLAN signal is important.
- A primary role of WLANs is network extension—even in modern networks.
- Everything you learned in relation to security while studying for the CWNA is still important for the CWSP candidate.
- Three key organizations drive the standards and certifications in relation to 802.11 security solutions: IEEE, Wi-Fi Alliance, and IETF.
- Home office networks should still ensure proper security. At the very least, they should use WPA- or WPA2-Personal.
- Small business networks vary greatly, but they should employ proper security solutions based on their budgetary constraints: WPA/WPA2 Personal or Enterprise, captive portals, and proper permissions on the available network resources.
- Large, modern enterprise networks nearly always use 802.1X/EAP for authentication.

- You will encounter legacy client devices that force you to make the best security decisions you can with what you have to work with.
- When possible, you should try to get legacy client devices replaced with devices that can support current security methods.
- Public networks must consider the security needs of the customer.
- Be sure to show a terms-of-use agreement that removes all responsibility from you for any incident that may occur while visitors are connected to your network.
- When working from remote locations, consider using VPN technology. Many enterprises require VPN.
- It often helps to think of the security technologies in relation to OSI Model layers. Many vendor documents refer to their technologies in this way.
- Wireless networking happens at the Data Link layer and the Physical layer, but it is important to understand how other layers are impacted by security measures.
- Wireless security is just one component of overall organizational network security.
- Whether the wireless network in question is small or large, security needs may well change over time. Network security is never a finished product.
- The 802.11 standards place great emphasis on backwards compatibility, which creates its own share of security concerns by allowing legacy devices to be accommodated on new networks.

Chapter 1: Review Questions

1. Wireless network security is built on the foundational concept of CIA, which stands for what?

    a. Configurations, Integrity, Applications
    b. Confidentiality, Integrity, Availability
    c. Configurations, Integrations, Availability
    d. Confidentiality, Integrations, Applications

2. The original WEP encryption specification used a key of which construct?

    a. 24-bit key with 40-bit Initialization Vector
    b. 40-bit key with 24-bit Initialization Vector
    c. 64-bit key with 24-bit Initialization Vector
    d. 104-bit key with 64-bit Initialization Vector

3. The 802.11i amendment does not allow which of the following?

    a. Shared Key Authentication
    b. Open System Authentication
    c. Four-way Handshake
    d. The use of STAs for WLAN

4. The concept of RSNA came about with _____ and stands for _____.

    a. 802.1X, Reasonably Secure Network Association.
    b. 802.11X, Robust Secure Network Association.
    c. 802.11i, Reasonably Secure Network Association.
    d. 802.11i, Robust Secure Network Association.

5. Which of the following is true regarding wireless networks?

    a. Wireless networks are easily confined.

    b. Wireless networks are considered to be unbounded.

    c. Wireless networks are immune to eavesdropping

    d. Wireless networks cannot be heard by authorized clients and intruders.

6. Which of these are a legitimate concern for personal usage threat assessment?

    a.   Intruders may exploit open wireless networks.

    b.   Intruders may compromise data base servers.

    c.   Intruders may access open switch ports.

    d.   Intruders may install rogue wireless access points.

7. Why are wired networks at risk from poorly secured 802.11 networks?

    a.   Users associate to both wired and wireless networks simultaneously.

    b.   Wired networks extend wireless networks.

    c.   Wireless networks extend wired networks.

    d.   It is very easy to eavesdrop on wired networks.

8. Which organization promotes wireless networking and has been instrumental in Wi-Fi interoperability?

    a.   IEEE

    b.   IETF

    c.   Wi-Fi Alliance

    d.   Wi-Fi Institute

9. WPA2 Enterprise makes use of which non-wireless standard?

   a. 802.1X
   b. 802.3X
   c. 802.11X
   d. PPTP

10. Shared Key Authentication uses _____ management frames, while Open Authentication uses _____ management frames.

    a. 2, 4
    b. 4, 2
    c. 4, 6
    d. 2, 6

11. Which of these is a valid reason why wireless networks need robust encryption?

    a. Many application layer programs use secure protocols.
    b. Undetected eavesdroppers can intercept traffic between authorized wireless stations.
    c. Wireless networks are becoming very popular for server connectivity.
    d. Intruders might piggyback on your wired network.

12. Two examples of Virtual Private Network protocols are:

    a. WPA2, CCMP
    b. PPTP, CCMP
    c. IETF, IPSec
    d. IPSec, PPTP

13. The Wi-Fi Alliance currently tests client devices for compatibility with how many EAP types?

    a. 4
    b. 8
    c. 16
    d. 18

14. A wireless network security method or practice that is no longer recommended because it has been found to be weak is said to be_____.

    a. Deprecated
    b. Retired
    c. Suspended
    d. Abandoned

15. At which OSI layer does RF in WLAN environments work?

    a. Layer 7
    b. Layer 4
    c. Layer 2
    d. Layer 1

16. WPA uses what encryption?

    a. CCMP/AES
    b. TKIP/RC4
    c. CCMP/RC4
    d. TKIP/AES

17. Which of the following are likely to be used in enterprise wireless networks?

    a. 802.1X

    b. 802.11

    c. 802.3

    d. All of the above

18. Which of the following should not be used on secure business wireless networks?

    a. WPA2

    b. CCMP

    c. Shared Key Authentication

    d. Open System Authentication

19. During active scanning, a client transmits a _____ and the access point responds with a _____.

    a. Key request, key response

    b. Keep alive, acceptance packet

    c. Authentication, acknowledgement

    d. Probe request, probe response

20. The three fundamental building blocks of RADIUS are:

    a. Supplicant, Authenticator, Authentication Server

    b. Client, Encryption Server, Authenticator

    c. Supplicant, Authenticator, Gateway Router

    d. Client, Authenticator, Authentication Server

21. A recommended example of reducing your attack surface is:

    a. Using additional switches and APs
    b. Removing all network devices
    c. Enabling many network services to confuse attackers
    d. Disable unused administrative services and change default passwords

22. Which organization is associated with RFCs?

    a. IEEE
    b. IETF
    c. CWNP
    d. Wi-Fi Alliance

23. Which of these are valid VPN protocols?

    a. PPTP, L2TP
    b. PPTP, IETF
    c. CCMP, L2TP
    d. SMTP, PPTP

24. Which of the following utilizes a clear text challenge that makes it weak and therefore a poor choice for wireless security?

    a. Shared Key Authentication
    b. Open System Authentication
    c. Shared System Authentication
    d. Open Key Authentication

25. Which of the following is NOT a typical security concern when using a public Wi-Fi hotspot?

  a. Someone looking over your shoulder
  b. Compromised switch ports
  c. Eavesdropping
  d. Peer to peer attacks

Chapter 1: Review Answers

1. **B** is correct. Confidentiality, Integrity, and Availability are design tenants of wireless (and wired) network security.

2. **B** is correct. The 40-bit key/24-bit IV combination is generally referred to as 40-bit WEP, but sometimes to as 64-bit WEP.

3. **A** is correct. Shared Key Authentication is not allowed by 802.11i.

4. **D** is correct. The concept of the Robust Secure Network Association was introduced with 802.11i.

5. **B** is correct. Propagating in free space, wireless networks are considered unbounded.

6. **A** is correct. The key word in the question is "personal." Individual users are at risk on open wireless (hotspot) networks.

7. **C** is correct. Wireless networks extend the wired network and can provide an attack vector against the LAN.

8. **C** is correct. The Wi-Fi Alliance has interoperability and promoting wireless use as two of its primary focuses.

9. **A** is correct. Remember that 802.1X is not a wireless standard, but it works elegantly with secure 802.11 networks.

10. **B** is correct. Shared key authentication has four management frames while open authentication has two.

11. **B** is correct. Given that there is no way to detect eavesdropping, encryption renders intercepted traffic useless to the intruder.

12. **D** is correct. IPSec is one of the most common VPN types in service today. PPTP is valid, but its use is discouraged.

13. **B** is correct. There are currently 8 EAP types included in the Wi-Fi Alliance's compatibility testing regimen.

14. **A** is correct. The word "deprecated" is quite popular in networking when a feature or command is considered obsolete.

15. **D** is correct. WLAN works at Layer 1 (RF) and Layer 2 (data frames).

16. **D** is correct. TKIP is exclusively used in WPA while AES is used in both WPA and WPA2.

17. **D** is correct. 802.1X (security), 802.11 (WLAN), and 802.3 (Ethernet) are all part of the enterprise WLAN environment.

18. **C** is correct. Shared Key Authentication is a relic of early 802.11 and has been deprecated.

19. **D** is correct. As a CWSP (or CWNA) you will get well familiar with probe requests and probe responses.

20. **A** is correct. These are the proper terms for RADIUS components.

21. **D** is correct. Reducing your attack surface results in a smaller overall number of targets that attackers might attempt to exploit.

22. **B** is correct. Regardless of which technology is being discussed, the IETF is responsible for RFC documents.

23. **A** is correct. Of all listed, only PPTP and L2TP are valid VPN choices.

24. **A** is correct. The clear text challenge is the main reason that Shared Key Authentication was deprecated.

25. **B** is correct. Switch ports are not typically exposed in public Wi-Fi situations.

Chapter 2:

Wireless Security Challenges

Objectives

1.1 Describe general network attacks common to wired and wireless networks, including DoS, phishing, protocol weaknesses, and configuration error exploits.

1.2 Recognize common attacks and describe their impact on WLANs, including PHY and MAC DoS, hijacking, unauthorized protocol analysis and eavesdropping, social engineering, man-in-the-middle, authentication and encryption cracks, and rogue hardware.

1.5 Explain and demonstrate the security vulnerabilities associated with public access or other unsecured wireless networks, including the use of a WLAN for spam transmission, malware injection, information theft, peer-to-peer attacks, and Internet attacks.

After you understand the fundamental security concepts that are discussed in the first chapter, you can begin to investigate the specific security challenges related to 802.11 networks. This chapter addresses several specific topics important to the WLAN security professional. It begins with an exploration of network discovery processes. As with Chapter 1, you may notice overlap with CWNA materials throughout this chapter as we add depth to security-related topics from CWNA. We begin with examining the process that an attacker or security auditor would go through to locate WLANs.

Next, the chapter investigates questionable recommendations that actually result in a false sense of security. These are called pseudo-security solutions and are as important to be aware of as legitimate security measures. We will progress with legacy security mechanisms that should no longer be used, along with basic network attack methods. Finally, we will consider a number of recommended practices as we begin the process of learning how to secure against the types of attacks mentioned in this chapter. There is a lot of ground to cover in Chapter 2, with much that is relevant to the daily work and worry of the typical CWSP working on wireless networks.

Passive WLAN Discovery

802.11 wireless network discovery is foundational to wireless network security associations. The wireless discovery process consists of passive scanning or active scanning, or both. As with many things related to 802.11 wireless, network discovery is both important for its overall functionality and as a potentially exploitable juncture in WLAN operations.

Passive discovery uses Beacon management frames, which are transmitted at regular intervals—usually every 100 "time units" or "TU's". One-time unit is equal to 1,024μs (microseconds). Therefore, the average Beacon interval is 100 times 1,024μs or roughly 100ms (milliseconds), or 102.4ms to be exact. Though Beacon intervals are adjustable on enterprise wireless APs, the 100ms interval tends to be the de facto default value across most WLAN products. This time interval between beacon intervals is also known as the Target Beacon Transmission Time, or "TBTT". You may recall from CWNA that during passive discovery, wireless client devices listen for Beacons. Clients use Beacons to identify available wireless networks and their characteristics, including the type of security that each network is capable of. From a security perspective it is important to understand what information is, and is not, broadcast in Beacon management frames.

Beacons contain a frame body that includes fixed fields and information elements. The security information elements (IEs) that appear in Beacon frames depend on the type of security mechanism for which the network is configured, such as TKIP/RC4 (WPA) or CCMP/AES (WPA2).

Devices that are certified for Wi-Fi Protected Access (WPA) include a WPA information element in Beacon management frames. To client devices, this information element identifies the supported security features, including the authentication methods, whether passphrase or 802.1X/ EAP, the encryption type, which is Temporal Key Integrity Protocol (TKIP), and the RC4 stream cipher.

Devices that are certified for Wi-Fi Protected Access 2 (WPA2) include a Robust Secure Network (RSN) information element in Beacon management frames. To client devices wishing to associate, this information element identifies the supported security features, including the authentication methods that are either passphrase or 802.1X/EAP, the encryption type which is Counter Mode Cipher Block Chaining Message Authentication Code Protocol, Counter Mode CBC-MAC (CCMP), and the Advanced Encryption Standard (AES) block cipher. Keep in mind that the 802.11i amendment that defined RSN parameters allowed TKIP/RC4 for backward compatibility in an RSN network. (As mentioned in Chapter 1, the notion of backwards compatibility is pervasive throughout 802.11 standards.)

 Note: **If a wireless device such as an AP is configured for WPA2 and WPA for backward compatibility, then both the RSN and WPA information elements appear in Beacon management frames. Wireless frames are discussed in greater depth in the Certified Wireless Analysis Professional (CWAP®) course and study guide.**

The Beacon management frame, which allows for the passive scanning process by wireless clients, includes the following basic information of potential interest to attackers:

- **Capability Information**—This includes information related to operational modes, whether it is a BSS or IBSS and other capabilities.
- **SSID**—This is the name of the BSS/ESS.
- **Supported Rates**—This is the list of data rates supported based on configuration and it is further expanded by the Extended Supported Rates field.
- **RSN-IE**—This shows the configured security capabilities of the network from a robust security perspective.

Active WLAN Discovery

Active scanning is another method of WLAN discovery, and uses both a Probe Request management frame (sent by client devices) and a Probe Response management frame (sent by the AP) in the discovery process. Wireless client network adapters scan all RF channels they support, which may include the 2.4 GHz band and the 5 GHz band (depending on model), in an effort to quickly locate WLANs that are available. The Probe Request is either aimed at a specific SSID or is very commonly used to find all SSIDs within radio range. When looking for any available network, the destination address (DA) is a broadcast address. All APs (infrastructure) or client devices (ad-hoc) on that RF channel that hear the Probe Request answers with a Probe Response frame.

It is important to understand what information is broadcast in the Probe Request and Probe Response frames, and the differences between the two. Like Beacon management frames, the Probe Request and Response frames each contain a frame body with fixed fields and information elements. Though there are commonalities, the contents of the frame body are different for both of these management frames. Some of the information contained with Probe Request frames is the Service Set Identifier (SSID), supported basic data rates, and extended supported rates. This frame contains limited information compared to the Beacon management frame.

The 802.11 standard requires that all devices (such as an AP in infrastructure mode or clients in an IBSS) that hear a Probe Request frame must answer with a Probe Response frame. The Probe Response frame contains much of the same information as the Beacon management frame, which identifies the specific capabilities of the service set. In addition to the SSID and supported data rates, the Probe Response frame also contains security-related information such as WPA and RSN information elements. The Probe Response frame is a Directed management frame and is sent to the MAC address of the device that sent the request.

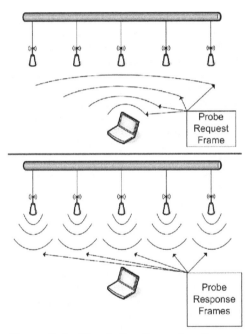

Figure 2-1: The Active Scanning Process

The Probe Request frame the client transmits may contain

- a specific SSID value, which identifies only the networks it associates to, or
- a "Broadcast SSID" as a wildcard (blank) SSID, allowing the device to connect to any wireless network that responds.

What determines whether a client only talks to a specific SSID or is interested in any available SSID? The way the client device is configured makes that determination. For example, the typical off-the-shelf configuration for wireless client devices' Probe Requests is to transmit the wildcard/any SSID, but a locked-down laptop in a corporate wireless environment might only allow for a specific SSID. More on this follows later in the chapter.

Discovery Hardware

In order to connect to a wireless AP, a client device with a wireless network adapter and client software is required. The discovery process is part of the normal procedure of connecting to a wireless network, so nearly any wireless device can be used as discovery hardware. Discovery hardware detects and connects to WLANs legitimately, or seeks out unprotected wireless networks and gains uninvited access to the resources of the network that are located behind the AP. Unauthorized intruders may prefer to use lightweight, unobtrusive equipment to perform discovery and exploitation of unprotected WLANs. Equipment such as laptops and tablet PCs make for powerful exploitation platforms, but the smaller size and convenience of handheld devices may be preferred when it comes to wireless attacks.

With the proliferation of high-end smartphones and small computers such as the Raspberry Pi, wireless users, IT staff, and attackers are all enjoying a range of very interesting client hardware options. Wireless support staff may use common client devices in tracking down wireless rogues, or they may use add-on hardware and/or utilities that provide Spectrum Analyzer or Packet Analysis functionality to help detect signals that should not be present in their environments.

> **Exam Moment:** When using a spectrum analyzer to locate rogue devices based on signal strength as an indicator of proximity, look at the **amplitude of the energy in the FFT view**. By contrast, when using a protocol analyzer to locate rogue devices, **use the signal strength value in frames from the target devices**. Similar information is being shown, but the spectrum analyzer works at Layer 1 while the protocol analyzer, in this case, is working at Layer 2.

All discovery devices require a wireless client adapter, an antenna, and discovery software. While most modern off-the-shelf client devices have built-in adapters and antennas, there is more than meets the eye in this space. There are many variations on the radio cards and antennas that are available, and custom configurations can offer extended range and sensitivity at surprisingly far distances and at surprisingly low prices—an advantage to the unauthorized intruder. A high-gain antenna connected to the right wireless client adapter can significantly increase the operating range of wireless intruders.

Wardriving is the term used to describe the act of performing a mass WLAN discovery activity while logging the discovered AP location information to a file for later analysis. The name wardriving is taken from the Matthew Broderick movie *WarGames* in which an automated software application was used to scan for open telephone modem connections—"wardialing." Wardriving is the act of performing a WLAN discovery while driving through a business park or residential area.

Wardriving is often conducted in a surreptitious manner and is usually considered to be an illicit activity. However, the legality of wardriving in the US is not clearly defined, and there has never been a criminal conviction. Most of those who fear wardriving are under the impression that the perpetrators are in the act of accessing the wireless networks they find (piggybacking), but the nature of most wireless network scanning applications, such as inSSIDer and Kismet, does not allow this. These applications take over control of the wireless network station adapter and do not allow them to associate to the discovered APs at the same time the discovery process is working. So wardriving can be construed primarily as a data gathering activity. Keep in mind that some client devices can use multiple adapters simultaneously to monitor and to connect. And even though "wardriving" implies a vehicle is involved, the same data gathering can be done while walking, cycling, or even from a boat.

The use of a Global Positioning System (GPS) device connected to a discovery PC can augment the effectiveness of wardriving. GPS greatly increases the effectiveness of location charting software by assigning a latitude and longitude position to each AP in the discovery listing. The GPS unit usually connects via USB, and is pivotal in automating location recording when covering a large area or while operating in unfamiliar locations. While this positioning information only indicates where the GPS receiver was located when it received each AP's signal, it can still be a very useful tool for locating nearby networks. Additional software can be used to take the raw discovery location logs and convert them into graphical map representations.

Figure 2-2: Spectrum Analyzer

A custom-built Spectrum Analyzer can be used as a protocol analyzer. This example is based on a Dell Windows 8 tablet with an external USB adapter.

Wireless network scanning applications that can be used for wardriving may operate in either active mode or in RF Monitor mode. Active mode applications such as the original NetStumbler issued probe requests to nearby listening APs using the standards-mandated broadcast (wildcard) SSID. Any APs that are not explicitly restrained from answering these probes respond with a matching Probe Response that contains—among other critical pieces of information—the current SSID of the answering AP. Listen-only RF Monitor mode applications such as the Linux-based Kismet listen quietly for various types of management messages such as authentication and association exchanges, which contain the SSIDs of the nearby networks. Active mode applications may be effective at gathering discovery information from devices that have been tailored with rudimentary security mechanisms such as SSID hiding.

Discovery Software

In addition to wireless cards and antennas, discovery stations require software in order to locate and connect to nearby APs. This software is typically called a client utility, or a client. Some computer operating systems include only basic wireless connectivity support from within the operating system itself, with few options beyond client credentials and basic wireless profile settings. More features tend to come with the wireless adapter's manufacturer utilities that usually accompany new Wi-Fi adapters. The Intel ProSet utilities are a long-running example.

A growing number of apps can be installed on some mobile devices, providing more features than those that are builtinto the mobile operating system. One multi-OS example of these apps is inSSIDer, which is a popular Wi-Fi discovery application. It is a favorite especially among Android users in the Wi-Fi support space, and brings functionality to Wi-Fi devices that the operating system itself cannot provide.

 Note: **If you are a Mac OS X user, you will find excellent tools from Adrian Granados in this wireless discovery category. He offers WiFi Explorer, an inSSIDer like tool, and AirTool for simplification of wireless capture with Wireshark. More information can be found here: adriangranados.com/apps.**

Specialized client applications may be used to perform wireless network discovery, site surveys, security auditing, wireless intrusion detection and mitigation, spectrum analysis, protocol analysis, and endpoint security. Linux is often the operating system of choice for wireless hackers, as it is typically the easiest to develop applications for. At the same time, every modern OS has some form of wireless utility that can be used for legitimate support or nefarious purposes.

Discovery software may fit into the category of online databases that are populated with information provided by the hacker community via web sites. Frequently, the information gathered during a wardrive is published to a publicly viewable, online repository. Several such databases exist, but they have varying degrees of accuracy and up-to-datedness. When performing an initial security audit in an organization that has a pre-existing WLAN installation, it may be a good practice to check the online databases to see if the organization's APs are currently listed there, and what vulnerabilities the hacker community claims are in play for those APs.

The following are popular public-access Wi-Fi databases:

- **openBmap**—openBmap.org
- **Skyhook**—www.skyhookwireless.com/coverage-map
- **Wigle**—www.wigle.net

Weakest Link

The overall security of any network is only as strong as the weakest link, and this certainly includes wireless networks. For example, let us say that you have 50 devices that are connected to the wireless network, and 49 devices use the strongest security available (WPA2—CCMP/AES) while one device uses WEP. The security of the entire network is assumed to be diminished to WEP because that is the lowest level of security that is in place on the network.

MAC address filtering is a popular control mechanism whose security value is frequently overestimated. Though MAC filters have their place in networking, relying on them for wireless network security is not recommended, as we will cover later in the chapter.

Another example of weak or mistaken security is when a networks SSID is hidden in an effort to secure the network. In reality, hiding the SSID does not offer any wireless security whatsoever. Some choose to hide the SSID for various reasons, but do not consider this as a security strategy. SSID hiding is covered in more detail in the next section.

Wireless networks have challenges from both the troubleshooting and security perspectives that you may not see in a wired network infrastructure. These challenges exist because the communication medium is RF in free space, which, as we have established in Chapter 1, is an unbounded medium. Taking this into consideration is critical when it comes to understanding and implementing wireless network security.

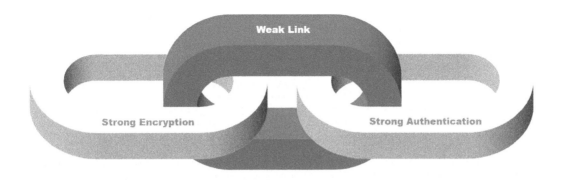

WEP, SSID Hiding and MAC Filtering

WPA/WPA2, 802.1X/EAP

Weak Links Break the Chain

The security of a wireless network is only as strong as the weakest link. In other words, if legacy security solutions such as Wired Equivalent Privacy (WEP) are in place you can consider that the best you will have.

Figure 2-3: Weak Links

At the same time, when it comes to security concerns, 802.11 networks are not completely different than wired networks. It is worth mentioning again that wireless networks extend the wired network, so there are common elements in play and threat factors to consider regardless of how network clients actually connect for access. Some of the attacks that may be common with both wired and wireless networks include, but are not limited to:

- Denial of Service (DoS) attacks
- Phishing attacks
- Protocol weaknesses
- Configuration error exploits

If this were an Ethernet security course, all of these would still be talked about. The particulars would be different, of course, but the overarching concerns pervade wired and wireless. Here we look at the wireless-specific characteristics of each of these attacks.

Common DoS attacks can exist at both the Physical layer and the Data Link layer. For Wi-Fi, RF jamming is the most obvious Layer 1 DoS. Other DoS attacks are due to exploits that have been discovered in the 802.11 protocol itself (MAC) at Layer 2. You will learn more about DoS attacks later in this chapter.

Phishing is a method used by attackers as a way to gather information that is valuable in some way to the person that is performing the phishing attack. This information can be of a sensitive nature and usually includes login credentials (usernames and passwords) and other information that may provide access to financial institutions, credit card accounts, and other sensitive resources. Various methods are used in phishing attacks, including email messages, web sites, telephone calls, and other electronic communications.

In the very basic sense, the 802.11 protocol was designed in a way that allows devices to politely share the wireless medium. Great care was taken when developing 802.11 in allowing each wireless device to have a turn in a protocol where only one STA (station) at a time can communicate, and there are many management and control frames required to keep it all orderly and precisely timed. Unfortunately, this comes with its share of security concerns due to exploits that have been discovered over the years. Some 802.11 management frames such as Deauthentication and Disassociation, which were designed for basic protocol operation, can be exploited with malicious intent. This includes hijacking authorized user devices and denial of service attacks. We will discuss how the concept of Management Frame Protection (MFP) can somewhat help prevent against management frame attacks later.

Incorrect configuration of infrastructure devices causes other potential security concerns. Though misconfiguration is more common in home and small business networks because the individual installing the device may lack the knowledge or skills required to correctly configure the devices, the stakes get much higher in business network settings. At home and in small business settings, simply following directions provided by the manufacturer of the infrastructure devices may be enough to provide a basic security posture. In some cases, it may be best to involve a professional to lock the devices down to the strongest possible configurations and to relax settings as needed and justified based on the use of the network. The configuration of infrastructure devices used with enterprise networks are driven by corporate security policy, which helps to lessen the possibility of misconfiguration. Policy alone cannot do much good if it is not put into practice by skilled administrators.

 Note: **Creating and using a checklist is a great way to ensure that all bases are covered when it comes to securing network devices. A checklist helps to lessen the possibility of misconfigurations. The book,** ***The Checklist Manifesto—How To Get Things Right***, **showed clearly that checklists work in projects large and small. Many high-importance tasks from military operations to flying an aircraft to building a house rely on checklists, which can be thought of as mini project-plans.**

SSID Hiding

Recall from CWNA that an SSID is more than just a network name. The Service Set Identifier (SSID) is used for wireless network identification and segmentation, and allows the naming of service sets much like Microsoft Windows uses workgroups to group computers and other devices. Other characteristics include:

- The SSID is included within several different management frames.
- Legacy security tactics suggest hiding the SSID from intruders, although doing so provides no security.
- Current security tactics adequately protect WLANs, making SSID hiding as unnecessary as it is flawed as a security mechanism.

SSID hiding (or sometimes called "cloaking") is a technique implemented by WLAN device manufacturers that removes the information found in the SSID information element from Beacon management frames. Depending on the implementation, SSID hiding may remove it from Probe Response frames sent from the AP. Hiding the SSID

- is intended to keep casual users from noticing a wireless network, but may be problematic for certain client devices, and

- does not offer any legitimate protection because many software utilities and all protocol analyzers can find the SSID in 802.11 management frames other than Beacons.

There simply is no hiding; the best that it does is reduce the obviousness of the SSID.

 Note: **The 802.11-2012 standard allows STAs to operate simultaneously with pre-RSNA and RSNA algorithms, but RSNA forbids the use of Shared Key 802.11 authentication, which Pre-RSNA allows. For RSNA, only the Open System Authentication mechanism can be used.**

WARNING: Disabling the broadcasting of the SSID within the Beacon frames is not an effective deterrent and adds no value to WLAN security.

Some organizations hide the SSID on all WLAN profiles except for the profile that is used for guest access. This decision is not for security purposes but rather to prevent users that do not belong to the organization from attempting to connect to wireless networks in which they do not have the proper credentials. This in turn may help lessen unnecessary technical support calls. Although this is not a recommended security procedure, it is a configuration option that may be used in some installations for management purposes.

Consider the explanation provided by one SOHO AP manufacturer:

"It is possible to make your wireless network nearly invisible. By turning off the broadcast of the SSID, your network SSID will not appear in a site survey. A site survey is a feature of many wireless network adapters on the market today. It scans the "air" for any available network and allows the computer to select the network from the site survey. Turning off the broadcast of the SSID helps increase security."

This type of messaging, though well meaning, can mislead inexperienced users to enable SSID hiding as a standalone security mechanism. Thankfully, most manufacturers have advanced past this sort of poor advice in their product literature.

To be clear, SSID hiding should not be considered a security solution at all. In some scenarios, it may play the role of assisting with management or usability of a given WLAN environment, but simply hiding SSIDs is never a security solution. It can help shape usability from the perspective that, if SSID broadcasting is disabled, normal users do not see WLANs to which they should not connect. Users who need to connect to hidden WLANs can be provided with the configuration profiles. Free utilities combined with low skill show hidden SSIDs. The point is that hiding the SSID provides management or usability, but in no way exemplifies WLAN security.

SSID Field in Other Frames

In addition to Beacon management frames, the SSID information is included in several other 802.11 management frames, which are:

- Probe Request
- Probe Response
- Association Request
- Reassociation Request

For protocol functional purposes, the Association Request and Reassociation Request frames always contain the SSID. The SSID cannot be removed from these frames or the 802.11 protocol would cease to function.

Hiding the SSID only removes it from the Beacon management frame. The information element in this frame is still intact; however, the SSID value is removed from the frame itself.

Authentication Request, Authentication Response, and Association Response frames do not contain the SSID Information Element.

Many current discovery software applications and most protocol analyzers are able to identify the SSID even if it is hidden in Beacon management frames. Once a user has associated to an AP, a discovery utility can gather the SSID from other management frames. An intruder could wait for a new association to occur or actively force users to deauthenticate and then quietly learn the SSID when the devices reassociate to an AP. So you can see that even if the SSID is not broadcast in the Beacon frame, most enterprise-quality packet analyzer tools (and some of the free ones) have the capability to learn what the SSID is from the other management frames and display the SSID value.

Broadcast SSID in Probes

The 802.11-2012 standard defines a Broadcast SSID as a wildcard (blank) SSID. 802.11-2012 requires APs to respond to all Probe Requests that contain either a matching SSID or a blank SSID. Many manufacturers provide the configuration option to prevent APs from responding to Probe Request frames, even though 802.11-2012 still requires it. Curiously, the Wi-Fi Alliance does not deny certification to manufacturers who disable Broadcast SSID responses.

From IEEE 802.11-2012:

8.2.4.3.4 BSSID field

The value of all 1s is used to indicate the wildcard BSSID. The wildcard value is not used in the BSSID field except where explicitly permitted in this standard.

10.1.4.3.2 Sending a probe response

STAs, subject to criteria below, receiving Probe Request frames shall respond with a probe response only if

a) *The Address 1 field in the probe request is the broadcast address or the specific MAC address of the STA, and either item b) or item c) below.*

b) *The STA is a mesh STA and the Mesh ID in the probe request is the wildcard Mesh ID or the specific Mesh ID of the STA.*

c) *The STA is not a mesh STA and*

    1) *The SSID in the probe request is the wildcard SSID, the SSID in the probe request is the specific SSID of the STA, or the specific SSID of the STA is included in the SSID List element, and*

    2) *The Address 3 field in the probe request is the wildcard BSSID or the BSSID of the STA.*

Probe Response frames shall be sent as directed frames to the address of the STA that generated the probe request. The SSID List element shall not be included in a Probe Request frame in an IBSS.

MAC Address Filtering

Although it should not be used to secure a wireless network, Media Access Control (MAC) filtering is considered by some to be an effective deterrent to prevent casual or unintentional system access to a wireless network. Again, before going any further, MAC address filtering should not be used as a stand-alone security solution in anything beyond a home network. Even then, there is no real reason to use MAC filtering any longer with the availability of WPA/WPA2-Personal in all consumer equipment today.

Since 802.11 WLAN device technology operates at the Physical and Data Link layers of the OSI model, the MAC address is a big part of the wireless networking process. The MAC address, which is defined at the MAC sublayer of the Data Link layer (Layer 2), identifies the network interface by the use of a manufacturer-assigned unique physical address or, potentially, a software-assigned address. MAC addresses on wireless devices are sometimes (incorrectly) called Ethernet addresses.

The purpose of MAC address filters is to allow or disallow access to the wireless network by restricting which MAC addresses can authenticate and associate to the network using 802.11 technology. Procedurally, MAC addresses are manually entered into the wireless AP or are entered by instructing the AP to add all currently connected MAC addresses, which identify the specific devices that are allowed or denied access to the wireless network. This is called a white list. When a black list is used, all MAC addresses are allowed except those in the list.

MAC address filters can be reasonably enabled for small numbers of client devices, but for large numbers of devices, it can be tedious and prone to entry mistakes. If MAC address filters are the only deterrent, intruders can easily discover the MAC addresses that are permitted and re-address their own station adapters with an allowed MAC address to gain access—software-assigned addressing. This process is also called spoofing, or, specifically, MAC spoofing. Therefore, MAC filtering should not be used as a WLAN security solution. Next, we will discuss how easy it is to carry out MAC spoofing.

Finding Valid MAC Addresses

MAC address-based access control lists (ACLs) can provide a degree of admission control for client devices, but discovering which MAC addresses are authorized on a system is easy when using a wireless scanner or protocol analyzer software program. Any device that is successfully passing data traffic to an AP on the wireless network is considered an authorized device and that MAC address can be used for connectivity to the wireless network. MAC addresses can be easily spoofed using operating system techniques or third-party freeware utilities.

Keep in mind that the MAC addresses cannot be encrypted as specified in the 802.11 standard. This physical identifier (MAC address) is broadcast in plain clear text and is shown in protocol analyzer frame decodes, among other places. Therefore, it is very easy for an intruder or anyone with a limited amount of technical knowledge and the proper software tools to identify authorized-wireless networking devices from a simple scan of the unbounded RF medium used by the WLAN.

One analogy to consider is the physical address of a home or building on a street. Each building is marked with a unique physical address to provide an identity for the building, for example, 123 Main Street. The street name is comparable to the SSID of the wireless network since all connected devices share the same SSID, and 123 would be comparable to the MAC address of a connected device, which is the unique identifier.

Anyone who wanted to visit this building could easily identify it from the marking of the numbers 123. If these identifying addresses from all of the buildings on the street were missing, encrypted or scrambled in any way, there would be no way for a visitor to find the correct building. But since they are not, the buildings can be found easily. On WLANs, the same is true. The addresses are not encrypted or scrambled and so they can be located easily.

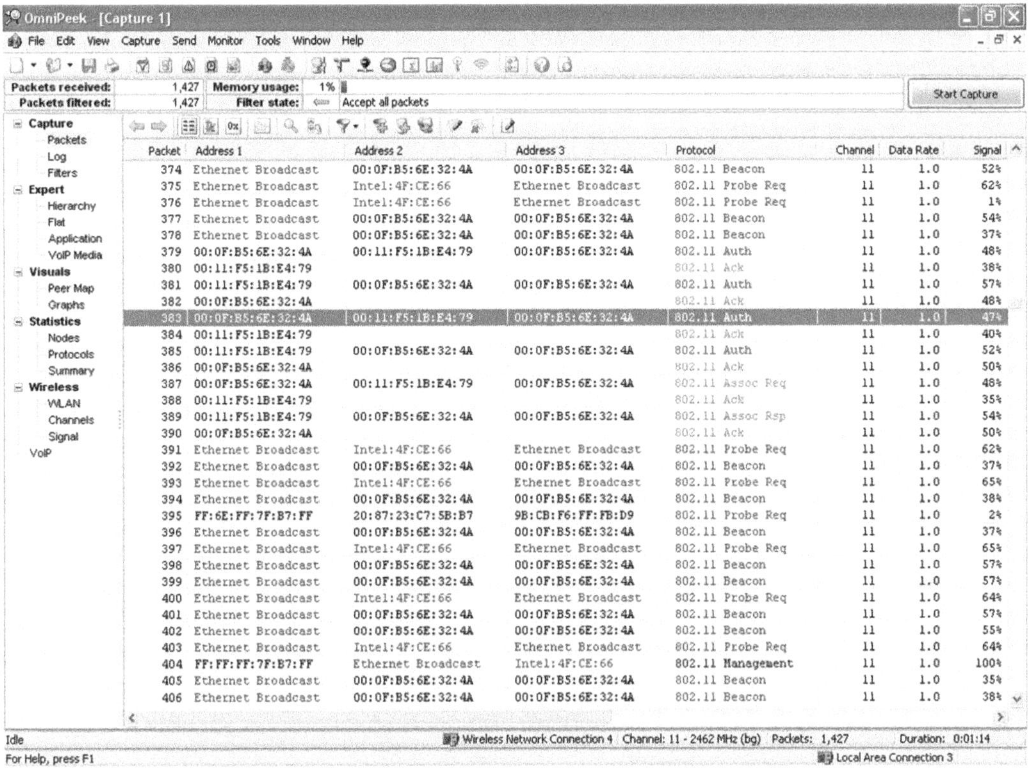

Figure 2-4: Protocol Capture Showing MAC Addresses

MAC-Address Spoofing

MAC-address spoofing is the process of altering a MAC address in a computer so that it matches a valid MAC address on the network. Each client device is given its MAC address at the time of manufacture, and you may sometimes hear of a MAC address referred to as burned-in address (BIA). This terminology might imply that MAC addresses are permanently written in some unalterable chip within the network adapter, but this is not true. The reality is that MAC address values can be re-written in software, so the network sees a different value than what the factory assigned. Several MAC spoofing utilities are freely available, including

- SMAC
- MAC Makeup

- A-MAC Address
- Nmap ("Network Mapper")
- Systems Lizard

MAC addresses may be reset with simple tools that are available by default on most computer OSes.

- Linux: ifconfig eth0 hw ether 03:a0:04:d3:00:11
- FreeBSD: ifconfig bge0 link 03:a0:04:d3:00:11

MS Windows: On Microsoft Windows systems, the MAC address is stored in a registry key. The location of that key varies from one MS Windows version to the next, but Internet searches help you find this value so you can edit it yourself. There are numerous free utilities you can download to make this change. For some NICs, you can modify the MAC address in the Device Manager using the following procedures:

1) Open the Device Manager.
2) Press Windows Key + S.
3) Type Device Manager and press Enter to select it in the results list.
4) Find the WLAN NIC in the Network Adapters node and double-click on it to open the Properties dialog.
5) On the Advanced tab, look for a property called Network Address, MAC Address, Locally Administered Address, or something similar.
6) Change it there.

 Note: **The MAC spoofing process does not always work on Windows systems, even when the feature is apparently available. The wireless drivers for some adapters just do not accommodate the capability.**

MAC-address spoofing is an effective way to bypass other MAC-based security or control mechanisms, such as those used for paid access to hotspots. Some service providers log allowed devices by MAC address. Those wishing to bypass this type of filter on a paid network can spoof their MAC address with an authorized device's

MAC address. This type of activity may be illegal along the lines of "theft of services" and, as with other capabilities you may learn in common with hackers, is not recommended. Hotspot providers should be aware of the limitations of their system.

Open System Authentication

802.11 Open System authentication must be performed every time a device connects to a wireless network or anytime it transitions from one AP to another. This process is a fundamental step in the basic operation of 802.11 wireless connectivity. Without performing this task, a wireless device would not be able to associate to the AP.

From IEEE 802.11-2012:

11.2.3.2 Open System authentication

> *Open System authentication is a null authentication algorithm. Any STA requesting Open System authentication may be authenticated if dot11AuthenticationAlgorithm at the recipient STA is set to Open System authentication. A STA may decline to authenticate with another requesting STA. Open System authentication is the default authentication algorithm for pre-RSNA equipment.*

> *Open System authentication utilizes a two-message authentication transaction sequence. The first message asserts identity and requests authentication. The second message returns the authentication result. If the result is 'successful,' the STAs shall be declared mutually authenticated.*

> *In the description in 11.2.3.2.2 and 11.2.3.2.3, the STA initiating the authentication exchange is referred to as the requester, and the STA to which the initial frame in the exchange is addressed is referred to as the responder. The specific items in each of the messages described in the following subclauses are defined in 8.3.3.11, Table 8-28, and Table 8-29.*

Based on this description, it should be obvious that Open System authentication alone provides no security whatsoever. Despite including the word authentication, there really is not any in this case, as any and every device (STA) is welcome to communicate with the AP.

Though "a STA may decline to authenticate with another requesting STA," it is pretty much a given that devices of like technical capabilities will authenticate with each other. Despite the lack of security, it is important to know that Open System authentication is used as part of the workflow by all strong enterprise security solutions today.

For example, when using WPA2-Enterprise, Open System authentication is performed first and then the EAP authentication occurs, followed by the 4-way handshake, which is used to generate the unicast encryption keys used between a single STA and the AP.

You will learn about these concepts in greater detail later in this book, but it is important to keep this fact in mind.

Wired Equivalent Privacy (WEP)

WEP should never be used today. It really is that simple. If you desire confidentiality and integrity for your data, you will not use WEP. All hardware released for the past several years will support at least WPA-Personal, which is an order of magnitude stronger in security than WEP. The weaknesses of WEP are briefly reviewed in this section. To better understand why currently accepted WPA variants are so much stronger, it is worth digging into the flaws of WEP just a bit more. In other words, we study WEP as CWSPs to learn from the past.

From IEEE 802.11-2012:

11.2.2.1 WEP overview

WEP-40 was defined as a means of protecting (using a 40-bit key) the confidentiality of data exchanged among authorized users of a WLAN from casual eavesdropping. Implementation of WEP is optional. The same algorithms have been widely used with a 104-bit key instead of a 40-bit key in fielded implementations; this is called WEP-104. The WEP cryptographic encapsulation and decapsulation mechanics are the same whether a 40-bit or a 104-bit key is used. Therefore, subsequently, WEP can refer to either WEP-40 or WEP-104.

The characteristics of WEP include:

- RC4 Stream Cipher
- Static Pre-shared Keys
- Manual Key Management

- Weak Implementation

WEP is unsafe for use under any circumstances or at either key size (40-bit or 104-bit) because it suffers from multiple weaknesses. Your top priority should be to move to a more secure solution and ensure that no wireless networks in your care ever use WEP.

WEP Weaknesses

WEP required the use of static keys. The selected key would have to be manually entered on all devices that were part of the same service set. In most cases, once the key was determined and entered on all of the devices it was never changed. In theory changing the key periodically, or at a specific regular interval, would help to provide a more secure network. The important words here are "in theory."

You learned earlier that the 802.11 standard defined a 40-bit WEP key. Also, a 104-bit key could be used. 40-bit and 104-bit is the actual key length. In addition to the key, WEP also used a 24-bit initialization vector (IV) as part of the encryption and decryption process. Therefore, with the addition of the IV, the key length would be 64-bit or 128-bit. The key can be made up of either hexadecimal or ASCII characters. The length for each is shown in the following table:

64-bit	13	5
128-bit	26	10

Table 2.1: WEP Key Lengths

The 24-bit IV transmitted across the wireless medium in clear text makes the WEP key vulnerable to intrusion. This reality was a primary flaw in the WEP implementation. RC4 is not necessarily a bad encryption algorithm, but the keys must be implemented in a way to avoid reuse in any reasonable window of time. It was not implemented in this way, and so WEP was vulnerable to key reuse attacks. Further explanation follows.

Two primary problems exist with how this IV mechanism was implemented.

- First, the 24-bit IV was transmitted across the air in clear text or plaintext.
- Second the 24-bit IV was used as encryption seed in conjunction with the WEP key and the RC4 stream cipher to create
  - a key stream, and
  - finally the encrypted cipher text message.

This was accomplished through the use of an exclusive OR process with the Integrity Check Value (ICV) providing an encrypted frame body for the wireless data frame. Though this process resulted in basic encryption of data, these two items created a bad combination. If someone was to capture enough of the encrypted frames, the WEP key could be found using any number of key cracking programs.

In addition to the weak IV scheme, the WEP process also suffered from weak integrity protection or ICV. The WEP ICV was computed using the CRC-32 and calculated over the plaintext MAC Protocol Data Unit (MPDU) field. This made the ICV vulnerable to what is known as a bit flip attack, which gave someone the capability to capture frames and flip bits in the data payload of the frame. Then the ICV would be modified and the frame would be retransmitted with the modified data payload. Unbeknownst to the receiver, the data was modified in transit, creating an additional vulnerability and losing integrity—the very purpose of the ICV.

In the early days of wireless, cracking WEP became a bit of a sport for the hacker community, as their obsession with Wi-Fi increased with the popularity of wireless networking. Since the advent of the 802.11n standard, no APs going forward should even support WEP as an option per the standard. This fact does not always play out in implementations, but it is the practice all vendors should follow. You do not have to memorize the explicit details covered here in the examination of WEP's weaknesses, but it is good to

- know why more robust encryption options were ultimately needed, and
- appreciate the evolution of this important component of wireless security.

WEP is no longer a primary testing area on the CWSP exam because we should have learned the lessons from it long ago. It is addressed here only to discourage its use in any modern WLAN implementation.

Shared Key Authentication

802.11 Shared Key Authentication is a deprecated authentication mechanism. Unlike Open System authentication which used WEP only for data encryption, Shared Key authentication required the use of WEP for both 802.11 authentication and for data encryption. While it may seem that adding an authentication exchange would enhance a network's security, Shared Key authentication may actually accelerate the exposure of a static WEP key. Like with other early security features, the intentions were not realized with Shared Key Authentication.

Figure 2-5: Shared Key Authentication Process

Notice that in the image, Shared Key authentication uses four authentication management frames that are exchanged between two stations, in this case a client station and an AP. Recall that Open System authentication only uses two authentication management frames. In order for Shared Key authentication to function, the same WEP key must also be installed on all stations that are part of the wireless service set.

In this example, the first frame is sent from the client station to the wireless AP, which initiates the Shared Key authentication process. The AP responds to the requesting client station with a clear text or plaintext challenge message. This challenge text can be seen by anyone monitoring the wireless medium with eavesdropping software (protocol analyzers and dedicated cracking tools such as those in Kali Linux). The third frame is sent back to the AP from the client station and now has an encrypted message, which was encrypted using the WEP key assigned to the client station. Keep in mind that this is the same key that is installed on all devices that are part of the same service set, including the AP. The AP validates the encrypted message and respond to the client device with the fourth frame showing a failed or successful authentication. Once this process has successfully completed, the 802.11 association process ensues and data communications can occur.

Shared Key Authentication Uses WEP

Let us break down what is wrong with Shared Key authentication a little deeper. Since Shared Key authentication requires the use of WEP, it introduces additional methods that may be used by an eavesdropping intruder to recover the static encryption key. This is because all that needs to be captured by an intruder are the four authentication frames as seen in the graphic. With the proper tools, such as a wireless protocol analyzer and key cracking software program, the WEP key can be discovered very quickly without the need to capture a single data frame that contains the IV. This vulnerability is part of the 802.11 Shared Key authentication process and allows for the easy discovery of the WEP key without the aid of any data frames that contain the plaintext 24-bit IV.

Once the WEP encryption key is discovered, an intruder can use it to join the wireless service set by configuring the client device as an authorized station in possession of the WEP key. It also allows for decryption of encrypted frames that traverse the wireless medium in protocol analyzers that support decryption of data.

From IEEE 802.11-2012:

11.2.3.3 Shared Key authentication

Shared Key authentication seeks to authenticate STAs as either a member of those who know a shared secret key or a member of those who do not.

Shared Key authentication can be used if and only if WEP has been selected and shall not be used otherwise.

This mechanism uses a shared key delivered to participating STAs via a secure channel that is independent of IEEE Std 802.11. This shared key is set in a write-only MIB attribute with the intent to keep the key value internal to the STA.

The following list summarizes the weaknesses of 802.11 Shared Key authentication:

- Requires the use of WEP—WEP is required and is used for both station authentication and data encryption.
- Uses a clear text or plaintext challenge message—This challenge text can easily be discovered by someone that is monitoring the wireless medium, which will result in discovery of the WEP key.
- Results in a weak authentication mechanism—Software tools are readily available for many operating systems, and are fairly easy to use, allowing for the Shared Key authentication process to be easily compromised.

Thankfully, even most on-the-market, new, consumer-grade wireless routers today do not offer the user the ability to implement WEP or Shared Key authentication. In all but the most ridiculous of cases, the only options are Open, WPA, or WPA2. In most of the newest equipment, the only options are now Open or WPA2 (or possibly WPS).

CWSP still requires a working familiarity with the WEP and Shared Key authentication's flaws, as security professionals should understand not just that they are weak methods, but also why they are weak. However, CWSP no longer required detailed knowledge of the inner-workings of WEP or Shared Key authentication.

EAP-MD5

You learned in Chapter 1 that 802.1X, which defines port based access control, helps to provide a secure, scalable, and manageable security solution for enterprise wireless networks. It is important to note that 802.1X is a framework that works in conjunction with an appropriate EAP method to allow for user-based security. Many EAP variants can be used to secure WLAN communications, and you saw in Chapter 1 that the Wi-Fi Alliance does interoperability testing for eight EAP types. This chapter explores some of the EAP types that are vulnerable to intrusion and that should not be used to secure a wireless network.

EAP-MD5 is one example of a weak EAP type. It was developed for use on the wired network to test basic connectivity between EAP participants. It does not provide dynamic encryption key management, mutual authentication (client trusts the authentication server, and the server trusts the individual clients), or any operational characteristic that would provide security for a wireless network. Because it creates numerous vulnerabilities, EAP-MD5 should never be used to secure an 802.11 network.

Proprietary LEAP

Earlier in this chapter you learned about 802.11 Open System authentication, Shared Key authentication, and WEP. You saw that all of these methods are inadequate for providing secure wireless communications on an 802.11 network. At one point on the 802.11 timeline, the realization hit the wireless industry that early security methods were not sufficient (by a long shot) as the popularity of Wi-Fi exploded. There was an urgent need for methods that would provide stronger wireless security, or wireless networking would be stunted in where and how it could be used. Something had to be done!

The answer to the security dilemma would eventually be addressed in the 802.11i amendment to the standard, which would provide enhanced strong wireless security mechanisms including CCMP/AES. However, in the early 2000 timeframe, the ratification of the 802.11i amendment was still some time away (it would not be ratified until 2004). In the interim, attempts were made to provide alternative wireless security options, such as LEAP.

Cisco systems developed its own EAP type known as Lightweight Extensible Authentication Protocol (LEAP). This proprietary EAP method was very popular because it provided secure wireless communications and was widely deployed with Cisco networks. Keep in mind that LEAP required the use of a Cisco infrastructure, which included Cisco client devices and wireless APs. One exception to this was the use of Cisco Compatible Extensions (CCX) technology. This enabled non-Cisco manufacturers to develop code that allowed their devices to use LEAP technology on the client device side. There have been several versions of CCX through the years, but non-Cisco adoption has been far from universal.

Figure 2-6: ASLEAP Capturing LEAP Information

LEAP included a vulnerability in which the username of the person attempting to authenticate was passed in clear text across the wireless medium and did not use any tunneling mechanisms to secure the communications. Theoretically, this behavior made authentication traffic that was captured susceptible to offline dictionary attacks on weak passwords since it used a variant of the MSCHAPv2 hash for the exchange of client credentials. Joshua Wright, a long-time WLAN security expert, created a software program (named ASLEAP) that made this theory a reality.

 Note: **In addition to developing wireless security tools, Joshua Wright has published a wealth of articles on Wi-Fi security and has taught classes on the topic. Heis very active in the wireless community and is one of those people that CWSPs would do well to follow as a resource for current WLAN security trends and concerns.**

After LEAP's vulnerabilities were discovered and published, Cisco Systems introduced a more secure EAP type, called EAP-FAST, which served as a replacement to LEAP. EAP-FAST has also since been replaced in many deployments by newer non-Cisco-specific EAP types, such as PEAP, EAP-TLS, and EAP-TTLS.

Eavesdropping

By now, you likely realize that unencrypted wireless traffic is easily intercepted by any and all nearby users with a protocol analyzer. Any client device that can receive the WLAN traffic is able to collect information that traverses the wireless medium. Modern protocol analyzers make it easy to collect and inspect unencrypted traffic. These wireless protocol analyzers use a special network device driver that allow the wireless adapter to operate in promiscuous mode, which in turn makes the analyzer a passive device. The monitoring analyzer is then unnoticed by any intrusion prevention methods. Not all wireless adapters can be placed into monitor mode or promiscuous mode, but USB variants can be purchased specifically for the task of wireless eavesdropping in monitor mode. Protocol analyzer software vendors recommend and sell adapters for this purpose. Such software and hardware are intended for analysis of WLANs aimed at performance and functional improvements, such as those covered in the CWAP® certification, but they are often used by hackers.

802.11-based encryption obscures Layer 3-7 data from protocol analysis, and is the basic deterrent to eavesdropping. Using adequate mechanisms to encrypt WLAN traffic is imperative to ensure security and privacy. Unauthorized protocol analysis with protocol analyzer software is the most common form of eavesdropping, but its effectiveness varies with the security of the WLAN being monitored.

Because of the passive methods used by wireless protocol analyzers, there is no way to detect or prevent this type of eavesdropping. The amount of information that can be gathered by eavesdropping on a WLAN with weak security is amazing, and what can be learned by passive listening is fairly shocking the first time you see network traffic exposed in this manner. Even with encrypted data payloads, you can learn significant information, such as:

- Supported data rates
- Allowed MAC addresses
- Security cipher suites and encryption algorithms used
- PHYs supported in the BSS
- MAC and PHY features supported
- The amount of data traversing the network

Though it is not the only method you can use, it is very easy to perform eavesdropping using the Kali Linux distribution and a compatible USB adapter. Kali can run in a virtual machine (VM) so that it need not even be your native OS. It comes with all the required tools for wireless eavesdropping preinstalled. The appendix to this text provides instructions for installing a Kali Linux VM using VirtualBox. It can be used in VMware Player—a free virtualization environment that can only run a single VM at a time. VirtualBox can run multiple VMs and, for this reason, it is the tool referenced in the appendix. However, here at CWNP, we have found that running Kali Linux in VMware Player typically results in better performance on the same machine.

Assuming you have a compatible USB adapter, (the Hawking HD45U or Linksys AE3000 both work well for 802.11n three stream captures) connected to your computer and passed through to VMware Player or VirtualBox running Kali Linux.

Use the following instructions to perform a capture on any channel you desire:

1) In the Kali Linux VM, logon as a user you have created or as `root` (the default password is `toor`).

2) On the desktop, click the Terminal icon to load a terminal (console) session.

3) In the console, execute `iwconfig` to determine the WLAN adapter name, for example, `wlan0` or `wlan1` are common.

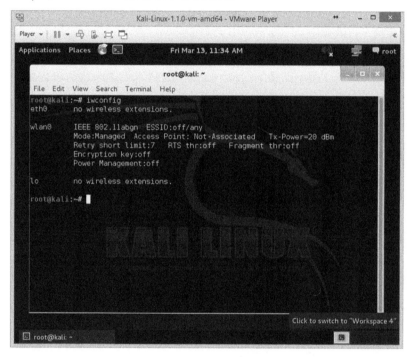

4) Turn on monitor mode by running `airmon-ng start wlan#`, while replacing # with the identifier of your adapter.

5) Execute `airodump-ng mon# --band g` to look for SSIDs on 2.4 GHz or `airodump-ng mon0# --band a` to look for SSIDs on 5 GHz, while replacing # with the appropriate identifier for your monitor interface created by airmon-ng, for example `mon0`.

```
CH 13 ][ Elapsed: 50 s ][ 2015-03-13 11:43

BSSID              PWR  Beacons    #Data, #/s  CH  MB   ENC  CIPHER AUTH ESSID

B4:75:0E:59:39:DD  -31        4        0    0   1  54e. WPA2 CCMP  PSK  OFFICE24

BSSID              STATION           PWR   Rate   Lost    Frames Probe

(not associated)   48:F8:B3:9B:99:95   0    0 - 6     0        2

root@kali:~#
```

6) Execute `airmon-ng stop mon#`, while replacing # with the appropriate identifier, for example `airmon-ng stop mon0`. You need to create a new monitor interface on the channel you want to scan.

7) Execute `airmon-ng start wlan# 1` to instantiate a monitor interface on channel 1 (change 1 to any other channel you desire, including 5 GHz channels), while changing the # as needed.

8) Run Wireshark by executing `wireshark` from the console.

9) Ignore any root errors, after all, you are performing wireless discovery.

10) After you are in Wireshark, click the `mon#` interface and then click `Start` to begin capturing, while replacing # with the identifier of your monitor interface created with `airmon-ng`.

Results: Depending on your adapter and its supported drivers, your results will vary. Excellent results have been achieved with the Hawking HD45U adapter, though this USB device is getting harder to acquire.

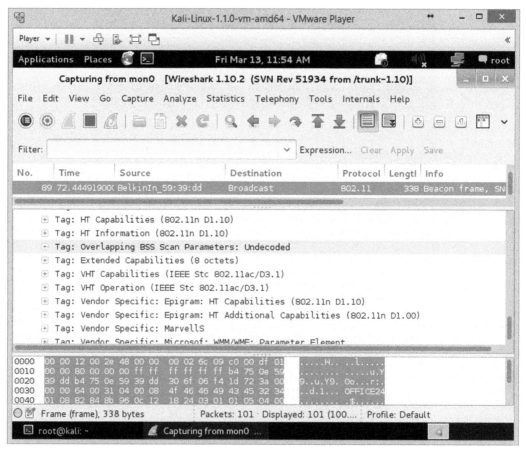

Figure 2-7: Capturing 802.11 Beacon Frames on Kali Linux

If you are unfamiliar with Wireshark, this is a great time to get your feet wet with it as it is

- a favorite of wireless and Ethernet network engineers and support staff
- a powerful Multi-OS tool for showing packet and frame-based activity that frequently leads to solving network problems, and
- a favorite for hackers.

"The packets never lie" is a popular saying among those skilled in protocol analysis and, as you get used to what Wireshark can tell you, you will understand why that expression is true.

For more detailed information on protocol analysis (as well as spectrum analysis), see the CWAP Official Study Guide published by CertiTrek Publishing.

Social Engineering

Social engineering is

- a collection of methods used by intruders to gather information that may in turn facilitate the ability to circumvent an installed wireless security solution, and
- perhaps one of the easiest ways for someone to bypass even the best security solutions because it takes advantage of the human component in network environments.

The people who use and support a network are often quite vulnerable to exploitation. Most individuals are trusting to a certain degree, so network users can be easily deceived by practiced intruders.

Consider a simple example, the company help desk. The purpose of the company help desk is to assist users with technical problems. In many computer network installations, the help desk is commonly the first place a user turns when experiencing wireless network problems and seeking assistance. If not properly trained and aware of social engineering practices, the help desk personnel can be targets for potential intruders. Some tactics include calling the help desk and befriending the person that is assisting them in order for the intruder to get information such as WLAN passphrases. Another method used is when the intruder places a call into the help desk and requests a password reset for an authorized user account. The social engineering variations are many, such as various phishing methods, talking-the-talk with the right people, dumpster diving, and others.

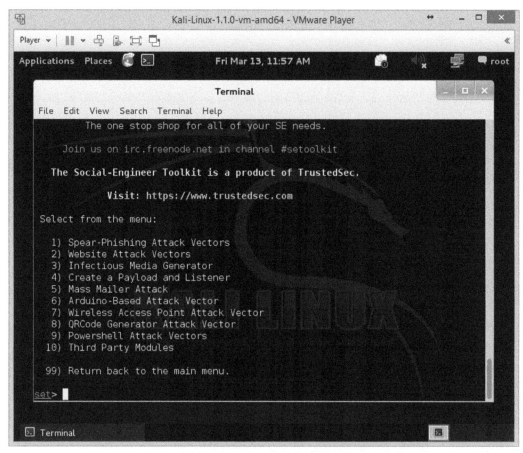

Figure 2-8: Social Engineering Toolkit Bundled in Kali Linux

A well-known hacker named Kevin Mitnick often addresses the vulnerability of social engineering. Many of his greatest network attacks occurred by exploiting this weak link in the security chain:

"My message today is primarily the same… I usually go around speaking on the threat of the human element, particularly on social engineering."—Kevin Mitnick

The Social Engineering Toolkit, shown in the image on the preceding page, includes several of the following attack vectors:

- **Spear-Phishing**—send emails with attached file payloads.

- **Website Attacks**—utilize multiple web-based attacks to compromise site visitors.
- **Infection Media Generator**—create USB, CD, and DVD autorun modules with a Metasploit payload.
- **Creating a Payload and Listener**—set up a payload to provide re-entry to compromised systems.
- **Mass Mail**—send emails to massive numbers through a private mail server or a junk Gmail account.
- **Arduino Attacks**— program Arduino hardware for attack purposes.
- **Wireless AP**—set up fake APs and captive portals to capture user information or infect user machines.
- **QRCode Generator**—generate QRCodes that can redirect people to attack sites.
- **Powershell**—take advantage of Powershell's power in modern Windows systems to perform attacks.
- **Third-Party**— extend the features of the toolkit with several add-ons.

This toolkit makes social engineering attacks easy, but the most powerful of these involve direct human interaction. For this, no software can give an attacker the ability to do what some gifted and charismatic people are able to do. Whether you claim to be the CTO (or his assistant) when you demand a password over the phone, or pose as a copier repair person to plant a rogue AP, the human interactions associated with social engineering can do the most damage.

Social engineering should be addressed in the corporate security policy for any type of computer network, including wireless networks. Training of all company personnel in awareness of social engineering should be explicitly defined and made mandatory. Training helps to

- explain and identify the techniques and methods used in social engineering attacks, and
- provide company-wide awareness as the primary countermeasure to such attacks.

RF DoS

Just as the name implies, a Denial of Service (DoS) attack prevents access to a service. Regarding wireless networking, one such attack is a RF DoS. This occurs when the radio frequency that is used for intended communications is impacted by external RF sources, preventing wireless communication from occurring at Layer 1. This type of attack may fall under one of two different categories, intentional or unintentional.

With standards-based wireless networking, the 802.11 PHYs specify raw RF Energy Detect (ED) thresholds, which causes the STA to defer transmissions on a given RF channel. If alternative RF channels with available APs are not available because the jamming spreads across multiple channels or because there are no other APs, a complete network outage may occur as a result of excess RF noise. This is known as is a PHY DoS.

The unintentional RF DoS is the first category of attack. This denial of service is usually caused by devices that are operating in the same radio frequency space as a wireless network. The RF could be modulated or unmodulated radio frequency information, which means it may or may not understand or implement 802.11 wireless network communications. An unintentional RF DoS attack could be caused by various devices that use radio frequency including:

- Microwave ovens
- Cordless telephones
- Baby monitors
- Wireless cameras
- 802.11 wireless networks

The intentional RF DoS is the second category of attack.. This type of denial of service attack, which is typically classified as an RF jamming attack, is used to interrupt valid, active RF communications with malicious intent. Intentional jamming can have serious implications on a wireless network, as all RF communications in the range of the jamming device can be stopped. The attack could be used by an intruder to force an authorized wireless network device to reauthenticate and roam to a rogue AP, or to shut down an RF channel or channels—effectively shutting down a wireless network. Such an attack can be performed by devices such as:

- RF Jammer, narrowband or wideband
- RF signal generator
- 802.11 wireless adapters using specialized software programs

The best way to protect against an intentional RF DoS is to realize that it is happening and to employ proper physical security techniques. The best tool to identify this type of attack is an RF spectrum analyzer that covers the correct frequency spectrum used, or a wireless intrusion prevention system (WIPS). While such solutions can detect the attack, they cannot stop it, if it is wideband. Intervention by an engineer, who locates and stops the transmission, is required. A narrowband attack may be mitigated through solutions like Radio Resource Management (RRM), which moves an AP to an alternate channel.

EXAM MOMENT: Intentional jamming is typically performed on 2.4 GHz spectrum as jammers are easily acquired (though absolutely illegal). If an intentional jamming attack were to occur on a modern WLAN that uses dual-band APs, chances are that only one band or the other would be impacted because any jamming tool likely to be used would not impact both 2.4 GHz and 5 GHz. A jamming attack can be extremely disruptive, but the range of jamming tools is limited. The same jamming that could lay waste to an SMB Wi-Fi environment would likely only impact a part of a larger WLAN, as even jamming signals are subject to free space path loss.

Layer 2 (MAC) DoS

As stated before, 802.11 wireless networks operate at both the Physical layer and the MAC sublayer of the Data Link layer in the OSI model. In addition to the PHY DoS attacks mentioned, 802.11 wireless networks are also vulnerable to MAC sublayer attacks. This is a result of the way the 802.11 protocol functions, with built-in vulnerabilities due to the nature of operation subject to exploitation.

Several different MAC sublayer DoS attacks are documented that can be used for wireless network exploitation. Due to the half-duplex shared-media nature of WLANs,

802.11 protocols specify behaviors that require Wi-Fi devices to play nice. These same protocols, specified for the good of the network, are also used to exploit the same network with a DoS attack.

Common Layer 2 wireless MAC sublayer DoS attacks include using Deauthentication and Disassociation management frames to subvert normal client connectivity.

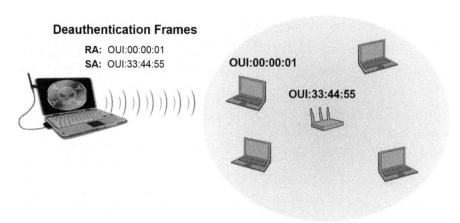

Figure 2-9: A Deauth DoS Attack

With common tools like protocol analyzers and a wireless intrusion prevention system (WIPS), Layer 2 DoS attacks can be identified and, in many cases, mitigated. Unlike the PHY DoS attacks, changes can be made to circumvent such attacks more easily.

Use the following procedure to perform a deauth DoS using Kali Linux with a compatible adapter:

1. Launch the Kali Linux VM (the appendix provides instructions for creating the VM).
2. Logon as `root` with a password of `toor`.
3. Launch a Terminal.
4. Determine the proper WLAN adapter identifier based on the instructions provided earlier.

5. Execute `airmon-ng start wlan0`, replacing `wlan0` with the proper identifier for your WLAN adapter.

6. Execute `airodump-ng mon0 --band a`, replacing `mon0` with the proper identifier of your monitor interface and `--band a` with `--band g` if you prefer to look for attack targets in 2.4 GHz instead of 5 GHz.

7. Note the `BSSID` of the AP you wish to target. This is the MAC address of the target AP. You can highlight it and then right-click and select COPY to make things easier.

8. Press `CTRL+C` to end the airodump-ng scan.

9. Execute `aireplay-ng -0 0 -a B4:75:0E:59:39:DE -c mon0`, replacing `B4:75:0E:59:39:DE` with your target MAC address and `mon0` with the identifier of your monitor mode interface.

Peer-to-Peer

Peer-to-peer network communications are when one wireless client device connects to another wireless client device. These communications can be accomplished by using an Independent Basic Service Set (IBSS) (also known as an ad-hoc WLAN) network in which client devices connect directly to each other or in infrastructure mode where wireless client devices connect to each other through an AP or directly when allowed. It is important to understand that ad-hoc networks are typically against most corporate security policies; however, they may be allowed in some cases. If they are used, proper security precautions must be taken. Even if they are not "allowed," it is important to remember that, if they are not restricted on the organization's devices, they can be created by the users. They can also be created on user-owned devices. Therefore, monitoring for them with WIPS solutions is important if the organizational policy is against them.

If infrastructure mode peer-to-peer connections are not required, then enable peer-to-peer blocking on the WLAN infrastructure (at the APs or controllers). WLAN equipment manufacturers use different methods to perform this task, but it is usually an easy configuration step. For networks that require this type of communications, such as wireless voice handsets or Apple Facetime, enable peer-to-peer communications.

Multiple types of peer-to-peer attacks exist, and they are most common with open public access networks (wireless hotspots) where unsuspecting users leave themselves vulnerable to attackers. If the establishment that is hosting the open wireless network did not implement proper security measures such as peer-to-peer blocking, many experienced attackers are able to identify this type of wireless network and use it for a variety of attacks. These attacks include data theft and accessing the client device directly because of weak security on the client system.

Man in the Middle (MITM)

A wireless man in the middle (MITM) attack is the result of an intruder placing an unauthorized wireless device between a legitimate wireless AP and a wireless client device that is authorized to connect to and use the wireless network. The intruder gains the capability to capture and exploit all information that is passed between the authorized wireless client device and the wireless AP as that information traverses the MITM device. The possibilities of how to leverage the ill-gotten data are endless once a MITM attack has been successful. Several steps must be taken to perform a MITM attack and slight variations exist to the basic construct. We will look at a common scenario here.

With minimal equipment and easily-acquired programs, a MITM attack can be fairly straightforward. It is important to understand what technology is used in this type of attack in order to protect your network from it.

One common method is to use a client device (usually a laptop) with two wireless adapters. One adapter is used in conjunction with a software AP and the other used to connect to the authorized AP. The intruder forces the unsuspecting authorized user to connect to the software AP, typically with a deauth attack, and retransmits to the authorized AP using the second wireless network adapter. The success of this process assumes that the

- attack is performed on an open wireless network (public hotspot), or

- intruder has the proper credentials to connect to a secured network.

Acquiring these credentials may have been the result of another attack, such as social engineering or shoulder surfing (looking over the shoulder of a target to view the username and password entered).

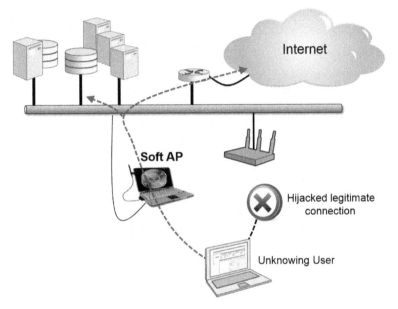

Figure 2-10: Hijacking Attack

To perform a successful MITM attack, the intruder must first hijack the authorized wireless client device. Hijacking is performed by forcing the authorized wireless client device to connect to the intruder's unauthorized wireless device. Given that a client connects to the AP with the strongest signal strength from the Beacon frame (or Probe Response frame), a deauth attack typically causes the client to connect to the attacker's software AP, assuming the software AP radio is closer to the target and provides a stronger signal than the authentic AP. Once an authorized client device is hijacked, several other attacks can be conducted.

MITM attacks may lead to very serious security issues, or they may simply be used for eavesdropping purposes in order to gather specific information about the network and the connected wireless devices for planning future exploits. For example, the attacker may be able to harvest website credentials used by the user, including credentials required to authenticate to a captive portal or some such system.

MITM attacks can be prevented with adequate protection and proper security measures in place. Using 802.1X/EAP authentication makes it very challenging for an attacker to launch such an attack. Using memes to indicate to the user that they are at a legitimate captive portal login page (such as those used by banking websites) can help, but these depend on the user actually observing that the proper meme (graphic selected by the user at account creation) is in view and not logging in when it is not.

You can effectively perform a MITM attack using Kali Linux on an Open System authentication-only network with three tools: arpspoof, driftnet, and urlsnarf. All three tools are included in the Kalie Linux distribution. Instructions can be found in many online forums; there are even videos online that walks you through the process.

Management Interface Exploits

Many home and small business network users do not realize the dangers of default configurations. Wireless equipment manufacturers publish their default configurations to ease the initial configuration process, but when these parameters are not changed, they are easy to exploit. One of the first steps in staging an AP prior to placing it into service is to change any and all default configurations. These changes include the login credentials (username and password), remote access configurations, securing all required access control protocols, and disabling all protocols that are not needed. Changing default configuration parameters should be performed with home, small business, and enterprise installations.

Enterprise network deployments typically specify configuration parameters as part of the corporate security policy. As a main defense against management interface exploits, the policy should document all required steps and help to ensure that everything related to staging and management of devices is covered.

Physical access to the infrastructure devices, such as an AP, is an important area that must be considered. Gaining physical access to these devices can introduce many security issues. Issues include theft, device replacement, resetting to factory defaults, access to the console port that is used for configuration, and other concerns. Many solutions are available to help control physical access to APs, including special enclosures and device locks. As with configuration parameters, physical access should be identified and documented in the corporate security policy.

Similarly, weak protocols such as HTTP and Telnet send session authentication traffic as clear text, and an eavesdropped session would allow access to an intruder. When management interfaces are accessible to intruders, complete DoS attacks—or worse—are very easy to perform.

Some best practices recommend managing wireless infrastructure devices from a wired network connection only, and never from a wireless connection. If this is not possible, proper security must be used to ensure eavesdropping provides no security credentials or parameters that may pose a security risk to the network infrastructure.

> **Exam Moment:** Management interface exploits can be prevented by implementing proper staging and management procedures. Staging includes all tasks during the initial setup of the equipment. Perform management procedures only over secure channels. Always use encrypted protocols such as HTTPS, sFTP, and SSH.

Authentication Cracking

Some authentication protocols that are used with 802.11 wireless networks may be weak and vulnerable to authentication cracking. These include, but are not limited to:

- 802.11 Shared Key authentication
- WPA/WPA2-Personal mode
- Lightweight Extensible Authentication Protocol (LEAP)
- EAP-MD5
- Point-to-point tunneling protocol (PPTP)
- PAP, CHAP, MSCHAP, MSCHAPv2

In most cases, if the above authentication methods are cracked, the process used to encrypt the data is cracked, exposing the network and user data to intruders. It should be noted that many of these authentication methods can be implemented today in a way that makes it nearly impossible to crack them, particularly WPA2-Personal with a very strong PSK, and MSCHAPv2 when properly implemented in a secure tunnel that is itself established through a mutual authentication process.

802.11 Shared Key Authentication—The shared key challenge hash is easily recovered and even accelerates recovery of the WEP key allowing an intruder to authenticate to the wireless network and have access to all encrypted data.

WPA-Personal and WPA2-Personal—Though both of these methods can be secured with sufficiently strong passphrases (used to create the pre-shared key or PSK), weak passphrases may jeopardize the network security. Weak passphrases can be discovered by capturing the 4-way handshake and the use of dictionary attack software. With the intruder knowing the passphrase, they have the ability to connect to the AP and potentially see user data. Additionally, many administrators actually use the same text for the passphrase that they use for their own administrative account password.

LEAP—Recall that ASLEAP is a well-known software utility that can be used to recover LEAP-authentication credentials. An intruder can capture the frames used for authentication that traverse the wireless medium in order to recover the user password. The ASLEAP software in conjunction with a dictionary file is able to recover weak passwords.

EAP-MD5—By capturing a few frames, EAP-MD5 authentication can easily be cracked. This is because it does not provide dynamic encryption key management, mutual authentication, or any characteristic that would provide security for a wireless network.

Point-to-Point Tunneling Protocol (PPTP)—and other legacy protocols such as PAP, CHAP, MSCHAP, and MSCHAPv2 are vulnerable to authentication cracking. Although PPTP is used with VPN solutions, the authentication process can be cracked and can introduce security vulnerabilities if used with wireless networking. Like LEAP, PPTP allows an intruder to capture the frames used for authentication that traverse the wireless medium in order to recover the user password. L2TP/IPSec has replaced PPTP in many installations where VPN technologies are in use.

Encryption Cracking

WEP is the best known weak encryption scheme used with standards-based wireless networking. Earlier you learned about the vulnerabilities of WEP and why it should be avoided. Several encryption cracking tools are available for its exploitation. Cracking WEP is a straightforward process and can be achieved with software programs designed for that specific purpose and minimal required effort. Modern software tools allow for WEP to be cracked even without capturing any data frames, which exposes the IV. Early WEP cracking methods required an intruder to capture potentially large amounts of data traffic (usually 300 or more MB). Later methods do not require this large amount of traffic and result in even more severe security concerns.

TKIP also has some known encryption weaknesses. In late 2009, it was widely publicized that new TKIP weaknesses were discovered, and much was made about these attacks. However, these weaknesses with the TKIP MIC function were known from its inception. TKIP was never intended as a long-term solution. Rather, it was introduced as a stop-gap solution for WEP/RC4 while 802.11i was being ratified and then implemented with CCMP/AES. The published TKIP weaknesses may allow an attacker to inject traffic to probe for wired side vulnerabilities and possibly conduct DoS attacks. As TKIP/RC4 is deprecated in the newest 802.11 specifications, it should be removed from networks as soon as possible. It was a transitional solution, so you should transition your network to the original end goal, which was CCMP/AES.

Although there are strong encryption methods used with 802.11 wireless networks, encrypted data still has the potential to be viewed by intruders. This weakness is based on how the technology operates. One example is both WPA-Personal and WPA2-Personal modes. Even though WPA2 can use strong encryption methods such as CCMP/AES, which is considered uncrackable, the way WPA2-Personal mode is designed may allow an intruder to view encrypted user data. This is because the passphrase used with WPA/WPA2 to secure the service set also is used as a seed to ultimately create a unique session encryption key known as the pairwise transient key (PTK). The PTK is basically used to encrypt unicast traffic that traverses the wireless medium. The PTK is created during the 4-way handshake after 802.11 authentication and association. If the passphrase is known, capturing the 4-way handshake will yield enough information to view encrypted data assuming the correct software tools are used.

 Note: **When using WPA- and WPA2-Personal, you must use a strong and long passphrase, preferably one that is 20 characters and not composed of words. Use a mixture of uppercase letters, lowercase letters, and digits. If you add in special characters, it is much stronger.**

In addition to WPA and WPA2, other authentication methods used with wireless networks, if cracked, leads to the ability to view encrypted data. These include LEAP and PPTP, mentioned earlier, to name two.

Other Common Concerns

Other attacks may take advantage of basic weaknesses in a computer network infrastructure, such as physically available (unlocked and accessibly mounted) APs or open and unsecured Ethernet ports that may allow for the placement of rogue APs. Rogue APs can be used to provide an access portal to the wired LAN, exposing all of your servers, data, and infrastructure devices.

The need for a physical security plan cannot be overstated. Theft of WLAN infrastructure is one concern, but tampering with installed devices can lead to other security issues. If an intruder were to have physical access to an installed wireless AP, there is the possibility (depending on the manufacturer) that the administrator or logon credentials could be reset to the default configuration or re-configured with a hacker's credentials, but still maintain the functional configuration of the device. This would allow the intruder free reign within the actual devices that he has access to, the ability to read configuration information, and the possibility of creating unauthorized access to the wireless network for later exploitation.

Physical access to unsecured Ethernet ports provides the opportunity for placement of rogue APs. Keep in mind that a rogue AP is one that is not authorized. Rogues APs can be

- installed for either innocent (but usually misguided) or malicious purposes, and
- placed on a network infrastructure with malicious intent and may provide an opening to the network for more serious attacks.

Rogues are classified as intended—installed by intruders—or unintended—placed on the wire by employees who did not know better.

Public Access Networks

Public access wireless networks, commonly called wireless hotspots, have their share of vulnerabilities, as discussed in Chapter 1. This type of network can be a big draw for intruders. Many times a business such as a restaurant or coffee shop may install a wireless AP for the convenience of its customers and to provide a draw of traffic for the business. Often the infrastructure devices that are installed for public hotspots are home- or small office/home office (SOHO)-grade devices and lack both enterprise security features and the in-house skill to know the difference. Therefore, they may not have the capability to provide additional security features such as peer-to-peer blocking. Other public access networks may use enterprise-grade equipment and be managed by the corporate IT group or outsourced to a provider with the capability to professionally manage the devices.

Most public access wireless networks do not have any wireless security authentication and/or encryption features enabled, because ease of use wins out over security in general for hotspots. They are configured to support standards-based 802.11 Open System authentication only because they want users to connect with the least amount of problems, given that there is likely no real support avenue. The security is typically left up to the end user when it comes to hotspots. In many cases, this can pose a security threat due to the end user's lack of security knowledge. Many users have no idea that their network communications that are traversing the wireless medium can be intercepted and viewed by intruders. End user education is the key factor in this situation.

Because of the way most public access networks are configured (for example, 802.11 Open System authentication), they are potentially subject to a variety of wireless network security threats, including:

- Spam transmission
- Malware injection
- Information theft
- Peer-to-peer attacks
- Various Internet attacks

If the operator of the establishment that is hosting the public access network has the knowledge to configure the APs correctly, it helps to lessen these potential threats to the network and the devices that connect. If they do not know how to perform these tasks or cannot outsource to someone that has that knowledge, then these threats are likely to frequently become security incidents. Some of the configurations that helps to lessen these types of threats include:

- Firewall configuration
- Port blocking
- Protocol blocking
- Peer-to-peer blocking

All of the security onus should not be put on the establishment that is hosting the public access network. Users also have the responsibility of securing the devices they use on the network. User responsibilities include using up-to-date anti-virus software, proper firewall configurations, and strong passwords; securing any file shares; and using VPN technology.

General Recommended Practices

Legacy security is wishful thinking, based on a simpler time when the WLAN industry as a whole was far more naïve about the threats to wireless networks. In the legacy surety mindset, an administrator's only hope is to try to hide from intruders or throw a few obstacles in the way of intrusion. This philosophy says that if you put enough inconveniences in the intruder's way, he will pick on someone easier. CWSPs know not to bet your livelihood on this—especially since modern 802.11 security mechanisms, if implemented correctly, provide strong protection, deterrence, and threat mitigation. Conveniently, modern security steps are actually easier to implement than things like MAC filtering and other weak solutions.

Recommended best practices include the following:

- Upgrade the security suite.
- Replace legacy solutions and clients.
- Upgrade firmware.

Upgrading to a WPA2 security mechanism is highly recommended. All modern Wi-Fi certified equipment should now be compatible of WPA2. However, some implementations may have older devices that are not WPA2-capable and only support WPA. Ideally these devices should be upgraded, but this may not always be feasible due to budgetary constraints, proprietary software implementations, specific use cases, or a variety of other situations.

Replacing legacy WEP security solutions is at the point where it is now a requirement. This is because of corporate security policy, the business model, and in some cases legislative compliance such as Health Insurance Portability and Accountability Act (HIPAA), Payment Card Industry Data Security Standard (PCI-DSS), and others.

Upgrading firmware in all devices (this goes for all networks, not just wireless) provides many benefits. These include adding new features to the hardware that may not have been available previously, resolving issues that may have been discovered after the older firmware was released, and opening up enhanced security features such as WPA2. In some cases, firmware updates may not be available because of embedded operating system form factors, end-of-life equipment, or other reasons. In these situations, it is highly recommended to work toward an appropriate replacement path even if it is inconvenient or expensive to do so.

From the Blogs

Security is Your Responsibility when using Free Wi-Fi

URL: dalewifisec.wordpress.com/2012/03/27/is-free-public-wi-fi-safe
Author: Dale Rapp
Blog: DALESWIFISEC—dalewifisec.wordpress.com

Coffee shops, restaurants, airports, and hotels, are just some of the locations that you may find an available public wireless network or a free Wi-Fi hot spot. These free wireless hot spots deliver a high-speed internet connection, but this convenient, no hassle access to the internet comes with a lack of security. It doesn't mean you should avoid accessing a free wireless hot spot, it just means you need to be aware of how to protect your device and data when you do.

To prove the point that security is your responsibility at a public hot spot, I captured the following screen shot from a Wi-Fi user agreement from a local restaurant I often visit. The user agreement clearly states security and privacy is the user's responsibility.

> 5. YOU ARE RESPONSIBLE FOR YOUR SECURITY AND PRIVACY. Although privacy and security are important to Panera and the Third Party Provider, you understand and agree that you shall have no expectation of privacy or security in your use of this Service. There are privacy and security risks associated with wireless communications and the Internet in general and you acknowledge that Panera and the Third Party Provider make no assurances that your communications, or activities while using the Services, will be (or will remain) private or secure, and you further agree that Panera and the Third Party Provider assume no responsibility in that regard. You agree that you, and not Panera or the Third Party Provider, are solely responsible for your own privacy and security in using this Service, and for implementing any protections you deem to be appropriate to protect and secure your privacy, and your activities, hardware, software and systems.

Other businesses that offer free wireless access have similar verbiage in their Wi-Fi usage agreements. With the user being responsible for the security of their device, I have outlined some general security tips that can help protect you when using a free public wireless hot spot.

106

1) Have an Antivirus Program Installed

Whether you access the internet from a wired or wireless network, your home, work, or Wi-Fi hot spot, an antivirus program should always be installed and running on your computer. Antivirus will prevent the unwanted programs from being installed on, or accessing data in your computer.

2) Make Sure The firewall is Enabled

A firewall acts as a bouncer to either allow or deny access to your computer. The firewall uses rules to control the traffic and prevent an unauthorized person from accessing your computer through an internet or network connection.

3) Use a VPN Connection

- Free public Wi-Fi provides no encryption or scrambling of the data as it travels the air waves, so anyone could capture the communications including passwords you are using to access websites. A VPN will allow you to create an encrypted tunnel through the hot spot network to the VPN server. An encrypted VPN tunnel is the best way to scramble your communications as they travel the network and prevent anyone that may be eavesdropping on the Wi-Fi hot spot from reading your traffic.

- There are a lot of personal VPN services available and a quick Google search will reveal numerous companies that provide the service. Most companies providing personal VPNs should offer a free trial of their service along with monthly and annual plans for a fee. If you travel a lot or you are constantly using public Wi-Fi you may find this to be money well spent to protect your traffic when accessing any unencrypted public Wi-Fi network.

4) Use HTTPS When Available

Any website you access that requires some sort of log in should be using HTTPS. HTTPS is the secure alternative to HTTP, and to verify if any site is using HTTPS look in the browsers address bar and make sure the web address of the site starts with HTTPS. Some sites such as Facebook may require the user to enable the HTTPS feature through the privacy settings.

When I travel or access free Wi-Fi I'm usually on my Windows 8 laptop, and while researching this blog post I found some great articles on the Microsoft site discussing Wi-Fi security tips. One of those articles is linked below and provides additional details and instructions to help protect you when using public Wi-Fi.

https://www.microsoft.com/en-us/safety/online-privacy/public-wireless.aspx.

Chapter 2 Summary

In this chapter, you explored the basics of WLAN security concerns. This began with a review of the 802.11 discovery procedures, both active and passive, and then moved on to look at additional important topics such as discovery hardware and software, weak concepts like SSID hiding and MAC filtering, weak authentication systems, and basic attack methods.

Facts to Remember

Be sure to remember the following facts as you prepare for the CWSP certification, and be sure that you can explain the details related to them:

- Passive discovery is based on Beacon frames, and active discovery uses the Probe Request and Probe Response frames.
- Discovery hardware can be a laptop computer, tablet, or even a mobile phone these days.
- Discovery software includes internal utilities and specialty software that shows more information, such as inSSIDer.
- The network is only as secure as its weakest link. One WEP client on the network can introduce a potential tragedy for your data.
- SSID hiding is not secure: the SSID is also in Probe Request, Probe Response, Association Request, and Reassociation Request frames.
- MAC filtering is not secure in and of itself because an attacker can easily discover valid MAC addresses and then spoof those addresses.
- Open System authentication is not secure by itself, but it is performed first before modern authentication solutions are invoked.
- Shared Key authentication should never be used: it is based on WEP and sends clear text challenge information across the network.
- EAP-MD5 and LEAP are both examples of what should be end-of-life EAP types. They are not secure.
- Social engineering attacks rely on human manipulation techniques.

- DoS attacks can be either RF (physical) or MAC (data link).
- Peer-to-peer attacks are common in public hotspots.
- A man-in-the-middle attack involves the attacker placing herself between the valid client STA and the AP to listen to or overtake the user session.
- Management interface exploits involve gaining access to management interfaces on devices and then reconfiguring them for easier access or attack purposes.
- Authentication and encryption cracking are easily performed against WEP networks, and may be performed against poorly configured WPA/WPA2-Personal networks as well.
- Rogue devices are devices that are not authorized on the network.
- Physical security is a key concern and should be implemented using specialized fasteners, lockable mounts, selective mounting locations, and NEMA enclosures for outdoor reachable devices.
- When using a Public WI-FI Network (hotspot), a VPN can assist in protecting the client STA. Additionally, endpoint security solutions prove beneficial.
- Recommended security practices include: use of a strong security suite, replacement of legacy products as quickly as possible, and updating firmware on existing products as needed at regular intervals.

Chapter 2: Review Questions

1. In one WLAN discovery scenario, Probe Requests and Probe Responses are exchanged between the wireless client device and access points. Which type of discovery is this?

    a. Synchronized discovery
    b. Active discovery
    c. Passive discovery
    d. RSN discovery

2. Which of the following SSID descriptions in a Probe Request elicit a Probe Response from all APs within range?

    a. Blank SSID
    b. Wildcard SSID
    c. Broadcast SSID
    d. All of these, as they mean the same thing.

3. An intruder wants to listen to your WLAN undetected as they eavesdrop. What operational mode will the intruder likely employ on their Wi-Fi adapter?

    a. Listen mode
    b. Stealth mode
    c. Monitor mode
    d. Silent mode

4. Wireless DOS attacks can occur at which layers of the OSI model?

      a.   Layer 1, Layer 2
      b.   Layer 1, Layer 7
      c.   Layer 2, Layer 7
      d.   Layer 2, Layer 3

5. Besides being present in the Beacon management frame, which one of the following frames also contains the SSID Information Element?

      a.   Association Request
      b.   Association Response
      c.   Authentication Request
      d.   Authentication Response

6. Which of the following regarding 802.11 wireless MAC addresses is true?

      a.   They are associated with the Physical layer.
      b.   They cannot be encrypted.
      c.   They cannot be spoofed.
      d.   They are assigned locally by DHCP.

7. Open System Authentication has been part of the 802.11 standard from the very beginning. On modern WLAN, how is Open System Authentication acceptably used?

      a.   As part of all strong encryption methods.
      b.   As a stand-alone security method.
      c.   As part of the 4-way handshake.
      d.   Never

8. WEP has a number of characteristics that make it weak for wireless network security. Which one of the following is not a characteristic of WEP?

    a.   RC4 stream cipher

    b.   Manual key management

    c.   40-bit key

    d.   Dynamic pre-shared keys

9. When using WPA2-Enterprise as your wireless network security solution, which of the following properly describes the order of functional events?

    a.   4-way handshake, EAP authentication, Open System Authentication.

    b.   4-way handshake, Shared Key Authentication, EAP Authentication.

    c.   Shared Key Authentication, EAP Authentication, 4-way Handshake.

    d.   Open System Authentication, EAP Authentication, 4-way Handshake.

10. When using 802.1X, which of the following EAP types work at Layer 2?

    a.   All EAP types

    b.   EAP-FAST

    c.   LEAP

    d.   PEAP

11. Shared Key Authentication uses WEP. What makes the implementation of Shared Key Authentication risky?

    a.   Only MAC addresses are needed to discover WEP key.

    b.   WEP Keys are shown in clear text.

    c.   Only four authentication frames are needed to discover WEP key.

    d.   Only four data frames are needed to expose the authentication keys.

12. LEAP is a _____ EAP type, crackable by the _____ utility.

    a.   Proprietary, Netstumbler

    b.   Private, LEAPCRACK

    c.   Public, ASLEAP

    d.   Proprietary, ASLEAP

13. Encryption methods specified by 802.11 standards obscure data from which layers of the OSI model?

    a.   1-3

    b.   2, 3

    c.   1-7

    d.   3-7

14. Which two EAP types were developed by Cisco for use with 802.1X-based secure wireless networks?

    a.   PEAP, LEAP

    b.   LEAP, EAP-FAST

    c.   PEAP, EAP-FAST

    d.   TLS, LEAP

15. An intruder has a number of cracks he plans on executing against a local business WLAN. His first step is to conduct eavesdropping from a nearby parking lot using a high-gain antenna and a Wi-Fi adapter in Monitor mode. What can the business do to protect itself from this kind of network discovery?

    a.   Use a WIPS overlay.

    b.   Use integrated WIPS.

    c.   Secure its switch ports.

    d.   There is no real defense.

16. Of the following potentially hostile behaviors, which one qualifies as an example of social engineering?

    a.   Impersonating a legitimate network user and contacting the help desk.

    b.   Using an unsecured network switch port to find the admin interface of an access point.

    c.   Installing a rogue access point to extend the wired network.

    d.   Performing a Layer 1 DoS using a signal generator.

17. A hacker has set up an attack in which he wants to force an authorized user off of the private wireless network and onto the intruder's own access point. What might he use to accomplish this?

    a.   Layer 3 redirection

    b.   RF DoS

    c.   Management interface exploit

    d.   Peer-to-peer attack

18. The new CIO of your company mentions that she is very fond of working on company business from a laptop at the local coffee shop. She asks your opinion about what she should be concerned about in this situation. Which of these would be appropriate to warn the CIO about?

    a.   Network equipment default credentials.

    b.   Weak enterprise encryption.

    c.   Intruders looking over her shoulder.

    d.   Open switch ports on the hotspot router.

19. Peer-to-peer attacks are most often associated with which of the following wireless network scenarios?

    a.   Public hotspot

    b.   Ad hoc networks

    c.   802.1X networks

    d.   VPN access

20. Which of the following are regulatory concerns that you may have to be familiar with along with general WLAN-related security if you support wireless in hospitals or places where financial transactions occur?

    a.   PCS and HIPAA

    b.   PCI-DSS and WECA

    c.   HIPAA and WECA

    d.   PCI-DSS and HIPAA

21. _____ was never intended as long-term WLAN security solution, but was created to bridge the gap between WEP and 802.11i.

    a.   RSN

    b.   TKIP

    c.   WPA2

    d.   CCMP

22. Which of the following choices are not true enterprise wireless security measures, but are sometimes mistaken as such?

    a.   MAC address filtering and broadcasting SSID.

    b.   802.1X and MAC address filtering.

    c.   Hiding SSIDs and MAC address filtering.

    d.   Hiding SSIDs and 802.1X.

23. Good practices of device staging and management help protect against with which type of attack?

    a.   Management interface

    b.   Physical layer

    c.   Peer-to-peer

    d.   Inventory harvesting

24. As a CWSP, you are educating wireless support technicians on the differences between intentional and unintentional jammers. Which of the following is an intentional jammer?

    a.   Cordless telephone

    b.   Microwave oven

    c.   Baby monitor

    d.   Signal generator

25. Passive discovery relies on which of these?

    a.   Probe Requests

    b.   Beacons

    c.   Acks

    d.   Probe Responses

Chapter 2: Review Answers

1. **B** is correct. Active discovery uses Probe Requests from the wireless client and Probe Responses from the access point.

2. **D** is correct. All of these choices are synonymous, and result in a probe response from all APs within range.

3. **C** is correct. Monitor mode is a "listen only" capability.

4. **A** is correct. Wireless DOS attacks can happen against the RF at Layer 1, or at Layer 2 against the 802.11 frames.

5. **A** is correct. The SSID IE is also present in the Association Request, the Probe Request, the Probe Response, and the Reassociation Request.

6. **B** is correct. MAC addresses are not encrypted by 802.11 standards-based security methods.

7. **A** is correct. Open System Authentication is largely an operational formality but is present in all strong encryption methods.

8. **D** is correct. Basic WEP did not make use of dynamic pre-shared keys.

9. **D** is correct. Remember that Open System Authentication comes first.

10. **A** is correct. 802.11 wireless works at Layer 2, therefore all EAP works at Layer 2.

11. **C** is correct. Only four authentication frames are needed for skilled attackers to discover the WEP key in Shared Key authentication.

12. **D** is correct. Created by Cisco, LEAP can be cracked by the ASLEAP utility.

13. **D** is correct. 802.11-based security encrypts from Layer 3 up.

14. **B** is correct. LEAP and EAP-Fast are both Cisco-authored EAP types.

15. **D** is correct. When it comes to passive eavesdropping, of the options given, there is no defense (though Faraday cages and RF paint/wallpaper technically can help defend against eavesdropping, these measures are rarely practical to implement).

16. **A** is correct. Social engineering takes advantage of the human side of networking.

17. **B** is correct. Using an RF DOS attack can force WLAN clients to join an attacker's network.

18. **C** is correct. Of the choices given, the CIO is most at risk of someone watching her type passwords, user names, etc.

19. **A** is correct. Users of poorly implemented public hotspots are at risk of peer-to-peer attacks.

20. **D** is correct. PCI-DSS is a financial regulation, whereas HIPAA is medical-oriented.

21. **B** is correct. TKIP was meant to be an interim security solution.

22. **C** is correct. MAC address filtering and SSID hiding are not valid security measures for enterprise WLAN.

23. **A** is correct. Proper staging practices ensure that management interfaces are secured before device deployment.

24. **D** is correct. Many devices just happen to transmit in the same frequencies as Wi-Fi, but signal generators can be used to intentionally attack wireless environments.

25. **B** is correct. Beacons can be heard by devices that are passively scanning.

Chapter 3:

Security Policy

Objectives

2.1 Explain the purpose and goals of security policies, including password policies, acceptable use policies, WLAN access policies, personal device policies, device management (APs, infrastructure devices and clients), and security awareness training for users and administrators.

2.2 Summarize the security policy criteria related to wireless public access network use, including user risks related to unsecured access and provider liability.

2.3 Describe how devices and technology used from outside an organization can impact the security of the corporate network, including topics like BYOD, social networking, and general MDM practices.

1.4 Describe and perform risk analysis and risk mitigation procedures, including asset management, risk ratings, loss expectancy calculations, and risk management planning.

Security policies are the true foundation of all effective security. The policies define minimum requirements for security in an environment based on the operational needs of that environment. Without policies, the best you can do is implement a few best practices and hope your environment stays functional and unchanged over time. With sound policies, you can implement the security you truly need for your organization, and provide a documented reference that keeps the entire organization grounded in a common security mindset.

This chapter explores the purposes and goals of various granular security policies, including password policies, acceptable use policies, WLAN access policies, personal device policies, and device management for both infrastructure devices and client devices. We will also address security awareness training for users and administrators.

Security Policy Defined

Generally speaking, a policy is a documented plan and management-endorsed agreement. The policy includes rules, regulations, and a course of action based on organizational needs and requirements. An organization has various policies based on its explicit business model. From an IT perspective, a corporate security policy is a very important written document that contains detailed information about protecting the integrity of the entire scope of corporate computer networking operations.

The content of a corporate security policy varies based on the type of organization or vertical market for which it is written. For example, educational institutions, financial firms, government, healthcare facilities, retail establishments, transportation companies, and other organizations have specific policies based on their individual business models. Even though many organizations have operational areas that are common amongst them, different types of organizations require sections of a policy to be tailored to their specific business needs. As an illustration, a healthcare organization and a company that deals in transportation both require a network password policy, but the healthcare organization must have a policy for specific industry regulatory compliance such as Health Insurance Portability and Accountability Act (HIPAA). Given that HIPAA generally does not impact transportation firms, the password policies of each company likely are not identical.

Every organization should have an IT security policy in place with specific focus on networking. If not, establishing this policy should be the highest priority, followed by immediate implementation. Some organizations may already have an existing security policy; however, it may not specifically address wireless networking. This is especially true with organizations that may be new to the WLAN technology arena. By now, you realize that WLAN concerns are unique enough to warrant their own operational guidance, and a security policy is part of that.

One of the hardest parts of creating a security policy is figuring out where to begin.

- If a good network security policy **exists**, it is a little easier than starting from scratch, because all that needs to be done is to add the appropriate sections pertaining to wireless networking technology.
- If a security policy **does not yet exist**, many organizations offer templates that could help to streamline the creation process. One such organization is the SANS Institute, at www.sans.org.

To view and modify a sample wireless security policy, follow the procedure below:

1. In your Internet browser, navigate to www.sans.org.
2. Select Resources > Security Policy Project from the menu.
3. In the Find the Policy Template You Need section, choose Network Security and then choose Wireless Communications Policy.
4. Download the DOC version so you can open it in Microsoft Word.
5. After downloading, open the document.
6. In the document, search for and replace <Company Name> with your company name.
7. Save the Word document when you are finished editing the policy.

 Note: **This policy depends on the Wireless Communications Standard document. It is quite common in a security policy document set and allows for less redundancy in information delivery.**

Regulations

The operation of a network in unlicensed or licensed frequencies are subject to the governing authorities of the network's locale. It is important to ensure that your network policy acknowledges and complies with the appropriate regulations of the governing authorities. These include agencies like the Federal Communications Commission (FCC) in the Unites States, the Innovation Sciences Canada (ISC) in Canada, and many others around the world. You are not required to memorize all such organizations for the CWSP exam, but you should understand (and recall from CWNA) that they dictate various parameters related to network usage.

Industry-specific compliance regulations are also becoming increasingly important and demanding. Data breaches have led compliance groups, such as the Payment Card Industry (PCI), to tighten their regulatory belts and have opened the eyes of many a security manager to the gravity of network-related data loss. PCI has developed the PCI Data Security Standard (PCI-DSS), which is becoming a mainstream part of retail implementations and an integral part of a growing number of security frameworks. Other compliance requirements such as Federal Information Processing Standard (FIPS) and additional government-related requirements are already very strict, demanding utmost care and attention by the network security staff for persistent compliance. Most companies realize the importance of a secure and compliant network, but budget constraints often keep administrators from achieving their intended security goals.

Industry regulations to be aware of include:

- PCI DSS
- HIPAA
- Sarbanes-Oxley
- FIPS 140-2 DoD Directive 8100.2

Legal Considerations

Several legal considerations related to WLAN security policy should be investigated. Of course, regulatory compliance requirements are of interest to a company's legal department. It may even be possible for IT personnel to leverage the legal department to help make the case for expenditure on resources to ensure that regulatory compliance is met.

Also, any effective security policy must have executive support behind it. If employees are to be reprimanded or employment terminated for a breach of security policy, it is important to have the legal counsel provide guidance for these decisions and for it to be coordinated with senior management. Similarly, when a breach is detected and forensics are being gathered and analyzed to provide a defensible court argument, it is important that the legal team be involved. These steps, among others (like active rogue mitigation), may require input from legal counsel to make sure that policy does not become a liability instead of the asset it should be.

Policy Importance

As you can see, there are several important reasons to create a well-defined security policy.

1) First, a policy is required if network security is to be maintained with consistency.
2) Second, the IT staff requires documented authority in order to enforce the policies they have defined and for which executive buy-in has been achieved.
3) Additionally, with large IT groups, it is important to have a single, central source of documentation that defines practices and procedures for everyone to follow to prevent a patchwork of departmental policies that don't align.

The following are important reasons for creating a security policy:

- Maintain desired level of network security
- Uphold compliance
- Legal protection

- Asset documentation
- Procedural continuity
- Authority

Traditionally, documented policies are often overlooked or neglected because their importance is not understood and responsibility for policy creation is often shared between IT and management staff, with frequent difficulty in finding common ground. With networking security, that trend cannot be tolerated anymore. As mobility and pervasive networking take deeper root in both the business and personal realms, the stakes are higher than they have ever been for security. Wireless networking is one of the more visible and obvious places where this is true.

When deciding which 802.11 security mechanisms to use, it is important to consider the circumstances, requirements, and uses of the organization implementing the network. It is essential that the organization document its plan in a wireless network security policy for a secure wireless environment. Due to the speed with which changes have occurred in the wireless industry, it is desirable to create a security policy that is easily modified after periodic audits and technology evolution to take advantage of on-going security enhancements.

Use the following steps to create a wireless security policy:

1) Perform risk assessment.
2) Define and document vulnerabilities and countermeasures.
3) Obtain support from management.
4) Provide communications between the departments or individuals that are involved.
5) Provide ongoing monitoring and security auditing.
6) Plan response, forensics, enforcement, and reporting tactics in advance of a security policy breach.
7) Revise and fine tune the policy as needed.
8) Publish all changes to the security policy and provide an educational forum to keep users apprised of current status.

Exam Moment: Management must support the security policy development process, and they must also support the enforcement of the policies for the policies to have a significant impact and result in a more secure environment. Without critical executive buy-in, policy can be worthless and unenforceable.

Planning

A WLAN addendum or special wireless section should be added to the general corporate security policy. Corporate security policy templates can be found at: www.sans.org/resources/policies/#template.

Risk Assessment

An important first step should be to perform a risk assessment of the organizational assets. This assessment is used to determine the level of vulnerability that exists, and to attempt to quantify the consequences that could result from an intrusion into the LAN and connected hosts from the wireless segment.

Ongoing Monitoring

Continuous monitoring and periodic security auditing are crucial in determining security policy adherence. All companies should perform continuous monitoring— especially those that have a no WLAN policy. It is just not enough to hope or assume that intruders leave your network alone.

Implementation

As mentioned before as an important underpinning of CWSP processes, the level of WLAN defensive countermeasures enacted should be proportional to the determinations of your risk assessment. Stated plainly, you should not implement more security than is required, and you should not implement less, assuming that security solutions equate to costs. Of course, if complete and total security were free (or even possible), we would all gladly implement it. But even open-source solutions are not truly free as there is a time cost factor associated with the implementation of any technology.

Risk and Impact

Risk assessment and impact analysis are somewhat related concepts. Together they comprise the evaluation of assets and vulnerabilities, and they help formulate the level of necessary security. This is an early step in the policy creation process.

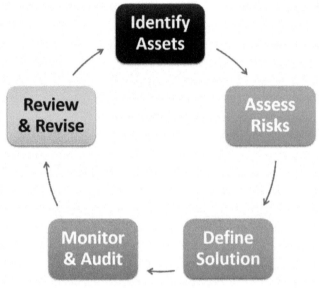

Figure 3-1: Risk Assessment Process

The risk assessment is basically an audit of the security in place, and helps to determine if the controls in use are adequate to provide the necessary security required by the specific organization. This can be performed in-house (typically by an unrelated department) or outsourced to a different organization that specializes in assessing network security. Standard penetration testing procedures help to provide the information needed to complete a full risk assessment and impact analysis. Clearly define and document all issues, concerns, and lack of compliance (whether incidental or intentional) as part of the risk assessment process. Evaluate the balance between potential security solution costs and how the organization benefit from specific security controls .The type of business or organization determines whether or not it is a significant target for intrusion and the likelihood of an attack. For example, a financial institution or a government entity is expected to have a higher risk of attack over a company who manufacturers widgets. At the same time, the widget maker also needs a policy even if the chance of its being targeted is smaller.

Understanding the impact of successful intrusions is also part of the risk assessment process. Not too long ago, the wireless network typically functioned as an extension to the wired network and allowed access to only a limited amount of company resources. The potential to gain access to specific types of information or to the network infrastructure was minimal. Today the wireless network is a primary access method, or is "the network" for many organizations, allowing access to all available resources and infrastructures. Therefore, the potential impact of a successful intrusion has grown tremendously.

The risk and impact analysis processes and procedures are not a one time shot, as shown in the Risk Assessment Process graphic. As technology evolves, so do the security risks and how they affect an organization. Think of this from a client device security perspective. In this example, you can purchase and install computer anti-virus software and run a full system scan. Any potential current threats are discovered and mitigated. But new and more sophisticated computer viruses are created every day. If the anti-virus software is not updated regularly and scans are not performed, the potential of a virus infecting the computer is greatly increased. The same premise holds true for the risk and impact analysis procedures. New threats are introduced constantly, so ensuring an organization is adequately protected is an ongoing process. Security policy should define the frequency of conducting risk analysis and what the subsequent analysis processes entail.

Exam Moment: Loss expectancy is a standardized calculation used in risk management. Annualized Loss Expectancy (ALE) is the result of the Single Loss Expectancy (SLE) multiplied by the Annual Rate of Occurrence (ARO). Though this formula may sound odd in a wireless security book, it helps illustrate how non-IT people measure loss from network insecurities.

Document and Define

After risk assessment, it is time to document and define the discoveries and deficiencies. When creating the policy document, do so based on the risk assessment, and ensure the following are addressed:

- It is accessible to all relevant parties via a public file share or on each user's computer.
- It is marketed/promoted/distributed within the company.
- It is kept up-to-date.
- Its importance is defined and communicated.

Buy-In and Training

For the security policy to have authority, management buy-in is necessary. For effectiveness, training must be performed and awareness must be promoted. If a strong and authoritative security policy is written, but employees are not aware of it, how can you expect them to follow it? Similarly, if you draft a policy, but management does not buy into it, what good is it? Security is as much of an organizational culture (and individual state of mind) as it is a technical and procedural framework.

Management buy-in offers the following benefits:

- Provides authority, as the policy is endorsed by top management.
- Allows for enforcement of technical policy requirements.
- Allows commitment of resources (people and money).
- Demonstrates commitment to disciplinary behavior when violations occur.

Training of end-users and administrators should include:

- Security awareness training with immediate training for new hires and periodic training updates for all the staff.
- Identify and report social engineering.
- The expectation that all abide by password policy.

- Prevention of rogue APs and clients.
- Understanding repercussions to policy violations.
- Acceptable Use and Abuse policies.
- Remote networking procedures.
- Creation of overall security awareness.

When management buy-in and training are implemented with these considerations, your policies result in a more secure environment.

Incident Response

The wireless security policy discussion is incomplete without addressing incident response. Incident response is the process or action taken when a security incident occurs. This response should be documented in an incident response plan, which also benefits from management buy-in and training for those staff members expected to respond.

Such a plan may be as easy as a one-page Visio flowchart or as complex as a multipage bound document. Either way, you should have a plan.

The response plan should address items such as the following:

- Forensic data analysis
- How to respond to rogue APs.
- Analyzing system logs.
- Accounting services
- What immediate reaction is taken with a compromised network infrastructure?
- What authorities are notified and involved?
- To whom do end-users and admins report security violations.
- The individual or department responsible for owning the response process and seeing it through to conclusion.

Enforcement

The security policy is of little value if it is too obtuse or impractical to be practiced and enforced. A workable and functional set of rules that can be realistically administered must be formulated. These rules determines how the wireless network is to be used. It is recommended to include the following criteria within the security policy functions:

- Use of passwords.
- Amount and frequency of training focused on use of the chosen security model and awareness of social engineering attacks.
- The methods to be used in order to provide awareness of security risks and vulnerabilities of WLAN implementation.
- Definition of acceptable and unacceptable uses of the WLAN.
- Employee awareness so that any or all of their WLAN traffic may be captured, filtered, and analyzed.
- Consistent procedures to implement and enforce the security policy .
- The creation and maintenance of a WLAN security checklist and a change management program.
- Possible security policy mandate of endpoint security, personal firewalls, and virus checking software for employee devices when:
  - Used on the corporate campus
  - Traveling and remotely connecting to the corporate network
  - Corporate information is contained on the employee's mobile computing devices
- Possible IT support department requirement for management of WLAN devices, including security applications installation, maintenance, and support.

The ongoing enforcement of functional policy is crucial. This can be a time-consuming task; and in some cases, depending on the size of the organization, it is a full-time job. One tool that can help with policy enforcement is a Wireless Intrusion Prevention System (WIPS) or a Wireless Intrusion Detection System (WIDS).

Properly implemented, configured, and tested, using a WIPS or WIDS can be very beneficial to an organization. Though it can add significant cost to the total cost of ownership (TCO) of a WLAN environment, the use of WIPS or WIDS can be a force-multiplier in ongoing support and will typically be less than the cost suffered as a result of a data breach. The difference between a WIPS and WIDS is that a WIPS can respond to detected incidents and a WIDS simply logs and alerts of the occurrence.

Advancements in technology such as multifunction mobile client devices bring many new security concerns to the forefront. In addition to a WIPS solution, consider a mobile device management (MDM) solution to aid in security policy enforcement for mobile device technology if it is allowed and used on the corporate network. MDM solutions help to administer and control how mobile devices such as smartphones, tablets, laptop computers, and even desktop computers can be used on a network and access company resources. The MDM market has become mature and impressive in the many options available.

Monitor and Audit

The initial security audit provides a baseline of all active wireless devices and is used to classify those devices as to their role. To ensure that the security audit baseline remains current, it is necessary to provide ongoing monitoring. This can be done manually in smaller environments, or through the use of automated sensing systems such as a WIPS.

Several wireless security manufacturers offer WIPS solutions that perform automated, around-the-clock monitoring, alarm notification, and reporting without administrator intervention. Many of these systems are equipped with the ability to isolate and nullify the actions of threatening wireless devices. This activity is referred to as "threat mitigation."

A WIPS solution uses distributed sensors that are either separate stand-alone infrastructure devices or that are integrated into wireless APs and strategically placed around a facility, campus, or other wireless service area. The sensors are passive monitoring devices that listen to the signals within the system's coverage area and gather a wealth of information that is used to report both performance metrics and security policy violations to a central analysis engine, or to a WIPS server.

Suggestions for WLAN monitoring include:

- 24x7x365 Monitoring
- Implementing WIPS
- Generating periodic and automatic reports
- Enabling appropriate alarms and notifications
- Keeping the WIPS sensors updated to match WLAN technology used by the WLAN

Audits provide spot-checks on organizational compliance with security policies and can be internal or external. An internal audit is one performed by the staff of the organization. An external audit is performed by an outside agency. Depending on your industry or the situation, an external audit may be required.

During the auditing process:

- Test for known weaknesses.
  - Authentication cracking
  - Social engineering
  - Rogue devices
- Generate detailed audit reports.
- Ensure compliance with industry regulations and guidelines.

The good news is that many modern and properly tuned WIPS solutions actually provide much, if not all, of this data to you without requiring manual actions. WIPS are further addressed in Chapter 9.

Review and Revise

As WLAN technologies and the company's IT and business needs change, it is important to review and revise the security policy to keep it up-to-date and relevant. Having an outdated policy is often as bad as having no policy. An outdated policy can give a false sense of security when action is actually needed.

A revision and review process should be implemented to keep the policy up-to-date. This process may be

- an annual process
- performed with each new system upgrade, and
- triggered by discovered vulnerabilities, but the trigger or schedule should be defined.

The process usually involves, at least, the following:

1) Perform a policy review.
2) Perform an internal/external audit.
3) Modify the policy based on results.
4) Set a time frame for policy updates to be complete.

Additionally, while it is important to review and revise your policies, it is important to stay informed regarding regulations and guidelines that may change for your industry. For example, if you work in healthcare, you want to know if anything changes in relation to HIPAA regulations or any other healthcare standard that could drive changes to your policy and operational framework.

Password Policy

Password policies define the required parameters for user, system and/or device passwords. When creating a password policy, consider the following elements:

- Password length (depends on the use case)
- Mixed alphanumeric with lowercase and uppercase and special characters
- Password change policies
- Password sharing policies
- Password access policies (who has access to passwords)
- Password storage policies

The following are example statements that can address the preceding list.

Note: These statements will vary greatly depending on the needs of the specific organization.

- Passwords used by individuals for authentication purposes must be 10 characters or longer.
- Passwords should include mixed characters and be case sensitive.
- Passwords used by individuals for authentication purposes must be changed every 60 days.
- Passwords used by systems or devices must be changed every 6 months.
- Passwords used by individuals may not be shared with anyone.
- Passwords used by systems or devices may only be shared with documented and authorized individuals.
- No individual will have access to the plaintext of any other individual's password.
- Only individuals with documented authorization should have access to system or device passwords.
- Passwords must be stored with sufficient encryption to avoid any currently known attack method that could extract the passwords within the password change requirement window.

Again, these are just examples of password-related policy statements and not fixed guidance. In addition to password policies, it is important that authentication requirements be addressed in the policy. Authentication requirements include the use of client credentials, sharing and storage of passwords/secrets and many other considerations.

 Note: Frustratingly, you may find that password policies conflict with wireless client device capabilities on occasion. Some devices only support passwords of limited length, and occasionally the use of special characters can be problematic for certain authentication databases.

Additional Policies

The following additional policies should also be addressed. While not covered in the previous examples of policy statements, these are equally important:

- **Acceptable use**—defines the intended use cases for the provided system.
- **WLAN access policy**—defines who can access the WLAN, and how they can access it.
- **Personal device or BYOD policy**—defines the allowed uses of personal devices and may include requirements such as onboarding (gaining authorized access to the system in an automated or manual process) and mobile device management.
- **Physical security policies**— relate to the protection of devices and the environment, and may include requirements such as security gates/doors, locks, enclosures and cameras.

Security Baselines

Security baselines provide a starting point to work from when striving for wireless network security. They give the minimum configurations that must be deployed when staging a new device. Security policies may define baseline security parameters, such as:

- SSID naming
- Authentication mechanisms
- Supported encryption types
- Device types used
- Rogue AP and client policy
- Endpoint security requirements
- Default configurations
- Remote networking
- Management protocols
- Monitoring

- Security layering
- Segmentation
- Role-Based Access Control

Device Management

Different business types require varying device management policies. A SOHO and some SMBs often only have one wireless AP, or possibly a few. In this case, the APs are often autonomous models that require each AP to be configured independently. The proper staging is required to ensure that there are no security holes that would allow for an intruder to gain access to the wireless network. This includes items such as:

- Changing the appropriate device default configuration values
- Securing the device login credentials
- Disabling remote access capabilities unless needed; if they are needed, using adequate security methods must be addressed
- Enabling firewall settings to meet the highest security requirements
- Disabling all protocols that are not used or needed

This is not a complete list, but includes some of the common items that need to be considered.

Enterprise wireless network device management policy is more involved due the size and complexity of the wireless network infrastructure. In addition to the items just mentioned that are used with smaller networks, infrastructure devices used in enterprise networks have the following management considerations:

- Wireless LAN security profiles
- Management protocols and software such as SNMP and third-party solutions
- Logging requirements
- Change management procedures

One important best practice for infrastructure device management recommends managing wireless infrastructure devices from the wired network only. If this is not possible, it is important to ensure adequate wireless security mechanisms are in place for the wireless devices that are accessing the management interfaces of the infrastructure devices. If an intruder were to get the administrator credentials, he would have the keys to the network kingdom, which could have catastrophic results.

Bring Your Own Device (BYOD) Policy

One of the important demands of enterprise networks that requires consideration is Bring Your Own Device (BYOD), which is the culture that allows employee-owned devices to not only be brought into the workplace environment, but also to access the corporate wireless network. It sounds simple, but BYOD adds significant complexity to network management. In addition to the potential impact on network capacity, network security is a big concern when personally-owned devices are part of the network. If employees are not allowed to use their own devices, then writing a BYOD policy is fairly straightforward. But if yours is among the growing number of organizations that allow BYOD on the network, then this part of the security policy can get very complex. If BYOD is not allowed, audit processes need to ensure that users are not violating the "no BYOD" policy.

One major benefit to BYOD is the fact that a given company, school, or hospital—to name a few examples—can leverage this technology for organizational business by allowing employees to use their own devices for operational processes under controlled circumstances. This could provide a large cost savings for the organization, as long as the paradigm is managed in a way that does not leave the door open to costly security risks. Items that should be addressed in a BYOD security policy include, but are not limited to:

- Allowed and supported device types, i.e., Android, Apple iOS, BlackBerry, Windows Mobile, and others
- Supported mobile operating systems
- Device provisioning and enrollment methods
- Containerization to separate corporate and personal data
- Permitted apps, distribution methods, and app stores used
- Remote device management
- Location services capabilities

- Data encryption methods
- Remote access security, virtual private network (VPN) use, and public access network behaviors
- Firmware, operating systems updates, and software patches or hot-fixes

Mobile Device Management Solutions

Another important technology popular with wireless network installations is mobile device management (MDM). With the large number of multifunction mobile devices that exist and those that are entering the workplace, management of these devices is vital to ensure corporate security policy is maintained and enforced. The MDM industry continues to grow, and many WLAN vendors are either providing built-in MDM capabilities or partnering with third-party MDM solutions as a competitive differentiator. MDM solutions provide a way to control and administer client devices that not only include portable devices such as smartphones and tablets, but also laptops and even the possibility of desktop computers. MDM can provide experience and configuration management capabilities for both corporate-owned devices and those belonging to employees.

Selecting the best MDM solution for specific networking requirements involves some careful consideration. As with any technology, the correct MDM solution must meet the needs of the organization and require planning to validate that it does so. MDM solutions are typically available in two forms: in-house (on-premise) solutions or cloud-based alternatives, which are provided as Software as a Service (SaaS) technology.

MDM solutions typically share common feature sets, which include:

- Multiplatform management and support
- Application distribution
- Device registration
- Remote lock and wipe
- Password control
- Feature lockdown

- Secure communications
- Policy enforcement

Notice several items on the above list are directly related to functional security and corporate security policy. Much of what you learned about earlier in this chapter applies here, including enforcement, monitor and audit, password policy, acceptable use, physical security, and device management. Mobile device management provides a way to ensure that, as wireless technology continues to evolve, it does so in a way that meets the security policy requirements of the organization.

Balancing mobile device security and usability is something to consider.

- If a policy is too tight, it may limit productivity or interfere with a user's ability to utilize her devices correctly.
- If policy is too loose, it could potentially compromise the security and integrity of the corporate network.

Therefore, how to provide an acceptable balance between the two must be carefully considered. A poorly balanced mobile device security policy is directly proportional to the potential for a policy failure. Consider the example of passcode or password policy. Most industry best practices agree that the longer and more complex a passcode/password is, the more secure it is. However, if it is too long or complex, a user may have difficulty remembering it or, depending on the device, it may be a challenge to type it into the device's interface. In cases like this, the policy did not meet the necessary goal.

As BYOD becomes more accepted in corporate culture for businesses of all sizes, an interesting new concern is becoming more common. Device loss or theft is of particular concern because the sheer number of small devices containing sensitive data is skyrocketing. Consider the CIO who leaves her smartphone in a taxi in a busy city, or the network administrator whose tablet gets stolen from his car in the parking lot of the local mall. These scenarios are commonplace, and could result in massive data breaches when you consider how much business is done over mobile devices that we all take everywhere we go. MDM solutions help make sure that highly mobile devices have a number of defenses configured in case of loss or theft. The ability to remotely lock or wipe a device through the MDM framework is the ultimate defense when theft or loss occurs. Even if other MDM features are not employed because of administrative overhead, it is common (and wise) to put into place mechanisms that wipe a device if a high number of bad passwords are entered.

Social Networking Policy

As with mobile device technology in general, social networking services such as LinkedIn, Twitter, and Facebook continue to grow in popularity. These services have proven to have business applicability that ranges far beyond personal use. Many organizations now use social networking extensively as part of their business practices. In some cases, this is a significant part of how many large businesses provide communications channels to their customer base and to the general public.

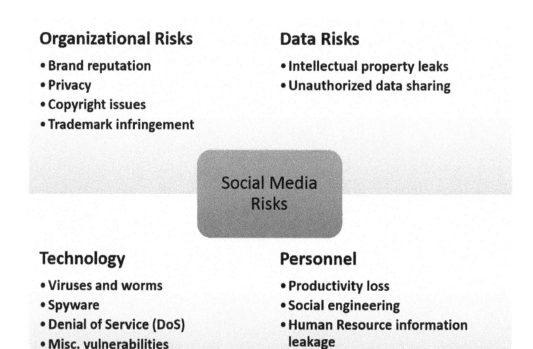

Figure 3-2: Social Media Risks

Despite potential benefits, social networking can introduce many potential security concerns for organizations that choose to use it as part of their business continuum. An appropriate social networking policy is important to help lessen the possibility of corporate security breaches that could come about through social media channels. Corporate security policy that addresses social media platforms is easy for companies to overlook, but it is important that social media be recognized for the threats it poses and made part of security policies. Here are some of the items that make social networking vulnerable to potential threats within an organization:

- Authentication / login management
- Phishing attacks
- Malware threats
- Corporate intellectual property (IP) integrity
- Reputation management

At a minimum, corporate security policy must consider how to deal with these threats. Unfortunately, chances are high that many organizations are lacking when it comes to addressing and maintaining policy with respect to social networking.

Some WLAN manufacturers provide "Social Wi-Fi" technology (either integrated or third-party solutions) that allow users to login to a guest network using their social media credentials. Behind the scenes, the use of Social Wi-Fi trades WLAN access for a varying amount of probing of your social media accounts for data that can be monetized. This type of captive web portal is a growing trend, and should be considered within the corporate security policy.

◾ From the Blogs

In Appreciation of White Box Guest Access

URL: wirednot.wordpress.com/2015/01/19/in-appreciation-of-white-box-guest-access

Author: Lee Badman

Blog: Wirednot—wirednot.wordpress.com

"Guest Access" means different things to different people, and organizations. Certainly if you're a traveler using hotel or conference Wi-Fi, you have a general set of expectations and desires. If you're a company or a school, the guest wireless service you provide is likely shaped by organizational policy. And for many of us, the guest environment also tends to act as a catch-all for client devices that don't fit on our secure WLANs—a place for "free passes" and MAC exceptions. But the devil is in the details, and I have found finding the right guest access feature set can be difficult.

1) What you WANT may not be what you can HAVE:

Having designed a number of guest environments for large and small networks, I'm always astounded to engage a WLAN vendor on the topic and to find how far their guest offering is from what I'm looking for (more on that in a bit). Worse, seldom do I hear "what are your requirements?" as it tends to be more like "this is what we think everyone should want and accept."

2) Simplicity? Fat chance:

Guest access can also have a lot of moving parts, depending on how it's implemented. Overall functionality tends to be broken up and scattered across APs, controllers, RADIUS servers, credential stores, web servers, and sometimes switches. It all has to click, or you have problems. And for me, despite the typical complexity of guest services, I still find myself frustrated at features that are not included.

3) **What worked for my environments:**

Years ago, for my big honkin' 3,000 AP environment (and our small branches alike), we arrived at a desired feature set that went more or less like this:

- Our guest SSID would equal a single dedicated guest VLAN.
- 24-hour individual self-sponsoring is a must.
- Alternatively, ANYONE authorized to use our wired or secure wireless network could sponsor a guest.
- For self-sponsoring, a ten-digit mobile number capable of accepting a text must be provided and within seconds a password would be sent.
- For large events, a shared account could be generated.
- All accounts were time limited with role-granularity.
- The system would have easily configurable firewall rules and (generous) rate limiting capabilities.
- On the admin side, we could add MAC exceptions and login-bypass.
- The system would provide NAT to preserve public IP addresses.
- Reporting would be easy, as would user quarantine (rarely used).
- ALL OF THIS WOULD HAPPEN UNDER ONE HOOD-VIA A SINGLE INTERFACE.
- A programmer would not be needed to stitch it all together.
- Ideally, it would have vendor support (for a number of reasons, open source was not desirable).

Going back those several years, our WLAN vendor (Cisco) didn't come close to being able provide what we wanted. In their defense, nor did any other market leaders at the time. We heard that Colubris Networks had a gateway that might fit the bill, but they had just been bought by HP and try as we might, we couldn't locate anyone that could talk with us about what we were looking for.

Then we found Bluesocket (now Adtran) and their BSC Controllers. When I first contacted Bluesocket, we came to the mutual realization that they could do about 75% of what I wanted. They weren't really initially open to developing the self-sponsored texting and "anyone authorized can sponsor a guest" features. So... we thanked each other for our time, and I kept searching. Then a week or so later

Bluesocket called back, and said they were game for a bit of development, and saw the value in what would become a feature set that they were able to market to others. They were able to do everything I was looking for in a single box in a matter of hours.

What Bluesocket was able to deliver after actually listening to our requirements has been in play for us for lots of years. We've served thousands and thousands of guests with it, along with using it as a mechanism for supporting wonky devices like Google Glass (turn head, spit) that weren't built with enterprise security support, and so can't be on the WLANs we'd rather they used.

It's been absolutely great, and I know of at least three other schools that pursued the same guest access model after experiencing ours.

Looking forward: Our old Bluesocket boxes are getting, well... old. They are appliances, and Adtran seemingly has no desire to virtualize what we need into an Open Virtual Appliance (OVA) or the like. In fact, on newer Adtran wireless products, what we appreciate about the BSC has been moved to Adtran APs that we'll never buy, so the research for a suitable replacement starts again.

The thing is, we absolutely love what we get out of our aging guest solution, and in a perfect world, I'll find a similar third-party, one-box bolt-on for our big Cisco WLAN. (I will give Cisco another chance to catch me up on how their native guest access services have improved, but I also know that my requirements are firm). I have also inquired to Adtran one last time about the possibility of somehow preserving this wonderful magic, but the silence thus far is pretty telling.

Which brings me to Meraki. The features I need for my guest environment are pretty much included in the WLAN side of the Meraki product line, and we use it with great success in our Meraki-enabled branch sites. But... to bolt the Meraki capability up to my Cisco WLAN in a way that would replace Bluesocket, I'd need the guest features made available in the Meraki MX security appliances and not just in the AP feature set. I'm hoping to get Meraki's ear on this anyway, because guest access needs also do tend to pop up on the wired side occasionally, too. Right now, wired guest needs are a gap in the MX.

If Meraki can accommodate, a big MX would snap in nicely where my Bluesocket sits now for guest access. If not, I'll have to consider things like pfSense, Packetfence and other one-offs that I'd rather not get into after being happy with a commercial solution. Or, I'll have to rethink our requirements, which would really suck, as they really are what we consider requirements, not just nice-to-haves.

Chapter 3 Summary

In this chapter, you reviewed the important factors related to security policies. First, policies were defined and then the details of various policies were explored. Additionally, the basics of the risk assessment process were addressed. Finally, modern issues such as BYOD and MDM were acknowledged with consideration of how policies should address them.

Facts to Remember

Be sure to remember the following facts as you prepare for the CWSP certification, and be sure that you can explain the details related to them:

- Security policies provide the foundation for effective security, and this is true in WLANs as well as wired networks.
- When developing policies, both internal and external regulations and guidelines, must be considered.
- Policies are important because they help you establish and maintain proper security.
- Risk assessment is a process that involves asset identification, assessment of risks, solution definition, monitoring and auditing, and reviewing and revising.
- Management buy-in is essential if policies are going to have the desired impact.
- Policies vary across organizations and are tailored to reflect an organization's goals and the value of the assets protected by the policy.
- An incident response plan should be developed as part of security policy, and well before an incident occurs.
- Auditing may be internal or external, using an outside agency to perform the external audit.
- With the influx of user devices, BYOD policies are more important than ever.
- MDM solutions control many aspects of the BYOD paradigm, and are becoming quite common.

- Loss or theft of mobile devices is a very real problem as users take their devices everywhere.
- Social media can be very positive for an organization, but it is a common attack point used by hackers.

Chapter 3: Review Questions

1. You are advising your management team on the benefits of having a process in place to deal with security incidents after they happen. Which of these are you describing?

    a.   Disaster Prep Plan

    b.   Incident Response Plan

    c.   Security Investigation Plan

    d.   Call-Down List

2. The capability of performing remote device locking and wiping comes with implementation of which system?

    a.   WIPS

    b.   Back Up

    c.   BYOD

    d.   MDM

3. In your role as Network Security manager, you are reviewing the company's security policy and realize that it is quite outdated. You find that there is no policy covering a fairly recent technology that could lead to copyright infringement, theft of IP, and productivity loss. What technology are you concerned with?

    a.   Social Media

    b.   MDM

    c.   BYOD

    d.   Mobility

4. Risk assessment is _____ in relation to security policy?

    a.   Easy
    b.   A one-time process
    c.   Optional
    d.   Critical

5. You are hired to do a security audit of the Wellington Company's wireless network. You find that the executive team at Wellington wants little to do with IT operations, and does not seem to know where to locate the wireless security policy or what is in it. What important component of wireless security policy is missing in this situation?

    a.   Audit process
    b.   Management buy-in
    c.   Incident response plan
    d.   Social media policy

6. When it comes to wireless network security policy, which of these applies to all organizations?

    a.   Policy is optional.
    b.   All policies are the same.
    c.   Policies will differ by company types.
    d.   Some companies do not need risk analysis.

7. For hospitals and medical facilities using wireless networking, which of these regulations help shape security policy?

    a.   HIPAA
    b.   FERPA
    c.   FIPS
    d.   PCI-DSS

8. A given company has not updated its wireless security policy in the last ten years. What important aspects are likely missing?

    a.   MDM

    b.   BYOD

    c.   Social media

    d.   All of these

9. What is the best approach for developing and communicating a wireless security policy?

    a.   Each department should create its own.

    b.   There should be a single company-wide policy.

    c.   To save money, employees should be trusted to follow their own common sense.

    d.   Senior management should not be part of the policy framework as they tend to not understand IT.

10. Security policy covering end devices would not include which of these?

    a.   Anti-virus software

    b.   Personal firewalls

    c.   Strong passwords

    d.   Administrative interfaces

11. What do we call the ability of a WIPS system to identify and nullify detected wireless threats?

    a.   Threat mitigation

    b.   Threat attribution

    c.   Threat classification

    d.   Threat isolation

12. Which of these is likely to not be part of a password security policy?

    a.   Password length

    b.   Password storage

    c.   Passwords at home

    d.   Password sharing

13. As you construct a security policy document, you are about to consult with your manager on the topic of Wireless Access Policy. What does this specifically cover?

    a.   Infrastructure administration

    b.   Members of Incident Response teams

    c.   How to communicate wireless policy to users

    d.   Who can access the WLAN, and for what reasons?

14. Which of these is not common among Device Management policies likely to be used in small business and enterprise wireless settings?

    a.   Use of SNMP

    b.   Securing management interfaces

    c.   Disabling unneeded protocols

    d.   Change device defaults

15. Which of the following can be used for automated auditing of wireless security policies?

    a.   MDM system

    b.   BYOD sensors

    c.   WIPS system

    d.   RADIUS server

16. Which of these is not going to be the typical wireless end user's responsibility under a formal wireless security policy?

    a. Preventing rogue APs
    b. Securing management interfaces
    c. Being aware of social engineering methods
    d. Abiding by password policy

17. What constituents in a large organization are likely to have a hand in writing, enforcing, and following wireless security policy?

    a. Management
    b. End users
    c. Legal team
    d. All of these

18. Which one of the following is not provided by a well-written wireless security policy?

    a. Regulatory compliance
    b. Legal protection
    c. Consistent user experience for clients
    d. Procedures for network implementation

19. Which of these steps most directly reduce the possibility of password theft?

    a. Not sharing passwords
    b. Using longer passwords
    c. Not writing passwords down
    d. Frequent changes

20. The process that involves asset identification, solution definition, monitoring and auditing is _____.

    a.   Risk assessment

    b.   Asset enumeration

    c.   Policy planning

    d.   Incident response

21. You support a wide range of customer types and sizes as a CWSP. Which of the following is likely to be the smallest target for security breaches?

    a.   Financial institution

    b.   Retail environment

    c.   Small business

    d.   Home user

22. Regarding MDM solutions, which of these is not accurate?

    a.   Becoming less relevant

    b.   Can be hosted on-site

    c.   Becoming more relevant

    d.   Can be hosted off-site as SaaS

23. Network security is always a trade-off between _____ and _____.

    a.   Security achieved, ease of use

    b.   Cost, policy

    c.   Size of organization, business model

    d.   Device types, proprietary protocols

24. What part of a wireless security policy would address the use of locks, locking enclosures, and tamper-proof fasteners?

    a.   Hardware security

    b.   Premise security

    c.   Physical security

    d.   Installation security

25. Which of the following would a response plan typically include?

    a.   Analyzing system logs

    b.   Password policy

    c.   Asset identification

    d.   Remote networking procedures

Chapter 3: Review Answers

1. **B** is correct. An incident response plan helps bring order to the chaos that can ensue after a security incident occurs.

2. **D** is correct. A Mobile Device Management system provides the ability to remotely act on client devices.

3. **A** is correct. Social media use brings a range of concerns that need to be addressed through policy.

4. **D** is correct. Risk assessment is critical to understanding what you are protecting.

5. **B** is correct. Without management's buy-in, security policy is doomed to failure.

6. **C** is correct. The final policy varies by company, but the process that leads to the policy being created is generally the same for all companies.

7. **A** is correct. The HIPAA regulations that govern hospital patient information policy has great impact on wireless security policy.

8. **D** is correct. All of these have generally come about in the last several years.

9. **B** is correct. A single, central policy is easier to write and keep updated, and has a better chance for successful implementation.

10. **D** is correct. Administrative interfaces are associated with network devices.

11. **A** is correct. Threat mitigation is a unique capability associated with WIPS.

12. **C** is correct. Though employees would do well to use strong personal passwords, the enterprise security policy is not likely to cover the use of passwords.

13. **D** is correct. Wireless network access policy deals specifically with who can use the WLAN, and for what purposes.

14. **A** is correct. The use of SNMP is generally beyond the scope of small network environments.

15. **C** is correct. A properly installed WIPS system augments an organization's ability to monitor and enforce security policy.

16. **B** is correct. End users play an important role in wireless security, but securing administrative interfaces is the job of IT staff.

17. **D** is correct. A good wireless security policy is the result of every part of the organization having some role in creating or following it.

18. **C** is correct. Policy does not really have a direct impact on network performance.

19. **C** is correct. Though all of these are good practices, passwords get stolen easily when written down.

20. **A** is correct. Risk assessment includes these tasks.

21. **D** is correct. The home user generally has the least valuable data when bad guys go looking for targets.

22. **A** is correct. MDM solutions most certainly are not becoming less relevant in today's wireless security paradigm.

23. **A** is correct. It is safe to say that stronger security can result in systems that are less convenient and less easy to use.

24. **C** is correct. All of these are examples of physical security.

25. **A** is correct. System logs can yield tremendous amounts of information when investigating what happened during a security incident.

Chapter 4:

Authentication

Objectives

4.1   Execute the preventive measures required for common vulnerabilities on
       wireless infrastructure devices, including weak/default passwords on wireless
       infrastructure equipment and misconfiguration of wireless infrastructure
       devices by administrative staff.

4.2   Identify the purpose and characteristics of IEEE 802.1X and EAP and the
       processes used, including EAP types (PEAP, EAP-TLS, EAP-TTLS, EAP-FAST and
       EAP-SIM), AAA servers (RADIUS), and certificate management.

4.3   Understand additional security features in WLAN infrastructure and access
       devices, including management frame protection, Role-Based Access Control
       (RBAC), Fast BSS transition (pre-authentication and OKC), physical security
       methods, and Network Access Control (NAC).

To quote something that wireless expert Tom Carpenter often says, "If your authentication is weak, little else matters in your security." This statement is true and the implications are many. The AAA security principle (authentication, authorization, and accounting) is built on this foundation. For example, if your authentication is weak, authorization is irrelevant from the perspective of strong security because an attacker could simply log onto the network posing as an individual with access to the resource. The same holds true for accounting: if authentication is weak, the attacker can log onto the network as another individual and the accounting system logs the improper actions to the wrong person. For that matter, it may log normal behavior because the attacker has connected as an authorized user in the first place. Strong authentication is the foundation of overall network security.

Authentication is the foundation of 802.11 WLAN security. For this reason, Chapter 4 explores available 802.11 authentication methods in depth. These methods range from passphrase authentication to the Extensible Authentication Protocol (EAP). But first, authentication itself must be introduced in more detail.

Authentication

Without a clear understanding of authentication and identity management, you will have difficulty configuring a secure wireless network. Both basic and advanced authentication methods exist, and many wireless systems include the ability to support both. For example, Windows Server systems allow for

- advanced authentication mechanisms through the Network Policy Server (NPS, Microsoft's RADIUS implementation), and

- basic authentication using simple passwords against the Active Directory database.

Both methods serve valid purposes and are best for certain scenarios. Determining which method is right for your scenario is the first step in implementing secure authentication.

Beyond selecting either advanced or basic authentication methods (or both), you must determine whom or what to authenticate.

- Do you need to authenticate the clients only?

- Is authentication of the authentication server required as well?

When both the client and the authentication server are authenticated, it is called mutual authentication. Mutual authentication helps prevent the introduction of rogue authentication devices into your network. Client-only authentication allows the network to have protection from unauthorized clients and is generally easier to implement, whereas mutual authentication allows both the clients and the network to have confidence and trust in the connections but with more administrative work required to bring accomplish it.

When considering authentication, it is good to understand where it fits in the paradigm of AAA (called "triple A"). Authentication should not be confused with authorization.

- **Authentication** is defined as *proving a person or object is who or what he or it claims to be.*

- **Authorization** is defined as *controlling or granting access to a resource by a person or object.*

Authorization assumes the identity has been authenticated. If authentication can be spoofed or impersonated, authorization schemes fail. From this, you can see why authentication is such an integral and important part of network and information security. In contrast to authentication, accounting processes log who or what performed a given action. Accounting assumes the authentication of the acting identity has been performed accurately and securely. Again, authentication is the foundation of strong security.

Advanced authentication systems generally utilize stronger user credentials and better protection of those credentials than basic authentication systems. The strength and protection of the user credential is determined by the effort it takes to exploit it. A password-protected credential is usually considered weak when compared with biometric-protected credentials, for example. However, in some cases this is a misconception because the strength of authentication really depends on how the authentication information (the credential and proof of ownership) is sent across the network. If you were to implement a biometric system, such as a thumb scanner, and the client sent the credentials and proof of ownership (a unique number built from the identity points on the user's thumb) to the server in clear text, it would be no more secure than a standard password-based system. Thankfully, no known biometric authentication system works in this way, but the point here is that seemingly secure methods can be defeated by lack of careful implementation.

The primary methodology of securing the authentication pathway is encryption, that is, the hashing of the user credentials or at least the proof-of-identity information. This protection can be accomplished with VPN technology or with well-designed authentication systems. One example of such an authentication system is 802.1X with a strong EAP type. 802.1X and EAP types are discussed in their respective sections in this chapter, and in later chapters as well.

You use authentication every day of your life. For example, when you are at a seminar and the speaker says that he is a subject matter expert, you use authentication mechanisms to verify this information. In other words, you listen to the information he delivers and use it to determine if he is truly an expert. In addition, suppose someone walks up to you and says, "Hi, my name is Bill and I am tall." You would look at him and compare his height with what you consider to be tall, and authenticate in your mind whether he is truly tall or not. If he is not tall by your standards, he loses credibility with you.

Remember the word *credentials?* Consider additional important "cred" words: credit, credibility, and credentials. Do you see how they are all related? They all have to do with having proof of something.

- When you have **good credit**, you have proof of your trustworthiness to pay debts.

- When you have **credibility**, you have proof that you are authentic, persuasive, and dynamic.

- When you have **credentials**, you have a title or the experience that proves your skill or identity.

All of these words originate in the Latin word *credere*, which means "to believe or trust." Authentication is the process used to verify credentials and establish trust.

Advanced authentication is more secure than basic authentication because advanced mechanisms are used to protect the credentials. This usually means protecting a username and password pair, but it can include protecting a user/certificate combination, a user/machine combination, or any other user/object combination used to identify a specific user. In addition to the extra protection offered by advanced authentication systems, when 802.1X-based systems are used, you have the benefit of standards-based security technology. Hardware and software from many different vendors are likely to support the authentication process when a standard is involved. A driver or firmware upgrade may be required, but a path often exists leading to the implementation of the authentication mechanism on most client devices.

Importance of Authentication in Wireless Networks

Authentication is important in any network, but it is particularly important in wireless networks. Wireless networks generally do not provide for location identification. For example, with a wired network, a smart switch can report to you the exact Ethernet port being used by a particular client. From there, a cabling record can tell you exactly where the premise wiring run goes that is connected to the switch port, so physically locating the connected client is very possible. But in a wireless network, the best that most systems can report is that a specific wireless client is connected to a certain AP. The client may be located anywhere within the three-dimensional transmit range of the AP, which can extend to multiple floors and several thousand square feet. For this reason, authenticating users becomes very important in wireless networks.

Triangulation systems are available that may be able to more finely locate a wireless client, but due to the mobility of 802.11-based connections, you may determine the location of the client only to arrive at that location and discover the attacker has physically moved and yet is still connected. A smart attacker is not going to stay connected from the same location for very long unless he knows there is no triangulation system in play. Further, a truly wily intruder might employ a partial Faraday cage, which could be placed around a portion of the antenna or a highly directional antenna in such a way that wireless sensors can only see it from one direction. This would effectively disable or cripple many triangulation systems—they would no longer properly calculate signals related to the antenna that they are analyzing because they often assume the use of omnidirectional antennas. Such a scenario would allow the attacker to communicate in the direction of the AP but not communicate—or be seen—from any other direction for sufficient triangulation.

Another issue is that the default Open System authentication mechanism of wireless networks allows anyone to be able to connect, resulting in the inability of network managers to track and control who is accessing their networks. Now contrast Open System to more robust methods. Through combinations of computer certificates and user credentials, an advanced authentication system can provide both the identity of the user and the exact machine he or she is using to connect to the wireless network. Effective authentication systems help enforce network policies such as who can gain access and what network resources they can use. These authentication systems make it very difficult for an attacker to gain access to your network in the first place. The attacker would have to steal both a computer certificate and user credentials to fully gain access. Granted, some networks do not desire or require the strongest authentication systems possible, but the good news is that they are available for wireless networks when required.

Choosing the Right Credentials

Many different credential solutions are available for securing your wireless networks. It is important to select the right system for your needs. In this process, consider the primary features of a credential solution and whether or not you need a multifactor authentication system. In addition, you should be aware of the various credential types available to you.

A credential solution should provide a means of user or computer identification that is proportional in strength to your security needs. You do not want to select a credential solution that places unnecessary burdens on the wireless network users and results in greater costs (of both time and money) than the value of the information assets you are protecting. You should determine whether the selected authentication solution provides for redundancy and integration with other systems, such as Active Directory or LDAP servers, as you evaluate how it would fit into the larger network picture for a given environment. The system should support the needed credential types, such as smart cards and/or biometrics.

In addition, consider the following factors when selecting a credential solution:

- The method used to protect the credentials

- The storage location of the credentials

- The access method of the credential store

The method used to protect the credentials: If an authentication system sends the credentials as clear text, there is no protection of the credentials. Advanced authentication systems protect the user credentials by encrypting them or avoiding the transmission of the actual credentials in the first place. Instead of transmitting the actual credentials, many systems use a hashing process to encode at least the password. Hashing the passwords means that the password is passed through a one-way algorithm resulting in a fixed-length number. The resulting number is known as the hash of the password, or as the message digest. The hash is stored in the authentication database and can be used as an encryption key for challenge text in a challenge/response authentication system.

The storage location of the credentials: The credentials, both username and password (or hash) or certificates, must be stored in some location accessible by other resources on the network that need to interact with it. The storage location

- should be both secure and responsive

- must be secure to protect against brute-force attacks, and

- must be responsive to service authentication requests in a timely fashion.

Certificates are usually stored in a centralized certificate store (known as a certificate server or certificate authority) as well as on the client, which uses the certificate for authentication. Both locations must be secure, or the benefit of using certificates is diminished. In addition to the standard certificate store, users may choose to back up their certificates to disk. Backups are usually password protected, but given enough time, brute-force attacks against the media store may reveal the certificate. For this reason, users should be well educated in this area and understand the vulnerability presented by the existence of such backups.

The access method for the credential store: Access methods vary by authentication system and storage paradigm, but standards exist that define credential access methods. One widely used example is Lightweight Directory Access Protocol (LDAP). LDAP is a standard method for accessing directory service information. LDAP information can include many objects but is usually inclusive of authentication credentials. LDAP is, or can be, used by Lotus Notes, OpenLDAP, Slapd, and Microsoft's Active Directory, among others.

Credential Categories

Sometimes, one credential category alone is insufficient for wired and/or wireless network security. In these cases, multifactor authentication can be used. Multifactor authentication is a form of authentication that uses more than one set of credentials. The generic credentials available are something you

- know (information: passwords, PINs, etc.)

- have (physical objects: smart cards, keys, etc.), and

- are (biometric: thumb scanners, retina scanners, etc.).

An example of a multifactor authentication process would be the use of both passwords and thumb scanners. Typically, the user would place her thumb on the thumb scanner and be prompted for a password or PIN (personal identification number) code. The password may be used for network authentication, or it may only be used for localized authentication before the thumb data is used for network authentication. However, in most cases the password and thumb data are used to authenticate to the local machine and then the network or just to the network alone. A common example of multifactor authentication would be an ATM card. The card is used and a PIN (something you have and something you know) must be entered. A username and password pair is not multi-factor authentication. Multi-factor authentication requires the use of multiple credential types and a username and password is a single credential.

Credential Types

Many credential types exist. They include:

- Username and password
- Certificates
- PACs (Privilege Attribute Certificates)
- Biometrics
- Tokens

Username and password pairs are currently the most popular type of credential. They are used by most network operating systems, including Mac OS X, Linux, UNIX, and Windows. Due to the human factor involved in the selection of the password, they often introduce a false sense of security. Because the chosen passwords are often too weak to withstand dictionary attacks and brute-force attacks, many users proceed with no knowledge that their credential could be compromised with common attacks. In addition, the passwords are often written down or stored in plaintext files on the system. And the passwords are changed infrequently, resulting in a longer attack opportunity window.

An alternative to username and password pairs is the digital certificate. In order to use certificates throughout an organization, a certificate authority (CA) must exist. The CA can be operated by the organization or by an independent third party. A CA is basically a server or service that issues and manages the lifecycle of a certificate. In either case, the costs are often prohibitive for widespread use due to the need for an extra server or even a hierarchy of servers. Small and medium-sized organizations usually opt for server-only certificates, or no certificates at all, because of the cost of implementation. A full PKI (Public Key Infrastructure) usually consists of more than one CA. Each CA would be a single server or cluster of servers. They are implemented in a hierarchy with one CA, called the root CA, at the top. The PKI is the mechanism used for generation, renewal, distribution, verification, and destruction of user and machine certificates.

The Privilege Attribute Certificate (PAC) is used by the Kerberos authentication protocol in Windows 2000 and higher (Windows XP, Windows Server 2003, Windows 2008 Server and R2, Windows Server 2012 and R2, Windows Vista, Windows 7, Windows 8 and 8.1, and Windows 10). The PAC contains the authorization data for the user and includes group memberships and user rights. This feature means that the user's group and rights assignments are transferred as a portion of the ticket-granting ticket (TGT)—a feature of the Kerberos authentication protocol.

Yet another credential is the individual authentication. Biometrics-based authentication takes advantage of the uniqueness of every human being and uses this for authentication purposes. For example, a thumbprint can be used as a unique identifier, as can your retina. The balancing of cost and security is important with biometric credentials. While hair analysis could potentially be used to authenticate a user, the cost and time involved is still too high for practical use. (Remember, the overall cost of security should not exceed the value of data being protected.) Today, both thumb scanners and retina scanners are becoming more popular.

There are two common types of authentication tokens: software-based and hardware-based.

- **Software-based** authentication token systems often run on tablets or cell phones. This allows users to launch the application on their mobile device and retrieve an authentication code. This code is usually used in conjunction with a password or PIN, essentially creating a two-factor authentication system. (Google Authenticator is an excellent free example of a software token that you can try out, if you have yet to see this type of authentication.)

- **Hardware-based** token systems usually provide a keychain-sized device that, with the press of a button, shows the current authentication code. This code is used with a password or PIN. Most token systems work off of a time-synchronized (or some other synchronization point) algorithm that generates proper codes in the software system or hardware device. This functionality means that a valid code today does not work tomorrow and provides greater security.

Figure 4-1: Hardware-Based Token Example

Passphrase-based Security

The preferred cipher suite from the current 802.11-2012 standard is CCMP (Counter Mode Cipher Block Chaining Message Authentication Code Protocol, Counter Mode CBC-MAC Protocol—yes, the first C in CCMP stands for nine words). CCMP is based on the advanced encryption standard (AES) encryption algorithm, and is available through any 802.11 equipment that supports the WPA2 interoperability certification. The personal version of WPA2 allows the use of a static passphrase to be entered by the administrator in lieu of using an EAP key generation and management technique. The use of a passphrase as the master session key (MSK) can be regarded as very strong, but only as long as the passphrase is selected using an unpredictable or unlikely-to-be-repeated methodology.

Many manufacturers allow for the entry of passphrases as either ASCII text or hexadecimal characters. ASCII-based passphrases are converted to a 256-bit pre-shared key (PSK) using a conversion hash, which is an important point to remember. The 802.11-2012 standard provides a passphrase-to-PSK mapping process.

Weak passphrases can be a security risk, and CWSPs need to understand why. Software is available that allows specific information that is captured over the unbounded wireless medium to be challenged against a "dictionary file." In this case, the dictionary is a file that contains common words and phrases. These dictionary files are available online. The software that is used to perform this attack compares the passphrase to every item in the dictionary, looking for a possible match. Continuous testing allows the intruder to try millions of combinations until they successfully discover one that works. With late-generation computing power, even a modest laptop can run this sort of analysis with ease. If a match is found, the security has been compromised. For this reason, if passphrases are to be used, it is critical to select the passphrase using a maximum-entropy technique and then keeping the passphrase secret. This means that long unique passphrases that you carefully control are recommended to help provide adequate security.

Additional attacks can be performed against WPS PIN-based security in Kali Linux using the following included tools:

- airmon-ng

- airodump-ng

- wash

- reaver

Reaver, in particular, can crack WPA and WPA2 PSKs when WPS is in use. To perform attacks with such utilities, you need to be able to inject frames onto the wireless network. Let us take a look at how that is done.

To test your adapter for this capability, perform this procedure in Kali Linux:

1. Open a Terminal window.

2. Execute the `airmon-ng start wlan0` command. Change `wlan0` to match your adapter identifier, if needed.

3. Execute `aireplay-ng -9 mon0` command. Change `mon0` to match your monitor interface identifier, if needed.

   Result: If injection works with your adapter, your output shows both "Injection is working!" and the percentage of directed probe requests successfully sent to various APs on the configured channel.

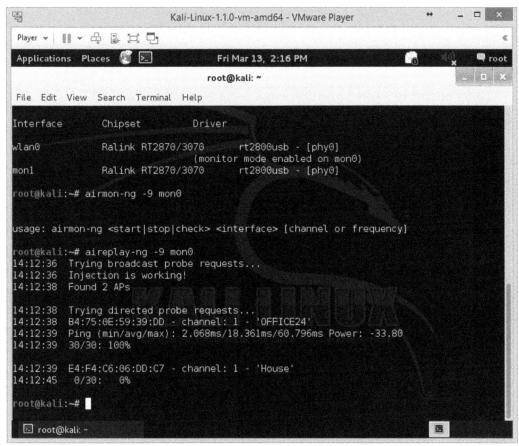

Figure 4-2: Testing Injection Ability in Kali Linux

Using default passphrases creates another issue. Most manufacturers publish the default credentials used to log into and manage their devices on their support pages online. They also frequently publicly share the default passphrases that may be used to secure the wireless service set. Your Security policy should address the issue of using default settings to include management interface credentials and proper passphrase security.

If an AP is not configured correctly with respect to passphrase security, it likely causes authentication issues. The same passphrase must be installed on all devices that are part of the same service set. Common errors in configuration include:

- Wrong passphrase entered

- Incorrect letter case used

- Errant spaces

It is important that all devices use the same exact passphrase and the correct alphabetic letter case. Otherwise, the device is not able to complete the authentication process because of a syntax mismatch between the devices. Controller-based WLAN systems are easier in this regard because you only have to provision the controller, and it then provisions the APs with the passphrase. When multiple controllers are used, the passphrase syntax must match on all controllers that host APs in the same service set. Regardless of whether the APs are controller-based or autonomous, the passphrase for a given SSID has to be consistently deployed across APs.

An important part of a CWSPs body of knowledge is the various keys that are used in WLAN authentication. The next several pages present key-related generation and use details. This is an important part of the book to read over, so take as many times as it takes to grasp the significant details.

WPA/WPA2-Personal mode authentication both happen by means of a shared pairwise master key (PMK). Both the supplicant (client device) and authenticator (AP) are configured with the same passphrase (or HEX ASCII), which is converted into a PMK. The PMK is used for dynamic encryption key generation during the 4-way handshake. Because the PMK is used as an input to dynamic encryption keys, if the PMK on both devices does not match, shared encryption keys are not generated and the 4-way handshake fails.

When a passphrase is used, rather than directly entering a hexadecimal PSK, the passphrase is converted into a PSK by the following method:

$$PMK = PRF(passphrase, ssid, ssidLength, 4096, 256)$$

In this formula, PRF refers to a pseudo-random function that is calculated against the string comprising the passphrase, SSID, and the SSID length. It is hashed 4096 times to generate a value of 256 bits, which becomes the very important PMK. The PMK is never transmitted across the unbounded wireless medium.

The PMK is used to generate a subsequent key known as the pairwise transient key (PTK). The derivation of the PTK is done by exchanging MAC addresses and randomly generated tokens known as *nonces* between the supplicant and the authenticator using the RSNA-defined 4-way handshake. The first two frames in the 4-way handshake contain all of the information required to create the PTK except the PMK. Did you get all that? If not, read it again, as its importance cannot be overstated. Now let us go even deeper with the 802.11 encryption and key paradigms.

WPA or WPA2 Personal

The original 802.11 standard specified WEP for a security level was only intended to prevent casual eavesdropping, which is exactly what it did. Hopefully by now you accept that WEP is unable to provide sufficient security on modern WLANs because it is easily compromised, as mentioned earlier in the book. Thankfully, most hardware no longer allows you to enable it. Let us review what we have already covered about WEP again, so we can expand on it. In the early 802.11 days, the perspective was that stronger WLAN security would be available with the eventual 802.11i amendment to the standard. Around the year 2001, however, the 802.11i amendment to the standard was still some time away. Stronger security was needed in order for standards-based WLAN technology to continue to evolve. Many organizations were reluctant to install 802.11 wireless networks because they lacked adequate security measures at the time. As happens today, there were early well-published wireless breaches on business networks that highlighted the dangers of insufficient security on the WLAN. The Wi-Fi Alliance developed a fix for WEP called TKIP, which was based on the pre-ratification draft of the 802.11i amendment. This interim solution served well until stronger security mechanisms, based on the 802.11i amendment, were finally ratified. IEEE 802.11i would ultimately provide very strong security that works well in home, small and medium-sized business, and enterprise wireless networks. That is, 802.11i would provide strong security where properly implemented.

TKIP provided security enhancements that improved the way WEP operated by fixing some of the inherent security flaws native to WEP. These enhancements included a longer initialization vector (IV), stretched to 48 bits instead of the original 24. TKIP provided an improved integrity check. In most cases, all that was required for legacy infrastructure devices to support TKIP was a firmware upgrade. For legacy client devices, driver updates, and an OS patch or two brought TKIP support to capable hardware.

Another important milestone in WLAN security was the creation of the Wi-Fi Alliance. Formed in 1999, this organization gained popularity, and provided an important service by providing interoperability certification testing for member companies that manufactured 802.11 standards-based WLAN devices. Early device certifications were for easy communications functionality and operation. With the demand for better wireless security and the lack of a ratified amendment, the Wi-Fi Alliance developed the Wi-Fi Protected Access (WPA) interoperability certification, which became available in 2003. WPA provided an interoperability certification for TKIP technology that allowed manufacturers of enterprise-grade wireless infrastructure devices to successfully build and market devices that provided a stronger wireless security solution that served well until the 802.11i amendment to the standard was approved. Once the .11i amendment was ratified, it would offer even stronger WLAN security by using CCMP/AES, which is certified by the Wi-Fi Alliance in WPA2.

Exam Moment: TKIP uses a per-MPDU TKIP sequence counter (TSC) to prevent replay attacks. A replay attack occurs when a frame is retransmitted, with or without modification.

Defining WPA and WPA2

TKIP (temporal key integrity protocol technology and the WPA certification provided a great interim wireless security solution ahead of the advent of 802.11i. However, the WLAN industry and its customers still required better wireless security before wireless could become the widely preferred access method of choice in business settings.

When the 802.11i amendment was ratified in 2004, it incorporated the use of CCMP/AES technology and introduced the Robust Security Network (RSN) concept. Although TKIP/RC4 did help to fix some of the problems associated with WEP, the arrival of 802.11i and CCMP offered the best and strongest security available for creating the RSN. It may have been slow in coming, but it was worth the wait as 802.11i is the backbone of enterprise wireless security today.

Figure 4-3: Configuring WPA2 in Windows 8

Given that certifying pre-802.11i WPA security was such a success, the Wi-Fi Alliance decided to certify equipment based on the 802.11i-ratified amendment. This new certification was named WPA2 and was made available in late 2004. Since then, manufacturers of enterprise-grade wireless equipment have been able to design, build, market, and sell 802.11 WLAN devices that supported the stronger CCMP/AES security mechanisms.

When deciding between WPA and WPA2, it is always advisable to use WPA2 with CCMP/AES, unless backward compatibility with legacy devices is required. Most equipment manufactured after mid-2005 supports CCMP/AES and therefore it should be used over TKIP/AES. In some cases, larger organizations may not be in a position to upgrade all of their older devices at any one time, therefore a mixed environment of TKIP (WPA) and CCMP (WPA2) was or still may be required. (You might be surprised how much really old infrastructure wireless is still out there.) Authentication of WPA-Personal and WPA2-Personal is basically the same, which leaves the encryption method as the only differentiation.

The RSN information element is very important to the CWSP, and it is contained within certain wireless management frames. This "IE" defines an Authentication Key Management Suite List field, which specifies the type of authentication supported in a network. The field populated with "00-0F-AC:02" delineates PSK-based authentication. We will see what other variants may be in the field in just a bit.

One significant indicator that these more modern security solutions such as WPA and WPA2 are in use is the presence of what is known as the 4-way handshake. These four unicast management frames are used to derive the necessary encryption keys that secure both unicast and broadcast/multicast wireless traffic on a per-user basis. You cannot progress in wireless security without understanding the basics of the 4-way handshake.

The 4-way handshake provides specific required information to be exchanged that allows the wireless AP and the wireless client device (in an infrastructure or personal network) to create the same encryption keys. These keys are used to encrypt and decrypt information that is sent over the wireless medium and are very critical to WLAN security.

With WPA-Personal and WPA2-Personal modes, "authentication" occurs during the 4-way handshake process via the fact that the client STA has the pre-shared key. After deriving the pairwise transient key (PTK), the supplicant (client device) message integrity check (MIC) protects frame number 2 of this exchange. The hash used to calculate the MIC value includes the key confirmation key (KCK), which is a part of the PTK. If the authenticator's (AP) PTK and the supplicant's (client device) PTK do not match, the MIC fails and the authenticator silently discards the frame, ceasing the 4-way handshake exchange. The same process happens for frames 3 and 4, so mutual possession of the PTK is confirmed. The point is that the pre-shared key, when properly configured to match on the AP and the client devices, results in a successful 4-way handshake. If the key is different, the handshake fails which results in authentication and key generation failures.

Note: An excellent white paper on 802.11i key management is available at https://www.cwnp.com/uploads/802-11i_key_management.pdf.

Per-User PSK (PPSK)

Typical implementations of WPA- and WPA2- Personal mode passphrase security use a single common passphrase that is shared by all users for a given SSID, as per the original intent of 802.11i. Potential security issues arise with standard uniform PSK because all users of the service set know the passphrase, or at least have the same passphrase configured. The passphrase is used to create a 256-bit pre-shared key that restricts access to the wireless network and is used to generate keys and secure individual user data. Manufacturer proprietary mechanisms allow for unique per-user passphrases, which limit the ability of users to get each other's passphrases. While the security offered by such a solution may not be as robust as secure implementations of 802.1X/EAP, this option provides many advantages over traditional one-for-all passphrases which include:

- Allowing granular user-specific control of network privileges, which is not provided by traditional shared passphrases.

- Alleviating management burden when a passphrase must be changed due to employees leaving or passwords being compromised.

- Providing enhanced accounting functionality.

- Enhancing security between users of the same network by preventing decryption of unicast traffic.

- Not conflicting with 802.11 protocol operations.

It is important to understand that PPSK is proprietary and is available from a limited number of WLAN manufacturers. Although it can enhance the way passphrase technology is used, it should not be used as a substitute for enterprise 802.1X/EAP security solutions.

Entropy

The 802.11-2012 standard provides for the use of a 256-bit pre-shared key to be entered directly as the pairwise master key (PMK). In addition, the standard allows the use of a more user-friendly 8-63-character passphrase from which the actual PSK can be derived using a key mapping technique. The 802.11 standard says, "The RSNA PSK consists of 256 bits, or 64 octets when represented in hex." The strength of the passphrase confidentiality mechanism can be considered sufficient for any non-governmental or non-military use as long as the administrator enters the PSK directly using a 64-octet hexadecimal pre-shared key.

The primary vulnerability in either the TKIP enhancement to WEP or the CCMP replacement for WEP becomes evident when a weak passphrase is used to create the 256-bit hexadecimal pre-shared key through the IEEE-recommended mapping routine. The 802.11 task group felt that it was too difficult to expect users to enter long hex keys as part of their configuration duties.

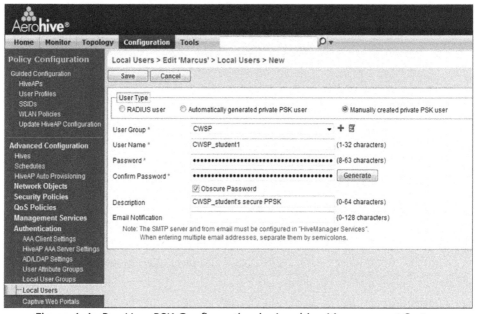

Figure 4-4: Per-User PSK Configuration in Aerohive Management System

From IEEE 802.11-2012:

M.4.1 Introduction

"Keys derived from the pass phrase provide relatively low levels of security, especially with keys generated form short passwords, since they are subject to dictionary attack. Use of the key hash [pass-phrase-to-PSK mapping process] is recommended only where it is impractical to make use of a stronger form of user authentication. A key generated from a passphrase of less than about 20 characters is unlikely to deter attacks."

The mapping algorithm is provided as a recommended practice. The IEEE 802.11i Task Group also detailed the weaknesses that this feature brings to the PSK mechanism. A passphrase typically has about 2.5* bits of security per character, so the passphrase mapping converts an n octet password into a key with about 2.5n+12** bits of security. Because of this, any dictionary-based brute force exploit can be modified to recover the hashed passphrase from the 4-Way handshake. This vulnerability does not exist if hexadecimal PSKs are used directly.

*This is due to the practice by most users of selecting easily-remembered key words that do not contain a mix of alphanumeric and special characters in their makeup. Because of this, an eight character passphrase (64 bits) would only contain 20-bits of entropy.

** Mixing in the SSID adds an additional (approx.) 12-bits of entropy.

In order to counteract the tendency of using repetitive patterns when creating cryptographic keys, it is necessary to intentionally add an additional measure of uncertainty into the selection process. In digital communications this uncertainty or randomness is called *entropy*, and it is measured in bits.

To visualize entropy, think about the act of flipping a coin. The coin has two possible states: heads or tails. We can be certain that the coin comes to rest in one of these two states but we cannot say for certain whether it ends up as heads or tails. A two-option scenario results in one bit of entropy. The following figure helps in understanding the randomness with which entropy is involved. Note that adding a single new slider lock (see fig. 4-5 below) always increases the possibilities by a factor of ten. The result is that a four-slider lock provides 100 times more possibilities than a two-slider lock—not twice as many possibilities.

Figure 4-5: Locks Representing Possibilities and Randomness

Simply defined, entropy is lack of order or predictability—or randomness. Technically speaking, passwords or passphrases themselves do not contain any entropy, or rather, they contain an entropy value of zero. It is the method you use to select the passphrase that contains the entropy. So, entropy is an estimate of how difficult it would be to deduce your passphrase. The more entropy (measured in bits) that is contained within the method you use to create your passphrase, the more difficult it is for someone else to deduce it.

Current information technology security best practices state that 72 bits of entropy should be safe for the foreseeable future while 128 bits is definitely safe for a very long time. Again, this assumes entropy and not some specific length alone. Longer passwords composed from a pool of fewer random options are not as strong as shorter passwords composed from a pool of more random options. This is why, using a minimum 20-character PSK that is not a common phrase and includes complexity (upper case, lower case, digits and special characters) results in strong WPA- and WPA2-Personal implementations.

Strong Passphrases

Is wireless passphrase technology (WPA/WPA2-Personal mode) strong enough and safe enough for use in a branch or remote office? If the preceding recommendations concerning the safe selection and storage of maximum-entropy passphrases have been followed, then there is only one remaining weakness that may be of concern for corporate usage. When using a passphrase/pre-shared key, there is one common pairwise master key (PMK) which is shared among all of the wireless devices that are part of the wireless service set. A potential security issue may arise from this configuration. Anyone who has knowledge of the PSK/PMK can decrypt encrypted data between a pair of stations (e.g., a wireless mobile device and an AP) if they capture the nonces from the 4-way handshake (sent in clear text across the unbounded wireless medium). Therefore, vulnerability to internal attacks are still possible. Use of profiles for configuration of WPA- and WPA2-Personal or direct entry by administrative staff limits the number of users who actually know the PSK.

Additionally, from the information that is contained in the captured 4-way handshake and with the help of additional dictionary attack software, there is a possibility that weak passphrases can be discovered. These captured frames and hacked passphrases then provide the 256-bit pre-shared key, which is in turn used to create the PMK for the service set. It is critical for users of this technology to use strong passphrases in order to protect the network. Several tools are available that aid in creating strong, secure passphrases.

The following are examples of password generation utilities and sites that are available to assist in adding entropy to the generation process:

- **LogmeOnce Password Security**
  - Password strength tester available as well
  - www.logmeonce.com/online-password-generator-to-generate-passwords

- **Gibson Research Free Online Passphrase Generator**
  - Ultra-high entropy, perfect for WPA/WPA2-Personal
  - https://www.grc.com/passwords.htm

- **DiceWare**
  - Let the dice create your maximum entropy passphrases in the form of easy to remember word groups
  - http://world.std.com/~reinhold/diceware.html

Use the following procedure to generate a random password in Kali Linux:

1. Open a Terminal window.

2. Execute the `openssl rand -base64 20` command.

 Note: **The password-like text generated, which is likely far more random than you would generate manually.**

3. If you desire shorter or longer passwords, change the last value, `20`, to the number you desire.

If PSK vulnerabilities are of concern to an organization, address them in the security policy and in their implementation. The policy should clearly state

- requirements for the creation of PSK passphrases, and

- identify the individuals who may be informed of the passphrases.

When using 802.1X/EAP as the authentication and key management (AKM) technology for 802.11 wireless networks, each individual 802.11 association has a unique PMK and a subsequent set of unique temporal keys. This unique key hierarchy does not allow for any keys to be discovered by capturing the contents of the 4-way handshake.

Authentication, Authorization, and Accounting (AAA)

"Triple A" plays an immensely important role in WLAN security for enterprise settings. The AAA framework/protocol can be thought of as a set of services provided within a network to securely manage and track access to network resources. The following helps to define this further:

Authentication—This process refers to the verification of an entity's identity. 802.1X/EAP is a common authentication protocol used with standards-based 802.11 wireless networks and validates that an entity is what it claims to be. Authentication can be accomplished in a variety of ways including username/password pair and user certificates. In summary, authentication can be thought of in relation to who a network user is.

Authorization—This term refers to the allocation of network resources in accordance with the privileges of a user or group. Authentication confirms a user's identity, and authorization provides access to network resources according to policy. Proper authorization ensures the authenticated user has access only to the network resources and services they have been explicitly assigned. In summary, authorization can be thought of in relation to what a network user can do.

Accounting—After resources have properly been authorized and a user has performed actions on a network, it is important to track and log those actions so that an accounting trail is made available. Accounting includes monitoring, analysis, and reporting of network events. In summary, accounting can be thought of in relation to what a network user did while connected.

Remote Authentication Dial-In User Service (RADIUS) is the most common AAA protocol in use with 802.11 wireless networks and it is used in almost every network that supports 802.1X/EAP. RADIUS server software is available for Windows, Linux, and even Mac OS/X servers.

RADIUS is a networking service that provides centralized authentication and administration of network users. RADIUS started as a way to authenticate and authorize dial-up networking users to allow access on a network, hence the name. A remote user would dial up to a network using the public switched telephone network (PSTN) and a modem. A modem from a modem pool on the receiver side would answer the call. The user would then be prompted by a remote access server to enter a username and password in order to authenticate. Once the credentials were validated, the user would have access to any resources for which they had permissions.

As computer networks grew in size and complexity and remote access technology improved, there was a need to optimize the process on the remote access server side. This is where RADIUS provides a solution. RADIUS took decentralized remote access services databases and combined them into one central location allowing for centralized user administration and centralized management. (If you can remember that far back, think of AOL's millions of customers and how difficult it might have been to manage that subscriber environment without a central database that RADIUS could query.) It eased the burden of having to manage several databases and optimized administration of remote access services. RADIUS is commonly used as an authentication server for wireless networks in 802.1X/EAP implementations.

Exam Moment: RADIUS servers can use return list attributes to set group membership, and this can be used to implement appropriate security profiles for authenticated users of the WLAN.

Mutual Authentication

The Internet Engineering Task Force (IETF) request for comment (RFC) specifying EAP, along with the 802.11-2012 standard, requires support for mutual authentication in the creation of a robust security network association (RSNA). Mutual authentication confirms the identity of the EAP peers, also known as the supplicant and the authentication server (AS). Most EAP methods implemented in modern standards-based wireless networks support mutual authentication.

Mutual authentication is a method used for two entities to authenticate each other. In 802.11 wireless security, this typically means that a client device and an authentication server authenticates each other. Though many EAP types are available to the wireless security professional, not all are good choices. For example, EAP-MD5 is an EAP type that does not provide for mutual authentication. It was not designed for wireless networks in the first place and should never be used with wireless, unless it is a tunneled authentication (and even then MS-CHAPv2 would be a better choice). Mutual authentication

- should always be supported for any authentication mechanism to be considered secure,

- is required for dynamic encryption key generation, and

- is essential because it prevents the easy implementation of rogue authentication servers.

If the server is authenticating the client (what is typically thought of when authentication is considered), but the client is not authenticating the server, evil twin attacks and other impersonation attacks are much easier. This alone should provide sufficient motivation to implement mutual authentication on the WLAN. Remember, it is no more complicated than the simple step of implementing a strong EAP type. When you do this, you have mutual authentication.

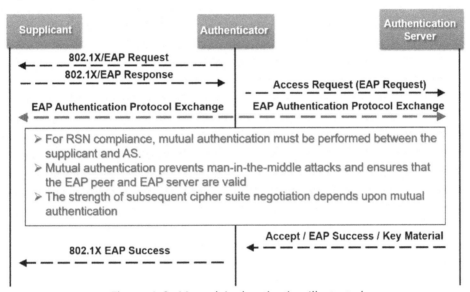

Figure 4-6: Mutual Authentication Illustrated

Some key points to consider:

- To be considered a robust secure network, mutual authentication must be performed between the supplicant and authentication server.

- Mutual authentication prevents client hijacking, which in turn

    o prevents man-in-the-middle attacks, and

    o ensures that the EAP peer and EAP server are both valid.

- The strength of subsequent cipher suite negotiation depends upon mutual authentication.

Authorization

Authorization may be performed in a number of different ways, but generally speaking, policies are defined and applied to users or groups of users via a profile mapping in the user database. Authorization includes the application of policies such as ACLs, VLANs, firewall policies, bandwidth controls, location/access permissions, traffic filters, and Quality of Service (QoS) policies.

RADIUS servers may use *attributes* in a RADIUS response to designate a specific role or policy for a user/group. This allows for simplification of the distribution of authorization rules in a WLAN.

Authorization can be allowed on a per-user or per-group basis and may include:

- **Access Control Lists (ACL)**—What the authenticated user can do on the network.

- **Stateful firewalls**—Allowing or restricting network services and ports.

- **Bandwidth controls**—How much data a user can transmit or receive, i.e., 5 Mbps.

- **Time controls**—What days and/or hours the network can be accessed.

- **Location permissions**—What can be done based on the user login location.

- **Traffic filters**—Restricting or allowing certain types of network traffic based on specified criteria.

- **QoS policies**—Specifies quality of service capabilities.

It is important to understand that authorization is also known as access control. You are controlling the resources to which the user has access by only authorizing access to appropriate resources.

Exam Moment: RADIUS supports ACCESS-REQUEST and ACCESS-ACCEPT packets to use for service authorization. When a RADIUS server receives an ACCESS-REQUEST packet, which includes a list of desired access rights, it must respond with an ACCESS-ACCEPT packet if all desired attributes are acceptable or an ACCESS-REJECT packet if one or more attributes are not acceptable.

Role-based Access Control

Role-based access control (RBAC) refers to the general process of

1. Applying roles or groups to users.

2. Applying filters, rules, and permissions to a security policy.

3. Mapping a security policy to a specific group or role.

In the end, a user is assigned a security policy through its role. The security policy sets the rights or permissions of the user.

RBAC should be required for most enterprise wireless networks and should be specified in the security policy. RBAC requirements should include:

- Defining network access roles

- Assigning authentication parameters to each role

- Assigning authorization parameters to each role

RBAC allows for access rules based on specific roles rather than an actual user identity. This is not to say that an actual user identity does not exist, but that the user is assigned a role or group membership and then authorization occurs based on the role or group rather than the user identity itself. RBAC was designed to ease the task of security administration on larger enterprise networks and shares characteristics similar to those of a common network administration practice, such as the creation of users and groups objects in an authentication database, which have been used in Windows and other systems for decades.

In computer network administration, to give a network user access to a network resource, such as a file share, best practices suggest

1. Creating a group object.

2. Assigning the group permissions to the resource.

3. Finally, adding the user object to the group.

This method allows any user who is a member of the group that was created to be granted access to that specific resource. The major benefit of this model is that the administrator can easily change the group permissions, which automatically changes all user permissions in the process.

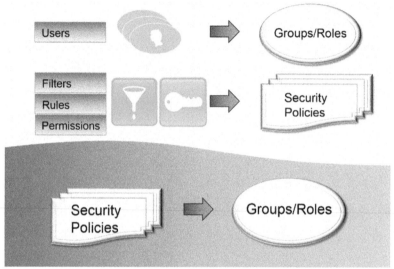

Figure 4-7: RBAC Represented Visually

RBAC, for the most part, works the same way and can be used for various activities users may perform while connected to a wireless network. Configuration options include:

- Enforcing time restrictions
- Bandwidth restrictions
- Controlling access to specific resources such as the Internet

Do some of the items on this list look familiar? Consider what was stated earlier with respect to authorization. RBAC is effectively an authorization system that is easier to manage in large-scale deployments with hundreds or thousands of users. It is not likely to be as beneficial in SOHO or small business deployments with less than 20-30 users. At the same time, cloud-managed WLAN is becoming quite popular with franchises that have small user counts, and RBAC can be rolled out to hundreds or thousands of small sites as if they were all one big enterprise via a well-designed cloud management dashboard.

Accounting

The final part of the AAA process is accounting. Accounting allows a network administrator to track all or selected activity an authenticated user has performed while connected to the network. The logged information is valuable when an incident occurs as it shows who performed a given action on the network. Of course, the accuracy of this data depends on strong authentication.

RADIUS supports network accounting via default port 1813 or 1646 as specified in RFC 2866, and must be enabled on both the AAA client and the AAA server.

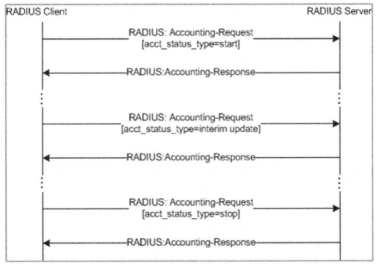

Figure 4-8: RADIUS Accounting

In addition, the wireless security professional must not lose sight of the accounting systems already available on the network. These include centralized log servers of infrastructure devices, such as Syslog servers, and operating system logs, like the

Event Viewer logs in Windows environments. One useful tool is the ManageEngine EventLog Analyzer, available at:

www.manageengine.com/products/eventlog

Tools like EventLog Analyzer can be used to aggregate logs from infrastructure devices, operating systems, and more. Once aggregated, it can then generate reports against terabytes of data to show you the important information you need.

Accounting logs on the RADIUS are extremely helpful in diagnosing why a given client failed authentication, and can be invaluable in troubleshooting. Some RADIUS servers do accounting logging far better than others, and this should be a differentiator when you are shopping for a RADIUS solution.

Network Access Control (NAC)

NAC is a security posture assessment tool. NAC may be stand-alone as appliance-based solutions, or as a set of features integrated with other key services. Before a client joins a network, the NAC service validates that the client complies with the network policy. Actions performed by a NAC solution may include:

- Assurance that all appropriate policies and security mechanisms are met by endpoints
- Application of policies to enforce security on a network
- Enforcement of requirements such as antivirus software version and scans, OS updates, security patches, firewalls, user restrictions, etc.
- Authentication and authorization
- Posture assessment
- Quarantine
- Remediation

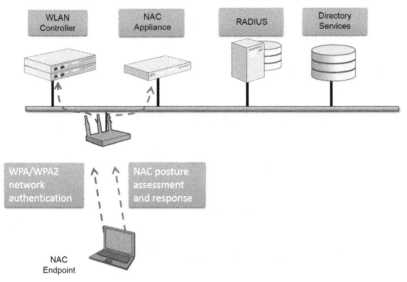

Figure 4-9: NAC Solution Illustrated

WPA and WPA2 Enterprise

The three primary authentication components of WPA-Enterprise and WPA2-Enterprise are:

- Remote Authentication Dial-In User Service (RADIUS)

- IEEE 802.1X—Port-based access control

- Extensible Authentication Protocol (EAP)

RADIUS allows for centralized authentication services and acts as the authentication server (AS). RADIUS can be used to query a local self-contained user database, or an external user database via Lightweight Directory Access Protocol (LDAP).

IEEE 802.1X is the standard that defines port-based access control. It specifies the roles of the components used in the authentication process. In a wireless network, regardless of vendor in use, these components are:

- **The supplicant**—client device to be authenticated

- **The authenticator**—the AP which provides the wireless connection

- **The authentication server**—the RADIUS server that validates user credentials

IEEE 802.1X contains virtual controlled and uncontrolled ports to filter pre-authentication and post-authentication user traffic.

The image, WPA2-Enterprise Illustrated, shows the basic flow of client authentication in a WPA- or WPA2-Enterprise network using RADIUS, 802.1X/EAP, and a LDAP-compliant user database.

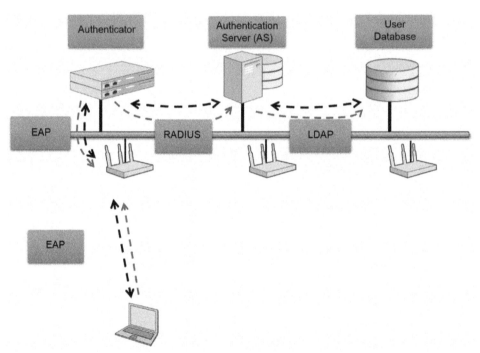

Figure 4-10: WPA2-Enterprise Illustrated

RADIUS Authentication

RADIUS services are the most often used for user-based authentication services in WLAN infrastructures. RADIUS services can be implemented either in a WLAN controller for smaller user counts, or on a stand-alone server computer (Windows, Linux, OS/X, etc.). RADIUS is based on UDP rather than TCP, though RFC 6613 supports RADIUS over TCP. When implemented on a server that runs a local firewall, it is important to open the following default ports where relevant:

- Port 1812 for authentication operations
- Port 1813 for accounting operations

A RADIUS server can have an integrated (native) database or it can proxy to SQL, older Windows Domains, newer Active Directory domains, Novell eDirectory, Lightweight Directory Access Protocol (LDAP), or another RADIUS service and is supported by all WLAN infrastructure providers.

Access points and WLAN controllers point to RADIUS servers in order to authenticate users (using 802.1X/EAP AKM) and to define authorization parameters to those users.

Several steps are required on different components in order to successfully configure 802.1X/EAP. Most RADIUS servers are relatively easy to configure because the user database that provides the authentication credentials is already configured and stored externally to the RADIUS service in most cases.

1. The first step in configuring a RADIUS server is licensing. The licensing paradigm varies by vendor, but is typically based on supported authenticator counts.

2. Once licensed, if the server is using digital certificates for server-side authentication, then the certificate needs to be imported or generated. If a certificate is generated, it needs to be distributed to client devices (via email, file transfer, etc.). If the certificate comes from a trusted party whose certificate is already stored on client devices, distribution of the server-side certificate is not necessary. It is important to remember that a digital certificate resides on the RADIUS server.

Exam Moment: RADIUS servers have digital certificates used to authenticate the RADIUS server itself. These certificates can be self-signed or provided by a trusted third-party.

3. Configuring an enterprise RADIUS server that is geared toward standards-based WLANs specifically is typically a straight-forward process, once you have defined what users or devices should be able to connect, and what EAP types should be used. As a reminder, solutions enforce policy, and RADIUS is no different. You need to know what you want out of the server before you can configure it! For WPA- and WPA2-Enterprise, configurations must be performed in three or four areas:

   a) Configure the client by selecting the WLAN profile, configuring the security parameters including EAP type, and selecting the certificate.

   b) Configure the WLAN Controller or AP with the IP address, correct port, and shared secret of the RADIUS server. Optionally, configuration of RADIUS services such as accounting may be performed.

   c) Configure the RADIUS server by adding the approved APs or network subnet. If user accounts are to reside on the RADIUS server (native RADIUS accounts), then they should either be imported or entered manually. Specific EAP and RADIUS services must be selected, configured, and enabled on the RADIUS server.

   d) Depending upon the user database, additional configurations may be required for database compatibility and functionality.

Of course, these steps are a simplification and additional options and services are often configured. This basic process helps to illustrate a common set of steps to be performed.

RADIUS Authentication Exchange

Beyond using the RADIUS server logs, a protocol or application analyzer can be useful when trying to troubleshoot an authentication failure. Depending on when the failure occurs within the authentication exchange, an analyzer can be used to pinpoint whether the fault is due to incorrectly supplied user credentials or misconfigured user database information. In addition, an extraordinarily high number of authentication failures may indicate vulnerability probing by a hostile intruder or a high number of misconfigured supplicants.

When using RADIUS authentication, frames are exchanged on both the wireless network connection—between the supplicant and the authenticator, and the wired side—between the authenticator and the authentication server. Therefore the appropriate tools are required in order to gather all of the necessary information and perform the adequate troubleshooting steps. A protocol analyzer must be placed between the authenticator and the RADIUS server, and another between the client STA and the authenticator to capture all communications related to the RADIUS authentication process.

You can build a RADIUS server for lab purposes using the Kali Linux VM. You need to install FreeRADIUS and configure it. Use the following steps to install FreeRADIUS:

1. Open a Terminal window.

2. Execute the command `apt-cache search freeradius` to view the available FreeRADIUS packages.

 Note: You may wish to run `apt-get update` first to ensure you are seeing the newest packages available to you.

3. View the following similar output :

> freeradius—high-performance and highly configurable RADIUS server
> freeradius-common—FreeRADIUS common files
> freeradius-dbg—debug symbols for the FreeRADIUS packages
> freeradius-dialupadmin—set of PHP scripts for administering a FreeRADIUS server
> freeradius-iodbc—iODBC module for FreeRADIUS server

freeradius-krb5—kerberos module for FreeRADIUS server

freeradius-ldap—LDAP module for FreeRADIUS server

freeradius-mysql—MySQL module for FreeRADIUS server

freeradius-postgresql—PostgreSQL module for FreeRADIUS server

freeradius-utils—FreeRADIUS client utilities

libfreeradius-dev—FreeRADIUS shared library development files

libfreeradius2—FreeRADIUS shared library

4. Run `apt-get install freeradius` to perform the installation.

5. When asked if you want to continue, type `Y` and press `ENTER`.

6. When the installation completes, you can add a web-based management interface by executing `apt-get install freeradius-dialupadmin`.

After these steps, you need to enable Apache with PHP and then create the appropriate MySQL configuration. More detailed information can be found here:

wiki.freeradius.org/guide/Dialup-admin

LDAP Authentication

LDAPv3 (RFC 3377) databases are often used in large enterprises to hold objects such as network users. RADIUS servers may query LDAP databases to authenticate wireless users. LDAP is based on the X.500 standard, and Microsoft Active Directory and Novell eDirectory are LDAPv3 compliant. Some WLAN infrastructure devices can interface with LDAPv3 directories directly without having to use RADIUS, but this functionality is being or has been phased out in many products.

802.1X/EAP Configuration

In addition to RADIUS configuration, the WLAN infrastructure must also be configured with the proper authentication server information. This configuration is typically limited to the creation of the WLAN profile which includes:

- The network name (SSID)

- 802.1X/EAP authentication

- The encryption scheme that is used

- Any SSID specific settings

- Configuration of a RADIUS server

RADIUS-specific parameters include:

- An IP address

- The shared secret

- Authentication and accounting ports

- Other required and optional parameters

The shared secret is a common password that is shared between the authenticator and the RADIUS server. This is one security mechanism that helps prevent the installation of rogue APs that may be connected to the wired network infrastructure, as rogues cannot send authentication to the RADIUS server without the RADIUS shared secret.

802.1X/EAP Client Configuration

Each supplicant has different 802.1X/EAP capabilities, and should be checked for compatibility prior to selection. Remember that the supplicant can be

- native to the operating system (Windows, OS X, Linux, etc.), or

- in the form of the client utilities provided by the wireless NIC vendor, or

- as a third-party supplicant sold separately.

Common configuration steps include:

1. Configure the SSID and basic 802.1X/EAP security parameters, including encryption type.

2. Verify the specific EAP type is selected and configured.

3. Select the proper server and client certificates to be used, and configure some tunneled EAP parameters.

4. Select advanced settings, such as user or machine authentication, as well as fast secure roaming features if required.

Certificates and Tunneled EAP

To use WPA- or WPA2-Enterprise, digital certificates are required with many EAP types. Following are a few examples of enterprise-grade RADIUS applications capable of generating self-signed digital certificates and acting as a trusted root certificate authority:

- **FreeRADIUS** (Open source)
- **Microsoft**—Network Policy Server NPS (Windows Server 2012 and R2)
- **Cisco**—Access Control Server (ACS), soon to be replaced by Cisco Integrated Services Engine (ISE)

Some of these applications provide methods of distributing the server-side certificate to client stations.

Many manufacturers of enterprise WLAN equipment provide built-in RADIUS, which is integrated into the platform or management software they provide.

Server-side Certificates

A self-signed server certificate must be created and imported into the client's trusted root certificate store. In many deployments with self-signed certificates, certificates are installed with installation-executable files or other automated processes. They may be installed during device staging and deployment. For example, when deploying Windows systems, the certificate can be installed before the system image is created.

WPA- and WPA2-Enterprise can provide mutual authentication of both the authentication server and the wireless client using several forms of extensible authentication protocol (EAP). The most popular of these EAP types use a digital certificate as the authentication credential for the authentication server. In addition, some of the EAP-types also use a digital certificate as the authentication credential for the wireless client.

 Note: **The Wi-Fi Alliance no longer lists WPA as a certification program they offer for new equipment on their certification programs page; however, they are still listing it on certificates. They do not recommend using it in any environment unless an upgrade is impossible.**

A digital certificate is a data file that is exchanged between the authenticating entities. Digital certificates are created, distributed, and authenticated by trusted certificate authorities (CA), which, in an enterprise deployment, are part of a Public Key Infrastructure (PKI). The CA certificate should be installed in the local store of trusted roots on all client devices so that certificates issued from the CA is trusted as well.

Several forms of EAP rely on transaction layer security (TLS) based protocol variants to provide authentication. TLS is based on the secure sockets layer (SSL) protocol originally developed by Netscape. The TLS standard does not specify how security is implemented. Instead, TLS leaves the decisions on how to initiate handshaking and how to authenticate credentials such as digital certificates and secret keys to the protocol designers. These credentials may be exchanged during or following the TLS handshake procedure.

TLS provides the mechanism to allow the client and server to authenticate each other and to negotiate an encryption algorithm and cryptographic keys, while guaranteeing privacy through the use of asymmetric cryptography and secure message integrity. TLS negotiations are secure from eavesdropping, hijacking, and man-in-the-middle intrusions, and thus have great importance in 802.11 security.

Authentication Models

When implementing authentication for a single building or campus, the model can be quite simple. However, when implementing authentication for branch offices and remote locations, the complexity increases. In this brief section, single building and branch deployments is considered.

Single Building or Campus

In a standard enterprise single-site network environment, it is most common to see one or more wireless controllers authenticating users against RADIUS, which in turn proxies to an LDAP directory service. Because all components that provide the authentication are contained within the local wired high-speed network, this authentication model should perform well if the network infrastructure has been designed correctly. The same authentication model used for the traditional wired networks are extended to the wireless network with the possible addition of a RADIUS server, if it is not already in place.

Branch Option #1

In a standard enterprise multi-site environment, it is common to see one or more WLAN controllers or management systems authenticating users against RADIUS, which in turn proxies to an LDAP directory service. In the multi-site deployment pictured below, both the headquarters and the branch office LANs are connected together using an Internet connection. This is a very common method that is used in many implementations.

 Note: **It is important to note that each location has its own**

- **RADIUS server used for authentication, and**
- **its own replica of the LDAP database which contains the user directory database.**

If there were a link failure between the sites, it would not cause any authentication issues as each location is, for the most part, a stand-alone entity because they have their own RADIUS services and user database. Of course, the branch office would not be able to access any resources at the headquarters locations, and any updates would not be replicated until the link between sites was restored.

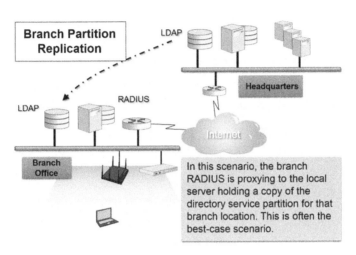

Figure 4-11: Multi-Site Directory Deployment

Branch Option #2

If the branch office does not have a local LDAP server (user directory database), RADIUS may proxy to a remote site (like the main office) to authenticate users. Doing this introduces a potentially slow and less reliable link (the Internet connection) into the equation. This slow link could cause extreme latency for initial 802.1X/EAP authentications, so it is imperative that fast/secure roaming mechanisms such as Opportunistic Key Caching (OKC) (discussed in Chapter 8) be considered on the branch WLAN controller and wireless stations when using this authentication option.

If the branch or remote office does not have a replica or a partition of the user database several potential problems may result, which include:

- Availability
- Latency
- Wide area network (WAN) utilization, and
- Fast secure roaming.

This option relies on an available connection (either leased-line or the Internet) between locations. In the event of a link failure (Internet connection), the branch office RADIUS services would not be able to contact the headquarters location to authenticate users that attempt to log into the network.

The connection speed of the link between locations is also an important factor. If a slow link is in place, the authentication could be slowed down since the RADIUS must cross the wide area network to perform the authentication. The same holds true with a WAN link that is heavily used. This can cause delays and long authentication times.

Depending on the fast secure transition method used, it could cause roaming delays when a user transitions from one AP to another AP at the branch office. If the fast roaming method used requires the RADIUS server to cross the WAN link, it could cause the connection to break, and to require reauthentication to occur.

IEEE 802.1X Port-based Access Control

The 802.1X standard specified port-based access control. This standard may be applied to wired and wireless networks. When implementing an 802.1X solution, three entities are always involved and these are the basic building blocks of 802.1X

Figure 4-12: 802.1X Entities

Remember, the 802.1X entities (basic building blocks) include:

- **Supplicant**—The client device/software requesting network connectivity.

- **Authenticator**—The AP or WLAN controller that acts as a port-based access control entity pending supplicant authentication.

- **Authentication Server (AS)**—A RADIUS (or similar) authentication server entity that supports an authentication method; the AS may host the user database or may communicate with an external user database to authenticate user credentials and profiles.

The use of 802.1X in a wireless environment introduces several key benefits. Reasons to use EAP with 802.1X include:

- Maturity and interoperability as a solution

- User-based authentication and authorization

- Dynamic encryption key management (generation and distribution), and

- Flexible authentication (many EAP types available).

The first step to creating a Robust Security Network Association (RSNA) in an infrastructure BSS is to become 802.11 authenticated and associated. As this happens, each STA receives the other's Robust Security Network (RSN) IE that describes their respective capabilities and requirements.

The second step in creating the RSNA is for the supplicant and authentication server to complete the mutual 802.1X/EAP authentication, and for the authentication server to pass the PMK to the Authenticator.

Note that an 802.1X Port consists of both a Controlled Port and an Uncontrolled Port. This notion is very important to understand, as it plays a significant role in wireless network authentication.

- **Uncontrolled Port**—Used for authentication. The 802.1X Controlled Port is blocked from passing general data traffic between two STAs until an IEEE 802.1X authentication procedure and key management process complete successfully over the 802.1X Uncontrolled Port.

- **Controlled Port**—Passes protected data. Once the Authentication and Key Management (AKM) completes successfully, data protection is enabled to prevent unauthorized access, and the 802.1X Controlled Port is unblocked to allow protected data traffic to flow for this particular STA. 802.1X supplicants and authenticators exchange protocol information via the 802.1X Uncontrolled Port.

Exam Moment: When using 802.1X virtual ports, the uncontrolled port is used for authentication, and the uncontrolled port also allows data communications across the controlled port after such successful authentication.

Remember that the uncontrolled port is for exchanging authentication frames and the controlled port allows for the communication of data frames. In an 802.11 wireless network, the controlled port is blocked during the entire EAP authentication process. Once the 4-way handshake has successfully completed, the controlled port is no longer blocked and encrypted data flows over the controlled port.

The uncontrolled port and the controlled port are virtual ports. They do not represent separate physical ports, and a virtual uncontrolled and controlled port are available to each association made with an AP in a WLAN implementation.

A Port Access Entity (PAE) operates the algorithms and protocols associated with the Port Access Control Protocol. A PAE exists for each port of a system that supports Port Access Control functionality in the supplicant role, the authenticator role, or both.

In the supplicant role, a PAE is responsible for providing information to an authenticator that establishes its credentials. A PAE that performs the supplicant role in an authentication exchange is known as a supplicant PAE.

In the authenticator role, a PAE is responsible for communication with a supplicant, and for submitting the information received from the supplicant to a suitable authentication server in order for the credentials to be checked and for the consequent authorization state to be determined. A PAE that performs the authenticator role in an authentication exchange is known as an authenticator PAE.

Both PAE roles control the authorized/unauthorized state of the controlled port, depending on the outcome of the authentication process. If a given controlled port has both authenticator PAE and supplicant PAE functionality associated with it, both PAEs must be in the authorized state in order for the controlled port to become authorized.

IEEE 802.1X/EAP Framework

The IETF RFC 5247, which defines EAP, does not specify a specific implementation of EAP (other than MD5, which is useful for nothing more than basic testing of link communications and should never be used for secure authentication in any scenario). Instead, the RFC specifies a generic EAP framework that can be adapted to the specific purposes of an EAP implementation, such as EAP-PEAP (often just called PEAP or PEAPv0 for short) or EAP-FAST.

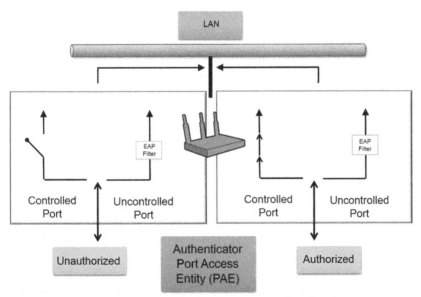

Figure 4-13: 802.1X Architecture Visualized

Exam Moment: EAP over LAN (EAPoL) packets are used across the medium between the wireless client STAs and the AP/controller. Encapsulated EAP over RADIUS is used between the AP/controller and the authentication server (RADIUS).

In addition to improved encryption and integrity algorithms, the 802.11 standard specifies the use of 802.1X port-based access control and Extensible Authentication Protocol (EAP) to provide user authentication and dynamic key distribution. EAP is a Layer 2 authentication protocol used by 802.3 and 802.11 networks as a flexible replacement for PAP and CHAP under Point-to-Point Protocol (PPP).

IEEE 802.1X restricts access to the network until a station has been authenticated by an authentication authority, usually residing within the wired network segment. Consider the following factors when planning for and implementing 802.1X authentication solutions:

- The same 802.1X framework that is used for secure WLAN can also service wired 802.1X-secured environments.

- Access to the network is managed through the use of controlled and uncontrolled ports, which are logical entities on the same physical connection. Prior to successful authentication, the client station may only communicate over the uncontrolled port and the use of this communication is authentication only.

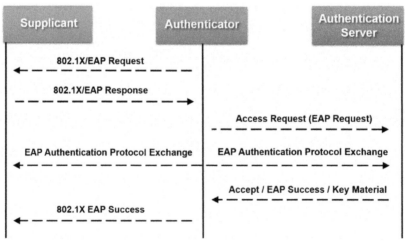

Figure 4-14: Basic Extensible Authentication Protocol (EAP) Framework

4-way Handshake

The third step in creating a RSNA is for the two STAs to have a matching pairwise master key (PMK). The PMK is used to generate the pairwise transient key (PTK) for encryption purposes. Gaining the shared PMK is accomplished in one of two ways:

- **Out-of-band**—This method uses a pre-shared key (PSK) that is entered on both STAs either directly or created from a passphrase. It is used with WPA/WPA2Personal.

- **In-band**—This method uses an 802.1X/EAP with RADIUS infrastructure where the 802.1X/EAP mechanism creates the PMK.

The final step in creating a RSNA is the 4-way handshake, which results in the availability of the unicast and broadcast/multicast encryption keys on both the supplicant and the authenticator. At the conclusion of the handshake, each STA has derived the same PTK. This PTK is used to

- secure unicast traffic, and

- exchange a group temporal key (GTK) to secure broadcast and multicast traffic.

In an 802.1X/EAP enterprise scenario and upon successful completion of the 4-way handshake, the authenticator and supplicant have authenticated each other and the 802.1X controlled port is unblocked, which allows encrypted data traffic to flow.

Exam Moment: The order of communication is ANonce, SNonce with MIC, transmission of the GTK and a final message to verify installation of the PTK sent from the supplicant to the authenticator.

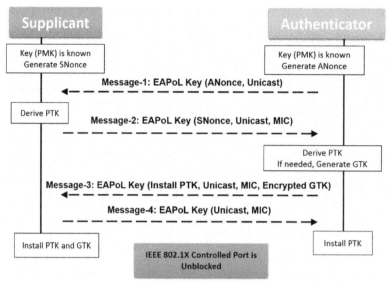

Figure 4-15: 4-way Handshake Illustrated

EAP Type Comparison

EAP is a Layer 2 authentication protocol used over 802.3 and 802.11 networks as a flexible replacement for PAP and CHAP under PPP. There are many EAP types, each with its own advantages and disadvantages. Choosing the right EAP type is essential in a WLAN security deployment.

Remember that EAP is an authentication framework and does not specify a specific authentication method. For that reason, multiple EAP types are used.

The following comparison chart shows the features of many common EAP types.

	EAP-MD5	LEAP	EAP-TLS	EAP-TTLS	PEAP	EAP-Fast
Mutual Authentication	No	Yes	Yes	Yes	Yes	No
Certificates Required	No	No	Client/Server	Server Only	Server Only	No
Dynamic Key Generation	No	Yes	Yes	Yes	Yes	Yes
Costs and Management Overhead	Low	Low	High	Low/Medium	Low/Medium	Low
Industry Support	Low	High	High	High	High	Medium
Credential Security	Weak	Weak	Strong	Strong	Strong	Strong

Figure 4:16: Common EAP Types and their Features

EAP-MD5 should never be used on a wireless network because of several vulnerabilities, including the fact that it requires no digital certificates at all. EAP-MD5 does not provide mutual authentication and it does not use tunneled authentication. When an authentication protocol sends too much information across the network without encryption, it is simply not a good protocol. EAP-MD5 is in that category. As stated previously, it may be used for testing the links in the authentication chain, but it should not be trusted for any real-world authentication scenarios.

EAP-LEAP is Cisco Systems proprietary and was cracked in early 2004; it is rarely used today if at all. Cisco's position statement was that if strong passwords are used, it is secure. That could be considered true; however, the problem is the enforcement of strong passwords. EAP-FAST was Cisco's replacement for LEAP and was used in the short term after it was released. The use of EAP-FAST decreased after other EAP types became available. There are much better non-proprietary EAP types available; therefore, LEAP should generally be avoided.

The following list shows EAP types that are more commonly used with wireless networks:

- **EAP-TLS**—client and server certificates required
- **TTLS** (EAP-MSCHAP-v2)—only server certificates required
- **PEAPv0** (EAP-MSCHAP-v2)—only server certificates required
- **PEAPv0** (EAP-TLS)—client and server certificates required
- **PEAPv1** (EAP-GTC)—used with token card and directory-based authentication systems; only server certificates required
- **EAP-SIM**—EAP for GSM Subscriber Identity Module—mobile communicators
- **EAP-AKA**—for use with the UMTS Subscriber Identity Module—mobile communications

The EAP type used really depends on the organization and network that is in place. Some EAP types such as EAP-TLS and PEAP (EAP-TLS) require the use of digital certificates on both the authentication server and the clients, and therefore require a full private key infrastructure (PKI). This can become an expensive endeavor with extra management overhead.

> **Exam Moment:** PEAP supports three different common internal methods on WLANs: MSCHAPv2, EAP-TLS, and EAP-GTC. EAP-GTC, specifically, is used with PEAPv1.

One common method used is PEAP (EAP-MSCHAP-v2). It is very popular because it is included in the Microsoft Windows operating system, Mac OS Z and Apple iOS, and Android. It can use a username/password credential set, and is widely available on several Linux variants as well.

EAP-MD5

As previously mentioned, EAPMD5 is only an authentication protocol. It does not handle encryption keys of any kind. All messages after authentication are transmitted in clear text and the authentication server is never authenticated by the client. EAP-MD5 requires only light processing, but has no use in the production WLAN market.

PEAP

Protected EAP is a common EAP implementation, and is often referred to as EAP-in-EAP because it uses a second EAP type for client authentication after the server is authenticated.

All PEAP versions require server-side certificates, which are used to establish a TLS tunnel for the client authentication exchange. Establishment of the TLS tunnel is often referred to as Phase 1. Client authentication happens in Phase 2 inside the TLS tunnel and is specific to the particular PEAP implementation. Client authentication may include the use of a username and hashed passphrase (EAP-MSCHAPv2), a client certificate (EAP-TLS), or a token card (EAP-GTC), among others (such as POTP).

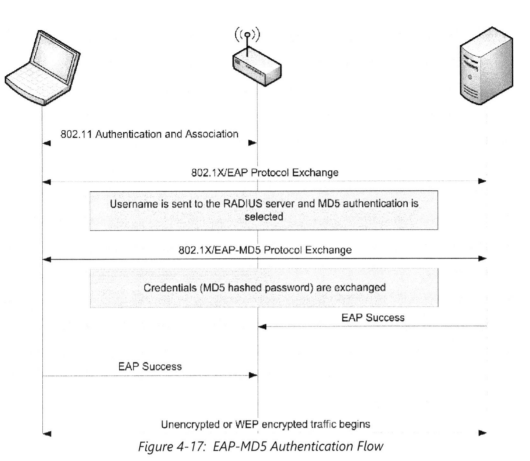

802.11 Authentication and Association

802.1X/EAP Protocol Exchange

Username is sent to the RADIUS server and MD5 authentication is selected

802.1X/EAP-MD5 Protocol Exchange

Credentials (MD5 hashed password) are exchanged

EAP Success

EAP Success

Unencrypted or WEP encrypted traffic begins

Figure 4-17: EAP-MD5 Authentication Flow

The following image shows the basic PEAP authentication flow for review.

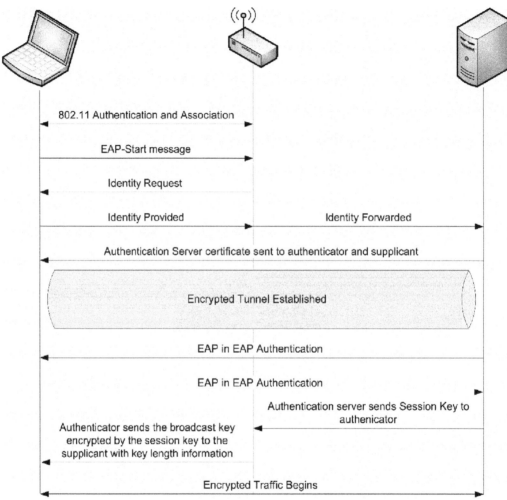

802.11 Authentication and Association

EAP-Start message

Identity Request

Identity Provided

Identity Forwarded

Authentication Server certificate sent to authenticator and supplicant

Encrypted Tunnel Established

EAP in EAP Authentication

EAP in EAP Authentication

Authentication server sends Session Key to authenicator

Authenticator sends the broadcast key encrypted by the session key to the supplicant with key length information

Encrypted Traffic Begins

Figure 4-18: PEAP General Authentication Flow

PEAPv0/EAP-MSCHAPv2

PEAP (EAP-MSCHAPv2) is commonly implemented because it only requires username/password credentials from the client, and because it is supported by many authentication servers. However, client-side certificates can be used instead of username/password credentials.

Phase 1 contains the establishment of the encrypted TLS tunnel and server authentication, while Phase 2 contains the client authentication and derivation of the session keys. PEAP requires EAP-in-EAP (e.g., PEAP/EAP-MSCHAPv2).

 Note: **The PEAPv0 may also be used with tunneled EAP-TLS. This is called PEAPv0/EAP-TLS and is modeled after the EAP-TLS protocol, but performs client authentication inside a TLS tunnel. The frame flow is very similar to that shown for PEAPv0/EAP-MSCHAPv2.**

As stated, this EAP type is very popular because it has broad support on a wide range of client devices and operating systems.

Cisco LEAP

LEAP provides mutual authentication, data encryption, and per-user/per-session keys, dynamic key rotation at intervals, and a strong MIC. However, it does have known weaknesses that prevent its utilization today.

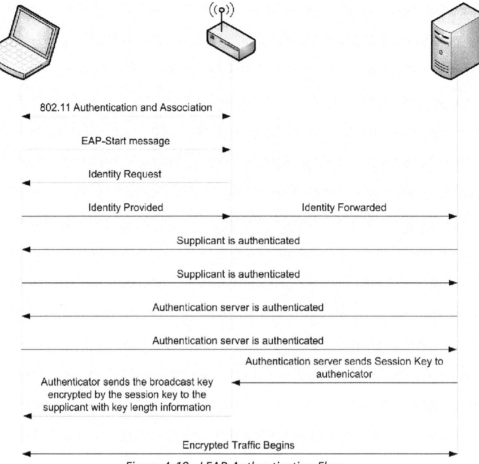

<figure>
802.11 Authentication and Association

EAP-Start message

Identity Request

Identity Provided   Identity Forwarded

Supplicant is authenticated

Supplicant is authenticated

Authentication server is authenticated

Authentication server is authenticated

Authentication server sends Session Key to authenicator

Authenticator sends the broadcast key encrypted by the session key to the supplicant with key length information

Encrypted Traffic Begins
</figure>

Figure 4-19: LEAP Authentication Flow

LEAP requires only username/password credentials for authentication. The username is passed across the wireless medium in clear text and an MD4 hash is used as part of MS-CHAP authentication.

- Capturing user credentials is easy when strong passwords are not used.

- 99% of all passwords users select can be broken through the use of comprehensive dictionary files.

- ASLEAP is an example of an offline dictionary attack utility.

- Originally used for active and passive attacks against LEAP, ASLEAP can also be used to recover passwords contained in PPTP.

      - ASLEAP has been updated to support large file sizes.

  - Creating large dictionary files is easy and relatively fast.

  - High-capacity, portable hard drives, currently up to 2TB, are not expensive and allow the use of terabyte-sized dictionary files with brute-force exploits.

LEAP was cracked in early 2004 and should be avoided. Any installations that still use LEAP should work on a migration path to eliminate it from the network as quickly as possible.

EAP-FAST

EAP-FAST is Cisco's response to the vulnerabilities found in LEAP. EAP-FAST consists of three phases (0-2).

  - **Phase 0** is for provisioning Protected Access Credentials (PACs), which can occur either manually or through MS-CHAPv2.

  - **Phase 1** is for building a TLS tunnel for encrypting the client credentials when sent to the authentication server.

  - **Phase 2** is when the supplicant authenticates to the authentication server. According to Cisco (www.cisco.com/c/en/us/products/collateral/wireless/aironet-1300-series/prod_qas09186a00802030dc.html):

EAP-FAST uses symmetric key algorithms to achieve a tunneled authentication process. The tunnel establishment relies on a Protected Access Credential (PAC) that can be provisioned and managed dynamically by EAP-FAST through the authentication, authorization, and accounting (AAA) server (such as the Cisco Secure Access Control Server [ACS] v. 3.2.3).

With a mutually authenticated tunnel, EAP-FAST offers protection from dictionary attacks and man-in-the-middle vulnerabilities:

- **Phase 1**—Establish mutually authenticated tunnel-Client and AAA server use PAC to authenticate each other and establish a secure tunnel.

- **Phase 2**—Perform client authentication in the established tunnel-—-Client sends username and password to authenticate and establish client authorization policy.

- **Optionally, Phase 0**—This phase is used infrequently to enable the client to be dynamically provisioned with a PAC. During this phase, a per-user access credential is generated securely between the user and the network. This per-user credential, known as the PAC, is used in Phase 1 of EAP-FAST authentication.

EAP-FAST supports 802.11key management. EAP-GTC is the only EAP type presently supported inside the EAP-FAST TLS tunnel. EAP-FAST was an acceptable interim solution for Cisco networks after LEAP was cracked and before newer EAP types became popular.

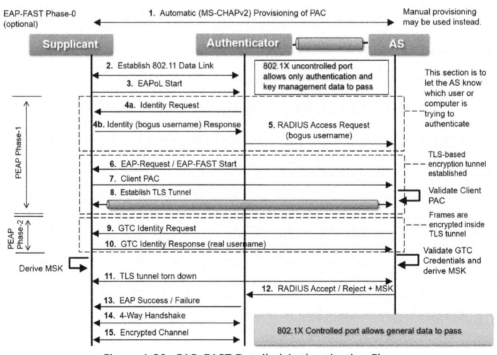

Figure 4-20: EAP-FAST Detailed Authentication Flow

EAP-TLS

EAP-TLS requires that the supplicant and authentication server have their own x.509 certificates installed. A TLS tunnel is constructed to secure the key generation process. In fact, EAP-TLS has two modes: normal and tunneled. Since secure server certificates are used for server and client authentication, EAP-TLS implementations often forego the tunnel.

EAP-TLS supports mutual authentication and encryption key generation either through proprietary mechanisms or through the 802.11 4-way handshake. EAP-TLS is an excellent choice in environments that distribute all hardware to be used on the network because client certificates are required. When the organization only allows self-distributed hardware to be used on the network, it can more easily control the distribution of client certificates. In environments with requirements for BYOD and heavy secure guest access, PEAP or EAP-TTLS are more likely to be utilized.

EAP-TTLS/EAP-MSCHAPv2

EAP-TTLS supports the 802.11 4-way handshake, uses a TLS tunnel for encrypted user credential exchange, and supports various legacy authentication protocols inside the TLS tunnel such as MD5, PAP, CHAP, MS-CHAP, and MS-CHAPv2. EAP may also be tunneled (e.g., EAP-TTLS/EAP-MSCHAPv2). EAP-TTLS was developed by Funk Software and Certicom and has gained a loyal customer base in the industry because it supports authentication protocols compatible with legacy user databases.

Notice several similarities between this EAP type (EAP-TTLS) and PEAP (EAP-MSCHAPv2). They are basically competitors with each other and were released within a short time of each other. One major disadvantage to EAP-TTLS is that it requires third-party supplicant software to be installed on devices running the Microsoft Windows operating system.

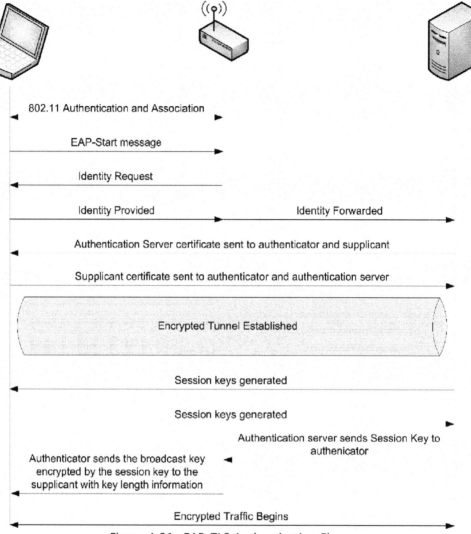

802.11 Authentication and Association

EAP-Start message

Identity Request

Identity Provided   Identity Forwarded

Authentication Server certificate sent to authenticator and supplicant

Supplicant certificate sent to authenticator and authentication server

Encrypted Tunnel Established

Session keys generated

Session keys generated

Authentication server sends Session Key to authenicator

Authenticator sends the broadcast key encrypted by the session key to the supplicant with key length information

Encrypted Traffic Begins

Figure 4-21: EAP-TLS Authentication Flow

802.11 Authentication and Association

802.1X/EAP Protocol Exchange

Selects the EAP-TTLS Authentication Protocol

802.1X/EAP-TLS Protocol Exchange – Client Authenticates Server

Encrypted Tunnel Established

User credentials are exchanged using any of the following: EAP-MD5, MS-CHAPv2, MS-CHAP or PAP

If EAP is successful, the user is authenticated and key materials are delivered

If EAP is successful, the WEP keys are set

Encrypted Traffic Begins

Figure 4-22: EAP-TTLS Authentication Flow

📖 From the Blogs

Is WPA2 Security Broken Due to DEF CON MS-CHAPv2 Cracking?

URL: www.revolutionwifi.net/revolutionwifi/2012/07/is-wpa2-security-broken-due-to-defcon.html

Author: Andrew von Nagy

Blog: Revolution Wi-Fi—www.revolutionwifi.net

Quick answer—No. Read on to hear why.

A lot of press has been released this week surrounding the cracking of MS-CHAPv2 authentication protocol at DEF CON. All of these articles contain ambiguous and vague references to this hack affecting Wi-Fi networks running WPA2 security. Some articles even call for an end to the use of WPA2 authentication protocols such as PEAP that leverage MS-CHAPv2.

But they fail to paint a true and accurate picture of the situation and the impact to Wi-Fi networks. I think this is misleading, and that any recommendations to stop using PEAP are flat-out wrong as of early 2015!

So let's clarify things.

1) Is MS-CHAPv2 authentication broken?

Answer—Based on what I've read, let's assume it is TOTALLY broken. You can read about the details in other Internet articles. But for the topic of this post, applicability to Wi-Fi networks, it really doesn't matter if it is broken or not.

2) What is the Impact to Wi-Fi Network Security?

Specifically, does this make much of an impact for Wi-Fi networks where 802.1X authentication is employed and MS-CHAPv2 is used (namely EAP-PEAPv0 and EAP-TTLS)?

Answer—No, it really does NOT. The impact is essentially zero.

Microsoft has released a security advisory (advisory 2743314) which recommends the use of PEAP encapsulation to mitigate this attack against un-encapsulated MS-CHAPv2 authentication.

Let me explain why.

3) EAP Tunneled Authentication Protocols

MS-CHAPv2 is only used in what we call "tunneled authentication protocols," which includes EAP-PEAPv0 and EAP-TTLS. These EAP protocol specifications acknowledge that many insecure and legacy authentication methods need protection and should not be used on their own. They deal with that by wrapping the insecure protocol inside of another, much more secure, TLS tunnel. Hence, these protocols are called "tunneled authentication protocols."

This tunneling occurs by relying on asymmetric cryptography through the use of X.509 certificates installed on the RADIUS server, which are sent to the client device to begin connection setup. The client verifies the certificate is valid (more on that in a second), and proceeds to establish a TLS tunnel with the server and begin using symmetric key cryptography for data encryption. Once the TLS tunnel is fully formed, the client and server use the less secure protocol such as MS-CHAPv2 to authenticate the client. This exchange is fully encrypted using the symmetric keys established during tunnel setup. The encryption switches from asymmetric key cryptography to symmetric key cryptography to ease processing and performance, which are much faster this way. This is fundamentally the same method used for HTTPS sessions in a web browser.

A reference ladder diagram of PEAP authentication in on the next page, which highlights the different phases of the connection process (outer TLS tunnel setup and inner MS-CHAPv2 authentication).

So, MS-CHAPv2 is not used natively for Wi-Fi authentication. We're safe right? Only if implemented properly.

4) **Importance of Mutual Authentication**

The key link in this chain then is the mutual authentication between the RADIUS server and the wireless client. The client must properly validate the RADIUS server certificate first, prior to sending it's credentials to the server. If the client fails to properly validate the server, then it may establish an MS-CHAPv2 session with a fake RADIUS server and send it's credentials along, which could then be cracked using the exploit that was shown at DEF CON. This is commonly referred to as a Man-in-the-Middle attack, because the attacker is inserting their RADIUS server in the middle of a conversation between the client and the user database store (typically a directory server).

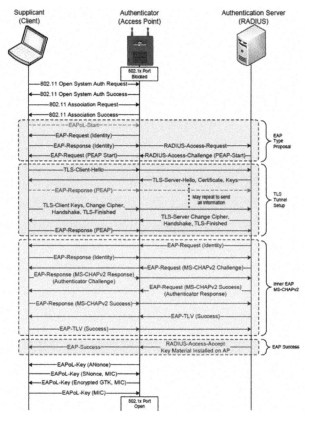

Figure 4-23: Mutual Authentication

The RADIUS server is validated as long as the certificate that it sends is trusted. For most client platforms, trusted certificates are provided by the manufacturer for public Certificate Authorities and PKI systems (such as Verisign, Thawte, Entrust, etc.) and are held in the certificate store or keychain on the device. In addition, for corporate environments, administrators can deploy certificates to managed devices in a number of different ways to enable trust for private Certificate Authorities and PKI systems, most common among these methods are Group Policy Objects (GPO) for Microsoft clients and Server Profile Manager or the iPhone Configuration Utility (iPCU) for Apple clients (including OS X and iOS devices).

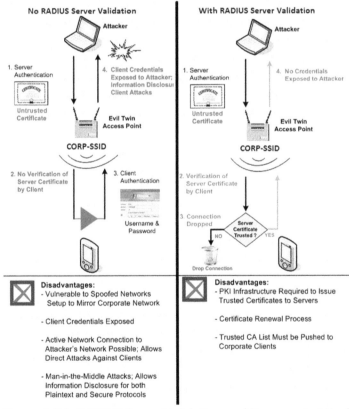

Figure 4-24: RADIUS Server Validation and Exposure to Attack

5) Enabling Server Certificate Validation on Clients

In Windows the RADIUS server validation is defined within each SSID profile. If you are looking directly on a Windows 7 workstation, you will want to view the SSID properties, select the Security tab, and go into the PEAP settings. Enable server validation, specify valid server names (which are checked against the Common Name—CN within the server certificate presented to the client), restrict which Root CAs the server certificate can be issued from, and prevent the system from prompting users to accept untrusted certificates (which is important, otherwise they could unknowingly accept a bad certificate and connect to an attacker's RADIUS server).

Figure 4-25: Windows RADIUS Server Validation

In Apple devices, including OS X and iOS, use the Server Profile Manger or iPCU to define a configuration profile which includes credentials and a Wi-Fi policy. I'll explain the iPCU in this example. First, add the Root CA certificate into the "Credentials" section. Next, define a Wi-Fi policy which specifies the trusted certificates and certificate names allowed.

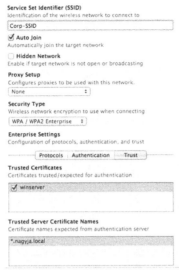

Figure 4-26: Apple RADIUS Server Validation

6) **Client Behavior for Server Validation**

In both vendor implementations, the behavior of the client device is dictated by what policy has been defined on the system.

If no policy for the SSID has been defined or pushed to the client device by an administrator, the default behavior is to prompt the user to validate the certificate. This is likely not ideal, since users typically have a hard time distinguishing what a certificate means and whether or not they should proceed. For example, when an Apple iPhone attempts to join a network when no profile has been deployed for that SSID, the user receives a prompt to accept the connection and proceed.

Therefore, for all corporate 802.1X environments, it is recommended to push profiles for all 802.1X SSIDs that end-users need on their systems. This goes for both production access and BYOD scenarios. The behavior on Windows 7, OS X, and iOS devices when a profile has been installed for a specific SSID, is to check the local certificate store or keychain to validate the RADIUS server certificate. It must also match the Root CAs and server names specified in the deployed profile. In the event that an untrusted certificate is presented, all of these systems will NOT prompt the user and the connection is rejected.

7) Outstanding Vulnerabilities

You should still be aware of a few indirectly related vulnerabilities that have not yet been resolved related to Wi-Fi authentication with 802.1X.

- First, the default behavior of all systems (especially personal devices) is to prompt users to validate the RADIUS server certificate. This is often confusing and can lead to bad actions being taken by users and attempted authentication through an attacker's RADIUS server. This can be mitigated by having corporate environments deploy configuration profiles for all SSIDs in their network, both production and BYOD. Don't fall into the trap for BYOD of letting users connect on their own and try to decipher the certificate prompt. Establish a sound personal device on-boarding process which deploys a configuration profile to the device upon successful enrollment and policy acceptance. There are numerous ways to do this, ranging from simple solutions such as sending them a profile in an email or providing a web URL where users can download the profile, to more complex solutions such as MDM integration that allow self-registration and zero IT involvement.

- Second, certificate binding to the SSID is still a manual process on wireless networks. It must be defined within the configuration profile. This is in contrast to SSL and TLS protocols that are used for secure web access where the end-user system can automatically verify if the FQDN within the URL matches the Common Name presented in the certificate. The manual binding process in Wi-Fi networks is born out of a lack of extensibility within the PKI system to handle network access scenarios such as this. A better solution is needed.

- Finally, certificate revocation checking cannot occur by Wi-Fi clients since they do not yet have a network connection with which they can query a certificate revocation list (CRL) distribution point or use Online Certificate Status Protocol (OCSP). This means that client devices cannot check the status of the presented server certificate to see if it has been revoked, which could be caused by valid certificates that have subsequently been compromised or certificates that were invalidly issued by a CA. However, there is hope that the 802.11u-2011 extensions to Wi-Fi (which are included in 802.11-2012, though very hard to locate because of all the section remapping that took place during the 802.11-2012 update) can eventually provide the means for this to occur through message exchanges prior to full network connection (thanks to Christopher Byrd for pointing this out to me during a Twitter conversation).

8) Revolution or Evolution?—Andrew's Take

We've known that MS-CHAPv2 is an insecure protocol for a long time. The recent DEF CON exploit has just taken that one step further. Development of modern Wi-Fi security recognized the possible value in using legacy protocols such as these. Therefore, EAP protocols that employed such protocols were designed to tunnel the insecure protocol within a much more robust protocol such as TLS. These "tunneled authentication protocols" such as PEAP ensure protection for these insecure protocols through the use of certificates.

The onus for proper security then falls on RADIUS server validation to ensure the other end of the connection is trusted before allowing the client authentication to proceed. In a properly implemented wireless network, this MS-CHAPv2 exploit is a non-issue.

There is no need for Wi-Fi network administrators to abandon PEAP. Period.

Security is a complex field. It may be hard to distinguish the FUD from fact. If you're interested in learning more about Wi-Fi security, then I highly recommend engineers take training provided in the CWSP (Certified Wireless Security Professional) course offered by CWNP, Inc. or the SEC-617 (Wireless Ethical Hacking, Penetration Testing, and Defenses) course offered by the SANS Institute.

Chapter 4 Summary

In this chapter, you learned about the importance of authentication and the different authentication methods available in 802.11 WLANs. You explored the 802.1X/EAP enterprise authentication solutions and the different EAP types. This information is essential for the CWSP exam, but it is also important to know so that you can make effective decisions when designing security in the real world.

Facts to Remember

Be sure to remember the following facts as you prepare for the CWSP certification, and be sure that you can explain the details related to them:

- Authentication is used to validate credentials and is the foundation of all other security technologies.

- Passphrase security, or a pre-shared key (PSK), is useful in SOHO and small business deployments with a few dozen clients.

- When using a PSK, the password used to generate the PSK should be random and difficult to guess. It should sufficiently long.

- WPA- and WPA2-Personal use a PSK implementation.

- WPA- and WPA2-Enterprise us an 802.1X/EAP implementation.

- WPA supports TKIP/RC4 and WPA2 supports CCMP/AES.

- You can identify the PSK authentication when the AKM Suite type is equal to 00-0F-AC:02.

- Triple-A (AAA), as a security principle, consists of authentication, authorization, and accounting.

- Mutual authentication means that both the authentication server and the client are authenticated.

- RBAC (Role-Based Access Control) is a method used to provide authorization through groups or roles.

- RBAC typically involves the creation of policies and the assigning of these policies to groups or roles.

- Accounting can be provided through RADIUS servers and Syslog servers.

- 802.1X provides port-based authentication.

- Extensible Authentication Protocol (EAP) is a framework on which different types of EAP authentication methods are built, such as EAP-TLS and PEAP.

- EAP-MD5 and LEAP should not be used.

- PEAP, EAP-TLS, EAP-TTLS, and EAP-FAST can all be implemented in a secure manner.

- Though many EAP types are available, most environments only use one of a few common types.

- Lightweight Directory Access Protocol (LDAP) servers are often used to provide a credential store for 802.1X/EAP authentication through RADIUS servers.

Chapter 4: Review Questions

1. Which of the following packets are used across the medium between the wireless client stations and the AP or controller?

    a. EAP over RADIUS

    b. EAPoL

    c. EAP over PEAP

    d. LANEAP

2. You are discussing possible credential types with a new WLAN customer. Which of these is not a valid WLAN credential type?

    a. Birth certificate

    b. Digital certificate

    c. Biometrics

    d. Tokens

3. Verification of a user's identity is the simple definition of _____.

    a. Authorization

    b. Accounting

    c. Enumeration

    d. Authentication

4. Where does the Master Session Key (MSK) originate on a PSK wireless network?

    a. RADIUS server

    b. Nonce credential

    c. Passphrase

    d. GTK

5. You have a client that is interested in alternatives to standards-based PSK wireless security, but she does not want the administrative overhead of keeping up a RADIUS server. Which of these might work for her?

    a. PPSK

    b. DPSK

    c. MS-CHAP

    d. 802.1X

6. Which of the following keys is used to secure broadcast and multicast traffic, but not unicast?

    a. PTK

    b. GTK

    c. MTK

    d. RSNK

7. EAP is a Layer _____ authentication protocol?

    a. 7

    b. 3

    c. 2

    d. 1

8. During the 4-way handshake, which method of gaining the pairwise master keys is considered "in-band"?

    a. 802.1X with RADIUS

    b. Pre-shared key

    c. Pre-shared RADIUS

    d. Token exchange

9. One available EAP type should never be used for wireless security because it only does authentication and not encryption. What EAP type is this?

    a. EAP-TLS

    b. EAP-CLEAR

    c. EAP-FAST

    d. EAP-MD5

10. During the 802.1X process, which virtual port is used for authentication only?

    a. EAP port

    b. Controlled port

    c. Uncontrolled port

    d. PAE port

11. Where is RADIUS server configuration information located on a WLAN infrastructure device such as an AP?

    a. Device registry

    b. WLAN profile

    c. Access control list

    d. Server repository

12. While talking with a client's firewall administrator about a new secure Wi-Fi rollout, she asks if you need UDP ports 1812 and 1813 open. What are these ports used for?

    a. 1812 is RADIUS accounting, 1813 is RADIUS authentication.

    b. 1812 is EAP verification, 1813 is EAP accounting.

    c. 1812 is 802.1X authorization, 1813 is 802.1X accounting.

    d. 1812 is RADIUS authentication, 1813 is RADIUS accounting.

13. Which of the following is not a valid example of a credential used in multifactor authentication?

    a. Something you know

    b. Something you can write

    c. Something you have

    d. Something you are

14. A new 802.1X-secured network has been implemented in your company headquarters, and you are explaining the key-related details to your WLAN technicians. Which key is used to secure unicast traffic?

    a. PTK

    b. GTK

    c. PMK

    d. APK

15. Which of the following is not a fundamental element of 802.1X?

    a. Supplicant

    b. Applicant

    c. Authenticator

    d. Authentication server

16. On wireless networks, the paradigm of assigning roles to users, and then a variety of permissions to the roles, is which of the following?

    a. GBAC

    b. UBAC

    c. CBAC

    d. RBAC

17. Which of these is a posture assessment tool?

    a. NAC

    b. Anti-virus

    c. Audit protocol

    d. ANC

18. When a station becomes authenticated and associated to an infrastructure BSS and exchanges RSN IE information with other STAs, which step is this in creating an RSNA?

    a. Final

    b. Third

    c. Second

    d. First

19. The RSNA PSK is how many bits, regardless of length of passphrase?

    a. 128

    b. 256

    c. 512

    d. 1024

20. Where are encryption keys generated in the overall secure authentication process?

    a. In the 4-way handshake

    b. In the Open System authentication

    c. In the MD5 tunnel

    d. In the pre-authentication

21. The packets that are used by RADIUS for attribute-related RBAC functions are?

    a. PERMISSION-REQUEST, PERMISSION-ACCEPT

    b. ACCESS-REQUEST, ACCESS-DENY

    c. PERMISSION-REQUEST, PERMISSION-DENY

    d. ACCESS-REQUEST, ACCESS-ACCEPT

22. In large WLAN environments, the 802.1X authentication server might query an external credential store using what protocol?

    a. ADAP

    b. LDAP

    c. CPAP

    d. PCAP

23. You have been called to troubleshoot a secure WLAN environment that uses client and server certificates. What EAP type is in use here?

    a. EAP-GTC

    b. EAP-MSCHAPv2

    c. EAP-TLS

    d. EAP-SIM

24. Which EAP type uses three phases, 0-2?

    a. EAP-LEAP

    b. EAP-FAST

    c. EAP-TTLS

    d. EAP-TLS

25. RADIUS server functionality may be _____?

    a. In a dedicated server or integrated into AP/controller

    b. Only in stand-alone servers

    c. Only integrated in infrastructure hardware

    d. Only in client devices

Chapter 4: Review Answers

1. **B** is correct. EAPoL packets are transmitted between the supplicant (client) and the AP/controller.

2. **A** is correct. There are many valid credential types you need to be aware of for secure WLAN. The birth certificate is not one of them.

3. **D** is correct. Authentication concerns verifying a user's identity (or a host's).

4. **C** is correct. On PSK networks, the MSK is derived from the passphrase.

5. **A** is correct. PPSK is proprietary, and does not come from any standard.

6. **B** is correct. The Groupwise Temporal Key (GTK) is used to secure broadcast and multicast traffic.

7. **C** is correct. Remember that all EAP and 802.11 security functions happen at Layer 2.

8. **A** is correct. For the 4-way handshake, 802.1X use is considered in-band, while PSK is considered out-of-band.

9. **D** is correct. MD5 is not an EAP type that should ever be used in WLAN security.

10. **C** is correct. The uncontrolled port is used for authentication only.

11. **B** is correct. The WLAN profile is the configuration set that has RADIUS server configuration.

12. **A** is correct. 1812 and 1813 ports are widely known RADIUS authentication and accounting ports.

13. **B** is correct. The multifactor paradigm includes something you are/have/know.

14. **A** is correct. The PTK secures unicast traffic.

15. **B** is correct. The fundamental elements of RADIUS are the supplicant, authenticator, and authentication server.

16. **D** is correct. RBAC is role-based access control.

17. **A** is correct. NAC is network access control, and is a posture-checking mechanism.

18. **D** is correct. The question describes the first step in creating an RSNA.

19. **B** is correct. The PSK hash results in a 256-bit key length regardless of PSK length.

20. **A** is correct. Encryption keys are generated in the 4-way handshake process.

21. **D** is correct. ACCESS-REQUEST and ACCESS-ACCEPT packets are supported by RADIUS for RBAC.

22. **B** is correct. LDAP servers are an integral part of many large wireless environments, and are communicated with by the RADIUS server.

23. **C** is correct. Of the options listed, only TLS uses client and server certificates (mutual authentication).

24. **B** is correct. EAP-FAST is the only EAP type to use this construct.

25. **A** is correct. RADIUS server services have flexible implementation options.

Chapter 5:

Authentication and Key Management

Objectives

3.2 Understand and explain 802.11 Authentication and Key Management (AKM) components and processes including encryption keys, handshakes, and pre-shared key management.

3.3 Define and differentiate among the 802.11-defined secure networks, including pre-RSNA security, Transition Security Networks (TSN), and Robust Security Networks (RSN), and explain the relationship of these networks to terms including RSNA, WPA, and WPA2.

As you learned in Chapter 4, authentication is essential to WLAN security. When required to troubleshoot authentication issues, you must first understand the authentication process in depth and how it eventually leads to the creation and distribution of encryption keys. Encryption itself, in greater detail, is addressed in Chapter 6. Here in this chapter, you will explore Authentication and Key Management (AKM), which addresses both authentication and the generation and distribution of encryption keys. The first step is properly grasping the terminology.

Terminology

The following definitions provide a foundation for learning about AKM in wireless networks:

- **RSN**—Robust Security Network. A security network that allows only the creation of robust security network associations (RSNAs). An RSN can be identified by the indication in the RSN information element (IE) of Beacon frames that the group cipher suite specified is not wired equivalent privacy (WEP).
- **RSNA**—Robust Security Network Association. The type of association used by a pair of stations (STAs) if the procedure to establish authentication or association between them includes the 4-way handshake. Note that the existence of an RSNA by a pair of devices does not of itself provide robust security. Robust security is provided when all devices in the network use RSNAs.
- **pre-RSNA**—Pre-Robust Security Network Association. The type of association used by a pair of stations (STAs) if the procedure for establishing authentication or association between them did not include the 4-way handshake.
- **TSN**—Transition Security Network. A security network that allows the creation of pre-robust security network associations (pre-RSNAs) as well as RSNAs. A TSN can be identified by the indication in the robust security

network (RSN) information element of Beacon frames that the group cipher suite in use is wired equivalent privacy (WEP).

- **MSK**—Master Session Key. Keying material that is derived between the Extensible Authentication Protocol (least EAP) peer and exported by the EAP method to the authentication server (AS). This key is at 64 octets in length.

- **PMK**—Pairwise Master Key. The highest order key used within this standard. The PMK may be derived from a key generated by an Extensible Authentication Protocol (EAP) method or may be obtained directly from a pre-shared key (PSK).

- **PTK**—Pairwise Transient Key. A value that is derived from the pairwise master key (PMK), authenticator address (AA), supplicant address (SPA), authenticator nonce (ANonce), and supplicant nonce (SNonce) using the pseudo-random function (PRF), and that is split up into as many as five keys, i.e., temporal encryption key, two temporal message integrity code (MIC) keys, EAPOL-Key encryption key (KEK), EAPOL-Key confirmation key (KCK).

- **GMK**—Group Master Key. An auxiliary key that may be used to derive a group temporal key (GTK).

- **GTK**—Group Temporal Key. A random value, assigned by the broadcast/multicast source, which is used to protect broadcast/multicast medium access control (MAC) protocol data units (MPDUs) from that source. The GTK may be derived from a group master key (GMK).

- **KCK**—EAPOL-Key confirmation key. A key used to integrity-check an EAPOL-Key frame.

- **KEK**—EAPOL-Key encryption key. A key used to encrypt the Key Data field in an EAPOL-Key frame.

- **PMKSA**—Pairwise Master Key Security Association. The context resulting from a successful IEEE 802.1X authentication exchange between the peer and authentication server (AS) or from a pre-shared key (PSK).

- **PMKID**—Pairwise Master Key Identifier. The PMK is an identifier of a security association.
  - PMKID = HMAC-SHA1-128(PMK, "PMK Name" || AA || SPA)

- **PTKSA**—Pairwise Transient Key Security Association. The context resulting from a successful 4-way handshake exchange between the peer and authenticator.
- **GTKSA**—Group Temporal Key Security Association. The context resulting from a successful group temporal key (GTK) distribution exchange via either a group-key handshake or a 4-way handshake.

This set of defined terms should become very familiar to you as you prepare for the CWSP exam, and as you work with secure wireless networks. While the list may seem daunting at first, you will quickly remember it through repeated exposure in designing and supporting networks that make use of these security mechanisms.

Pre-Robust Security Networks

You learned in Chapter 1 that the 802.11i amendment to the 802.11 standard defines two different types or classes of WLAN security. These are:

- Pre-Robust Security Network Association (pre-RSNA)
- Robust Security Network (RSN)

In this section you will learn more about the pre-RSNA. The RSN is discussed next.

A wireless network that is classified as a pre-RSNA network consists of WEP and 802.11 entity authentication methods. With the exception of the 802.11 Open System authentication method, all pre-RSNA security mechanisms have been deprecated due to failure to meet their original security goals. The reality of the situation is that early attempts at WLAN security were not good enough to be sustainable. New 802.11 standards-based implementations should support pre-RSNA methods only to aid in the migration toward RSN security and as part of a Transitional Security Network (TSN).

It is important to understand the concept of a TSN with respect to wireless networking. A TSN is typically a security network that allows a transition from one security solution to another more secure solution. In relation to 802.11 wireless networking, the TSN includes the creation of pre-RSNAs, which use WEP, as well as RSNAs. So we say WEP is bad and must not be used. At the same time, it is not always easy to drop WEP without significant planning and budget implications. It is for these kinds of circumstances that TSN is intended.

A TSN can be identified by the inclusion of WEP in the group cipher suite in the RSN information element of Beacon frames. By contrast, pre-RSNA APs/STAs generate Beacon and Probe Response frames without an RSN information element, and ignore the RSN information element in TSNs because it is unknown to them. This allows an RSNA STA to identify the pre-RSNA STAs from which it has received Beacon and Probe Response frames. In reality, most WLAN administrators should not have to deal with the TSN paradigm anymore. Little excuse for TSN exists from the client side as very few clients remain in service that do not support at least WPA. An organization's infrastructure should

- be designed to support only required clients, and
- should not continue to support weak security solutions that are no longer required by any past generations of clients.

When working in an environment that still runs a TSN, verify that no clients require WEP and move quickly to a robust security network. If some clients do still require WEP, create a plan for transitioning from those clients so that you can move to a robust security network. If for whatever reason WEP clients cannot be upgraded, give serious consideration to how they can be isolated to minimize network exploitation through them.

Robust Security Networks (RSN)

As a reminder, an RSN is a wireless network that allows only the creation of robust security network associations (RSNAs). An RSN can be identified by the indication in the RSN Information Element (IE) of Beacon frames that the group cipher suite specified is not WEP. Stated plainly, if WEP is allowed, it is not considered an RSN because RSNs do not allow WEP.

An RSNA is the type of association used by a pair of STAs if the procedure to establish authentication or association between them concludes with the 4-way handshake. It is important to know that the existence of an RSNA by a pair of devices does not of itself provide robust security. Robust security is provided when all devices in the network use RSNAs, such as those that support only CCMP/AES. One device allowed on the network (BSS) using WEP prevents it from being an RSN, as the weakest security in use anywhere in the BSS defines the entire BSS.

The security afforded by the 802.11-2012 standard meets the following requirements:

- Protects user data
- Replaces legacy wireless security options
- Can meet governmental requirements for security, if implemented properly
- Is composed of two levels; one level for historical compatibility, and one level for future security. Both levels provide the following:
    - Continuously-changing encryption keys
    - A choice between two levels of user authentication
    - Replay protection
    - Removal of weak IVs
    - Better integrity protection than legacy ICV
    - Dynamic key management

RSN Information Element

The RSN IE is a set of frame fields included in certain WLAN management frames that are part of a RSN

- The RSN IE defines the cipher suites used and authentication key management (AKM) suites that are required and supported in the RSN.
- It also defines additional capabilities, such as preauthentication support.
- The RSN IE is contained within the following 802.11 WLAN management frames:
    - Beacon
    - Probe Response
    - Association Request, and
    - Reassociation Request.

Exam Moment: The RSN IE is important as it defines the security parameters of the BSS. It is included in beacon, Probe Response, Association Request, and Reassociation Request frames.

The following graphic shows a packet trace with an expanded view of the RSN IE.

Figure 5-1: RSN IE Shown in WiFi Explorer on Mac OS X Yosemite

The two main fields are

- the "PairwiseKey Cipher Suite List" field, which shows the supported 802.11 cipher suites (encryption methods) for the BSS (in this case CCMP/AES), and
- the "AuthKey Management Suite List" field, which shows if the service set is configured for pre-shared key (PSK) Personal mode or 802.1X/EAP Enterprise mode.

It is important to note that in order to be considered an RSN, the service set must support CCMP; however, TKIP is allowed as an optional cipher suite for backward compatibility.

Recall that if WEP is supported, then the service set does not qualify as an RSN. One way to identify this is in the RSN IE "Group Key Cipher Suite Type" field. If this field did show support for WEP, then this BSS would not qualify as an RSN.

In the next image, notice the "PairwiseKey Cipher List" shows that both TKIP and CCMP cipher suites are enabled for this service set; therefore, it does qualify as an RSN since CCMP is supported and WEP is not. However, devices (STAs) that do not support CCMP but do support TKIP would still be able to associate with the AP because of the supported TKIP cipher suite (encryption method).

In the next image, notice the "Authenticated Key Management Suite List" field which shows a value of **00-0f-ac:02** for the "Authenticated Key Management Suite OUI." The fact that this ends in **02** indicates that this service set is configured as pre-shared key (PSK) and not 802.1X/EAP. The AKM suite list is either 01 (802.1X) or 02 (PSK).

Exam Moment: The AKM Suite List field defines whether PSK or Enterprise (802.1X) authentication and key management is used. Stated differently, it defines whether Personal or Enterprise WPA or WPA2 is in use.

The Cipher Suite Type or Cipher Suite OUI always starts with 00-0F-AC and is followed by a number indicating the actual suite. Suite values include:

- 00—Use the Group Suite
- 01—WEP-40
- 02—TKIP
- 04—CCMP
- 05—WEP-104

It is important that you know these values.

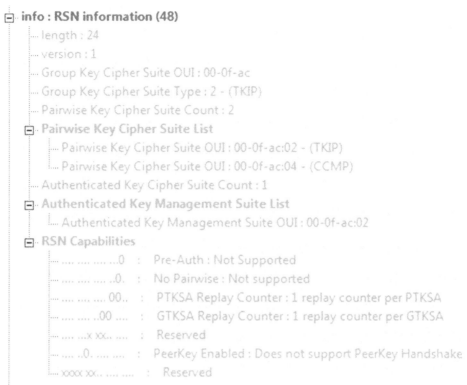

Figure 5-2: RSN Information Element in a Protocol Analyzer

The RSN Capabilities fields shows additional supported features available for the service set that is configured as an RSN.

The group cipher type identifies what cipher type (encryption) is used for group traffic that traverses the wireless medium for the service set. This group cipher is identified in the "Group Cipher Type" field. When a service set is configured only for CCMP and not TKIP, it makes sense that CCMP would be used for group traffic encryption as well as for unicast traffic, because it is the only cipher suite available. The group cipher is always the lowest possible encryption type that is used in the service set. For example, if you have a service set that is configured for both CCMP and TKIP, the lowest common type is TKIP, so the group cipher used to encrypt group traffic is TKIP. Any device that is capable of CCMP would also be able to understand TKIP; so there are no compatibility issues with the group traffic.

Another important field contained within the RSN IE is the "PMKID Count" field. PMKID stands for pairwise master key identifier. The PMKID is a unique identifier that is created for each pairwise master key security association (PMKSA) that has been established between the AP and the client (STA) when an RSNA is created. This is only used when fast secure transition (roaming) features are enabled on the service set. The PMKID field is visible only in Association Request and Reassociation Request management frames. You will learn about fast secure transition methods later in Chapter 8.

802.11 Association

The first step in creating an RSNA between two STAs (for example, client device and AP) in an infrastructure BSS is to become 802.11 authenticated and associated. Anytime an STA (device) connects to an infrastructure BSS or transitions to a different AP, the authentication and association process must occur. This allows for the STA to be connected to the AP. At this time, no wireless security measures are in place. In most public wireless hotspot networks, simple authentication and association are all that is required because these networks are open. With secure wireless networks, additional security methods must be put in place in order to protect the transmissions.

The next step in creating an RSNA is to continue with securing the wireless transmissions between STAs. This is the stage where each STA receives the other's RSN information element describing its respective capabilities and requirements using the appropriate management frames. Notice that, in the following image, the Probe Response from the AP and the Association Request from the client STA contain the RSN IE information. If the capabilities match, the STA will be able to successfully associate to the AP.

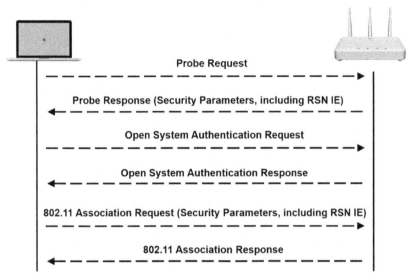

Figure 5-3: Authentication and Association

Key Hierarchy

One of the most confusing parts of security in 802.11 WLANs is the key hierarchy. This is because a single key is not generated and then used for encryption, as one unfamiliar with the topic might assume. A simple paradigm such as that would not work in the complex communications environments of 802.11 networks. Think back to your CWNA studies; remember that sending a single file across the WLAN involved many frames. Management frames, control frames, and data frames—they all have to traverse the network. Some frames are sent to every STA connected to the BSS, while others are passed only between the AP and a single STA. The notion of several different keys being used for wireless security has to fit within this framework. For this reason, a key hierarchy is required. If you can grasp this key hierarchy, you will better accept the complexity introduced in the following pages.

The 802.11-2012 standard specifies an RSN key hierarchy for authentication and dynamic encryption keys. This is often referred to as authentication and key management (AKM). 802.11 AKM has several parts, but the overall scheme is illustrated in the pyramid structure below. The process works from the top down starting with either a passphrase, PSK, or Master Session Key (MSK). This pyramid illustrates the key derivation process for both pre-shared key and 802.1X capable wireless networks.

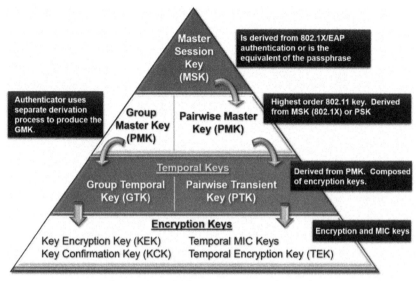

Figure 5-4: 802.11 AKM Key Hierarchy

Authentication and key management should first be understood as it is used in PSK mode. When using PSK mode and if passphrases are used, the passphrase is used to create a 256-bit PSK which is equivalent to the master session key (MSK). The MSK is then used to generate the PMK for the session. Therefore, when a passphrase is entered into the wireless client utility and the configurations of the wireless AP, wireless controller, or cloud-managed WLAN device, the passphrase is used to create the PSK. This PSK is equivalent to the MSK used in 802.1X AKM. It is used to derive the other required keys in the hierarchy.

Alternatively, in some cases, the PMK can be entered directly as the PSK without the use of a passphrase. When the PMK is present on both STAs (AP and client device for example) the 4-way handshake is the next step in the AKM process. The 4-way handshake uses "nonces" (arbitrary values that are only used once in the process) and other inputs with the PMK to create temporal unicast encryption keys which include the Pairwise Transient Key (PTK). The temporal keys are composed of encryption and MIC keys. The 4-way handshake is discussed in more detail later in this chapter.

The Temporal Encryption Key (TEK), simply called the temporal key (TK) in the 802.11-2012 standard, is the actual key used to encrypt and decrypt unicast frames. It is part of the PTK. The Key Encryption Key (KEK) is used for encryption during the 4-way handshake and is also part of the PTK. The Key Confirmation Key (KCK) is also part of the PTK and is used during the 4-way handshake to provide for data origin authenticity.

If user-based 802.1X/EAP authentication is used instead of the pre-shared key method, authentication and key management is a somewhat different process. The MSK is now derived as part of the 802.1X authentication workflow. In this case, a series of frames is exchanged between STAs which in 802.1X terminology are the supplicant and the authenticator. These frames are used to derive the MSK with the aid of an authentication/RADIUS server. The derivation process continues as it does for pre-shared key, and the PMK is generated. The 4-way handshake would then follow to create the PTK as it did with the pre-shared key model.

It is important to note that the authenticator (usually the AP or the wireless controller) is what derives a Group Master Key (GMK) using a separate derivation process, and it uses the GMK to generate the Group Temporal Key (GTK). The GTK is then used to secure group traffic, which is both broadcast and multicast traffic.

PSK Key Hierarchy

WPA- and WPA2-Personal mode can secure wireless communications without the need for a RADIUS infrastructure by using a PSK security mechanism. The security input entered into all STAs that is part of the service set can be a passphrase, instead of directly entering a 256-bit key. The objective for using the passphrase is to lessen the chance of errors when a user manually inputs a key into their device settings. Since most users are familiar with using passwords, entering a passphrase is fairly straightforward and, therefore, decreases the possibility of typographical errors. The passphrase entered uses a published algorithm to generate a 256-bit PSK, using a passphrase to PSK mapping. Using PSK results in a far simpler AKM key hierarchy.

The trade-off to the ease of using PSK is that the way passphrases are used may pose somewhat of a security risk depending on the length and complexity of the passphrase. After the 802.11 authentication and association completes, the 4-way handshake occurs. At the start of the 4-way handshake, the PMK is known by both STAs that are part of the frame exchange because it was entered into both devices. If an intruder were to capture the 4-way handshake with a protocol analyzer and use the right dictionary attack software, they may be able to extract the passphrase that can be used to access the network and to possibly see encrypted traffic. If a weak passphrase is used, this attack is not difficult to accomplish. Therefore, passphrases should be strong and of sufficient length to lessen the chance of dictionary attacks. The 802.11-2012 standard specifies that a key generated from a passphrase of less than about 20 characters is unlikely to deter attacks. It is recommended to use long, complex passphrases. Interestingly, the Wi-Fi Alliance suggests an 8-character non-word passphrase on its website. CWNP recommends the longer 20-character passphrase instead.

With WPA2-Personal mode, both TKIP/RC4 and CCMP/AES can be used with passphrases. Key derivation and distribution is identical with both models. WPA2-Personal mode uses strong CCMP/AES for encryption, but has the same authentication weakness as WPA-Personal (i.e., if the passphrase is too short, it can be recovered by a dictionary attack).

It is important to distinguish the difference between unicast and multicast/broadcast encryption keys because unicast is encrypted differently from broadcast.

- **Unicast** information is directed, or a "one-to-one" exchange between STAs. User Data and directed management frames, such as Authentication or an Association Request frames, are considered unicast communications.
- **Broadcast** communications are intended for all STAs that are part of the BSS. This means any STA within radio range should be able to hear broadcast traffic.

- **Multicast** traffic is similar to broadcast traffic in the sense that it is not one-to-one but is intended for a subset of STAs that are part of a multicast group, instead of all STAs.

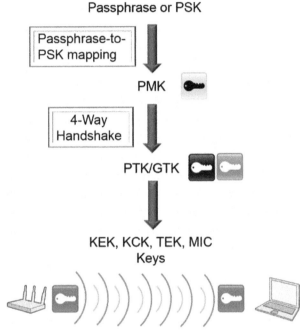

Passphrase or PSK

Passphrase-to-PSK mapping

PMK

4-Way Handshake

PTK/GTK

KEK, KCK, TEK, MIC Keys

Figure 5-5: The AKM Key Hierarchy with PSK

Unicast Encryption—The pairwise transient key (PTK) is a single key that is unique to each STA association and is used to encrypt all unicast traffic. The PTK is created during the 4-way handshake process using the PMK as the seed. Therefore, the PTK is unique between each pair of stations. A STA pair can be a wireless client device and an AP, or two client devices connected together in ad-hoc mode. Even though all devices in a PSK service set share the same PMK, the PTK is different for each pair of associated devices, thereby providing secure communications for all transmissions. You need to know the roles of the PMK and PTK here.

Broadcast / Multicast Encryption—A different key is used to secure broadcast and multicast traffic as compared to unicast traffic. This key is the group temporal key (GTK). Recall, earlier in this chapter it was stated that the GTK is derived from the GMK. This is a separate process than the PTK derivation process for unicast traffic described previously. The GMK is derived by the authenticator—which is an AP, wireless controller or cloud-managed device. The GMK works as a seed to then derive the GTK. As with the PTK, the installation of the GTK occurs during the 4-way handshake process. In order for all STAs to share and understand group traffic, the GTK is common for all devices that are part of the same service set. Again, you need to understand well the role of the GTK.

It is important to understand that in both WPA- and WPA2-Personal networks, each member of the network knows the PMK (or passphrase from which a PMK is derived). Since the other inputs to the PTK can be collected by observing the 4-way handshake, unicast encryption keys can be recreated by other members of the BSS. This is a potential security vulnerability if all members of a BSS cannot be trusted. In other words, in a PSK network, the network is only as secure as the users that know the PSK or passphrase treat it.

From a network security management perspective, PSK networks are considered limited in scalability. This is because all STAs or devices that are part of the service set must have the same passphrase or PSK entered into the device. In a home or small network this is easily attainable. In enterprise networks, managing a PSK WLAN can be challenging. It is time-consuming to enter the keys when the network is first implemented, and to change the keys at responsible intervals. For the most part, PSK administration is a manual process; however, some proprietary and automated solutions are available to help ease the burden of the passphrase or key management. PSK use and management should be defined in the corporate security policy.

802.1X/EAP Key Hierarchy

When using WPA- or WPA2-Enterprise, the 802.11 authentication and key management (AKM) scheme uses 802.1X port-based access control with EAP user-based authentication. In this scheme, the MSK is sometimes referred to as the authentication, authorization, and accounting (AAA) key. The MSK/AAA is exported out of the EAP process, and the first 256 bits of the MSK are considered to be the PMK from which encryption keys (PTKs and others) are generated during a 4-way handshake. This process is similar to that used with a PSK network discussed earlier. The main difference is that, when 802.1X/EAP is used, the session key is derived from a series of exchanged EAP messages.

Recall that WPA Enterprise uses 802.1X/EAP user-based authentications with the TKIP cipher suite for encryption. With Enterprise mode, the 802.1X/EAP method allows each new association between a pair of STAs to have its own unique key sets of both the PMK and PTK. Remember that in a PSK network, all STAs that are part of the same service set share a common PMK.

WPA2-Enterprise uses 802.1X/EAP user-based authentication with support for the mandatory CCMP and optional TKIP cipher suites for encryption. As with WPA enterprise, this method allows each new association between a pair of STAs to have its own unique key sets of both PMK and PTK, making this potentially a very secure solution. You can see why WPA2-Enterprise is so strongly recommended as a security solution.

An important stage in 802.11 AKM is the exporting of dynamic encryption keys, which are created during the 802.1X/EAP authentication process. These keys are derived on both the authentication server (AS) and the supplicant (client STA). The AS must securely distribute this information to the authenticator (wireless AP or controller) before the 4-way handshake can use these keys to generate actual encryption keys. Creation of keying material is EAP method-specific. Similarly, the EAP framework does not define how the AS securely distributes the keys to the authenticator. This is left up to the developers of the individual EAP types, allowing for great flexibility in the framework.

Keying material must be exported by the specific EAP type for RSN compliance. Mutual authentication is required for the creation of dynamic keying material and ensures the security of subsequent cipher suite encryption. Not all EAP methods included in RFC 3748 provide key generation. Those that do not include EAP-MD5, EAP-OTP, and EAP-GTC. EAP methods that do export dynamic keying material include PEAP (including PEAPv1), EAP-TLS, EAP-TTLS, EAP-LEAP, and EAP-FAST, among others.

In the 802.1X/EAP authentication model, the method used for generation of dynamic encryption keys is EAP type-specific. The key generation, when offered, is defined in the documentation that specifies the EAP method. After mutual authentication has occurred, both the authentication server and the supplicant will export an MSK, from which the PMK is derived.

The basic requirements that are common to all strong EAP types are:

- Mutual authentication is required for management of dynamic encryption keys.
- The dynamic keys must be securely distributed from the AS to the client. The distribution is beyond the scope of the EAP framework, and is defined by the specific EAP type.

The 802.11 standard defines mutual authentication as a dependency of an RSNA.

From IEEE 802.11-2012:

4.3.4.3 Robust security network association (RSNA)

"An RSNA depends upon the use of an EAP method that supports mutual authentication of the AS and the STA, such as those that meet the requirements in IETF RFC 4017."

RFC 3748, Section 7.10 (Emphasis Added)

"In order to provide keying material for use in a subsequently negotiated cipher suite, an EAP method supporting key derivation MUST export a Master Session Key (MSK) of at least 64 octets, and an Extended Master Session Key (EMSK) of at least 64 octets. EAP Methods deriving keys MUST provide for mutual authentication between the EAP peer and the EAP Server."

RFC 3748, Section 7.2.1

"Mutual authentication -- This refers to an EAP method in which, within an interlocked exchange, the authenticator authenticates the peer and the peer authenticates the authenticator. Two independent one-way methods, running in opposite directions do not provide mutual authentication as defined here."

From IEEE 802.11-2012:

11.1.6 RSNA assumptions and constraints

"When IEEE 802.1X authentication is used, the specific EAP method used performs mutual authentication. This assumption is intrinsic to the design of RSN in IEEE 802.11 LANs and cannot be removed without exposing both the STAs to man-in-the-middle attacks. EAP-MD5 is an example of an EAP method that does not meet this constraint (see IETF RFC 3748 [B26]). Furthermore, the use of EAP authentication methods where server and client credentials cannot be differentiated reduces the security of the method to that of a PSK due to the fact that malicious insiders can masquerade as servers and establish a man-in-the-middle attack."

"In particular, the mutual authentication requirement implies an unspecified prior enrollment process (e.g., a long-lived authentication key or establishment of trust through a third party such as a certification authority), as the STA must be able to identify the ESS or IBSS as a trustworthy entity and vice versa. The STA shares authentication credentials with the AS utilized by the selected AP or, in the case of PSK, the selected AP. The SSID provides an unprotected indication that the selected AP's authentication entity shares credentials with the STA. Only the successful completion of the IEEE 802.1X EAP or PSK authentication, after association, can validate any such indication that the AP is connected to an authorized network or service provider."

Stated plainly, for effective and secure distribution of dynamic encryption keys, mutual authentication is both intrinsically and explicitly required.

After the PMK is generated, the 4-way handshake should transpire to generate the actual PTK used for encryption. The 802.11 standard defines the 4-way handshake explicitly.

From IEEE 802.11-2012:

11.6.6.1 General

4-Way Handshake

"RSNA defines a protocol using IEEE 802.1X EAPOL-Key frames called the 4-Way Handshake. The handshake completes the IEEE 802.1X authentication process. The information flow of the 4-Way Handshake is as follows:

Message 1: Authenticator → Supplicant: EAPOL-Key(0,0,1,0,P,0,0,ANonce,0,DataKD_M1) where DataKD_M1 = 0 or PMKID for PTK generation, or PMKID KDE (for sending SMKID) for STK generation

Message 2: Supplicant → Authenticator: EAPOL-Key(0,1,0,0,P,0,0,SNonce,MIC,DataKD_M2) where DataKD_M2 = RSNIE for creating PTK generation or peer RSNIE, Lifetime KDE, SMKID KDE (for sending SMKID) for STK generation

Message 3: Authenticator → Supplicant: EAPOL-Key(1,1,1,1,P,0,KeyRSC,ANonce,MIC,DataKD_M3) where DataKD_M3 = RSNIE,GTK[N] for creating PTK generation or initiator RSNIE, Lifetime KDE for STK generation

Message 4: Supplicant → Authenticator: EAPOL-Key(1,1,0,0,P,0,0,0,MIC,DataKD_M4) where DataKD_M4 = 0."

4-way Handshake Frames

Four EAP over LAN (EAPoL) Key frames are used, with each acknowledged in a 4-way handshake, hence the name. The process of exchanging these four frames allows for the creation of the PTK. The PTK is used to encrypt unicast traffic between STAs.

Remember that in a pre-shared key network/service set, all STAs share a common PSK that is entered into the STA as a 256-bit key, or created from a common passphrase that is entered on all STAs. The 4-way handshake occurs immediately following the 802.11 Open System authentication and association process. This is an indicator that the packet trace in the following image was likely taken from a PSK network, since no 802.1X/EAP frames display. However, it is not 100% guaranteed based on the information below. The possibility exists that this could be an 802.1X/EAP session that is using fast secure transition. The only way to be certain is to expand a frame that contains the RSN IE and view the authentication key management suite list field, which identifies either PSK or 802.1X/EAP.

Source	Destination	BSSID	Flags	Channel	Signal	Data Rate	Size	Relative Time	Protocol
Intelorate:50:5...	ArubaNetwo:14:F...	ArubaNetwo:14:F...	*	161	58%	6.0	34	0.000000	802.11 Auth
ArubaNetwo:14:F...	Intelorate:50:5...		#	161	69%	6.0	14	0.000010	802.11 Ack
ArubaNetwo:14:F...	Intelorate:50:5...	ArubaNetwo:14:F...	*	161	72%	6.0	34	0.000257	802.11 Auth
Intelorate:50:5...	ArubaNetwo:14:F...		#	161	58%	6.0	14	0.000264	802.11 Ack
Intelorate:50:5...	ArubaNetwo:14:F...	ArubaNetwo:14:F...	*	161	58%	6.0	114	0.000831	802.11 Assoc Req
ArubaNetwo:14:F...	Intelorate:50:5...		#	161	72%	6.0	14	0.000839	802.11 Ack
ArubaNetwo:14:F...	Intelorate:50:5...	ArubaNetwo:14:F...	*	161	72%	6.0	122	0.007198	802.11 Assoc Rsp
Intelorate:50:5...	ArubaNetwo:14:F...		#	161	56%	6.0	14	0.007209	802.11 Ack
ArubaNetwo:14:F...	Intelorate:50:5...	ArubaNetwo:14:F...		161	72%	6.0	159	0.011639	EAPOL-Key
Intelorate:50:5...	ArubaNetwo:14:F...		#	161	58%	6.0	14	0.011650	802.11 Ack
Intelorate:50:5...	ArubaNetwo:14:F...	ArubaNetwo:14:F...		161	56%	6.0	161	0.018900	EAPOL-Key
ArubaNetwo:14:F...	Intelorate:50:5...		#	161	72%	6.0	14	0.018910	802.11 Ack
ArubaNetwo:14:F...	Intelorate:50:5...	ArubaNetwo:14:F...		161	72%	6.0	193	0.020660	EAPOL-Key
Intelorate:50:5...	ArubaNetwo:14:F...		#	161	58%	6.0	14	0.020671	802.11 Ack
Intelorate:50:5...	ArubaNetwo:14:F...	ArubaNetwo:14:F...		161	56%	6.0	137	0.021873	EAPOL-Key
ArubaNetwo:14:F...	Intelorate:50:5...		#	161	69%	6.0	14	0.021883	802.11 Ack

Figure 5-6: 4-way Handshake with no EAP Authentication

It is important to consider that if the 4-way handshake is captured with a packet analyzer and PSK is used, software programs are available that allows the collected information to be challenged against a dictionary to possibly determine the passphrase. Therefore, using a strong passphrase lessens the chances of an intruder discovering it. There is a possibility that this same process can be used for legitimate reasons, such as troubleshooting or auditing. Many packet analyzer programs have built-in functionally that allow a network administrator to see encrypted traffic if the passphrase is known. The passphrase and SSID are entered into the analyzer and, once the 4-way handshake is captured, the administrator would be able to view the encrypted information. This option may be necessary for various support reasons.

Using a packet analyzer to reassemble VoIP communications is a common troubleshooting process. In a WLAN with a VoWi-Fi implementation, assuming encryption is in use, only a PSK deployment of VoWi-Fi would allow for the decryption of the voice stream in a packet analyzer. This is because the actual PMK is unknown in an enterprise deployment using 802.1X/EAP and is not exposed in any interface in a way that it can be retrieved. Even with the 4-way handshake data, the PTK cannot be derived.

A packet trace that is captured from a network configured for 802.1X/EAP shows a series of EAP messages after the 802.11 Open System authentication, and the association process completes before the 4-way handshake starts. This is a key indicator that 802.1X/EAP is in use on the network. If you were to view the authentication key management suite list field in a frame that carries the RSN IE, it would be identified as such.

Note that the 4-way handshake being shown does not necessarily mean this connection is part of an RSN BSS, as the service set may be using TKIP/RC4, which alone is not considered an RSN. Remember, CCMP is mandatory to have an RSN and TKIP is optional, though now deprecated in the standard. The only way to be certain whether an RSN is in use is to

- expand a frame that contains the RSN IE, and
- view the pairwise key cipher list, which would show CCMP for an RSNA.

Group Key Handshake

The group key handshake is a group key management protocol defined by the 802.11 standard. It is used only to issue a new group temporal key (GTK) to peers with whom the local STA has already formed security associations.

Once the initial PTK and GTK are in place via the 4-way handshake, the group key (GTK), which is used to encrypt broadcast and multicast data traffic, may be changed by the authenticator (AP) for a number of reasons. Updating the stations with the new GTK is performed through a simple two-step group key handshake, as shown in the Figure 5-7.

The authenticator may initiate a group key handshake when an STA is disassociated or deauthenticated to protect the integrity of BSS multicast or broadcast communications.

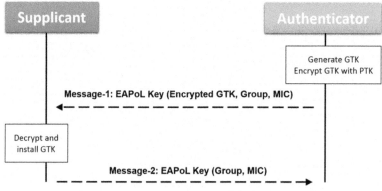

Figure 5-7: Group Key Handshake Protocol

🔲 From the Blogs

RSN Information Element

URL: mrncciew.com/2014/08/21/cwsp-rsn-information-elements
Author: Rasika Nayanajith
Blog: mrn-cciew—mrncciew.com

The RSN-IE (Robust Security Network Information Element) is an optional field of variable length that can be found in 802.11 management frames. The RSN-IE element has an element ID of 48 and is present in the following different management frames:

1. Beacon frames (sent by AP)
2. Probe Response frames (sent by AP)
3. Association Request frames (sent by Client)
4. Reassociation Request frames (sent by client)

All 802.11 radios will use one cipher (pairwise) suit for unicast encryption and another cipher (group) for encrypting multicast/broadcast traffic. The following are the different cipher suite values:

- 00-0F-AC-04 (CCMP) is the default
- 00-0F-AC-02 (TKIP) is optional
- 00-0F-AC-01 (WEP-40)
- 00-0F-AC-05 (WEP-104)

When a station supports several ciphers, it always chooses the strongest one first (for example, CCMP, TKIP, WEP-104, WEP-40).

The RSN-IE also used to indicate what authentication methods are supported. The Authentication Key Management (AKM) suite indicates whether the station supports 802.1X or PSK authentication. Following are the 3 different AKM suite values depending on the Authentication method used:

- 00-0F-AC-01 (802.1X)

- 00-0F-AC-02 (PSK)
- 00-0F-AC-03 (FT over 802.1X)

Here is the structure of RSN element:

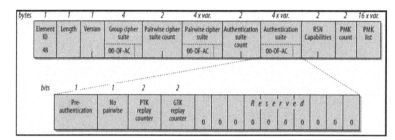

The following sample wireless frames show captures of the four different type of frames in which the RSN-IE field exists.

1) **Here is a beacon frame**. You can filter Beacon frames in Wireshark using the *(wlan.fc.type == 0)&&(wlan.fc.type_subtype == 0x08)* filter. As you can see below both the Group and Pairwise cipher is CCMP-AES (00-0F-AC-04) and the AKM suite is PSK (00-0F-AC-02).

```
⊞ Frame 15: 237 bytes on wire (1896 bits), 237 bytes captured (1896 bits) on inte
⊞ Radiotap Header v0, Length 18
⊟ IEEE 802.11 Beacon frame, Flags: ........C
    Type/Subtype: Beacon frame (0x0008)
  ⊟ Frame Control Field: 0x8000
      .... ..00 = Version: 0
      .... 00.. = Type: Management frame (0)
      1000 .... = Subtype: 8
    ⊞ Flags: 0x00
    .000 0000 0000 0000 = Duration: 0 microseconds
    Receiver address: Broadcast (ff:ff:ff:ff:ff:ff)
    Destination address: Broadcast (ff:ff:ff:ff:ff:ff)
    Transmitter address: 64:a0:e7:af:47:4e (64:a0:e7:af:47:4e)
    Source address: 64:a0:e7:af:47:4e (64:a0:e7:af:47:4e)
    BSS Id: 64:a0:e7:af:47:4e (64:a0:e7:af:47:4e)
    Fragment number: 0
    Sequence number: 2210
  ⊞ Frame check sequence: 0x31b69ef4 [correct]
⊟ IEEE 802.11 wireless LAN management frame
  ⊟ Fixed parameters (12 bytes)
      Timestamp: 0x000000051d8bb822
      Beacon Interval: 0.104448 [Seconds]
    ⊞ Capabilities Information: 0x0011
  ⊟ Tagged parameters (179 bytes)
    ⊞ Tag: SSID parameter set: TEST1
    ⊞ Tag: Supported Rates 12(B), 18, 24(B), 36, 48, 54, [Mbit/sec]
    ⊞ Tag: Traffic Indication Map (TIM): DTIM 0 of 0 bitmap
    ⊞ Tag: Country Information: Country Code AU, Environment Any
    ⊞ Tag: QBSS Load Element 802.11e CCA Version
    ⊞ Tag: HT Capabilities (802.11n D1.10)
    ⊟ Tag: RSN Information
        Tag Number: RSN Information (48)
        Tag length: 20
        RSN Version: 1
      ⊟ Group Cipher Suite: 00-0f-ac AES (CCM)
          Group Cipher Suite OUI: 00-0f-ac
          Group Cipher Suite type: AES (CCM) (4)
        Pairwise Cipher Suite Count: 1
      ⊟ Pairwise Cipher Suite List 00-0f-ac AES (CCM)
        ⊟ Pairwise Cipher Suite: 00-0f-ac AES (CCM)
            Pairwise Cipher Suite OUI: 00-0f-ac
            Pairwise Cipher Suite type: AES (CCM) (4)
        Auth Key Management (AKM) Suite Count: 1
      ⊟ Auth Key Management (AKM) List 00-0f-ac PSK
        ⊟ Auth Key Management (AKM) Suite: 00-0f-ac PSK
            Auth Key Management (AKM) OUI: 00-0f-ac
            Auth Key Management (AKM) type: PSK (2)
      ⊟ RSN Capabilities: 0x0028
          .... .... .... ...0 = RSN Pre-Auth capabilities: Transmitter does not su
          .... .... .... ..0. = RSN No Pairwise capabilities: Transmitter can supp
          .... .... .... 10.. = RSN PTKSA Replay Counter capabilities: 4 replay co
          .... .... ..10 .... = RSN GTKSA Replay Counter capabilities: 4 replay co
          .... .... .0.. .... = Management Frame Protection Required: False
          .... .... 0... .... = Management Frame Protection Capable: False
          .... ...0 .... .... = Joint Multi-band RSNA: False
          .... ..0. .... .... = PeerKey Enabled: False
    ⊞ Tag: HT Information (802.11n D1.10)
    ⊞ Tag: Vendor Specific: 00:40:96: Aironet DTPC Powerlevel 0x11
    ⊞ Tag: Vendor Specific: 00:50:f2: WMM/WME: Parameter Element
    ⊞ Tag: Vendor Specific: 00:40:96: Aironet Unknown (1) (1)
    ⊞ Tag: Vendor Specific: 00:40:96: Aironet CCX version = 5
    ⊞ Tag: Vendor Specific: 00:40:96: Aironet Unknown (11) (11)
    ⊞ Tag: Vendor Specific: 00:40:96: Aironet Client MFP Disabled
```

2) **Here is a Probe Response frame**. You can filter Probe Response frames using the *(wlan.fc.type == 0)&&(wlan.fc.type_subtype == 0x05)* Wireshark filter.

```
⊓ Frame 38: 231 bytes on wire (1848 bits), 231 bytes captured (1848 bits) on
⊞ Radiotap Header v0, Length 18
⊟ IEEE 802.11 Probe Response, Flags: ....R...C
    Type/Subtype: Probe Response (0x0005)
  ⊟ Frame Control Field: 0x5008
      .... ..00 = Version: 0
      .... 00.. = Type: Management frame (0)
      0101 .... = Subtype: 5
    ⊞ Flags: 0x08
    .000 0000 0011 0000 = Duration: 48 microseconds
    Receiver address: 00:1b:d4:58:e6:1a (00:1b:d4:58:e6:1a)
    Destination address: 00:1b:d4:58:e6:1a (00:1b:d4:58:e6:1a)
    Transmitter address: 64:a0:e7:af:47:4e (64:a0:e7:af:47:4e)
    Source address: 64:a0:e7:af:47:4e (64:a0:e7:af:47:4e)
    BSS Id: 64:a0:e7:af:47:4e (64:a0:e7:af:47:4e)
    Fragment number: 0
    Sequence number: 2599
  ⊞ Frame check sequence: 0x019f4cee [correct]
⊟ IEEE 802.11 wireless LAN management frame
  ⊟ Fixed parameters (12 bytes)
      Timestamp: 0x000000051dafba18
      Beacon Interval: 0.104448 [Seconds]
    ⊞ Capabilities Information: 0x0011
  ⊟ Tagged parameters (173 bytes)
    ⊞ Tag: SSID parameter set: TEST1
    ⊞ Tag: Supported Rates 12(B), 18, 24(B), 36, 48, 54, [Mbit/sec]
    ⊞ Tag: Country Information: Country Code AU, Environment Any
    ⊞ Tag: QBSS Load Element 802.11e CCA Version
    ⊞ Tag: HT Capabilities (802.11n D1.10)
    ⊟ Tag: RSN Information
        Tag Number: RSN Information (48)
        Tag length: 20
        RSN Version: 1
      ⊟ Group Cipher Suite: 00-0f-ac AES (CCM)
          Group Cipher Suite OUI: 00-0f-ac
          Group Cipher Suite type: AES (CCM) (4)
        Pairwise Cipher Suite Count: 1
      ⊟ Pairwise Cipher Suite List 00-0f-ac AES (CCM)
        ⊟ Pairwise Cipher Suite: 00-0f-ac AES (CCM)
            Pairwise Cipher Suite OUI: 00-0f-ac
            Pairwise Cipher Suite type: AES (CCM) (4)
        Auth Key Management (AKM) Suite Count: 1
      ⊟ Auth Key Management (AKM) List 00-0f-ac PSK
        ⊟ Auth Key Management (AKM) Suite: 00-0f-ac PSK
            Auth Key Management (AKM) OUI: 00-0f-ac
            Auth Key Management (AKM) type: PSK (2)
      ⊞ RSN Capabilities: 0x0028
    ⊞ Tag: HT Information (802.11n D1.10)
    ⊞ Tag: Vendor Specific: 00:40:96: Aironet DTPC Powerlevel 0x11
    ⊞ Tag: Vendor Specific: 00:50:f2: WMM/WME: Parameter Element
    ⊞ Tag: Vendor Specific: 00:40:96: Aironet Unknown (1) (1)
    ⊞ Tag: Vendor Specific: 00:40:96: Aironet CCX version = 5
    ⊞ Tag: Vendor Specific: 00:40:96: Aironet Unknown (11) (11)
    ⊞ Tag: Vendor Specific: 00:40:96: Aironet Client MFP Disabled
```

3) **Here is an Association Request frame**. You can filter Association Request frames using the *(wlan.fc.type == 0)&&(wlan.fc.type_subtype == 0x00)* Wireshark filter.

```
⊡ Frame 89: 114 bytes on wire (912 bits), 114 bytes captured (912 bits)
⊞ Radiotap Header v0, Length 18
⊟ IEEE 802.11 Association Request, Flags: .........C
    Type/Subtype: Association Request (0x0000)
  ⊟ Frame Control Field: 0x0000
      .... ..00 = Version: 0
      .... 00.. = Type: Management frame (0)
      0000 .... = Subtype: 0
    ⊞ Flags: 0x00
      .000 0000 0010 1100 = Duration: 44 microseconds
      Receiver address: 64:a0:e7:af:47:4e (64:a0:e7:af:47:4e)
      Destination address: 64:a0:e7:af:47:4e (64:a0:e7:af:47:4e)
      Transmitter address: 00:1b:d4:58:e6:1a (00:1b:d4:58:e6:1a)
      Source address: 00:1b:d4:58:e6:1a (00:1b:d4:58:e6:1a)
      BSS Id: 64:a0:e7:af:47:4e (64:a0:e7:af:47:4e)
      Fragment number: 0
      Sequence number: 801
    ⊞ Frame check sequence: 0xbdce004c [correct]
  ⊟ IEEE 802.11 wireless LAN management frame
    ⊟ Fixed parameters (4 bytes)
      ⊞ Capabilities Information: 0x0a31
        Listen Interval: 0x0001
    ⊟ Tagged parameters (64 bytes)
      ⊞ Tag: SSID parameter set: TEST1
      ⊞ Tag: Supported Rates 12(B), 18, 24(B), 36, 48, 54, [Mbit/sec]
      ⊞ Tag: QoS Capability
      ⊞ Tag: Vendor Specific: 00:40:96: Aironet CCX version = 4
      ⊞ Tag: Vendor Specific: 00:40:96: Aironet Unknown (1) (1)
      ⊟ Tag: RSN Information
          Tag Number: RSN Information (48)
          Tag length: 20
          RSN Version: 1
        ⊟ Group Cipher Suite: 00-0f-ac AES (CCM)
            Group Cipher Suite OUI: 00-0f-ac
            Group Cipher Suite type: AES (CCM) (4)
          Pairwise Cipher Suite Count: 1
        ⊟ Pairwise Cipher Suite List 00-0f-ac AES (CCM)
          ⊟ Pairwise Cipher Suite: 00-0f-ac AES (CCM)
              Pairwise Cipher Suite OUI: 00-0f-ac
              Pairwise Cipher Suite type: AES (CCM) (4)
          Auth Key Management (AKM) Suite Count: 1
        ⊟ Auth Key Management (AKM) List 00-0f-ac PSK
          ⊟ Auth Key Management (AKM) Suite: 00-0f-ac PSK
              Auth Key Management (AKM) OUI: 00-0f-ac
              Auth Key Management (AKM) type: PSK (2)
        ⊞ RSN Capabilities: 0x0028
      ⊞ Tag: Vendor Specific: 00:50:f2: WMM/WME: Information Element
```

4) **Here is a Reassociation Request frame**. You can filter these frames using the *(wlan.fc.type == 0)&&(wlan.fc.type_subtype == 0x02)* Wireshark filter. As you can see it uses the AKM suite of 00-0F-AC-01 (802.1X) & CCMP-AES (00-0F-AC-04) encryption ciphers.

```
⊞ Frame 2429: 195 bytes on wire (1560 bits), 195 bytes captured (1560 bits) on i
⊞ Radiotap Header v0, Length 18
⊟ IEEE 802.11 Reassociation Request, Flags: ........C
    Type/Subtype: Reassociation Request (0x0002)
  ⊟ Frame Control Field: 0x2000
      .... ..00 = Version: 0
      .... 00.. = Type: Management frame (0)
      0010 .... = Subtype: 2
    ⊞ Flags: 0x00
    .000 0000 0011 0000 = Duration: 48 microseconds
    Receiver address: b8:38:61:84:c2:ff (b8:38:61:84:c2:ff)
    Destination address: b8:38:61:84:c2:ff (b8:38:61:84:c2:ff)
    Transmitter address: 04:db:56:35:fe:46 (04:db:56:35:fe:46)
    Source address: 04:db:56:35:fe:46 (04:db:56:35:fe:46)
    BSS Id: b8:38:61:84:c2:ff (b8:38:61:84:c2:ff)
    Fragment number: 0
    Sequence number: 376
  ⊞ Frame check sequence: 0x79a0b5c0 [correct]
⊟ IEEE 802.11 wireless LAN management frame
  ⊟ Fixed parameters (10 bytes)
    ⊞ Capabilities Information: 0x1011
      Listen Interval: 0x0014
      Current AP: b8:38:61:84:c2:ff (b8:38:61:84:c2:ff)
  ⊟ Tagged parameters (139 bytes)
    ⊞ Tag: SSID parameter set: LTUWireless2
    ⊞ Tag: Supported Rates 12(B), 24(B), 36, 48, 54, [Mbit/sec]
    ⊞ Tag: Power Capability Min: 5, Max :24
    ⊞ Tag: Supported Channels
    ⊟ Tag: RSN Information
        Tag Number: RSN Information (48)
        Tag length: 20
        RSN Version: 1
      ⊟ Group Cipher Suite: 00-0f-ac AES (CCM)
          Group Cipher Suite OUI: 00-0f-ac
          Group Cipher Suite type: AES (CCM) (4)
        Pairwise Cipher Suite Count: 1
      ⊟ Pairwise Cipher Suite List 00-0f-ac AES (CCM)
        ⊟ Pairwise Cipher Suite: 00-0f-ac AES (CCM)
            Pairwise Cipher Suite OUI: 00-0f-ac
            Pairwise Cipher Suite type: AES (CCM) (4)
        Auth Key Management (AKM) Suite Count: 1
      ⊟ Auth Key Management (AKM) List 00-0f-ac WPA
        ⊟ Auth Key Management (AKM) Suite: 00-0f-ac WPA
            Auth Key Management (AKM) OUI: 00-0f-ac
            Auth Key Management (AKM) type: WPA (1)
      ⊞ RSN Capabilities: 0x000c
    ⊞ Tag: HT Capabilities (802.11n D1.10)
    ⊞ Tag: Vendor Specific: 00:10:18
    ⊞ Tag: Vendor Specific: 00:90:4c: HT Capabilities (802.11n D1.10)
    ⊞ Tag: Vendor Specific: 00:50:f2: WMM/WME: Information Element
```

As a final note, when you have multiple cipher suites (because of the need for mixed client support), the Group Cipher must be always the lowest denominator. For example, if the CCMP and TKIP ciphers are both used in the same SSID/BSS, the group cipher must be TKIP. 🔲

Chapter 5 Summary

In this chapter, you learned about the key derivation processes based on the authentication system in use. This is known as authentication and key management (AKM). You learned how to identify AKM in formation in the RSN information element (IE), and the meaning of many terms, such as PMK, PTK, GTK and more, all related to AKM.

Facts to Remember

Be sure to remember the following facts as you prepare for the CWSP certification, and be sure that you can explain the details related to them:

- Remember the many terms related to AKM, including RSN, RSNA, Pre-RSNA, MSK, PMK, GTK, and PTK.
- Know that a RSNA always includes the 4-way handshake; however, not all authentication systems that conclude in the 4-way handshake are CCMP-based because TKIP also concludes with it.
- The RSN IE contains valuable information to allow the CWSP troubleshooter to identify the security in use on the network.
- The RSN IE is in Beacon, Probe Response, Association Request, and Reassociation Request frames.
- When using 802.1X, the MSK is used to acquire the PMK, which is used to acquire the PTK and GTK.
- When using PSK, the PSK is used to acquire the PMK.
- The PTK is used for unicast traffic and the GTK is used for broadcast and multicast traffic.
- The group key handshake is used should the AP require to update all STAs with a new GTK.

Chapter 5: Review Questions

1. When is WEP specified in the RSN IE of Beacon frames on Robust Security Networks?
    a. When RSNAs are in use
    b. After 4-way handshakes
    c. When TSNs fail
    d. Never

2. Which of the following is not a valid term in authentication and key management?
    a. TSN
    b. MSK
    c. GSK
    d. GMK

3. The security parameters of a given BSS are defined in which Information Element (IE)?
    a. RSN IE
    b. SSL IE
    c. MSK IE
    d. PMK IE

4. Which key is derived from the 802.1X process or from the PSK in pre-shared networks?
    a. RSK
    b. PMK
    c. GMK
    d. PTK

5. Of the following, which is not a valid Cipher Suite type value?
    a. 00-0F-AC-00
    b. 00-0F-AC-01
    c. 00-0F-AC-03
    d. 00-0F-AC-05

6. The _____ key secures group traffic, while the _____ secures unicast traffic.
    a. GTK, PTK
    b. PTK, GTK
    c. GTK, MSK
    d. MSK, PTK

7. With WPA2-Personal mode, which of the following can be used?
    a. CCMP/AES
    b. WEP
    c. Neither
    d. Both

8. Only one of these EAP types provides key generation. Select the one that does:
    a. EAP-GTC
    b. EAP-MD5
    c. EAP-FAST
    d. EAP-OTP

9. When is the PTK used to encrypt unicast traffic generated?
   a. During the 4-way handshake
   b. During Open System authentication
   c. During the group key handshake
   d. After the EAP is created

10. Which of the following is required for secure distribution of encryption keys?
   a. Bounded medium
   b. 802.1X
   c. Unicast encryption
   d. Mutual authentication

11. For WPA- and WPA2-Enterprise, the MSK is exported out of what?
   a. The EAP process
   b. The GMK
   c. The PTK
   d. The PSK

12. When a Cipher Suite Type of 00-0F-AC-05 is in use, what cipher suite is present?
   a. WEP-40
   b. TKIP
   c. WEP-104
   d. CCMP

13. Which of these represents the Authenticated Key Management Suite List value for 802.1X?
   a. 00-0f-ac-00
   b. 00-0f-ac-03
   c. 00-0f-ac-01
   d. 00-0f-ac-02

14. The RSN IE defines _____ and _____ in certain WLAN management frames.
   a. Cipher suites, AKM suites
   b. Cipher suites, SSID suites
   c. RSNA suites, Cipher suites
   d. AKM suites, RSNA suites

15. Select the option that represents the proper AKM key hierarchy.
   a. MSK, GTK, PMK, KCK
   b. KCK, PMK, MSK, GTK
   c. MSK, PMK, GTK, KCK
   d. MSK, PMK, GTK, TEK

16. Traffic that is sent from one station to another on a WLAN is what kind of traffic?
   a. STA traffic
   b. Multicast traffic
   c. Directed traffic
   d. Unicast traffic

17. Any device that is capable of CCMP is certainly able to process which one of the following?
   a. PPTP
   b. L2TP
   c. IPSec
   d. AES

18. The unique identifier created for each pairwise master key security association (PMKSA) when an RSNA is created is which of these?
   a. PMKID
   b. PMKAS
   c. PMKMP
   d. IDPMK

19. A TSN network allows for the creation of _____?
   a. Pre-MSK and MSK
   b. Pre-RSNA and RSNA
   c. Pre-PSK and PSK
   d. Pre-GMK and GMK

20. As a security consultant, you audit a new customer site and find that WEP clients are still in use. What should you do?
   a. Shut down the WLAN.
   b. Create new security policy.
   c. Create plan to transition WEP clients to robust security.
   d. Ensure clients understand social networking dangers.

21. The group cipher will always be the _____ possible encryption type that is used in the service set.
    a. Highest
    b. Most secure
    c. Lowest
    d. Least complicated

22. Regardless of length of passphrase used in WPA-PSK/WPA2-PSK, it is always hashed to a key length of _____ bits?
    a. 56
    b. 128
    c. 184
    d. 256

23. What is the minimum recommended length of a PSK pre-share?
    a. 8 characters
    b. 20 characters
    c. 32 characters
    d. 64 characters

24. When PSK is in use, what attack might be executed against a captured 4-way handshake?
    a. DoS attack
    b. EAP flooding
    c. Dictionary attack
    d. Broadcast attack

25. When might an authenticator initiate a group key handshake?

    a.   When an STA is disassociated or deauthenticated

    b.   After an RF jamming attack

    c.   When WEP and multicast are in use

    d.   When BSS members cannot be verified

Chapter 5: Review Answers

1. **D** is correct. WEP is not allowed in the RSN framework.

2. **C** is correct. There are no shortage of acronyms in wireless networking. GSK does not exist as a valid WLAN security term.

3. **A** is correct. The RSN IE is the only valid choice, and it includes security parameters of a given BSS.

4. **D** is correct. It is important that you learn about the PTK.

5. **A** is correct. -00 is not valid.

6. **A** is correct. The Group Temporal Key secures multicast and broadcast traffic, while the Pairwise Transient Key secures unicast traffic.

7. **A** is correct. WPA2-Personal requires support for CCMP/AES and may optionally support TKIP/RC4. WEP is not supported.

8. **C** is correct. Of those listed, only EAP-FAST provides keying material used in key generation.

9. **A** is correct. The PTK is generated during the 4-way handshake.

10. **B** is correct. 802.1X is used for secure distribution of encryption keys, among its other discrete functions.

11. **A** is correct. MSK is exported out of the EAP process.

12. **C** is correct. You will need to memorize the Cipher Suite types, an -05 is used for WEP-104.

13. **C** is correct. -01 is the AKM Suite List value for 802.1X.

14. **A** is correct. Cipher suites and AKM suites are defined in the RSN IE of certain management frames.

15. **D** is correct. Understanding key hierarchy is critical to the CWSP exam and understanding WLAN security.

16. **D** is correct. Unicast traffic is between individual stations, as opposed to Multicast and Broadcast which deal with some or all stations.

17. **D** is correct. CCMP uses AES for encryption. CCMP is the authentication and key management protocol.

18. **A** is correct. PMKIDs are unique identifiers for each PMKSA.

19. **B** is correct. Transitional Security Networks support Pre-RSNA and RSNA.

20. **C** is correct. WEP clients should be replaced as soon as possible when discovered.

21. **C** is correct. The lowest encryption in use determines the overall group cipher.

22. **D** is correct. WPA-PSK and WPA2-PSK passphrases are hashed to 256 bits.

23. **B** is correct. 20 characters is the minimal recommended PSK key length.

24. **C** is correct. A dictionary attack can be used against captured PSK traffic.

25. **A** is correct. A group key handshake might be initiated by an authenticator (AP or controller) when a station associates or disassociates.

Chapter 6:

Encryption

Objectives

3.2   Understand and explain 802.11 authentication and key management (AKM) components and processes, including encryption keys, handshakes, and pre-shared key management.

Encryption is defined as the process of modifying information (data) with an algorithm called a cipher that results in data being unreadable or meaningless to those without the key used in the algorithm. Encryption is very important in wireless communications because wireless networks use an unbounded medium (RF waves). For this reason, a CWSP must understand the basics of encryption as it relates to WLANs. First, let us explore the foundational terms and definitions related to encryption that is needed for this chapter.

Terminology

The following terms should be understood by the CWSP:

- **Encryption algorithm**—Encryption algorithms are mathematical procedures used to obscure information so it appears as seemingly meaningless data to an unintended recipient without a key. AES RC4, RC5, and RC6 are examples of encryption algorithms.
- **Hash function or hashing algorithm**—A cryptographic hash function is a deterministic procedure that takes an arbitrary block of data and returns a fixed-size bit string, the (cryptographic) hash value, such that an accidental or intentional change to the data will change the hash value.
- **Cipher suite**—A cipher suite is a named combination of authentication, encryption, and message authentication code (MAC) algorithms used to negotiate the security settings for a network connection.
- **Stream cipher**—A stream cipher is a symmetric key cipher where plaintext bits are combined with a pseudorandom cipher bit stream (keystream), typically by an exclusive-or (xor) operation. In a stream cipher, the plaintext digits are encrypted one at a time, and the transformation of successive digits varies during the encryption.
- **Block cipher**—In cryptography, a block cipher is a symmetric key cipher operating on fixed-length groups of bits, called blocks, with an unvarying transformation.

- **Symmetric key encryption**—Symmetric key algorithms are a class of algorithms for cryptography that use trivially related, often identical, cryptographic keys for both decryption and encryption.
- **Asymmetric key encryption**—Asymmetric key algorithms are a class of algorithms for cryptography that use separate key pairs for encryption and decryption. Key pairs are typically deployed as shared public and secret private keys.

Symmetric Key Encryption

Two common encryption techniques used with electronic information are symmetric key encryption and asymmetric key encryption. Here you will learn about symmetric key encryption. Asymmetric key encryption is discussed next.

Symmetric key encryption is the primary standardized frame encryption technology used with IEEE 802.11 standards-based wireless networks today.

- With **symmetric key encryption**, matching keying material is passed to both parties over an encrypted link that has been created.
- With **static key implementations** (such as WEP), the keying material is used as a direct input to the encryption process as it is entered manually on all devices that belong to the wireless service set.
- With **dynamic key implementations** (such as TKIP and CCMP using 802.1X/EAP), this initial keying material is used to generate subsequent encryption keys that are
    - used for encryption, and
    - created during the 4-way handshake process as discussed in the previous chapter.

In this process, the actual encryption keys are never transmitted across the wireless medium. Instead, some of the required key inputs such as authenticator, supplicant, nonces, and other required information are transmitted, and then each participating device derives (generates) the keys. This adds a layer of security to the key creation process.

The following image illustrates that the dynamic encryption key generation process begins with symmetric keys. The 4-way handshake is used to derive mutual frame encryption keys that are used to encrypt information that traverses the wireless medium. These frame encryption keys are symmetric encryption keys.

Symmetric encryption is less processor intensive than asymmetric encryption. For this reason, many file encryption systems use a symmetric key and algorithm to encrypt data (Microsoft calls this the File Encryption Key [FEK]) and an asymmetric encryption key and algorithm to encrypt the data encryption key. The asymmetric encryption key is typically a digital user certificate, and the symmetric data encryption key is usually unique to a file or encryption process. The main takeaway is that the symmetric encryption process is less computationally intensive and is typically better for large-scale encryption tasks.

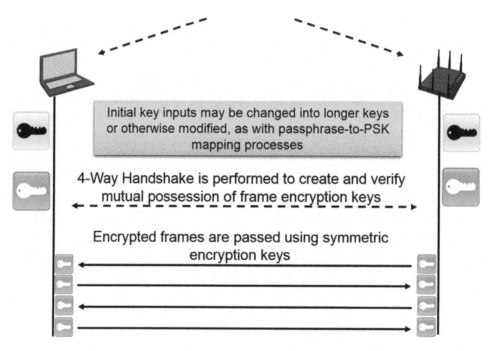

Figure 6-1: Symmetric Keys Used in 802.11

Asymmetric Key Encryption

Many different types of asymmetric key encryption exist, and each of them works a bit differently. Asymmetric key encryption is also called public key cryptography.

In the simplest terms, asymmetric key encryption uses both a public and a private encryption key. An initial entity (often a server, which we call Entity A) possesses a matched private and public key (the asymmetric keys).

- The public key is passed to any and all entities (Entity B) with whom a secure connection is desired.
- The private key is never shared with other entities.

When a frame is encrypted with the public key by Entity B, it can only be decrypted by the private key. Thus, only Entity A can successfully receive this information, because Entity A is the only one with the private key. Others who possess the public key cannot decrypt a frame that is encrypted with the public key. Hence, asymmetric encryption.

The following image illustrates just one use of asymmetric encryption.

Figure 6-2: Use of Asymmetric Encryption

This type of cryptography generally requires two sets of keys. Each communicating entity has a private/public key pair for secure information exchange. The public key is distributed to others, but the private key is kept by only one entity.

In some cases, asymmetric keys are used initially so that symmetric encryption keying can be established. Symmetric keying material can be transmitted inside an asymmetrically encrypted frame. The benefit of asymmetric key encryption is that initial keying material must only be distributed to one device at the beginning of the process.

Outside of the WLAN space, we see other examples of comparable encryption. For instance, when using a public hotspot and accessing HTTPS-based web sites, you are using asymmetric encryption based on the HTTPS server certificate (which contains the public key of the server). This is a perfect example, because the server sends the session encryption key (symmetric key) or materials used to generate the key to the client using asymmetric encryption processes.

Stream Ciphers

A cipher is a mechanism that allows for the encryption and decryption of information to occur. Stream ciphers take an initial plaintext input data stream and encrypt this stream one bit at a time. The plaintext input is typically processed using exclusive OR (XOR) math against a keystream and, bit-by-bit, an encrypted cipher text results. 802.11 WLAN technology uses the RC4 stream cipher with WEP and TKIP.

The following image shows how the stream cipher process works. You can see the plaintext information, in this case WLAN computer data, is combined with a created keystream. The logical combination of the plaintext data and the keystream using an XOR process results in ciphertext (encrypted information) that is sent across the wireless medium.

Figure 6-3: Stream Cipher Process
(Showing the importance of protecting the key and the keystream.)

Stream ciphers can be fast, and by comparison are often computationally faster than block ciphers. If not implemented correctly though, stream ciphers can allow for security weaknesses. This is one reason why WEP had its share of vulnerabilities and was cracked early in its tenure. WEP's use of a plaintext initialization vector that was sent across the wireless medium was certainly problematic. This IV was also used as a seed with the WEP key that was entered into the client software to create the needed keystream.

Stream ciphers lack integrity protection. When using WEP or TKIP, the integrity check value (ICV) is added to the process. The ICV as it was implemented in WEP was also vulnerable to a bit flip attack (used to alter transmitted data), another weakness of WEP.

Remember that RC4 is used with TKIP. However, changes were made in TKIP to help combat the problems associated with RC4 that were part of the WEP process. You will see more about TKIP later in this chapter.

Block Ciphers

There are several different types of block ciphers. In contrast to stream ciphers, block ciphers encrypt plaintext data in blocks, or chunks of bits, instead of sequentially one bit at a time. Block ciphers specify the size of the block to be encrypted, and CCMP/AES uses a 128-bit block.

The CBC block cipher mode is used with CCMP and, as shown in the following image, uses a chaining process whereby each encrypted block is used as an input to the encryption of the next block. This type of encryption adds strength to the cipher because it builds upon the strength of the previously encrypted blocks.

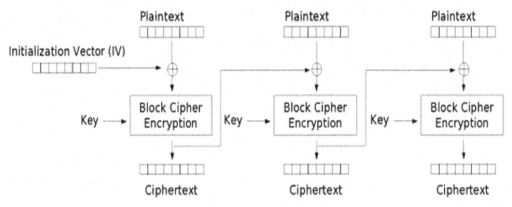

Figure 6-4: CBC Block Cipher Model

Like stream ciphers, block ciphers use an XOR process to process plaintext information. Block ciphers can be slower than stream ciphers, and to operate correctly and efficiently may require more powerful hardware. This requirement is why many older APs and client devices could not be upgraded to support WPA2 through firmware, but required hardware replacement.

Frame Encryption

It is important to understand what protection is afforded by any specific type of encryption. We often describe an encryption scheme in accordance with the OSI layer at which it is applied. For example, 802.11 standardized encryption methods, such as TKIP and CCMP, use Layer 2 encryption mechanisms. This phraseology means that they are applied at Layer 2 of the OSI model, protecting only the higher layer data, and not the MAC sublayer data (headers).

If you recall from CWNA and previous networking studies, the OSI model has 7 layers: Physical, Data Link, Network, Transport, Session, Presentation, and Application, listed from Layer 1 to Layer 7. The Physical (Layer 1) and Data Link (Layer 2) layers are subdivided into two sublayers.

- The Data Link layer sublayers are the MAC and the LLC.
- The Physical layer sublayers are the PLCP and the PMD.

Since WLAN encryption is applied at the MAC layer, it protects the LLC sublayer and the higher layer contents, but it does not protect MAC sublayer data. MAC sublayer information, such as MAC addresses, must remain unencrypted in order to be correctly transmitted and received. In many cases, the application data is what we are trying to protect, but it is also helpful to obscure IP-layer information as well as other pieces of the networking puzzle. The following image illustrates the encrypted portion of the 802.11 frames.

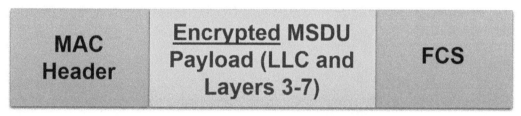

Figure 6-5: Illustrating 802.11 Frame Encryption

Capturing encrypted WLAN frames with a packet analyzer shows the MAC layer information that is transmitted in clear text. However, the frames that carry Application layer (Layer 7) data payload are obfuscated and not viewable. These nuances are critical to both CWSP study and in supporting secure wireless networks.

Encryption and Decryption

Encryption and decryption can either be centralized or distributed.

- When centralized, a WLAN controller performs the encryption and decryption processes.
- When distributed, these processes occur in the AP.

Most deployments today use distributed data forwarding and, therefore, perform distributed decryption as the encryption is only employed for the benefit of the wireless link.

Older model APs did not adequately secure secret keys in their configuration settings, which posed a security threat if the AP was stolen. Attackers could potentially recover network passwords/secrets. For that reason, it was advisable to move the keys to a centralized WLAN controller. The centralized mode of encryption/decryption protects the encrypted data all the way from the client (edge) to the WLAN controller (core).

Conversely, distributed data forwarding models require key storage and encryption/decryption processes locally on the AP. This allows for more expedient processing and forwarding of data frames directly to a destination from the edge, instead of going through the WLAN controller and then on to the destination. Because the unbounded wireless medium poses the greatest security vulnerability (attackers can easily intercept traffic with simple eavesdropping techniques), this method provides sufficient security in most cases.

As you can see, neither method is necessarily better all the time. Business and security requirements dictate the type of encryption/decryption model to be used. Government networks often see the centralized model as an advantage, as some wired privacy is provided. However, distributed forwarding and entirely distributed WLAN architectures are pushing encryption and decryption to the edge in most deployments today.

Part of the encryption method selection decision may be dependent upon the other network security features supported, such as firewalls. If the firewall can only be applied in the WLAN controller, then it makes sense to store keys there. If, on the other hand, the AP can perform policy and firewall services, the keys must be stored there. Understanding the various paradigms makes you better at your WLAN duties, and helps you to guide clients to the best solutions for their circumstances.

Encryption Algorithms

Encryption algorithms are mathematical procedures used to obscure information so it appears as seemingly meaningless data to an unintended recipient without the correct key.

These are some of the more common algorithms:

- Rivest Cipher 4 or "Ron's Code 4" (RC4)
- Advanced Encryption Standard (AES)
- Data Encryption Standard (DES)
- Triple Data Encryption Algorithm (3DES)
- Rivest Cipher 5 (RC5)
- Rivest Cipher 6 (RC6)

Here we focus only on RC4 and AES, as these are commonly used with 802.11 standards based WLAN technology.

RC4 was developed by Ron Rivest of RSA Security in 1987. In 802.11 WLAN technology, RC4 is used in conjunction with WEP and TKIP. As you know from earlier lessons, WEP was cracked early on. However, the problem with WEP was not RC4, but how RC4 was used within WEP technology and with the plaintext Initialization Vector (IV). TKIP provided a fix for some of the weaknesses in WEP as an interim solution until the 802.11i amendment was ratified, which we learned earlier provided much stronger security. Interestingly, the use of TKIP lasted much longer than the intended interim period, as it is still used heavily in many environments today—particularly in PSK deployments within small businesses. TKIP also uses RC4 but with several enhancements to provide stronger security than WEP.

In 802.11 standards-based WLAN technology, AES is used in conjunction with CCMP. AES uses the Rijndael algorithm and is a block cipher that was established by the U.S. National Institute of Standards and Technology (NIST) in 2001 to replace the older 1970s DES encryption algorithm. AES has a block size of 128 bits and can use three different key lengths, 128-bit, 192-bit and 256-bits. AES is considered to be extremely secure with today's available technology. It would take a large amount of computing power and many years to be able to crack AES.

WEP (Pre-RSNA)

By now, you are well-versed that WEP was the initial security solution provided in 802.11 and that WEP is no longer appropriate for securing any wireless environment. The stated goal of WEP was to provide an equivalent level of security to that which is normally found in a wired LAN, but it fell short. If you have older hardware that does not support the newer WPA/WPA2 specifications, you should consider upgrading the deficient hardware. With the low-cost computing power available today, WEP can be cracked in minutes with the free utilities available on the Internet. This means it is not good enough for even the smallest of businesses run out of someone's home.

The best practice is to state in your wireless use policy that WPA or WPA2 (preferably only WPA2) must be used in place of WEP and, where WEP must be used, to require tests to ensure the signal does not reach outside of your building. Only then can WEP be considered. If the signal never leaves your building, WEP is nearly as secure as a wired port that is left open for anyone to connect a device. Of course, in the real-world, it is nearly impossible to say that you are certain WEP frames are not reaching outside of your building. Remember that the signal may not appear with standard equipment, but if an attacker has a wireless NIC with a very good receive sensitivity rating and a high gain antenna, they may be able to pick up the signal from surprising distances. For this reason, you should opt for no WEP at all. We are now more than ten years past 802.11i's ratification and it is time to move away from WEP once and for all.

The MAC service data unit (MSDU) contains upper layer information that is present at the Data Link layer (Layer 2), and which has passed down the OSI model from the Application layer. The MSDU has the appropriate layer-specific information added as it traverses the upper layers on its way "down the stack." As the name implies, this is a data unit that is serviced by the MAC sublayer of the Data Link layer. Once the MAC sublayer header is added, this data unit becomes what is known as the MAC protocol data unit (MPDU).

WEP encapsulates the MPDU data payload with a 4-octet IV and a 4-octet ICV, and extends the length of the MPDU by a total of 8 octets. This is what is known as frame expansion. Prior to the 802.11n amendment to the standard, the maximum frame body size was 2304 bytes. With the additional 8 octets used for WEP, the frame size would increase to 2312 bytes. It is important to note that newer WLAN technology such as 802.11n/ac allows for larger frame body sizes.

WEP Weaknesses

WEP was never intended to provide impenetrable security, but was meant to protect against casual eavesdropping (see 802.11-prime and still 802.11-2012 clause 11.2.2.1). With the rapid increase in processor speeds, cracking WEP has become an easy task. WEP can no longer be considered for protection for any wireless network. The specific weaknesses in WEP include the following:

- Brute-force attacks
- Dictionary attacks
- Weak IV attacks
- Re-injection attacks
- Storage attacks

In late 2000 and early 2001, the security weaknesses of WEP became public knowledge. After that, many attack methods were developed and tools created that made these attack methods simple to implement for even entry-level technical individuals.

A brute-force attack method is a key guessing method that attempts every possible key in order to crack encryption. Each failed attempt is followed by another automated attempt with a new key, until the attack is successful. In the early days of Wi-Fi, with 104-bit WEP, brute-force was really not a feasible attack method for most attacks. However, 40-bit WEP could usually be cracked in one or two days with brute-force attacks using more than 20 distributed computers. The short timeframe was accomplished using a distributed cracking tool like jc-wepcrack. The jc-wepcrack utility was actually two tools: the client and the server.

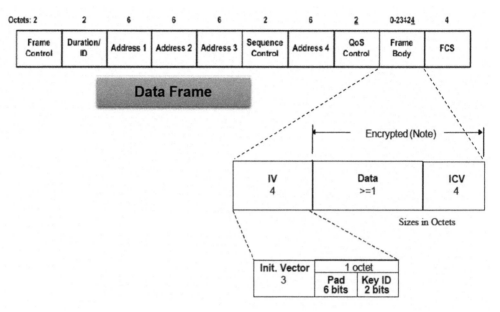

Figure 6-6: Expanded WEP MPDU

1) You would start the tool on the server and configure it for the WEP key size you thought was in use on the wireless LAN that you were cracking.

2) You would provide it with a PCAP file (a capture of encrypted frames) from that network.

3) You launched the client program and configured it to connect to the server. The client program would request a portion of the keys to be guessed and would attempt to access the encrypted frames with those keys.

With the modern addition of Field Programmable Gate Arrays (FPGAs)—which were add-on boards for hardware acceleration—the time to crack could be reduced by more than a factor of 30x. In fairness, the 20 computers would have to have been Pentium P4 machines or better, which were fairly hard to come by in the early half of the last decade (2001-2010). If you chose to go the FPGA route, you would have been spending a lot of money to crack that WEP key in those days.

Note: Since smart enterprises are no longer using WEP, this weakness and all others to follow are spoken of in the past tense.

Dictionary attack methodology relies on the fact that humans often use words or common strings as passwords. When using dictionary attacks against WEP, the key step was to use a dictionary cracking tool that understood the conversion algorithm used by a given hardware vendor to convert the typed password into the WEP key. This algorithm was not part of 802.11 and so was implemented differently by the different client vendors. Many vendors allowed the user to type a passphrase that was then converted to the WEP key using the Neesus Datacom or MD5 WEP key generation algorithms. The Neesus Datacom algorithm was notoriously insecure, and had resulted in what was sometimes called the Newsham-21-bit attack because it reduced the usable WEP key pool to 21 bits instead of 40 when using a 40-bit WEP key. This smaller pool could be exhausted in about 6 or 7 seconds on a P4 3.6 GHz single machine using cracking tools against a PCAP file. Even MD5-based conversion algorithms were far too weak, and should not have been considered as secure because they were still used to implement WEP, which was insecure due to weak IVs as well.

Weak IV attacks were based on the faulty implementation of RC4 in the WEP protocols. The IV was prepended to the static WEP key to form the full WEP encryption key used by the RC4 algorithm. This meant than an attacker already knew the first 24 bits of the encryption key, since the IV was sent in clear text as part of the frame header. Additionally, researchers Fluhrer, Mantin, and Shamir identified "weak" IVs in a paper released in 2001. These weak IVs resulted in certain values becoming more statistically probable than others, making it easier to crack the static WEP key. The 802.11 frames that used these weak IVs had come to be known as interesting frames. With enough interesting frames collected, you could crack the WEP key in a matter of seconds. This reduced the total attack time down to less than 5 or 6 minutes on a busy wireless LAN.

Note: **The weak IVs discovered by Fluhrer, Mantin, and Shamir are now among a larger pool of known weak IVs. After 2001, many more classes of weak IVs were discovered by David Hulton (h1kari) and KoreK. Thankfully, wireless security flaws are made public so they can then be fixed.**

What if the WEP-enabled network being attacked was not busy and you could not capture enough interesting frames in a short window of time? The answer was a re-injection attack. This kind of attack usually re-injected ARP packets onto the wireless LAN. The program aireplay could detect ARP packets based on their unique size and did not need to decrypt the packet. By re-injecting the ARP packets back onto the wireless LAN, it would force the other clients to reply and cause the creation of large amounts of wireless LAN traffic very quickly. For 40-bit WEP cracking, you usually wanted around 300,000 total frames to get enough interesting frames, and for 104-bit WEP cracking you wanted about 1,000,000 frames. Though these seem like high counts, automated attacks made short work of it.

Storage attacks are those methods used to recover WEP or WPA keys from their storage locations. On Windows computers, for example, WEP keys had often been stored in the registry in an encrypted form. An older version of this attack method was the Lucent Registry Crack. Surprisingly, the problem has not been fully removed from newer operating systems. An application named wzcook could retrieve the stored WEP keys used by Windows' Wireless Zero Configuration. This application recovered WEP or WPA-PSK keys (since they were effectively the same, WPA just improves the way the key is managed and implemented) and came with the Aircrack-ng tools used for cracking these keys. The application only worked if you had administrator access to the local machine; but in an environment with poor physical security and poor user training, it was not difficult to find a machine that was logged on and using the wireless LAN for the storage attack.

WEP makes up the core of pre-RSNA security in 802.11 networks. We hope the reality that WEP can be cracked in less than 5 minutes is enough to make you realize that you should not be using it on your networks. The only exception would be an installation where you are required to install a wireless LAN using older hardware and you have no other option. This scenario occurs even today in some very small deployments (and even a fewer large ones). The problem is not usually with the infrastructure equipment in any of the scenarios. The problem is with the client devices that the organization wants to continue allowing connectivity to the wireless LAN. Thankfully, most vendors have resolved this problem by taking WEP configuration out of their interfaces altogether, or at least removing it from the graphical configuration interfaces.

In the end, businesses and organizations that have sensitive data to protect must take a stand for security and against older technologies. This means that you should not be implementing WEP anywhere in your organization. When you have the authority of a corporation, the government, or even a non-profit oversight board, you can usually sell them on the need for better security with a short (5 minutes or less) demonstration of just how weak WEP is (or for that matter, WPA-PSK with weak passphrases). By thoroughly understanding the attack vectors used against WEP, the CWSP is better equipped to educate customers and clients against its use.

Dynamic WEP

Dynamic WEP was a non-standard interim solution introduced prior to the 802.11i amendment. Using the 802.1X/EAP framework to produce dynamic keys, manufacturers began supporting a proprietary WEP solution that used these keys dynamically. Many of the same weaknesses are present in dynamic WEP, and if enough frames are transmitted with dynamic WEP keys, the key can be recovered. As with 802.11's WEP, this proprietary WLAN security solution is not recommended.

Dynamic WEP does not use static keys, instead using the 802.1X framework to produce dynamic encryption keys. Dynamic WEP is one of the more curious stories in the history of wireless security, and never really saw wide-scale adoption.

TKIP (WPA)

TKIP was introduced to resolve the weaknesses of WEP. TKIP was part of the draft 802.11i amendment when the Wi-Fi Alliance chose to certify it as WPA so that vendors could begin implementing it in firmware for existing devices and out-of-the-box with new devices. TKIP/WPA added four new algorithms to WEP in order to address the security weaknesses it had:

- Michael—Message Integrity Check (MIC) to prevent forgery attacks (yes, it is really referred to as "Michael" for whatever reason)
- 48-bit Initialization Vector and IV sequence counter to prevent replay attacks
    - MPDUs received out-of-order are dropped by receiver
- Per-packet key mixing of the IV to de-correlate IVs from weak keys
    - 48-bit IV called TKIP Sequence Counter (TSC)
    - TSC updated each packet
    - 2^{48} frames allowed per single temporal key, would require 100 years to exhaust key space
- Dynamic re-keying mechanism to change encryption and integrity keys
    - Temporal key, transmitter address, and TSC combined into per-packet key
    - Split into 104-bit RC4 key and 24-bit IV for WEP compatibility

Earlier you saw that WEP encapsulates the MAC protocol data unit (MPDU) payload with a 4-octet IV and a 4-octet ICV, for a total of 8 octets. When TKIP is implemented, it adds the additional overhead of an extended IV of 4 octets (32 bits) and an additional MIC of 8 octets inside of WEP's encapsulation, which is a total of 12 additional octets. The total encryption overhead becomes 20 octets per frame vs. 12 octets for WEP, so the maximum frame body becomes a total of 2324 octets.

Michael is the name of the integrity algorithm used with TKIP that enhances the legacy ICV mechanism. Michael is meant to improve integrity protection while remaining backwards compatible with millions of limited-feature legacy radios since it is required to operate within a very small computing budget.

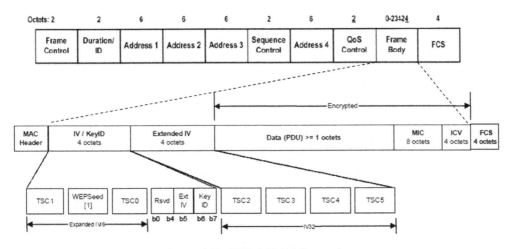

Figure 6-7: TKIP MPDU Expansion

The Michael MIC contains only 20 bits of effective security strength and is vulnerable to brute force attacks. For further protection, Michael is able to implement countermeasures if it detects an attack. Using these countermeasures, STAs or APs that detect two MIC failures within 60 seconds of each other must disable all TKIP receptions for 60 seconds.

These MIC failures should be logged for follow-up by a security administrator. It should be noted that the Michael countermeasure mechanism could be used as a DoS exploit although there are much easier DoS attacks that could be used. The TKIP-mandated 60-sec disablement period can also cause problems in healthy WLANs when a client has a defective driver or similar situation that triggers the countermeasure. Nearby clients are essentially disabled for Wi-Fi during the penalty period, and the effect can feel like a malfunctioning network. It is not uncommon for network administrators to override the 60-second non-transmit period to avoid false alarms related to Michael, but this negates an important security feature of TKIP.

Michael, MIC, was designed to help prevent forgery attacks which are a vulnerability of WEP.

In a frame decode that uses TKIP, but does not support CCMP, you will not see an RSN IE. This is because, in order to qualify as a RSN, the service set must support CCMP. Instead of the RSN IE, you will see a manufacturer-specific information element, commonly "WPA Information" or "WPA IE (221)," with either containing most of the same information as an RSN IE.

One thing to note is that, if support for both CCMP and TKIP is enabled on the wireless infrastructure device (which includes APs, WLAN controllers or cloud managed devices), in the appropriate management frame decode you see both the RSN IE and the WPA IE. This makes sense as a TKIP-only device would not be able to interpret the RSN information contained within the management frame.

The following image shows the 802.11 TKIP Data field in a protocol decode.

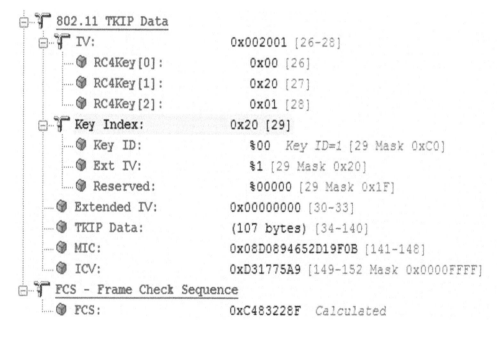

Figure 6-8: TKIP in an 802.11 Frame

CCMP (WPA2)

CCMP is based on the CCM of the AES encryption algorithm. CCM combines CTR (counter) mode for data confidentiality and CBC-MAC for authentication and integrity. CCM protects the integrity of both the MPDU Data field and selected portions of the 802.11 MPDU header. The AES algorithm is defined in FIPS PUB 197-2001. All AES processing used within CCMP uses AES with a 128-bit key and a 128-bit block size.

Note that WPA2:

- Replaces RC4 with the Advanced Encryption Standard (AES) (Rijndael algorithm) in Counter mode (for data privacy) with Cipher Block Chaining-Message Authentication Code (CBC-MAC) for data authenticity—CCMP/AES
  - AES is a symmetric, iterated block cipher.
- Uses 128-bit encryption key size, and encrypts in 128-bit fixed length blocks
- Has a 48-bit IV (called Packet Number or PN) derived from AES Key
- Does encryption and MIC calculation in parallel
- Renders per-packet keys unnecessary due to strength of AES cipher
- Features an 8-byte MIC which is considered much stronger than Michael
- Uses a separate chip to perform computation-intensive AES ciphering

Earlier you saw that prior to 802.11n, the largest frame body size was 2304 bytes. This was without any encryption methods used. When encryption is used, the frame body is expanded.

WEP added 8 octets of overhead, which increased the frame body to a maximum of 2312 bytes. TKIP added an additional 12 octets of overhead (which is in addition to the 8 octets for WEP) and increased the maximum frame body size to 2324 bytes.

Since CCMP is much more efficient than WEP and TKIP, and some of the CCMP encryption processing is handled by improved hardware technology, less overhead is required in the frame body. Therefore, CCMP adds only an additional 16 bytes of overhead to the frame body; 8 octets for the CCMP header and another 8 octets for the MIC. The maximum frame body size that uses CCMP is 2320 bytes in pre-802.11n deployments.

Exam Moment: The CWSP exam no longer tests on frame overhead knowledge when considering WEP, TKIP, and CCMP. This has been removed from the exam because organizations should only be using CCMP moving forward. It is provided here for current operational knowledge only.

Even though CCMP is much stronger and more secure that WEP and TKIP, it does not require any additional overhead in the frame body.

 Note: **Frame body sizes vary greatly now with 802.11n and 802.11ac and aggregation features. You are not tested on frame sizes on the CWSP exam at all, but a general knowledge serves you in your wireless duties.**

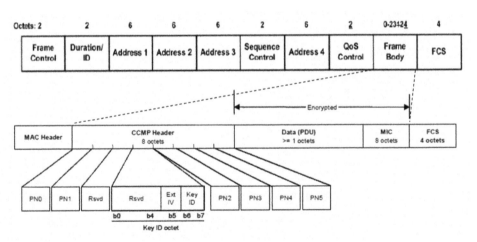

Figure 6-9: CCMP Frame Expansion

It is important to note that with newer WLAN standards such as 802.11n and 802.11ac, if TKIP is used but not CCMP and the 802.11 standard is followed, no MCS rates will be available. With TKIP, the highest achievable data rate is only 54 Mbps and TKIP should no longer be used on enterprise networks desiring the data rate advantages offered by 802.11n and 802.11ac. In reality, if you use TKIP in an 802.11n network, you are really running an 802.11g or 802.11a network, because 802.11n no longer allowed for use of any cipher suite but CCMP.

According to 802.11-2012, "The use of TKIP is deprecated. The TKIP algorithm is unsuitable for the purposes of this standard." (Section 11.1.1) Further, it says explicitly in 11.1.6, "An HT STA shall not use either of the pairwise cipher suite selectors: "Use group cipher suite" or TKIP to communicate with another HT STA. This, of course, applies forward to the 802.11 VHT PHY as well.

💬 From the Blogs

WPA/TKIP only going away in Cisco WLC release 8.0

URL: sc-wifi.com/2014/04/29/wpatkip-only-going-away-in-cisco-wlc-release-8-0
Author: Sam Clements
Blog: SC-WiFi—sc-wifi.com

Cisco is readying the next major release of their WLC code, version 8.0. At the advocation of the WFA, this brings with it a very significant change in security capabilities that you may find impacting if you are caught unaware. In an attempt to raise awareness, Cisco has approved a discussion of this change first mentioned here:

www.cisco.com/c/en/us/support/docs/wireless-mobility/wireless-lan-wlan/82463-wlc-config-best-practice.html

Cisco, in accordance with the new WFA guidelines, will no longer be allowing an SSID configuration with WPA/TKIP only security. If you are currently using an SSID that has WPA/TKIP only security, your configuration will automatically be updated to enable WPA2/AES connectivity as well as WPA/TKIP. You may want to start validation testing now if you are currently supporting legacy devices on a WPA/TKIP only SSID today. The easiest way to ensure you are not caught by this change is to

- o enable WPA2/AES along with WPA/TKIP, and
- o check to make sure your devices still behave as expected.

I have confirmed in the lab that this change will be automatic:

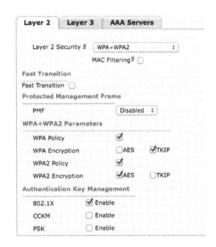

WPA-TKIP only SSID configuration, Pre-8.0

Same SSID with WPA2/ AES enabled post-update

To summarize the variety of allowed and disallowed potential configuration options you have available and if they will be supported in WLC 8.0:

- WPA1-TKIP (Disallowed due to eliminating TKIP)
- WPA1-AES (Allowed by Extension Policy)
- WPA1-TKIP/AES (Disallowed since not used in conjunction with WPA2-AES)
- WPA2-TKIP (Disallowed due to eliminating TKIP)
- WPA2-AES (Certified and allowed)
- WPA2-TKIP/AES (Disallowed due to WPA2-TKIP)
- WPA1-TKIP + WPA2-TKIP (Disallowed—no AES support)
- WPA1-TKIP + WPA2-AES (Certified and allowed)
- WPA1-TKIP + WPA2-TKIP/AES (Disallowed due to WPA2-TKIP)
- WPA1-AES + WPA2-TKIP (Disallowed due to WPA2-TKIP)
- WPA1-AES + WPA2-AES (Allowed by Extension Policy)
- WPA1-AES + WPA2-TKIP/AES (Disallowed due to WPA2-TKIP)
- WPA1-TKIP/AES + WPA2-TKIP (Disallowed due to WPA2-TKIP)
- WPA1-TKIP/AES + WPA2-AES (Allowed by Extension Policy)
- WPA1-TKIP/AES + WPA2-TKIP/AES (Disallowed due to WPA2-TKIP)

Other SSIDs and security configurations are not impacted, including Open SSIDs, any SSID that currently has AES enabled, and WEP SSIDs.

Due to user feedback, Cisco and the WFA finally settled on making the above restrictions in the GUI only.

- If you still have a business need for a WPA/TKIP SSID, you can configure it from the CLI.
- If you were building an SSID on a Cisco WLC with an ID of 6, you would use the following commands for example:

  config wlan create 6 TKIP-ONLY
  config wlan security wpa wpa2 disable 6
  config wlan security wpa wpa1 enable 6
  config wlan security wpa wpa1 ciphers tkip enable 6

Using the show commands, you can validate that this configuration took at the CLI:

show wlan 6

- Wi-Fi Protected Access (WPA/WPA2)   Enabled
- WPA (SSN IE)   Enabled
- TKIP Cipher   Enabled
- AES Cipher   Disabled
- WPA2 (RSN IE)   Disabled

Chapter 6 Summary

In this chapter, you studied encryption and its uses in 802.11 networks. You began by learning or reviewing definitions of several key terms related to encryption, and then explored the various encryption solutions in 802.11. First, it is enforced that WEP is not a suitable solution for use of RC4 or for any modern network. Then you learned that TKIP enhanced the RC4 implementation so that the weaknesses of WEP were overcome. However, you learned that the IEEE no longer recommends the use of TKIP despite its enhancements over WEP, and that it is only included in the standard in a deprecated manner. All new wireless networks should be implemented with CCMP (WPA2). We highlighted that implementing 802.11n or later equipment with TKIP (if the configuration interfaces even allowed it) would result in only basic 802.11a/g data rates. The blog post that ended the chapter showed just how much flux still exists in real implementations, with Cisco only recently disallowing TKIP-only networks, much less CCMP-only, as a requirement. In the next few years, we will see the transition complete.

Facts to Remember

Be sure to remember the following facts as you prepare for the CWSP certification, and be sure that you can explain the details related to them:

- Remember the terms defined in this chapter, including encryption, encryption algorithm, hash function/algorithm, cipher suite, stream cipher, block cipher, and others that were highlighted.
- Symmetric encryption uses the same key to both encrypt and decrypt data.
- Asymmetric encryption uses one key to encrypt and another key to decrypt.
- Stream ciphers work by passing a bit stream through the process and encoding or encrypting one bit at a time.
- Block ciphers work on blocks (several bits) of data at a time.
- RC4 is a stream cipher and AES is a block cipher.

- When dealing with basic 802.11 frame encryption, the upper layer payload (Layers 3-7) is encrypted, but not the MAC and PHY bits.
- Pre-RSNA security is WEP security.
- RSNA security is TKIP or CCMP; however, TKIP is now deprecated.

Chapter 6: Review Questions

1. Which two encryption algorithms are commonly used with 802.11 standards?
    a. AES and 3DES
    b. AES and RC4
    c. RC4 and 3DES
    d. RC5 and AES

2. A procedure that takes an arbitrary block of data and returns a fixed-size bit string is _____?
    a. Hashing algorithm
    b. Cipher suite
    c. Encryption algorithm
    d. Keying suite

3. Two valid dynamic key implementations related to secure 802.11 networks are:
    a. RC5 and TKIP
    b. 3DES and CCMP
    c. TKIP and CCMP
    d. RC4 and CCMP

4. You are using a public Wi-Fi hotspot and are accessing a web site using HTTPS. Your encryption is _____?
    a. Unequal
    b. Deprecated
    c. Symmetric
    d. Asymmetric

5. Which of the following is a valid statement comparing asymmetric encryption to symmetric encryption?
    a. Symmetric is more processor intensive.
    b. Asymmetric is more processor intensive.
    c. Symmetric is better.
    d. Asymmetric is better.

6. In 802.11 networks, where in the OSI model are standardized encryption methods applied?
    a. Layers 1 and 2
    b. Layer 1
    c. Layer 2
    d. It depends on the encryption type

7. CCMP /AES uses what size block to be encrypted?
    a. 40-bit
    b. 128-bit
    c. 256-bit
    d. A variable size bit that changes with packet sizes

8. As implemented in WEP, what specific attack was the ICV vulnerable TO?
    a. Bit-blasting
    b. RF DOS
    c. MTM
    d. Bit-flipping

9. Layer 1 is made up of two sublayers. What are they?
    a. PLCP and LLDP
    b. PMD and PLCP
    c. LDP and PMD
    d. PPTP and PMD

10. With centralized mode of encryption in use on 802.11 networks, encryption protects data from _____ to _____.
    a. Client to access point
    b. Access point to core
    c. Client to Internet
    d. Client to core

11. Which method uses public and private encryption keys?
    a. Public/Private
    b. Asymmetric
    c. Symmetric
    d. Reflexive

12. The weak IV attacks used against WEP were based on faulty implementation of what?
    a. RC4
    b. AES
    c. TKIP
    d. CCMP

13. What sort of attack would be used to recover WEP or WPA keys from the registry of the Windows operating system?
    a. Key probe attack
    b. Stored value attack
    c. Storage attack
    d. Bit-flip attack

14. Michael was a _____ associated with which encryption type?
    a. Message Integrity Check, WEP
    b. Error Correction Protocol, WPA
    c. Message Integrity Check, WPA
    d. Error Correction Protocol, CCMP

15. What makes up the core of pre-RSNA security in 802.11 networks?
    a. TKIP
    b. RC4
    c. AES
    d. WEP

16. Which following is a symmetric key cipher where plaintext bits are XOR'd with a pseudorandom bit stream?
    a. Stream cipher
    b. Stone cipher
    c. Block cipher
    d. Serial cipher

17. Which of the following attacks is not specific to WEP?
    a. Weak IV attack
    b. Storage attack
    c. Re-injection attack
    d. Layer 2 DoS attack

18. AES processing within CCMP uses a _____ key and a _____ block size.
    a. 64-bit, 256 bit
    b. 64-bit, 128-bit
    c. 128-bit, 128-bit
    d. 128-bit, 256-bit

19. You are examining a frame decode on a wireless network that uses TKIP but not CCMP. Which one of these is not a valid IE option for this decode?
    a. WPA information
    b. WPA IE (221)
    c. RSN IE
    d. Manufacturer-specific information

20. Which encryption type makes use of a separate processing chip for ciphering?
    a. Dynamic WEP
    b. Dynamic TKIP
    c. TKIP
    d. CCMP

21. One encryption type used in 802.11 wireless networks features a 60-second period where all STAs must suspend reception under certain conditions. Which is it?
    a. RSN
    b. TKIP
    c. CCMP
    d. Dynamic WEP

22. What is the performance penalty to using TKIP in 802.11n and 802.11ac networks?
    a. Only the lowest MCS values can be used.
    b. WEP must also be supported.
    c. The networks are effectively reduced to 11a/g rates.
    d. To go to CCMP, all access points must be replaced.

23. Which of the following has the curious distinction of being deprecated, but still allowed, under RSNA security?
    a. TKIP
    b. Dynamic WEP
    c. WEP2
    d. VPN

24. Which attack method tries to guess every possible key to crack the encryption in use?
    a. Dictionary attack
    b. Stream cipher attack
    c. Brute-force attack
    d. Key barrage attack

25. Select the proper pairing of encryption algorithm and encryption type.
    a. AES, WEP
    b. RC4, CCMP
    c. RC4, RSN
    d. AES, CCMP

Chapter 6: Review Answers

1. **B** is correct. AES and RC4 are common encryption algorithms used with today's 802.11 secure networks.

2. **A** is correct. This is the definition of a hashing algorithm.

3. **C** is correct. TKIP and CCMP are dynamic key mechanisms—do not confuse them with encryption algorithms.

4. **C** is correct. HTTPS uses asymmetric encryption.

5. **B** is correct. Asymmetric encryption is more processor-intensive than symmetric encryption.

6. **C** is correct. 802.11 encryption takes place at Layer 2.

7. **B** is correct. CCMP/AES uses a 128-bit block cipher.

8. **D** is correct. Bit-flipping took advantage of the weak WEP ICV.

9. **B** is correct. Layer 1 is made up of PLCP and PMD sublayers.

10. **D** is correct. Client to core encryption is the hallmark of centralized WLAN encryption.

11. **B** is correct. Asymmetric encryption uses public and private keys.

12. **A** is correct. RC4 itself was not the problem with WEP, it was the way it was implemented.

13. **C** is correct. Storage attacks are used to find WEP keys in Windows' registries.

14. **C** is correct. Michael is the oddly named Message Integrity Check used in WPA.

15. **D** is correct. WEP is the main element of pre-RSNA security.

16. **A** is correct. This describes the stream cipher process.

17. **D** is correct. Layer 2 DoS attacks are not specific to WEP environments.

18. **C** is correct. AES uses 128-bit block, and 128-bit key.

19. **C** is correct. Without CCMP, you cannot have an RSN IE.

20. **D** is correct. CCMP uses a separate processing chip due to its computational overhead, which is why older hardware cannot run CCMP.

21. **B** is correct. TKIP features the mandatory 60-second quiet period when two MIC failures within 60 seconds are detected.

22. **C** is correct. Without CCMP, the data rates of 11n and 11ac WLANs are seriously constrained.

23. **A** is correct. TKIP is deprecated, but not forbidden.

24. **C** is correct. The brute-force attack tries every possible key combination.

25. **D** is correct. AES and CCMP are the only legitimate pairing shown.

Chapter 7:

Security Design Scenarios

Objectives

3.5   Recognize and understand the common uses of VPNs in wireless networks, including remote APs, VPN client access, WLAN controllers, and cloud architectures.

3.8   Explain the role, importance, and limiting factors of VLANs and network segmentation in an 802.11 WLAN infrastructure.

3.10 Explain the purpose, methodology, features, and configuration of guest access networks and BYOD support, including segmentation, guest management, captive portal authentication, and device management.

3.6   Describe, demonstrate, and configure centrally managed client-side security applications, including VPN client software and policies, personal firewall software, mobile device management (MDM), and wireless client utility software.

With the first six chapters securely under your belt, you are ready to begin exploring a few specific security design scenarios. In this chapter, you will learn about virtual private networks and their practical use with 802.11 wireless connections. You will also explore various remote client access scenarios and the features provided by captive portals, segmentation, Mobile Device Management, and more. First, the basics of virtual private networks are explained.

Virtual Private Networking Basics

A virtual private network (VPN) is used to provide the capability to create private network communications over a public network infrastructure such as the Internet. VPN technology is used in many different networking scenarios, including 802.11 wireless networking. In fact, VPN is one of the most pervasive security mechanisms in use across LAN, WLAN, and WAN alike. VPNs are Internet Protocol (IP) based, so they commonly operate at Network layer (Layer 3) of the OSI model. However, some VPN protocols operate at other layers or even over multiple layers. VPN technology can consist of different configurations, such as client-to-server or site-to-site (gateway-gateway), and include various protocols such as:

- Point-to-point tunneling protocol (PPTP)
- Layer 2 tunneling protocol (L2TP) with Internet Protocol Security (IPSec)—L2TP/IPSec
- Internet Protocol Security (IPSec)
- Transport Layer Security (TLS), Secure Sockets Layer (SSL)—SSL/TLS
- Secure Shell (SSH)
- Datagram Transport Layer Security (DTLS)

VPN technology was very common in enterprise network deployments prior to the ratification of the .11i amendment to the 802.11 standard, and is still a very common remote access security solution. Due to advancements in WLAN security protocols and Wi-Fi Alliance (WPA and WPA2) certifications, Data Link layer (Layer 2) security solutions have become stronger, to the point where VPN technology is not as widely used within enterprise LANs for client access as it once was. However, VPN still remains a powerful security solution for remote access in both wired and wireless networking, and does see limited use within the borders of WLAN environments where specific security needs are in play.

VPNs consist of two parts, a tunneling component and an encryption component. A standalone VPN tunnel does not necessarily provide data encryption in and of itself, and VPN tunnels are created across Internet Protocol (IP) networks.

In a very basic sense, VPNs use encapsulation methods where one IP frame is encapsulated within a second IP frame. The encryption of VPNs is performed as a separate, stand-alone function in many implementations.

A VPN consists of endpoints, which are the devices that create the tunneled architecture. VPN endpoints can consist of various infrastructure devices including:

- Computers
- Layer 3 routers
- Wireless LAN controllers
- Wireless APs
- Dedicated servers
- VPN concentrators
- Firewalls
- Network Management System (NMS) platforms

Figure 7-1: Client VPN Example

The most common uses of VPNs in the WLAN space are for remote APs, remote client access to network resources across the Internet, proprietary bridging, and vendor-defined proprietary communications between WLAN devices, such as WLAN controllers or APs. Knowing these use cases is important for CWSPs.

Common VPN Protocols

Two common types of VPN protocols are:

- Point-to-Point Tunneling Protocol (PPTP)
- Layer 2 Tunneling Protocol (L2TP)

PPTP was developed by a vendor consortium that included Microsoft. PPTP

- was very popular because of its ease of configuration
- has been included in all Microsoft Windows operating systems starting with Windows 95
- uses Microsoft Point-to-Point Encryption (MPPE-128) protocol for encryption, and
- operates at Layer 2 and uses generic routing encapsulation (GRE) tunneling to encapsulate point-to-point protocol (PPP) packets. (You will find GRE tunnels are fairly common in a number of wired and wireless applications in modern networking environments.)

The PPTP VPN process provides both tunneling and encryption capabilities for the user's data. Vulnerabilities have been proven to exist; however, in the implementation MSCHAP authentication is used along with MPPE encryption. Although PPTP is easy to configure and did provide necessary security at its initial implementation, the VPN protocol lost much ground after the introduction of Layer 2 tunneling protocol (L2TP) and the discovery of several vulnerabilities.

It is important to note that with respect to wireless networking, the authentication process of PPTP has been cracked and should not be used with a wireless network. This statement applies when MS-CHAPv2 is used for the user authentication. If the authentication process (wireless frames) were captured using a wireless protocol analyzer and dictionary attack software, the user credentials can be discovered. This allows the intruder that captured the necessary frames the capability to logon to the network with stolen credentials. Recall from past chapters that a dictionary attack is performed by software that challenges the encrypted password (or pre-shared key, or whatever is being targeted) against common words or phrases in a text file that is the dictionary in this scenario. This is very similar to the process that is used to crack Cisco Systems LEAP. Therefore, using PPTP VPN on a wireless network with MS-CHAPv2 (or MS-CHAPv1) should be avoided.

By contrast, L2TP is the combination of two different tunneling protocols:

- Cisco's Layer 2 Forwarding (Layer 2F), and
- Microsoft's Point-to-Point Tunneling Protocol (PPTP).

L2TP defines the tunneling process, which requires some level of encryption in order to function. With L2TP, a popular choice of encryption is Internet Protocol Security (IPSec), which provides authentication and encryption for each individual IP packet in a data stream. Since it was published in 1999 as a proposed standard, and because it is more secure than PPTP, L2TP has gained much popularity and is a recommended replacement for PPTP. As such, many systems no longer provide the option to use PPTP and only support L2TP. L2TP/IPSec is a very common VPN solution in use today. You should note that L2TP should always be used instead of PPTP.

IPSec is a VPN protocol designed to authenticate and encrypt packets using the Layer 3 Internet Protocol. IPSec includes two possible implementations:

- **Authenticated Header (AH)**—Provides only authentication.
- **Encapsulation Security Payload (ESP)**—Provides encryption for the data payload in addition to authentication and integrity verification.

Furthermore, ESP operates in two modes:

- **Transport mode**—This mode with ESP would be appropriate for client-server or site-to-site communications. This excludes remote WLAN endpoint connectivity, where only tunneled mode should be used with ESP. With transport mode, endpoint devices encrypt/decrypt the data between each endpoint.

- **Tunneled mode**—This mode is able to communicate from one private IP address directly to another private IP address because the devices build a virtual tunnel. Again, remote WLAN endpoints should only use tunneled mode.

An additional VPN protocol that is gaining popularity in Microsoft environments is Secure Socket Tunneling Protocol (SSTP). SSTP implements HTTPS on TCP port 443 in order to allow passage through common firewall configurations. Interestingly, EAP-TLS is a common authentication protocol used with this VPN solution because it allows the passing of PPP traffic over the connection. SSTP is supported on all currently supported Microsoft operating systems (as of 2015), starting from Vista and Windows Server 2008 and going forward.

Proprietary VPN protocols may also be used to secure communications between wireless bridge links or possibly infrastructure devices, such as WLAN controllers. This is one area where WLAN vendors very much do their own thing, and why you cannot typically uses Vendor A's wireless controllers with Vendor B's in the same WLAN.

Exam Moment: When IPSec is used for VPN establishment, ISAKMP packets can be seen using a protocol analyzer. While the packets are encrypted, it can be determined that IPSec is in use even though you cannot see into the encrypted packets.

VPN Functionality

A client-server VPN solution consists of three components:

- Client side endpoint
- Network infrastructure (public or private)
- Server side endpoint

As mentioned earlier, the client side and server side are known as VPN endpoints. The infrastructure in many cases is an unsecured public access network such as the Internet, although some may use dedicated private leased lines from telecomm providers. The client side endpoint typically consists of software on a PC, tablet, or smartphone, which allows it to be configured for the VPN connection. This software is available at a nominal cost from a variety of manufacturers, if it is not already built into the device operating system. Newer Microsoft Windows and Apple operating systems include VPN client software for both PPTP and L2TP. The VPN can terminate either at an AP or across the Internet to a VPN endpoint on the corporate network set up for terminating remote connections.

Typically, there are three steps in creating a VPN after the basic configurations have been accomplished:

1. Perform the required authentication.
2. Build the virtual tunnel.
3. Encrypt the data.

VPN networks encapsulate one IP packet into another IP packet. The packet that has been encapsulated contains the data payload. This action prevents unauthorized users from being able to see any data that is sent over the secure tunnel.

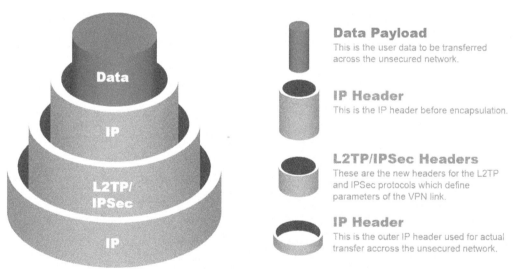

Data Payload
This is the user data to be transferred across the unsecured network.

IP Header
This is the IP header before encapsulation.

L2TP/IPSec Headers
These are the new headers for the L2TP and IPSec protocols which define parameters of the VPN link.

IP Header
This is the outer IP header used for actual transfer accross the unsecured network.

Figure 7-2: IPSec Tunnel Mode Illustrated

Common Wireless Uses

Remote networking has become very common as wireless access has proliferated to the home and branch office networks. Some manufacturers have developed dedicated remote APs that automatically build a tunnel to a remote WLAN controller or VPN concentrator. After establishing a secure tunnel, the AP receives a WLAN policy, which it then broadcasts locally for wireless access. This approach securely tunnels remote users to corporate networks for access to network resources. It may also be used to protect users from unknowingly compromising their corporate resources on their computer.

Three common uses of wireless VPNs that CWSPS must know include:

- Remote APs
- Wireless bridging
- Remote client connectivity

Remote APs allow a user to connect a wireless AP to remote Local Area Network with an active Internet connection. The remote AP uses the Internet to create a secure connection to the organization's corporate network. This in turn provides secured wireless access from the remote location to the corporate network. This is a common scenario for remote offices or home office users and for those that work "on the road," such as sales or field service personnel.

A wireless bridge connects two or more local area networks (LANs) together, and is a common tool for the wireless professional. Wireless bridges can provide cost savings for the organization because it does not require a physical infrastructure to be installed between the end sites, and there are no recurring monthly fees as with leased lines. Since many wireless bridging technologies use proprietary protocols and do not provide client connectivity, they often use proprietary VPN protocols for security. Securing a bridge is critical as the connection can span for long distances and the signal is not contained within a physical space. As with WLANs, wireless bridges use the unbounded medium of RF in free space.

Similar to the remote AP scenario described above, individual clients connecting to unsecured networks often use VPN technologies to secure their data traffic. This type of technology employs VPN software (instead of hardware, as with remote APs) that runs on the client computer. The software establishes an encrypted tunnel with a remote VPN terminator for access to network resources or for protection from local threats associated with using open public wireless networks.

Let's look at each VPN use case in more detail.

Remote AP

Remote APs provide secure access to travelling and home users by linking organizationally provided APs back to the corporate network. One of the great benefits of remote AP technology is that administrators maintain control of remote APs and can provision them in a way that reliably maintains the corporate security policies. Similarly, the users' connectivity experience does not have to change when they are at home, on the road, or at the office. If configured for it, they connect to the same WLAN profiles (does not require end-user control), they retain mobility and access to corporate resources, which is only limited by the organizational network to which they are connected—and not by their local infrastructure.

A remote AP is very easy to use. Typically, these devices are configured by the wireless network administrators of the organization. The remote user plugs the AP into an available Ethernet port on the network to which they wish to connect. This could be a home office, hotel conference room, company branch office, or anyplace with an active Internet connection where the user wishes to connect from.

Once the AP is connected locally, it uses the Internet to create a secure VPN tunnel from the remote location to the corporate office. The process is very similar to the client-server VPN model in which a client device uses VPN software to connect to the corporate office. The difference is that the remote AP has been configured to handle everything behind the scenes.

Remote Client Access

Remote client access is the most common use of a wireless network client-server VPN solution. With the continued growth of open public access wireless hotspot networks (free access in many cases), this type of solution is used every day by many people who have been educated on the importance of network security. Remote client VPN solutions:

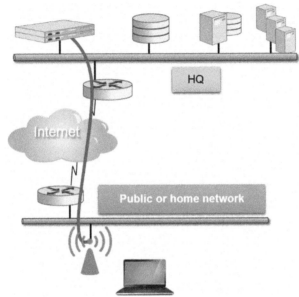

Figure 7-3: Remote AP Illustrated

- provide adequate security when connected to an open access public hotspot, and
- allow for communications between a remote wireless client and a corporate network across the Internet.

As wireless hotspots have become more common and wireless security vulnerabilities have received greater publicity, VPN implementations for remote clients have become increasingly popular. Client VPN technologies that are maintained along with client endpoint software or NAC solutions can offer a strong amount of protection for remote users connecting to open networks. The primary issue with this type of

VPN is that it can only be applied after the user has associated to the open network. This often leaves users open to other vulnerabilities, such as hijacking or man-in-the-middle (MITM) attacks.

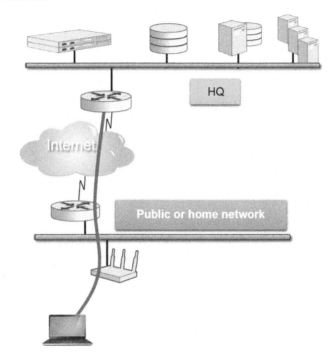

Figure 7-4: Remote Client Access Illustrated

It is not uncommon for less savvy users to assume that a VPN connection solves every potential security problem, but this is just not true. VPN by itself is only a secure connection, and not a complete security environment. Basic security policies and solutions should be enforced for users operating from unsecured wireless networks. These include personal firewalls, up-to-date antivirus software, endpoint software/agents, and network access control (NAC) solutions.

The network security policy should define the requirements for remote client connectivity. Several considerations must be made here. First, enterprises should define the operating system rights/permissions of the end-users. Are they capable of making configuration changes to client utilities? Are they allowed access on open wireless networks? Restricting the privileges of the wireless client is not always popular from the user satisfaction standpoint, but best practices for security demand tight control of corporate assets.

For the best security, client endpoint agents should be used to manage the wireless network to which a client has access, as well as to track usage and monitor network behavior and threats. Endpoint agent software provides powerful, unique views from the client perspective. At the same time, distributing and up-keeping agents can be challenging. If you desire to work with a VPN server that is free and works on Kali Linux, install and configure Openswan. A tutorial on the installation and configuration options is available here:

https://github.com/xelerance/Openswan/wiki

Tunneling and Split Tunneling

VPNs are examples of secure tunneling. As we just learned, tunneling is the process of encapsulating one IP packet within another IP packet.

- The original packet becomes the payload of the second packet.
- The source and destination IP addresses of the second packet typically point to the virtual IP address of the VPN client software (source) and the IP address of the VPN end point (destination).

Secure tunneling encrypts the original packet and obfuscates the original source and destination IP addresses. The VPN endpoint decapsulates (sometimes "de-encapsulates" is used in conversation) the tunneled packet onto the trusted network. This restores the original packet with its original source and destination addresses intact. This process works very well and is widely accepted and supported as a network security solution.

There are many different tunneling protocols available. Two common examples that we have already touched on are PPTP and L2TP. When configuring a VPN tunnel both endpoints must

- understand the specific mechanism used for that tunnel, and

- agree on the configuration which includes various settings such as encryption type and any other required parameters.

Data that is transferred between the endpoints and over the tunnel is typically sent using a protocol such as user datagram protocol (UDP), for example. However, other protocols may be employed and special protocols are used to build and teardown the tunnel.

Split tunnels were designed to reduce the processing overhead incurred by VPN usage, and are very empowering in branch-office and remote client VPN situations. In a split tunnel scenario, traffic sent to and from the private network is protected by VPN, but all other traffic, including local LAN activity and web-based activities, are not encapsulated within secure tunnels. The positive aspects of split tunneling include keeping traffic that does not "need" to be in the tunnel out of it, but there are trade-offs. For example, split-tunneling can result in a vulnerability whereby a malicious intruder in the public WLAN space may be able to

- piggyback the secure connection through the unsecured local connection
- inject a Trojan horse, malware, root kit, backdoor, or virus into the corporate environment, and
- allow access to the wireless client's local resources.

For this reason, CWNP's position is that only full-tunnel VPNs, which send all TCP/IP traffic through the VPN tunnel, should be allowed by remote access endpoints.

Public Access Networks

Public access wireless networks are commonly known has wireless hotspots and are increasingly available in many different locations and business types. This type of wireless network can be found at places including, but not limited to:

- Hotels
- Airports
- Coffee shops
- Restaurants
- Retail chain stores

- Public libraries
- Cruise ships
- Transportation—automobiles, airplanes, trains and other public transportation methods
- Sporting venues

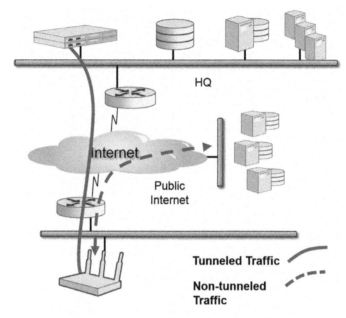

Figure 7-5: Split Tunneling Illustrated

In some cases, these networks are available for free while others are fee based. Those that are offered at no cost are typically provided as a draw to bring customers into the business as a value added service. Those that charge a fee use guest Wi-Fi for a revenue stream.

Depending on how the public access WLAN was implemented, there could certainly be security risks for the user. You will learn about these risks next. Proper configurations including client-to-client blocking features should be enabled to help lessen the chances of certain types of wireless intrusion techniques that may be used. Others may block protocols or ports to help prevent spamming and other Internet related attacks. In some cases, content filtering may be used to control access. Keep in mind that practices such as these may be controversial since the user is limited in what they can do while connected. This is yet another example of the frequent tension between security and ease of use which is a fact of life for CWSPs.

Public Access Risks

Several common security considerations arise when talking about public access networks. For starters, these popular networks typically provide no authentication or encryption, so users are vulnerable to a number of textbook attacks right away.

Public networks are attractive for intruders that want to gather information, and in some cases can yield information that can be used for financial gain or even identity theft. In many cases the client device that is connected to the unsecured network is not properly secured and may have the following vulnerabilities:

- outdated or no anti-virus software
- improperly configured or disabled firewalls
- weak or missing passwords
- unsecured file shares
- missing operating system updates or service packs, and/or
- saved password and account files in plaintext.

The service provider also has a number of concerns to address, such as limiting their own liability with a use/abuse policy, restricting network access in accordance with usage guidelines, and maintaining a captive portal for user pass-through.

Educating and informing end users of potential security risks is also beneficial. Many users on public wireless networks do not fully understand the risks and potential threats associated with open public networks.

The providing host of public Wi-Fi needs to be aware of the pros and cons that come with making WLAN available to customers and visitors. If the host is a coffee shop or small restaurant that provides free wireless access to its patrons as a business draw, they may not be knowledgeable enough to put much thought into the process beyond simply plugging an AP into an Ethernet port that has access to the Internet.

In these do-it-yourself scenarios, the host may use an inexpensive residential-grade AP or wireless router that lacks enterprise-quality security features like client-to-client blocking or protocol/port blocking features, for example. Others may not want to address risks because they might view security as an impediment to the free hotspot service that is used to attract customers. If you are consulting in this kind of situation, you should encourage the business to implement a solution that provides a balance of security and usability to both their organization and the customers.

Other host networks, especially those that are fee based, tend to use more elaborate enterprise-grade wireless equipment and often follow a specific policy that was written for this type of wireless network. This network may be handled by IT resources within the corporation, or it could be outsourced to a third-party service provider.

Public access users should follow best practices when connecting to a public host network. Some of the threats mentioned earlier can be mitigated if proper client-side security features are installed, enabled, and configured. These client-side security settings include:

- anti-virus software installed and up-to-date
- firewall enabled and correctly configured
- operating system updates installed and configured; this is important for all operating systems as none are immune to attack
- no open or unsecured file system shares
- use of strong login credentials, and
- use of virtual private networking.

Taking these steps into consideration helps to lessen potential security threats, and should provide the user with a secure connection on the host wireless network. Unfortunately, many users do not give proper attention to their own devices, and CWSPs often have to educate on the topic.

Captive Portals

Captive portals (sometime referred to as captive web portals, or abbreviated as CP) can serve many different functions depending upon the network provider's goals. To start, they are often used to usher users through an acceptable use agreement, which offloads some amount of legal liability to the service provider by clearly spelling out the terms and conditions associated with using their network.

Other implementations may be provided as for-profit services, in which the ISP wants to collect money in exchange for network access. For those network hosts who want to restrict network access to paying customers only, a captive portal can be used for authentication or to provide verification of services, such as with a receipt or customer number.

A captive portal works by redirecting a user to an authentication source of some type before they are allowed wireless network access. This authentication source, in the form of a web page, requires a user to "authenticate" in some way and may require the following:

- entering user credentials (username and password)
- inputting payment information, and/or
- agreeing to terms and conditions.

When one or more of these methods is complete, a wireless device is then able to access the network and use whatever resources they have permissions for. Most public access wireless networks have some type of captive portal enabled. A captive portal may help to protect both the provider (host) and the user of the wireless network. Many organizations use captive portals minimally to have the user agree to the wireless network terms and conditions. Most enterprise-grade wireless APs, including cloud-based APs and WLAN controllers, have built-in captive portal capabilities that are fairly straightforward to implement.

Captive portals have their place, but can complicate the user experience. From the client perspective, some mobile devices, such as smartphones or tablets, may experience problems while trying to connect to a network with a captive portal enabled. This could happen because of the mobile operating system in use, or other application related issues. For example, some devices have custom web browsers installed on them and such browsers may not function properly when connecting to a captive portal.

Most captive portals work such that when the user connects to the WLAN, DNS requests are intercepted so that no matter what URL the user attempts to access, they are directed to the captive portal web page. Additional interception methods may also be utilized to capture direct IP connection attempts.

Captive Portal Configuration

Captive portal configuration options allow administrators to specify all the specific parameters they would like to apply to their network. These parameters may include VLAN segmentation, requiring an acceptable use agreement along with bandwidth and time limitations for users. In many captive portal implementations, system configuration is a fairly intuitive process. The precise steps to create a captive portal varies based on the specific infrastructure device or software used. Here are some common basic steps:

1. Create a WLAN profile; this is commonly the guest wireless profile.
2. Do not enable any security features; this should be 802.11 Open System authentication.
3. Assign the profile to the captive portal functionality.

Once a user connects to the captive portal enabled SSID, they need to perform additional steps in order to gain access to wireless network resources. This restriction includes opening a web browser and attempting to access any web page. When web access is attempted, the user

- is "captured" or redirected to the specific web page that is configured for the wireless network, and
- must meet any requirements specified, such as accepting terms and conditions or entering provided credentials.

After the requirements are validated, and the user is able to perform any task or access any resources for which the user has been granted access.

Although not as common, in some cases Data Link layer security such as WPA/WPA2-Personal or WPA/WPA2-Enterprise may be used in conjunction with captive portal implementations. This configuration provides some level of security (through encryption) for users that have connected to the captive portal network.

It is very important for those that use wireless networks with captive portals to be properly educated about the potential security concerns regarding their use. In the setup steps above, it was stated that the WLAN profile used is often configured for Open System authentication. This setup results in all data being sent and received to the client device in clear text unless other security measures, such as VPN or other secure protocols, are used.

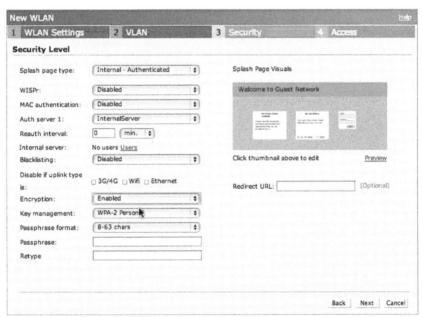

Figure 7-6: Captive Portal Configuration in Aruba Instant

If the captive portal page required any kind of authentication such as a personal identification number (PIN) or other credentials that were supplied by the host, it may give the user a false sense of security because they were required to enter credentials of some sort and therefore fall under the impression that the wireless transmissions are secure. It is important that the terms of service for the captive portal spell out what security is or is not provided.

Some wireless infrastructure device manufacturers provide built-in services for the management of billing plans (just one example of how WLAN systems are now going beyond providing simple access). Other implementations use dedicated gateway appliances for this function.

Network Segmentation

Segmentation is a pervasive networking technique that is used to limit the resources to which a device has access, and is not limited to just the WLAN domain. Segmentation commonly includes the use of virtual local area networks, (VLANs), access control lists (ACLs), and firewalls to filter and funnel users to specific resources. For a guest network, the target resource to be accessed is usually the Internet, and no "internal" network resources. By isolating guest clients to the Internet, internet service providers (ISPs) prevent guest users from accessing and/or exploiting corporate network resources, which are in place only for corporate users.

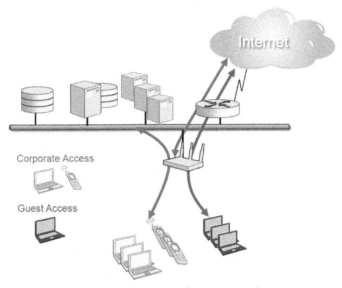

Figure 7-7: Network Segmentation

Most current network infrastructure devices have the capability to securely segment different types of network traffic. These infrastructure building blocks include devices that are used with wireless networking, including APs and WLAN controllers. If configured correctly, the corporate network traffic remains completely separate for the guest network traffic. Segmentation of wireless traffic can be accomplished using

- role-based access control methods, or
- WLAN profiles with correct policies and access control.

As you can see in the preceding image (Network Segmentation), a single AP is used to provide secured wireless access to

- the corporate network using the corporate SSID, and
- Internet-only access using a separate guest SSID.

This configuration allows users that are properly authenticated to the corporate segment to access both corporate network resources and to the Internet. Conversely, the guest SSID only allows connected users access to the Internet, and guests are not able to access secured corporate network resources. This is the prevailing model of typical guest access used for the exam, but CWSPs may be called on to be more creative with guest topologies in cases where guest privileges are more nuanced and may actually include specific internal resources.

In many cases, a captive portal is enabled on the guest wireless segment in order to restrict access to the guest SSID to only those that comply with whatever connection parameters are specified in the captive portal web page. Also, the captive portal might be configured to keep corporate users and devices that should be on the secure business WLAN out of the guest topology.

VLANs provide an excellent management technique for wireless LANs. VLANs are supported on most enterprise class APs for the purpose of extending VLAN functionality all the way though network switching out to the mobile client device. 802.1Q VLAN tagging is the only non-proprietary implementation available, so most WLAN devices use it.

While the full criteria for each wireless VLAN deployment is likely to be unique, some standard characteristics exist for most rollouts including:

- Common applications used by all WLAN end users. The wireless network administrator should define:
    - Wired network resources commonly accessed by WLAN users
    - Quality of service (QoS) level required by each application
- Common devices used to access the WLAN. The wireless network administrator should define:
    - Security mechanisms (WEP/WPA, WPA2/802.1x/EAP, VPN, etc.) supported by each device type
    - Wired network resources commonly accessed by wireless LAN device groups
    - QoS level needed by each device group

After specific wireless VLAN deployment criteria have been defined, the deployment strategy must be determined. Two standard deployment strategies are:

1) **Segmentation by user groups**—Segmentation of the WLAN user community and enforcement of specific access-security policies per user group.

For example, three wired and wireless VLANs in an enterprise environment could be created for full-time employees, part-time employees and guest access.

2) **Segmentation by device types**—Segmentation of the WLAN to allow different devices with independent access-security "levels" to access the wireless network.

For example, it is not recommended to allow handheld computers that support only 40/128-bit static-WEP to co-exist with other wireless LAN client devices using 802.1X with dynamic WEP in the same VLAN. In this scenario, devices should be grouped and isolated with different "levels" of access security into separate VLANs.

Implementation criteria such as those listed above are then defined to include:

- Use of policy filters to map wired policies to the wireless side.
- Use of 802.1X to control user access to VLANs using either RADIUS-based VLAN assignment or RADIUS-based SSID access control.
- Use of separate VLANs to implement different Classes of Service (CoS).

Market leader Cisco Systems recommends the following best practices for the wired infrastructure when 802.1Q VLAN tagging is extended to access points and bridges. These best practices are dependent on the features being supported by the wired infrastructure to which the wireless devices are connected.

- Limit broadcast and multicast traffic to the access point and bridge by enabling VLAN filtering and Internet Group Management Protocol (IGMP) snooping on the switch ports. Where 802.1Q trunks are used to extend VLANs to access points, filter to allow only active VLANs in the ESS. Enabling IGMP snooping prevents the switch from flooding all switch ports with Layer 3 multicast traffic.
- Map wireless security policies to the wired infrastructure with ACLs and other relevant mechanisms.
- The access point does not support Virtual Terminal Protocol (VTP) or Generic Attribute Registration Protocol VLAN Registration Protocol (GVRP) protocols for dynamic management of VLANs because the access point acts as a "stub"

node. The wireless LAN administrator must use the wired infrastructure to maintain and manage the wired VLANs.

- Enforce network security policies via Layer 3 ACLs on both the "guest" and management VLANs. The wireless LAN administrator
  - could implement ACLs on the wired infrastructure to force all "guest" VLAN traffic to the Internet gateway, and
  - should restrict user access to the native/default VLAN of the access points and bridges with the use of Layer 3 ACLs and policies on the wired infrastructure.

With wireless VLANs, each SSID is mapped to a default VLAN-ID on the wired side of the access point (or controller). The wireless LAN administrator may wish to impose RADIUS-based VLAN access control using 802.1X or MAC address authentication mechanisms. For example, if the wireless LAN is configured such that all VLANs use 802.1X/EAP and similar encryption mechanisms for wireless LAN user access, then a user can hop from one VLAN to another by simply changing their SSID and successfully authenticating to the access point (using 802.1X/EAP). This may not be preferred if the wireless LAN user is supposed to be confined to a particular VLAN. There are two different ways to implement RADIUS-based VLAN access control features:

1) **RADIUS-based SSID access control**—Upon successful 802.1X/EAP or MAC address authentication, the RADIUS server passes back the allowed SSID list for the wireless LAN user to the access point or bridge. If the client device used an SSID on the allowed SSID list, then it is allowed to associate to the wireless LAN. Otherwise, the user is disassociated from the access point or bridge.

2) **RADIUS-based VLAN assignment**—Upon successful 802.1X/EAP or MAC address authentication, the RADIUS server assigns the user to a predetermined VLAN-ID on the wired side. The SSID used for wireless LAN access does not matter because the user is always assigned to this predetermined VLAN-ID.

In order to have RADIUS return the appropriate attributes to the access point, the RADIUS server must implement the AP vendor's Vendor Specific Attributes (VSA) that define the allowed SSIDs or static VLAN assignment. As you can see from the explanation above, wireless VLAN functionality gives the access point somewhat similar functions to wireless middleware (EWGs) while maintaining infrastructure security at the network edge (the AP). The use of Vendor Specific Attributes can be very powerful when complex WLAN security requirements are in play.

Bring Your Own Device (BYOD)

The concept of BYOD continues to grow at a fast pace, and is being adopted in more organizations every day. When a user works for an organization that allows BYOD, there are a number of specific security concerns that must be dealt with. The core premise of BYOD is that a user can access the corporate wireless network in addition to home and other public access networks from the same device that is the personal property of the employee. Personally owned devices generally have access to both corporate and personal apps and data. Segmentation is often used to separate BYOD client devices (and certainly guest users) from the corporate users.

Security policy is very important when it comes to BYOD due the potential security threats that come with this usage paradigm. All of the previously-mentioned concerns associated with other types of client devices and public access networks exist in BYOD situations, along with more risks that are specific to BYOD's unique framework.

Concepts such as *data containers* should be considered. Tools are available that allow network administrators to logically separate corporate data from personal data on the same device (containerization) according to well-defined security policy. Containerization helps to ensure the integrity of the corporate data as it lives on personal BYOD devices. Tools also allow for remote access and control features such as remote lock, unlock, and remote wipe features to help ensure the integrity or verifiable destruction of the data in the event a device is lost or stolen.

BYOD in many cases foster personal satisfaction and potentially increase user productivity because the users are allowed to use their own devices. This concept provides a certain comfort level because BYOD users are already familiar with the hardware now being used with corporate apps. As a bonus to the users, they are able to access their own personal data and apps from their own devices when allowed as specified in corporate security policy.

Onboarding is an important additional process related to BYOD and a topic that CWSPs must firmly grasp. Onboarding allows devices to join the network through either pre-registration or self-registration.

- With **pre-registration**, the devices are added by an administrator before the users can connect.
- With **self-registration**, the user goes through a process which allows them to gain access to the network in a secure manner. Self-registration is often done via a web form.

Mobile Device Management (MDM)

MDM solutions are used to manage devices that are connected to a corporate wireless network. Because of the increase in popularity of mobile devices in general, MDM solutions are also becoming more common.

MDM is a great example of an industry unto itself that has grown alongside the WLAN market. Some manufacturers of enterprise wireless infrastructure devices integrate MDM solutions within their platforms, while others partner with third-party companies that specialize in the technology. Many MDM solutions are available as both on premise and cloud-based Software as a Service (SaaS) solutions. It is important to ensure that the one selected and used meets the needs of the organization, especially when it comes to security.

MDM solutions provide a plethora of BYOD-oriented security strategies and features that help to ensure corporate security policy is followed and maintained. Some of these security features include, but are not limited to:

- Compliance reporting

- Device registration (self-service portal)
- Location-based services
- Password control
- Policy enforcement
- Remote lock, unlock and wipe
- Secure communications (virtual private network)
- Location based services
- Geofencing
- Geolocation
- App management, containerization

Choosing the best MDM solution to use in your environment is an important decision to make. Evaluation of these products and the security features that they provide is something that needs to be closely considered before the purchase and implementation of the solution.

Client Management Strategies

MDM is but one client-side management strategy that can be used to manage both personal and corporate-owned mobile devices. There are other client management solutions available from a variety of companies, offering a range of interesting functionality. Although different solutions may contain common feature sets, it is still important to evaluate various solutions in order to choose the one that is best for the organization's specific needs. MDM may be used in conjunction with other management solutions, such as a WLAN management system (WNMS), in order to provide a complete wireless network management solution.

Client management strategies depend on the type of client devices used on the network, the features and capabilities of the devices, and the corporate security policy that is in place. Like MDM solutions, manufacturers of WLAN infrastructure devices may offer integrated client-side management features. Most management products provided by manufacturers are created to work only with the specific infrastructure devices they make, but are able to manage a variety of different client devices. Others provide a more vendor-neutral approach that work with any manufacturers infrastructure devices. As WLAN systems get more feature rich, multi-vendor WLAN management strategies become scarcer on the market.

Depending on the organization and the user population, different strategies can be used when it comes to managing connected devices. In some circumstances the user may have complete access and full control over the wireless device, in which case they are responsible for maintaining proper security control. In other situations, the user has little or no administrative control and the network manager is responsible for ensuring proper posture and security compliance.

Figure 7-8: Client Management Strategies in Secure WLANs

How corporate security policy is written and what the security goals of the organization are a major influence on the management of client devices. This includes what hardware, applications, and behaviors are either permitted or disallowed. Options such as remote access, the use of removable devices, installation or removal of applications and operating system permissions are a few examples that varies according to corporate security policy.

⬛ **From the Blogs**

Thoughts on Eliminating VLANs at the Access-Layer Edge

URL: transmitfailure.blogspot.com/2014/07/thoughts-on-eliminating-vlans-at-access.html
Author: Jake Snyder
Blog: Transmit Failure—transmitfailure.blogspot.com

There's a lot of talk in the industry about getting away from VLAN segmentation and relying on stateful firewalls at our access-layer edge to govern control over what users can access. This is a great idea; it solves issues with IPv6 and it simplifies network design. But there are some significant challenges that make it a no-go for today's enterprise networks. Most vendors are saying that their "stateful" firewalls in the AP and edge switches solve those challenges. But I find the current generation of these solutions inadequate to solve this issue in enterprise networks.

Issue #1: I need your identity at more places that the access-layer edge

Web Content Filtering is a great example of needing your identity elsewhere in the network. In a restrictive corporate environment, there is Active Directory integration that helps solve these problems, but what about non domain devices? What about organizations with the Internet of Everything?

I've seen solutions from Radius Accounting integration to agents on Domain Controllers, but these are usually point solutions and I personally have not had good luck with these nor are they widely supported. Also they are single device specific, so you can't send it to multiple devices for identity determination. Datacenter firewalls are another place where this falls apart. How do I write an ACL based on your identity when I may or may not have your identity? The solution inevitably leads to more identity verification: Captive Web Portals, VPN clients, etc.

Issue #2: Scalability of ACLs

Anyone who has tried to write complex ACLs to govern what a client can or can't get to, can tell you that ACLs become very unwieldy very quickly. You CANNOT effectively write ACLs for every resource and port that every potential client should be able to get to. It's also not effective as these ACLs take up precious TCAM space in our network equipment.

Solutions?

The solution to this problem is an identity exchange. Cisco has a pair of technologies called SGT and SXP with ISE or ACS (part of their TrustSec solution) that attempts to solve this problem. Instead of filtering traffic with ACLs on ingress to the network, they identify identity at the edge and pass that identity information to the rest of the network and filter packets on egress of the network. Both protocols are Cisco proprietary, but the idea is sound. While I'm not a fan of having to have special hardware to pass this info around the network, the idea of a central identity repository that all devices have access to solves the issue of having to filter all packets at the access-layer edge, we allow the rest of the network to share in this burden and create a solution that scales.

Jake's Opinion:

Personally, I don't think we will see single VLAN designs successfully implemented for quite some time. The wide variety of firewalls, web content filtering, lack of network-wide identity and complex nature of BYOD policies really prevent us from completely abstracting out the devices IP addressing. My hope is that, with the upcoming SDN-apocalypse, we will see SDN solutions providing ways to distribute identity throughout the network that get us closer than ever to the simplified access layer edge, which so many vendors are suggesting today.

Chapter 7 Summary

In this chapter, you studied several specific design scenarios, including the use of VPNs to secure public access. Additionally, you learned about captive portals and their basic operation. You also explored client management strategies and the factors that impact the selection process related to client management solutions.

Facts to Remember

Be sure to remember the following facts as you prepare for the CWSP certification, and be able to explain the details related to them:

- A VPN encrypts data in a tunnel between two endpoints so that all communications passed between them are secured.
- PPTP, L2TP/IPSec and SSTP are all commonly available protocols today.
- Split tunneling may be used to allow a remote client to communicate directly with the Internet when required, but also simultaneously communicate with the remote office via a VPN for secure transfer of organizational data.
- Public access networks introduce the threat of data theft and peer attacks.
- Using a VPN when accessing the Internet from a hotspot helps to protect against data theft.
- Running updated anti-malware and a client firewall on PCs that use public access Wi-Fi can assist in protecting against peer attacks.
- Captive portals allow for organizations to implement wireless access but control who gains access, what they can access, and how long they can access the resources for.
- Segmentation, using VLANs, firewalls, and router ACLs are commonly used to isolate and protect corporate data from non-corporate users.
- When considering client management, a good MDM solution for your scenario will be one that addresses the appropriate types of clients, matches the capabilities of the network and complies with corporate security policy.

- Remember BYOD concepts such as containerization, onboarding, segmentation, and the use of MDM in general.
- If remote APs connect across the Internet to a centralized location with a WLAN controller provisioned, the AP should establish some kind of VPN connection to either the controller or a VPN endpoint in the centralized network.

Chapter 7: Review Questions

1. Choose the option that specifies two valid VPN modes used to secure communications on wireless networks.
   a. Tunneled and overlay
   b. Tunneled and transport
   c. Transport and split
   d. Split and tunneled

2. Which of the following is not a valid defense against attack for a wireless user on a public access wireless network?
   a. Use of VPN
   b. Personal firewall
   c. Up to date anti-virus
   d. Wireless controller

3. Of the following VPN protocols, which is known to have been cracked and is therefore typically not recommended for use in enterprise wireless environments?
   a. PPTP
   b. L2TP/IPSec
   c. SSH
   d. SSL/TLS

4. Which one of these is not a common use of wireless VPN?
   a. Site-to-site tunnels
   b. Remote APs
   c. Wireless bridging
   d. Remote client connectivity

5. Split-tunneling has a major disadvantage. What is it?
   a. Data is encrypted
   b. Increased processing overhead
   c. Exposure to the public network
   d. Encryption keys must be made public

6. Using open public wireless access networks exposes users to a number of risks. Which of the following is typically not one of those risks?
   a. Weak passwords
   b. Unsecured file shares
   c. Improperly configured firewalls
   d. Poorly constructed WEP keys

7. There are typically three steps in building a VPN connection. One the following is not part of that process. Select the option that is not part of building a VPN connection.
   a. Perform required authentication
   b. Build virtual tunnel
   c. Traverse captive portal
   d. Encrypt the data

8. What WLAN security posture is typically present on SSIDs that make use of captive portals?
   a. WPA2 Pre-share
   b. WEP
   c. VPN
   d. Open System Authentication

9. Which of the following is used to segment guest traffic from corporate data?
    a. ACLs
    b. Firewalls
    c. VLANs
    d. All of the above

10. What standard is associated with VLANs?
    a. 802.1Q
    b. 802.11q
    c. 801.2q
    d. 802.1X

11. What aspect of a captive portal implementation is leveraged to protect the service provider from liability?
    a. Walled garden
    b. Encryption
    c. Terms of service
    d. VPN statement

12. Which of these is not a fundamental component of VPN?
    a. Server side endpoint
    b. Network infrastructure
    c. Client side endpoint
    d. Security tunnel broker

13. What should guide every security solution, including VPN, captive portals, VLANs, and MDM implementations?
    a. Security policy
    b. Client behavior
    c. Government regulations
    d. Client device capabilities

14. The ability for network administrators to remotely lock or wipe a lost or stolen device is a functional feature of _____.
    a. Security policy
    b. MDM
    c. Roaming admin platform
    d. Super user role

15. The ability to automatically place an authenticated user on a specific VLAN is enabled by which of these?
    a. VLAN attributes
    b. 802.1X attributes
    c. Policy attributes
    d. RADIUS attributes

16. Which VPN protocol makes use of HTTPS port 443 to allow passage through common firewall settings?
    a. PPTP
    b. MSTP
    c. SSTP
    d. PTSD

17. At which model of the OSI model does VPN typically work?
    a. Layer 2
    b. Layer 3
    c. Layer 4
    d. Layer 7

18. What security solution employs a web page or IP address capture mechanism that prevents users from proceeding until some credential is entered or action is taken?
    a. Captive portal
    b. MDM
    c. VLANPN
    d. Firewall

19. Corporate data and personal data are logically isolated from each other using _____ in an MDM solution.
    a. Segmentation
    b. Containerization
    c. Quarantine
    d. Private files

20. The concept of using logical data containers is to isolate corporate data is associated with which of the following?
    a. Guest access
    b. Private networks
    c. Isolation networks
    d. MDM systems

21. The BYOD function that involves either pre-registration or self-registration of client devices is which of these?
    a. In-processing
    b. Onboarding
    c. Side-loading
    d. Integration

22. Compliance reporting, geofencing, and location based services are features of what security solution?
    a. MDM
    b. Captive NMS
    c. BYOD
    d. Regulatory subscriber

23. When pre-registration is in use, what function is being employed and who registers the clients?
    a. Onboarding, clients register themselves
    b. MDM, administrator registers clients
    c. Onboarding, administrator registers clients
    d. MDM, clients register themselves

24. Your company is deploying remote access points in branch locations, and plans on connecting them back to the corporate network. From the perspective of security, what must be done with the remote APs?
    a. They need VPN connectivity to WLAN controller or endpoint.
    b. They need to be registered on the corporate network.
    c. The remote administrator's name should be recorded.
    d. Client access should be limited to prevent any users on the AP.

25. Which of these is not a common VPN endpoint type?
    a. WLAN controller
    b. Firewall
    c. NMS platforms
    d. Public access wireless AP

Chapter 7: Review Answers

1. **B** is correct. Tunneled mode and transport mode are two common VPN modes.

2. **D** is correct. There are a number of recommended practices to protect individual wireless users, but wireless controllers are infrastructure devices.

3. **A** is correct. PPTP is considered a cracked VPN protocol at this point.

4. **A** is correct. Site to Site VPN tunneling is common, but not generally applicable to wireless VPN.

5. **C** is correct. Split tunneling exposes traffic directly to the Internet.

6. **D** is correct. WEP is usually not utilized on open public networks.

7. **C** is correct. Captive portals have nothing to do with VPN per se.

8. **D** is correct. Captive portals generally do not use encryption.

9. **D** is correct. ACLs, VLANs, and firewalls are all common segmentation methods.

10. **A** is correct. 802.1Q is the VLAN standard for wired and wireless networks.

11. **C** is correct. Terms of Service are included in Captive Portal pages to protect the WLAN provider from liability.

12. **D** is correct. VPN requires server side endpoint, client side endpoint, and network infrastructure.

13. **A** is correct. The security policy is the overarching touchstone for any potential security solution and cannot be left out of the planning process.

14. **B** is correct. MDM's remote wipe capability is a powerful security feature for lost or stolen devices.

15. **D** is correct. RADIUS attributes can steer users to the VLAN that policy says they should be on.

16. **C** is correct. SSTP is a Microsoft-authored VPN protocol that uses port 443.

17. **B** is correct. VPN typically works at Layer 3, while 802.11 encryption works at Layer 2.

18. **A** is correct. The capture mechanism is fundamental to the captive portal paradigm.

19. **B** is correct. Do not confuse containerization with segmentation. Containerization keeps corporate data and personal data separate on BYOD devices.

20. **D** is correct. MDM systems use logical containers.

21. **B** is correct. Onboarding has become a popular feature for bringing clients onto the WLAN.

22. **A** is correct. These are just a few MDM features, make sure you get a handle on all of them.

23. **C** is correct. With pre-registration in MDM, the administrator registers clients-in contrast to self-registration, where clients register themselves.

24. **A** is correct. VPN should be used for remote APs.

25. **D** is correct. Public Wi-Fi networks generally do not provide VPN endpoints.

Chapter 8:

Secure Roaming

Objectives

3.9　Understand additional security features in WLAN infrastructure and access devices, including management frame protection, Role-Based Access Control (RBAC), Fast BSS transition (pre-authentication and OKC), physical security methods, and Network Access Control (NAC).

When WLANs were first implemented, the focus was on providing wireless access to laptop computers and the occasional desktop PC. Since the adoption of 802.11a/g that steadily changed. We have come a long way since basic client access was the only purpose of the WLAN. Modern business WLAN is far more complicated, and many critical and/or latency-sensitive applications are used over Wi-Fi. As device and application sophistication has increased, so has the complexity of WLAN configuration.

Today, WLANs are accessed by laptops, desktops, tablets, specialty devices, and mobile phones. Included under the heading of mobile phones are growing numbers of VoIP Wi-Fi handsets. While all wireless devices can benefit from properly designed roaming between Wi-Fi cells, VoIP phones require it in nearly all scenarios. The roaming must be fast, and it must allow for security throughout the roaming process to protect the privacy of the conversation.

The primary focus of this chapter is on roaming techniques that are available in current vendor solutions that are based on both standard and proprietary technologies. We will also look briefly at the latest roaming capabilities introduced by 802.11r, which is now part of 802.11-2012. We will see that even though .11r is formally here, many vendors still rely on earlier developed techniques. We will explain why.

IEEE 802.11 Roaming Basics

An 802.11 roam includes the movement of a client association from one AP to another. Of course, it is not as easy as simply moving the association. The new AP must

- authenticate the roaming client, and
- establish dynamic encryption keys and temporal encryption keys.

These processes take time, especially in WPA-Enterprise or WPA2-Enterprise networks. This is why special roaming procedures are required to facilitate fast roaming. The 802.11-2012 standard actually refers to this as a *transition*; however, most in the industry use the term "roam" with respect to 802.11 WLAN technology.

When a wireless client device moves an association from one AP to another, the process can be straightforward, but may be quite complex depending on the scenario. You learned in earlier chapters that every time a WLAN client device connects to an AP, it must perform an 802.11 Open System authentication and association. This process is what provides the Physical layer and Data Link layer connections to the network.

If a client device roams from one AP to another, it has to perform what is called a reassociation. 802.11 Association and Reassociation frames are almost identical, but CWSPs must recognize the subtle differences. A client device can only be 802.11 associated to one AP at any one time; therefore, moving the association or reassociating is required when a device moves to another AP.

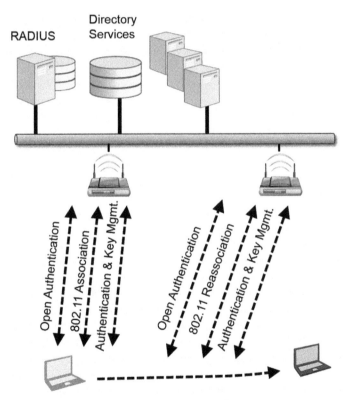

Figure 8-1: Basic Roaming Infrastructure

In addition to the reassociation, the client must perform an 802.11 Open System authentication. Therefore, when a client device moves to another AP it must perform an 802.11 Open System authentication and association; however, this is considered a reassociation as a device moves through the WLAN after the initial association. This process pertains to an open network connection without any Layer 2 security features. If 802.11 standard security features are enabled, the process gets more complicated, as you will see later in the chapter.

To assist your understanding of roaming, you should be aware of the following terms referenced in earlier chapters, but having a larger role here:

- **PMKSA**—Pairwise Master Key Security Association. The context resulting from a successful 802.1X authentication exchange between the peer and Authentication Server (AS), or from a pre-shared key (PSK).
- **PMKID**—Pairwise Master Key Identifier. The PMKID is an identifier of a security association.
  - PMKID = HMAC-SHA1-128(PMK, "PMK Name" || AA || SPA)
- **PTKSA**—Pairwise Transient Key Security Association. The context resulting from a successful 4-way handshake exchange between the peer and authenticator.

PSK Roaming

In previous chapters you learned about 802.11i, now incorporated into 802.11-2012, and WPA/WPA2-Personal and Enterprise modes. Remember that if an 802.11 wireless network is configured for WPA- or WPA2-Personal mode, the wireless client device performs a 4-way handshake after the 802.11 Open System authentication and association have completed. Also recall that the purpose of the 4-way handshake is to allow wireless devices that are connecting together, i.e., (AP and client device) to exchange some keying material in order to create the keys required to encrypt unicast and broadcast/multicast traffic for that device.

The following image shows a capture of the 802.11 Open System authentication and association, in addition to the 4-way handshake. Notice that the relative time, which is the time it took from the first Authentication frame to the final Acknowledgement frame, was 44ms in this example. This time is not as significant in an initial 802.11 authentication and association as it is when a device roams from one AP to another AP. The reason is this: if the time it takes to connect to a new AP and perform the necessary frame exchanges for wireless security is too long, chances are the client device will have to perform an entire new authentication process. For some wireless applications, such as wireless voice, this can cause serious performance or connectivity issues.

IEEE 802.11 wireless networks supporting WPA-Personal and WPA2-Personal typically do not require any special enhancements for fast roaming between APs. A full authentication typically takes less than 50 ms, so there is no need to improve upon this time. In this case there would be no roaming issues.

Packet	Source	Destination	BSSID	Flags	Channel	Signal	Data Rate	Size	Relative Time	Protocol
968	Intelorate:50:16:B1	02:18:1A:30:05:D6	02:18:1A:30:05:D6	*	44	100%	6.0	34	0.000000	802.11 Auth
969	02:18:1A:30:05:D6	Intelorate:50:16:B1		*	44	70%	6.0	14	0.000014	802.11 Ack
970	02:18:1A:30:05:D6	Intelorate:50:16:B1		*	44	70%	6.0	34	0.007421	802.11 Auth
971	Intelorate:50:16:B1	02:18:1A:30:05:D6	02:18:1A:30:05:D6	*	44	100%	6.0	111	0.008124	802.11 Assoc Req
972	02:18:1A:30:05:D6	Intelorate:50:16:B1		*	44	70%	6.0	14	0.008216	802.11 Ack
973	02:18:1A:30:05:D6	Intelorate:50:16:B1	02:18:1A:30:05:D6	*	44	70%	6.0	205	0.033179	802.11 Assoc Rsp
974	02:18:1A:30:05:D6	Intelorate:50:16:B1		*	44	70%	6.0	37	0.035667	802.11 Action
975	Intelorate:50:16:B1	02:18:1A:30:05:D6	02:18:1A:30:05:D6	*	44	94%	6.0	37	0.036510	802.11 Action
976	02:18:1A:30:05:D6	Intelorate:50:16:B1		*	44	70%	6.0	14	0.036535	802.11 Ack
977	02:18:1A:30:05:D6	Intelorate:50:16:B1	02:18:1A:30:05:D6		44	68%	0.0	137	0.036724	802.1x
978	Intelorate:50:16:B1	02:18:1A:30:05:D6	02:18:1A:30:05:D6		44	94%	6.0	161	0.043849	802.1x
979	02:18:1A:30:05:D6	Intelorate:50:16:B1		*	44	68%	6.0	14	0.043861	802.11 Ack
980	02:18:1A:30:05:D6	Intelorate:50:16:B1	02:18:1A:30:05:D6		44	68%	0.0	241	0.044696	802.1x
981	Intelorate:50:16:B1	02:18:1A:30:05:D6	02:18:1A:30:05:D6		44	94%	6.0	137	0.046558	802.1x
982	02:18:1A:30:05:D6	Intelorate:50:16:B1		*	44	68%	6.0	14	0.046567	802.11 Ack

Figure 8-2: Time for Authentication, Association, and 4-Way Handshake

But what happens when what is known as a *slow roam* occurs in a wireless network that is enabled for 802.1X/EAP with no fast roaming features? In a standard roaming environment, also known as a slow/secure roaming environment (when you are dealing with a robust security network [RSN]), each reassociation requires a full 802.1X/EAP reauthentication. This requirement is especially true in autonomous AP environments, but is often the case in controller-based and other environments as well. If there are no Fast BSS Transition (FT) protocols in place on the supplicant (client device) and authenticator (AP or WLAN controller), each reassociation may take 500ms or more, depending on a number of variables. At best, un-enhanced roaming nearly always takes more than 200–250ms.

A roam that takes 500ms is much too slow to maintain the integrity of the Wi-Fi connection. Many wireless networking best practices recommend roam times to be less than 150ms maximum. Longer roam times causes issues for the wireless client device that is making the move.

These steps occur during the slow roam process:

1. Open System authentication
2. Association
3. 802.1X/EAP authentication
4. 4-way handshake

As you can see, the same basic processes occur as those in the preceding image (time for Authentication, Association and the 4-way handshake), which required just under 50ms alone, but the added requirement of 802.1X/EAP authentication is significant. Keep in mind, the time delay between the AP and the client STA is no longer the only consideration. Now, the time delay between the AP and the RADIUS server must also be considered, along with added time for interaction between the RADIUS server and LDAP server. In addition, processing delay must be considered as the RADIUS server may be overtaxed at times, or the LDAP server may slow in high-usage periods. With all of these individual opportunities for processing delay, you can see why full slow roams can take more than 500ms to complete.

VoIP clients are among the most susceptible to issues that come from long roam times. This is because real-time VoIP protocols have stringent requirements in order to provide toll quality calls. Voice data packets come with demands that are not seen in traditional data packets.

For example, if you are sending a file to a server via FTP, it does not matter if a few packets arrive out of order, or if a delay occurs between the arrival of one packet and the next packet that is greater than a particular threshold. If an extended delay occurs it certainly slows the communications down, but the data eventually arrives at the destination with no ill effects. Voice traffic does not tolerate such occurrences. If an extended delay occurs with voice traffic, the call is dropped or its quality suffers. If you think about it for a moment, you will hopefully understand why this low tolerance for delay by voice data is so important.

Humans are at both ends of a Voice over IP (VoIP) communications link. They both talk and listen, and they have expectations that have been set by the analog telephone network. If they do not hear any sound for some variable length of time, they assume that the call has been dropped or the person on the other end has disconnected. If the sound quality is inferior, particularly to the point where they cannot understand one another, they may give up on the conversation. Expectations of session quality and predictability exist with voice over Wi-Fi. Those expectations must be met with VoIP data even though they have not traditionally been required of other data types. In fact, you often see reference to "carrier grade," "carrier quality," or "toll quality" VoIP communications. These terms mean that a sound quality and communication speed that is minimally equivalent to the traditional PSTN has been accomplished.

Because VoIP packets are transmitted over the same physical network as traditional data packets (such as e-mail, database access, file transfer, printing, etc.), you can say that voice is layered over the data network. The same network devices, cables, and software that are used for traditional data are also used to transfer voice data. This layering places a new demand on the network. This demand is that the data network must be able to differentiate between packet types, and give priority to voice packets so that the quality expectations of the VoIP users are met. The technology that enables this differentiation is known as Quality of Service (QoS), and is beyond the direct scope of this study guide (although it is addressed in the CWDP® Official Study Guide in detail). In addition, fast and secure roaming is needed on the wireless network.

Because voice traffic must move rapidly across the network, and because retransmissions of lost or corrupted voice packets would provide no functional value, UDP is used to send most VoIP data packets. UDP is a connectionless protocol, unlike TCP. TCP has far too much overhead to transmit voice packets as rapidly as they must be transmitted.

If you have not worked with VoIP, you may wonder why there is no benefit from resending corrupted or lost voice packets. The reason is simple. Think about how long it takes you to say the word "don't." If you are like most people, it takes you far less than a second. Now, imagine you are having a conversation on a VoIP phone and you say the following sentences, "Don't push the button. Pull the lever." Next, further imagine that the word "don't" was lost in transmission and the system decided to resend it. Because of the sequencing problem, the user on the other end hears the following, "Push the button. Don't pull the lever." This reordering could theoretically happen because the phrase "push the button" made it through while the word "don't" did not make it through. When the word "don't" was retransmitted, it was placed before the phrase "pull the lever." The result is the transmission of what amounts to the complete opposite of the intended message. Do you see why retransmitting lost audio packets would be useless and possibly damaging?

Now, this exact scenario is not likely to occur, even with retransmissions. It would definitely not occur in real VoIP implementations because they do not retransmit lost packets. Instead, the listener would likely just not hear the word "don't"; however, in reality it all gets a bit more complex. More than likely the listener would hear something like, "D---t pu—the ---ton. Pu-- --- --ver." The dashes represent either sounds that are unintelligible, or complete silences. The point is that the network does not usually drop exact words, but rather portions of audio much less than a complete word. This results in what we usually call a "bad connection."

These VoIP problems are rarely related to bandwidth or throughput. Rather they are related to a more precise term: *delay*. When delay is excessive in a WLAN link, the call can suffer in quality or be dropped. Although bandwidth and modulation can certainly impact delay because they limit the total amount of data that can be transmitted, the network can typically be engineered to sustain voice traffic. With a limited number of allowed concurrent calls, a properly configured wireless network can provide call quality, even given old 802.11b data rates. But when you introduce roaming-based delays, all of the other engineering benefits are lost as soon as users begin to move around the Wi-Fi environment while talking.

VoIP systems typically require less than 150ms of unidirectional delay. The ITU-T recommends in Recommendation G.114 that the round trip time (RTT) or round trip delay not exceed 300ms in a telephone network. A quick calculation reveals that this RTT cannot be met unless the unidirectional delay is 150 ms or less as an average.

So, what are the solutions? You can do one of three things to reduce delay, using traffic on a highway as an analogy:

1. Install more generic lanes.
2. Identify one or more lanes as high-occupancy lanes.
3. Teach people to drive better.

Installing more generic lanes increases the lane width (similar to network bandwidth) and reduces your delay. However, this solution is a very expensive one, and can slow down traffic while the extra lanes are being installed. If we apply this concept to the data network, we face the same negative impacts. If we simply install more APs with the same efficiency as current ones, we may reduce delay in the WLAN while greatly increasing the cost of doing so.

The second option, of identifying a lane for high-occupancy vehicles (HOV), does not have the same impact as adding more lanes, but it is far less expensive and should not result in as many delays during initial implementation. Installing HOV lanes is analogous to implementing QoS on a network or fast secure roaming techniques in a WLAN. QoS and roaming methods cannot increase the available data rates, but they can indicate that specific traffic types have a higher priority.

The third and final option for managing priority traffic is probably the most difficult in real life. Teaching people to drive better is a coded way of saying that we want to entice people to work together so that all drivers arrive at their destination in a window of time that is relatively acceptable to all. Stated differently, one driver is not gaining an advantage while he or she delays other drivers. Ultimately, we are talking about implementing better collaborative driving algorithms. Thankfully, while this task is very difficult with human drivers on the highway, it is fairly easy to accomplish with data that is transmitted across our wireless networks.

Remember that 802.11ac provides a higher throughput and data rate than 802.11n, even though they may be using the same 40 MHz of frequency bandwidth. You could say that both 802.11ac and 802.11n use 40 lanes for data transfer, but 802.11ac potentially gets more data through. How is this difference in throughput possible? The answer is that 802.11ac drives better, with more efficiency.

Basic Roaming Review

Basic roaming works in one of three primary ways:

- Layer 2 roaming across APs within a single controller or without a controller
- Layer 2 roaming across APs connected to separate controllers
- Layer 3 roaming

When Layer 2 roaming occurs, the IP configuration on the device in motion is not lost. With the same IP address and roaming times of typically less than 40 milliseconds, Layer 2 roaming on non-secured WLANs can support streaming technologies such as VoIP. Layer 2 roaming across APs

- within a single controller is called *intracontroller roaming*, and
- when connected to separate controllers is called *intercontroller roaming*.

Vendors handle the actions that take place within or between the controllers according to their proprietary algorithms. The 802.11 standards

- define only what should take place as a client STA roams from one AP to another, and
- do not specify exactly how the communications must occur within the infrastructure in every detail.

This flexibility allows the vendors to provide competitive features in this area, while working against the mixing of different vendors' network hardware in the same WLAN. With the demand for VoIP support, some WLAN solutions are eliminated from consideration if the vendor's roaming solutions are inefficient. The good news is that the major WLAN vendors all have both intracontroller and intercontroller Layer 2 roaming solutions that can accomplish the roaming speeds required for wireless voice over IP.

Layer 3 roaming occurs when the client STA roams to an AP that cannot provide the same IP configuration because that AP is located on a different wired network. In this roaming scenario, the IP address must be reallocated from the DHCP server, and the client STA is placed on a new network subnet. The problem with this simple operation is that the client's Layer 3 connections is lost, which is likely to be disruptive to any network host actions in progress. If a file was in the process of copying from the client to a server, the file copy process most likely has to be started again from the beginning. The same is true in the reverse scenario where the file is copying from the server to the client. While this situation is painful for the users, it cannot begin to compare with frustrations of dropped calls due to Layer 3 roaming on voice over WLAN phones. To solve this problem, *fast secure roaming* must be implemented, and the APs across which users would roam must somehow be part of the same wired network, or provide some other solution to this problem. The access points may be part of the same wired network through tunneling solutions within the infrastructure, or they may be connected to the same controller, but they must somehow allow the client STA to maintain its IP address during the roaming process.

Implementing Layer 2 roaming without IP configuration loss is not actually very difficult on open wireless networks without security. This capability has been available for many years on networks with no wireless security. But previous to 802.11i and 802.11r, WLAN administrators faced difficulties in implementing a standards-based secure wireless network that offered very fast roaming. For secure wireless networks to support fast roaming, the 802.1X authentication process has to be accommodated in rapid fashion so that the user can roam without requiring a complete 802.1X authentication exchange to occur. This is typically accomplished using some form of key caching, as discussed in the later sections of this chapter.

Finally, in order for roaming to work in a seamless manner, the coverage cells of the APs must overlap. Though this is more of a design issue than it is security, CWSPs must also understand the importance of proper cell overlap. If there is no point of overlap, the client STA always loses network connectivity for a brief time as the user moves the STA across the non-covered area. Vendors recommend cell overlaps ranging from 15 to 30 percent. Realize that you cannot really measure overlap, but you can determine how many APs can be seen from a given location. Therefore, the goal is to have at least two visible and usable (meaning sufficient signal strength and SNR) APs at any location where real-time devices may be used.

As a side note, when a user moves his or her laptop around within the coverage area of a single AP, roaming is not required. The user has mobility, but no roaming occurs while the connection to a single AP is maintained.

Wi-Fi Voice-Personal Certification

Wi-Fi Certified Voice-Personal is an optional Wi-Fi Alliance certification that wireless devices may acquire once they are certified for the basic 802.11 standards with which they comply (that is, they have been certified as 802.11n or 802.11ac compliant by the Wi-Fi Alliance). The goal of the Voice-Personal certification is to provide a certification of compatibility across vendors for Wi-Fi phones and infrastructure devices such as APs. It is referenced here as an example of the network demands required related to latency or delay features. Per the Wi-Fi Alliance website:

Voice-Personal: Voice over Wi-Fi—extends beyond interoperability testing to test the performance of products and help ensure that they deliver good voice quality over the Wi-Fi link.

As you can see by this definition, the goal is to show that interoperable devices can also perform well with voice communications traveling across the wireless network. The Voice-Personal certification requires that devices be tested in a test network that:

- Consists of a single AP serving multiple clients that may include PCs, phones, gaming devices, printers, etc.; handoffs between APs are not tested in this certification program.
- Supports at least four simultaneous simulated voice calls from four voice devices associated with the same AP.
- Carries data and video traffic to and from multiple devices, in addition to voice traffic.

- Assigns priority to voice over traffic from other applications.
- Provides security-protected access through WPA2-Personal.
- Supports power-saving capabilities in the AP and in battery-operated client devices.
- Has a single Internet connection.

Clearly, this test network is not as complicated as an enterprise-class network. But remember, the certification is called Voice-Personal and not Voice-Enterprise. Eventually the Wi-Fi Alliance developed a similar certification that tests large scale voice over WLAN deployments called Voice-Enterprise.

In order to acquire the Voice-Personal certification, the devices tested in the network must achieve the following minimum performance requirements:

- Packet loss of less than 1 percent
- Less than 50 milliseconds of latency
- Less than 50 milliseconds of maximum jitter

According to the Wi-Fi Alliance, *"If a device does not perform to these levels, the voice call may drop in and out, may end suddenly, or the conversation may suffer from excessive delays, making it unintelligible. Products that do not meet these requirements will not receive Voice-Personal certification."*

In addition to the performance requirements within the test network, devices must meet the minimum Wi-Fi Alliance certifications in order to even be considered for testing:

- 802.11a, 802.11b or 802.11g
- WPA2-Personal (notice WPA-Personal is not allowed)
- WMM
- WMM-Power Save (this is only required for APs and is optional for client STAs)

The Voice-Personal certification only validates the portion of the voice communication that occurs on the wireless link. The end-to-end performance of the voice communication as it traverses the wired network is not tested or guaranteed based on Wi-Fi Alliance product certification.

Wi-Fi Voice-Enterprise Certification

Now, the Voice-Enterprise certification are briefly addressed to help you see what is needed when roaming is added to the business WLAN picture. The Wi-Fi Alliance defines a typical enterprise voice network as:

- APs and STAs are 802.11-compliant members of an enterprise Wi-Fi network.
- The Wi-Fi network is likely to have other traffic at the same time that voice calls are active.
- The network consists of multiple APs and a variety of STAs, such as voice handsets, PCs, printers, etc.
- The system is designed to support multiple concurrent voice calls.
- Wireless security is high, and likely includes a RADIUS infrastructure.

As described for this environment, the target performance of a Voice-Enterprise certified solution is 50ms handovers (roams), although breaks of up to 100ms may be acceptable. This is based on the reality that 50ms is probably less than four 20ms speech frames.

Additionally, Voice-Enterprise requires that some 802.11r technologies be implemented as well as 802.11e (QoS) and 802.11k (radio resource measurements) to allow for effective VoIP operations. The certification only became available in 2012, and so a low percentage of current production environments employ hardware that is fully certified or configured according to the certification. This will change drastically in the coming years as VoIP over Wi-Fi continues to gain acceptance.

Why is all this important? Cisco forecasts that by 2018, Wi-Fi calling traffic volume will surpass voice over LTE, and this Wi-Fi voice traffic will account for at least 53 percent of mobile IP voice traffic as measured in minutes of use by 2019. By 2019, the number of Wi-Fi-capable tablets and PCs will be nearly 3.5 times the number of cellular-capable tablets, with 1.9 billion of them in use (source: Wi-Fi Alliance whitepaper: Wi-Fi Calling in the Spotlight).

Exam Moment: Troubleshooting roaming problems for voice communications on Wi-Fi requires specific hardware and software. A protocol analyzer and multiple supported adapters used to simultaneously monitor different channels may be used in such cases. Additionally, multiple laptops could be used with later merging of the separate protocol captures.

Preauthentication

Preauthentication is the first way of removing delay from the roaming process. It is used by a wireless station that hears other APs to which it may choose to connect during the scanning process. The full 802.1X/EAP authentication is performed over the Ethernet infrastructure for the purpose of remaining on-channel with its current AP, while preparing for connectivity with another AP. Preauthentication support is optional and not supported by all manufacturers.

Preauthentication is an IEEE standardized fast secure roaming (FSR) method. Because of this, interoperability should be effective. None the less, preauthentication has the drawback of requiring a full 802.1X/EAP authentication for each potential AP to which the client might consider roaming. This stipulation requires the client to perform predictive authentications, which can add unnecessary traffic to both the wireless and wired mediums, as well as to the backend authentication infrastructure.

CWSPs must remember that preauthentication has to occur over the Ethernet medium. EAPoL frames use non-standard Ethertype values, and are treated as standard data frames and forwarded to the distribution system (DS). A special Ethertype value (88-C7) is specified for use by the 802.11 standard for wired-side (Ethernet) communications of the roam.

The strengths of preauthentication are:

- Standardized by the IEEE.
- Can be supported on any WLAN architecture.
- Performed prior to roaming and allows for preauthentication with many different nearby APs.

The weaknesses of preauthentication are:

- Still requires 802.1X/EAP authentication after association.
- Is not considered an efficient solution as it preauthenticates to APs it may never touch.
- Must happen prior to the roam.
- Does not scale well.
- Only trims 1 to 3ms off of the roam time.

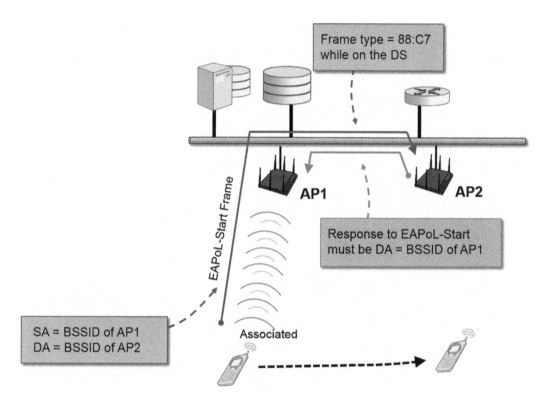

Figure 8-3: Preauthentication Architecture

Pairwise Master Key (PMK) Caching

PMK caching is also known as *fast roam-back*. In the following image you can see the steps required for this type of roaming to occur. The following paragraphs explain the process.

The 802.11 standard allows pairwise master key security associations (PMKSAs) to be cached at the AP (or WLAN controller) and on the wireless station for the purpose of fast roam-back. When a PMKSA is built (through a full 802.1X/EAP authentication) with an AP, the station and AP may continue to use that PMKSA at any point in the future when the station might roam back to the AP in which it was previously associated. The purpose of this feature is to avoid the slow 802.1X/EAP reauthentication process. In order to implement this feature, the client station must include the appropriate pairwise master key identifier (PMKID) in the Reassociation Request frame when it reassociates. Provided the AP still has the PMKSA cached, 802.1X/EAP authentication is skipped, and the 4-way handshake immediately ensues.

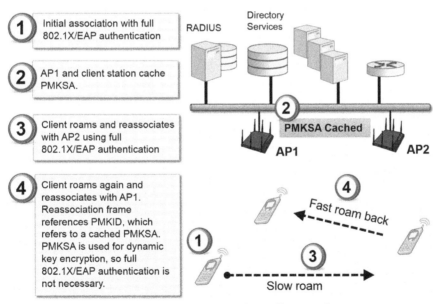

Figure 8-4: PMK Caching Illustrated

From IEEE 802.11-2012:

11.5.9.3 Cached PMKSAs and RSNA key management

"In a non-FT environment, a STA might retain PMKSAs it establishes as a result of previous authentication. The PMKSA cannot be changed while cached. The PMK in the PMKSA is used with the 4-Way Handshake to establish fresh PTKs.

If a STA in an ESS has determined it has a valid PMKSA with an AP to which it is about to (re)associate, it includes the PMKID for the PMKSA in the RSNE in the (Re)Association Request. Upon receipt of a (Re)Association Request with one or more PMKIDs, an AP checks whether its Authenticator has retained a PMK for the PMKIDs, whether the AKM in the cached PMKSA matches the AKM in the (Re)Association Request, and whether the PMK is still valid; and if so, it shall assert possession of that PMK by beginning the 4-Way Handshake after association has completed. If the Authenticator does not have a PMK for the PMKIDs in the (Re)Association Request, its behavior depends on how the STA performed IEEE 802.11 authentication. If the STA performed SAE authentication, then the AP STA shall send a Deauthentication frame. If the STA performed Open System authentication, it begins a full IEEE 802.1X authentication after association has completed."

The robust security network information element (RSN IE) of Reassociation frames contains PMKID, which refers to a PMKSA shared between the client and AP. It is important to note that the PMKID Count and PMKID List fields are present only in Reassociation frames.

From IEEE 802.11-2012:

8.4.2.27.5 PMKID

"The PMKID Count and List fields are used only in the RSNE in the (Re)Association Request frame to an AP and in FT authentication sequence frames. The PMKID Count specifies the number of PMKIDs in the PMKID List field. The PMKID list contains 0 or more PMKIDs that the STA believes to be valid for the destination AP. The PMKID can refer to

    a) A cached PMKSA that has been obtained through preauthentication with the target AP

    b) A cached PMKSA from an EAP or SAE authentication

    c) A PMKSA derived from a PSK for the target AP

    d) A PMK-R0 security association derived as part of an FT initial mobility domain association e) *A PMK-R1 security association derived as part of an FT initial mobility domain association or as part of a fast BSS transition.*

See 11.6.1.3 for the construction of the PMKID, 12.8 for the population of PMKID for fast BSS transitions, and 11.6.1.7 for the construction of PMKR0Name and PMKR1Name.

NOTE—A STA need not insert a PMKID in the PMKID List field if the STA will not be using that PMKSA."

When multiple PMKIDs are listed in the Reassociation frame, the AP (or controller) decides which PMKSA to use. If it does not find an applicable PMKID, it carries on with the full 802.1X/EAP authentication. If it finds a relevant PMKSA, it indicates which PMKID was used and proceeds with the 4-way handshake.

The strengths of PMK caching are:

- Standardized by IEEE
- Can be supported by any WLAN architecture
- Introduces no traffic overhead, and amounts to simple design

The weaknesses of PMK caching are:

- Provides fast roaming only on return to a previously associated AP (Roam back)
- New AP roams still require full 802.1X/EAP authentication

Opportunistic Key Caching (OKC)

Opportunistic Key Caching (OKC) is a key caching method not defined in the 802.11 standard, although it does have some commonality with 802.11r (now incorporated into 802.11-2012). OKC is used both at the supplicant and authenticator for fast roaming. The PMK and PMKID are retrieved from the initial AP with which the wireless station associates. An identical algorithm is used on the wireless station and WLAN controller/AP, and a unique PMKID is given to the original PMK when it is passed to each AP. The unique PMKID is based on the BSSID of the AP to which the PMK is sent.

At this point, OKC remains a proprietary and generally undocumented solution. It is important to note that for OKC to function, it must be supported by both the authenticator and the supplicant.

From IEEE 802.11-2012:

11.6.1.3 Pairwise key hierarchy

"A PMK identifier is defined as:
PMKID = HMAC-SHA1-128(PMK, "PMK Name" || AA || SPA)"

To understand this formula, you should know that AA is the authenticator's MAC address and SPA is the supplicant's MAC address.

Reassociation frames are the only frames that carry PMKID Count and List fields.

In normal OKC operation, Reassociation frames sent by the wireless client device list the PMKIDs to be chosen by the AP. OKC may be implemented such that it gains the PMKID from the Reassociation frames, or it may be implemented so that the AP does not require a PMKID from the client. Instead, the AP matches the client's MAC address to its PMKID table to identify an applicable match. If one is found, the PMKID is indicated in the first frame of the 4-way handshake. If none are found, the AP transmits an EAPoL-Start frame, and requires a full 802.1X/EAP authentication. CWSPs need to keep the following complexities in mind when they contemplate the use of OKC.

The strengths of OKC are:

- A good solution until Voice-Enterprise (802.11r) solutions are widely available and implemented
- Scales well
- Only requires a single initial 802.1X/EAP authentication

The weaknesses of OKC are:

- Not standardized
- Not all clients support it
- Not implemented in a compatible way across all vendors

802.11-2012 (802.11r) Fast Transition (FT)

To understand the impact of 802.11r FT on roaming, it is helpful to have a reminder of how 802.11i impacted it. To understand how 802.11i affected roaming, you must first understand the different keys used in 802.11i networks. Remember, the keys are used to secure communications on the wireless link. The following keys are used (as you have previously learned):

- **Pairwise Master Key (PMK)**—This is the top-level key used in the standard. The PMK is derived from a key generated by EAP, or from a pre-shared key (PSK) in smaller WLAN implementations.
- **Pairwise Transient Key (PTK)**—This is the key derived from the PMK, Authenticator (AP) address (AA), supplicant (client) address (SPA), Authenticator nonce (number used once) (ANonce), and supplicant nonce (SNonce). A pseudo-random function is used to generate up to five keys. The five keys are the EAPOL-Key confirmation key, the EPOL-Key encryption key, the temporal encryption key, and two temporal message integrity code keys.
- **Group Master Key (GMK)**—This is a supporting key that may be used to generate a group temporal key. The GMK may be regenerated within the AP periodically to reduce the exposure of the group temporal key.
- **Group Temporal Key (GTK)**—This is the key used to protect broadcast or multicast MPDUs on a wireless link.

The term *pairwise* refers to two devices associated with each other. A pairwise master key, for example, is a key used between an AP and a client STA to secure the communications. This is where roaming is an issue, because the 802.11 security was designed to be between a single AP and STA pair. Therefore, some method of quickly acquiring a PTK after a roam was needed.

Once an STA is associated and authenticated to the wireless network, with 802.11i, a PMK secure association (PMKSA) exists between the authentication server and the STA. A PTK secure association (PTKSA) exists between the AP and the STA once the 4-way handshake is completed. The problem, when discussing roaming, is that the accomplishment of such a PMKSA and PTKSA takes time. It can take too much time for real-time applications if some additional mechanism is not in play.

The 802.11i solution to the delay caused by establishing a PMKSA is PMK caching. With PMK caching, as you previously read, the authenticator (the AP) and the STA can cache PMKSAs so that regeneration of the PMKSA is not required at the time of roaming. Instead, the first step in the 4-way handshake is that the authenticator specifies the identifier of the PMK in the first message (Message 1) of the handshake. This functionality means that the required process of PMKSA establishment is removed, and only the PTKSA must be established. Always remember this rule: if you can remove steps from a process, you typically reduce the time required to complete the process. By removing the step of PMKSA establishment at roaming time, we speed up the process or reassociation with the new AP.

The 802.11r amendment was the first standards-based attempt to truly define fast secure roaming in any level of detail. It was ratified in 2008, and is now part of the 802.11 standard as amended (802.11-2012). The 802.11r amendment assumes the 802.11i amendment—as would be expected, since 802.11i was ratified in 2004. You must always remember, when studying IEEE standards, that an amendment ratified today is based upon the original standard and all prior amendments ratified. If you do not keep this in mind, the standard becomes very confusing to you very quickly.

 Note: **While 802.11r is standardized, and has been for almost a decade, few vendors have existing implementations that use it heavily. As much as the incompatibilities between different vendors are discussed, the vast majority of environments implement only one vendor in a facility, or at least per network in that facility. The result is that OKC is still commonly used as the solution in late 2016, but 802.11r is gaining acceptance.**

To begin the explanation of 802.11r, a few key definitions from the standard are in order:

- **Fast basic service set (BSS) transition**—A station (STA) movement that is from one BSS in one extended service set (ESS) to another BSS within the same ESS, and that minimizes the amount of time that data connectivity is lost between the STA and the distribution system (DS)

- **Fast basic service set (BSS) transition (FT) 4-way handshake**—A pairwise key management protocol used during FT initial mobility domain association; this handshake confirms mutual possession of a pairwise master key, the PMK-R1, by two parties and distributes a group temporal key (GTK)
- **Fast basic service set (BSS) transition (FT) initial mobility domain association**—The first association or first reassociation procedure within a mobility domain, during which a station (STA) indicates its intention to use the FT procedures
- **Mobility domain**—A set of basic service sets (BSSs), within the same extended service set (ESS), that support fast BSS transitions between themselves and that are identified by the set's mobility domain identifier (MDID)
- **Over-the-air fast basic service set (BSS) transition (FT)**—An FT method in which the station (STA) communicates over a direct IEEE 802.11 link to the target AP (AP)
- **Over-the-DS (distribution system) fast basic service set (BSS) transition (FT)**—An FT method in which the station (STA) communicates with the target AP (AP) via the current AP

As painful as it may be, memorizing the preceding list of definitions—at least in your own words—is a key part of preparing for the CWSP exam. Make sure you understand these definitions and what they mean for 802.11 roaming. In addition to these terms, you need to understand that a single PMK is not considered in an 802.11r implementation as a sole entity, such as was introduced in 802.11i. Instead, we must deal with a fast transition key hierarchy. The following definitions help you understand this hierarchy:

- **PMK-R0**—The first level (or top level) PMK
  - The PMK-R0 is derived from the master session key (MSK) when 802.1X/RADIUS is used, or from the pre-shared key (PSK) when personal implementations are used.
- **PMK-R1**—The second level PMK
  - The PMK-R1 keys are derived from the PMK-R0 key.

Remember this hierarchy. The first level is not PMK-R1, but it is PMK-R0.

The core of what 802.11r is all about is allowing a non-AP STA to preauthenticate with an AP to which it may roam at a later time. During the preauthentication process, in an FT implementation, the PTK is derived from the PMK-R1. It is important to remember that the PTK is not derived directly from the PMK-R0, but that it is derived from the PMK-R1.

Preauthentication is optional. If it is to be used, it must be available and enabled on both the APs and the client devices. Remember that preauthentication is not required of an 802.11-compliant device; however, it is very useful for wireless networks that must carry voice or other real-time traffic and provide for roaming ability.

As you have seen from the information in Chapter 5 (robust security network [RSN] and authentication and key management [AKM]), the key hierarchy follows a process of derivation. If you understand that key derivation process, this part which pertains to IEEE 802.11r fast transition is not as painful.

Basically, the fast transition (FT) process consists of different levels of the PMK. For example, a WLAN controller may hold PMK-R0, while AP1 has PMK-R1 (#1) and AP3 has PMK-R1 (#2). Both PMK-R1 (#1) and PMK-R1 (#2) are derived from PMK-R0. For standard authentication and key management processes, there is only one PMK that is created for the authenticated session. In 802.11 fast transition, there are many PMKs at different levels in the device authentication hierarchy.

The FT Initial Mobility Domain Association is similar to a non-FT initial association; however, a few new elements are introduced into the frame exchange.

From IEEE 802.11-2012:

8.4.2.49 Mobility Domain element (MDE)

"The MDE contains the Mobility Domain Identifier (MDID) and the FT Capability and Policy field. The AP uses the MDE to advertise that it is included in the group of APs that constitute a mobility domain, to advertise its support for FT capability, and to advertise its FT policy information."

The MDIE is broadcast by the AP in Beacons and probe response frames. The supplicant includes an MDIE in the (re)association request frame, and the authenticator compares this with its MDIE parameters. If a match is found, the exchange will continue.

8.4.2.50 Fast BSS Transition element (FTE)

"The FTIE includes information needed to perform the FT authentication sequence during a fast BSS transition in an RSN."

12.4 FT initial mobility domain association

12.4.1 Overview

"The FT initial mobility domain association is the first (re)association in the mobility domain, where the SME of the STA enables its future use of the FT procedures.

FT initial mobility domain association is typically the first association within the ESS. In addition to association frames, reassociation frames are supported in the initial mobility domain association to enable both FT and non-FT APs to be present in a single ESS."

12.4.2 FT initial mobility domain association in an RSN

"A STA indicates its support for the FT procedures by including the MDE in the (Re)Association Request frame and indicates its support of security by including the RSNE. The AP responds by including the FTE, MDE, and RSNE in the (Re)Association Response frame. After a successful IEEE 802.1X authentication (if needed) or SAE authentication, the STA and AP perform an FT 4-Way Handshake. At the end of the sequence, the IEEE 802.1X Controlled Port is opened, and the FT key hierarchy has been established."

Over-the-Air FT

The Over-the-Air FT protocol is a reassociation process that expedites reassociations in FT-enabled networks. As you review the following image, compare these contents and processes with a non-FT reassociation process. As you can see, fewer frames are used (8 in a non-FT reassociation; 4 in an over-the-air FT reassociation), and new contents are added to the 802.11 Authentication Request/Response and Association Request/Response.

From IEEE 802.11-2012:

12.5.2 Over-the-air FT Protocol authentication in an RSN

"The FTO and AP use the FT authentication sequence to specify the PMK-R1 security association and to provide values of SNonce and ANonce that enable a liveness proof, replay

protection, and PTK key separation. This exchange enables a fresh PTK to be computed in advance of reassociation. The PTKSA is used to protect the subsequent reassociation transaction, including the optional RIC-Request."

In an over-the-air FT reassociation, the new PTK is established before the reassociation occurs. Notice that the nonce values are included in the 802.11 Authentication Request and Response frames, which provide the necessary information to create new keys.

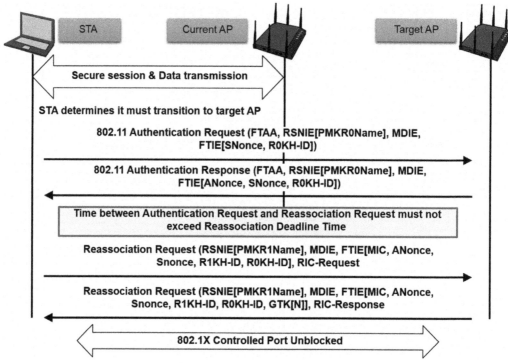

Figure 8-5: Over-the-Air FT

Over-the-DS FT

The Over-the-DS (distribution system) FT protocol is a reassociation process that expedites reassociation in FT-enabled networks. In an Over-the-DS exchange, the Open Authentication process is established via FT Request and Response Action frames. These frames are transmitted to the current AP, which then relays these frames to the target AP via the current DS. The FT Request and Response frames replace the Authentication Request and Response frames we are all familiar with. After the FT response is received, new PTKs are created on both the supplicant and target AP (authenticator), and the reassociation may then commence via the wireless medium.

The strengths of 802.11-2012 FT are:

- Standards-based fast roaming
- Required by Voice-Enterprise certification
- The most efficient fast roaming method available today
- Increasingly heavy support among users

The weaknesses of 802.11-2012 FT are:

- Has been very slow to market given its 8+ year life
- Available only since Wi-Fi Alliance Voice-Enterprise certification began in 2012
- Introduces many new terms and concepts requiring enhanced education for implementers

Single-Channel Architecture

The single-channel architecture represents a proprietary solution to the problem of slow RSN transitions. While the majority of enterprise wireless vendors use multiple non-overlapping channels and a concept known as channel reuse, single channel architecture (SCA) vendors configure all APs (within a mobility group) on a single channel.

The pioneer and primary vendor with this architecture is Meru Networks (now part of Fortinet). With all APs operating on a single channel, providing pervasive coverage across the service area, clients are not required to roam from one channel to another. Of course, roaming across channels is not the primary roaming concern. The problem for most networks comes when clients roam from one AP to the next, regardless of channel.

Because they operate on a single channel, SCA APs are able to use proprietary functions to broadcast a single BSSID across all APs. By using a single BSSID for all access points, the client does not realize that there are actually multiple physical APs. Instead, the client sees a single large virtual access point. Of course, the infrastructure must handle client handoffs from one AP to another, but this process is transparent to the client.

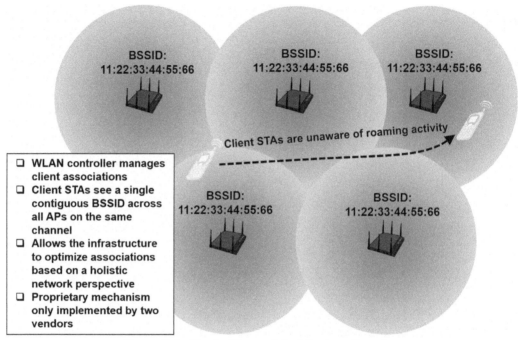

Figure 8-6: Single-Channel Architecture Roaming

A similar method of accomplishing the same result is to create per-client BSSIDs. When new clients join the network, a per-client BSSID is created, and this BSSID is broadcast on each AP. Again, the client does not realize that there are multiple APs, but rather sees only a single large and seamless AP. From the client's perspective, this negates the requirement to roam.

Despite the many negative marketing materials from competing vendors about SCA solutions, this solution is quite elegant and solves the traditional roaming problem.

The strengths of SCA roaming are:

- This is one of the best in-use roaming solutions today.
- Infrastructure devices have full control over roaming actions.
- Transitions are imperceptible to the client STA.

The weaknesses of SCA roaming are:

- Proprietary to the given vendor
- Requires SCA, which many feel is an inefficient architecture in comparison to multiple-channel architecture (MCA)

🔲 From the Blogs

A Sticky Problem—Wi-Fi Clients that Won't Roam

URL: www.wifikiwi.com/cwap/a-sticky-problem-wi-fi-clients-that-wont-roam
Author: Chris Lyttle
Blog: WiFi Kiwi's Blog—www.wifikiwi.com

I work in a very interesting industry. It seems like in no time, WLANs have gone from being a nice to have but definitely optional thing to something that everyone must have in order to operate their businesses. Part of the issue with this rapid change is that we are left with some decisions made in the past that have turned out not so great in the present day. One of those issues is caused by the decision to leave roaming decisions (if a WLAN client moves to a new AP and BSSID) up to the client. At the time I'm sure this seemed like a good solution. Craig Mathias over at *NetworkWorld* gave a bit of history (www.networkworld.com/community/node/83080) around this decision that I wasn't aware of before. Apparently it was felt that 'few sites would be purchasing APs, so it was assumed that most networks would be peer-based'.

We who deploy WLANs professionally know well the pain caused by buggy client drivers and the wide variance between different vendors on how they decide to do something as simple as roaming to a new AP. In comparison, cellular networks largely leave the roaming decision in the hands of the cell tower in many cases, which results in much smoother changes (such as not dropping your calls) in the main for clients as the move about. Two factors are converging to make this issue into a bigger problem for Wi-Fi networks. The first is that speeds are increasing on wireless (with 802.11ac it will go much higher) and people are using the WLAN because of this for more and more critical applications such as voice and video. The second is that the sheer number of devices using Wi-Fi as their only means of accessing the network has exploded since the introduction of the iPad in 2010. As Wi-Fi access becomes something that is relied on to run businesses, people naturally expect to be able to access it from wherever they need to work without a lot of hassle. They are not aware of such issues as limited bandwidth and contention caused by the increase in clients. They only want to know why their video doesn't run smoothly or why their voice call was dropped.

Yesterday, I attended Aruba Network's 802.11ac day (as part of Tech Field Day where they announced their newest AP, the AP-220, and had several other things to talk about). Foremost in the information was the announcement of their new ClientMatch technology to help with the issues with roaming caused by sticky clients. What is happening here is that clients are not making a decision to roam when a much better connection is available to them or when an AP is overloaded with other clients and a much lighter loaded AP is nearby. We have, in fact, a standardized way of dealing with this issue in the 802.11k and 802.11v standards, but not all clients support these standards. Aruba's solution to this is to build intelligence into the AP and controller to help 'match' the client with the best AP from the client's point of view. This intelligence is happening on several levels. At Layer 1, the link is being optimized by moving the clients either using 802.11k/v or by disassociating the client and only offering association to the 'better' AP. At layers 2-3 the load on the APs is taken into account and then for layers 4-7 the application's activity are taken into account.

Interestingly enough, Aruba believes that what they are doing is particularly unique and therefore patentable. They have submitted a patent which describes what they are doing for the clients that do not support 802.11k. Essentially they are creating the beacon reports used in the standard by collecting information from the APs when the client sends probe requests, authenticates or associates with the AP. What happens then is the AP takes the SNR information, does an adjustment and then sends the information upstream to either a controller, IAP or Airwave and that is used to figure out which AP is best for the client. This is a quite clever indirect way of figuring out how the client sees the network. The information that could be gathered is SNR, MAC address (as a key), channel, band, timestamp, noise floors, channel loading, AP capabilities and more. This combined with data the controller already has about applications means a decision can be made to whitelist or blacklist a certain STA on a group of APs. I've been told that they discovered in testing this that the actual SNR on the client was off from the readings they were getting from their algorithm by a constant amount, so they were able to just adjust to account for that.

Once you have built up this database of information, the next decisions you have to make is how to use it. Aruba told me that they decided to push this back down to the APs in a distributed way, so that the decision to associate a client wouldn't suffer from having to look back to a controller or other device. As was pointed out on Twitter, moving active voice or video streams off of a poorly performing AP is not a decision to take lightly. Most voice calls use a metric called a mean opinion score (MOS) to figure out what the quality of the call is. Aruba is using, as much as they can, information from the call itself to figure out the MOS on a real-time basis and then move other, non-voice clients off the AP, if that will interfere with the call quality. This was particularly highlighted by the Microsoft presenter who spoke about how they had opened an API up so that Aruba could gather this type of information about the Lync call. It wasn't discussed, but I think that the basic client roaming algorithm would move a voice client if it got too far away from an AP for its inbuilt MOS to be sufficiently high. In this case, the Aruba ClientMatch system would encourage it to pick a much better AP by only offering those that would be good for the client. One final point to make: Aruba was very careful to point out they took a cautious approach with ClientMatch so they were not moving clients with an 80% score just to get a 90% score. They wanted to make sure they concentrated on the bottom percentage of clients so that the improvement would be much larger and this would increase stability of the WLAN in general.

There are some additional uses that can come from being able to track what is happening from the client point of view. These uses come in Aruba's Airwave product where the information is being used to add to the ability of Airwave to troubleshoot user's connectivity. Aruba has created additional reports to give more visibility into client behavior, one of which is called the steering report. This report gives you information about what clients are being steered by ClientMatch and how often they have been steered. This gives you some clues into which clients might have firmware or driver issues that should be looked at because they are constantly sticking to poor AP connections. VisualRF additionally shows the status of client connections, indicating in a nice red color when a client has a poor connection. All this builds your control over what is happening on your Wi-Fi network and especially control over the client behavior that you haven't had before.

Chapter 8 Summary

In this chapter, you learned about the basic components required to implement fast secure roaming. You learned about the applications requiring secure roaming and of the standards-based and proprietary solutions available. You also learned about the 802.11 amendments that relate to roaming, including 802.11i and 802.11r, which are both included now in 802.11-2012.

Facts to Remember

Be sure to remember the following facts as you prepare for the CWSP certification, and be sure that you can explain the details related to them:

- Slow roaming can take longer than 200ms and as much as 500ms with 802.1X/EAP causing serious problems for VoIP.
- Preauthentication can save some time by authenticating to nearby APs before actually roaming to them.
- PMK caching works when an AP keeps the PMK as the STA roams away so that, on roam back, it is not required to recreate it.
- OKC is a non-standard solution, but it is implemented in many vendors and is the most widely used fast roaming solution.
- OKC, though popular now, started slowly because it is not a standard solution and had little client support.
- 802.11-2012 (802.11r) FT is a standardized fast roaming solution that is slowing working into the market and will become the eventual dominant method.
- Voice-Enterprise is a Wi-Fi Alliance certification for WLANs that requires 802.11r compliance.
- Voice-Personal is a Wi-Fi Alliance certification that sets requirements for performance without roaming.
- SCA roaming is controlled by the controller and not the client STA.

Chapter 8: Review Questions

1. What is another word for "roam" in 802.11 networks?
    a. Traversal
    b. Transition
    c. Travel
    d. Mobility

2. Which wireless network security type is inherently better when it comes to roaming?
    a. PSK
    b. RSN
    c. WPA2 Enterprise
    d. 802.1X

3. The fundamental risk associated with long roaming times on enterprise secure networks is _____.
    a. Traffic will be buffered.
    b. Client devices will not get back on the WLAN.
    c. Client devices will have to perform full associations all over.
    d. False associations can accumulate.

4. Best practices recommend that roam times in general should be less than how long?
    a. 500 ms
    b. 300 ms
    c. 200 ms
    d. 150 ms

5. Which of the following is not a step that is part of the slow roam process?
    a. Open systems authentication
    b. Reassociation
    c. 802.1X/EAP authentication
    d. 4-way handshake

6. VoIP protocols can be described as which of these choices?
    a. Real-time and TCP
    b. Full-duplex and TCP
    c. Real-time and UDP
    d. Half-time and UDP

7. Why do CWSPs most need to understand the nuances of roaming and the effects of roaming on wireless traffic?
    a. Because CWSPs design networks.
    b. Because roaming is an unsecure process.
    c. Because hackers can jam roaming frames.
    d. Because different security features can impact roaming in different ways.

8. You are troubleshooting roaming in an SCA environment. What controls client roaming in this WLAN scenario?
    a. The 802.11 standard
    b. The clients themselves
    c. The wireless controller
    d. Enterprise Voice algorithms

9. Which roaming method is currently the most efficient?
    a. 802.11-2012 FT
    b. OKC
    c. Preauthentication
    d. Enterprise roaming

10. Advantages of preauthentication include all of these, except ____?
    a. Is standardized by IEEE.
    b. Allows for preauthentication with a single AP.
    c. Supported on any WLAN architecture.
    d. Performed prior to roaming.

11. Target performance of Voice Enterprise includes handovers of how many milliseconds?
    a. 20
    b. 50
    c. 150
    d. 500

12. The capability to classify specific types of network traffic and to give priority to certain traffic types is called what?
    a. Quality of experience
    b. Fast pass
    c. QoS
    d. Degree of service

13. Which of the following statements is true about roaming and the 802.11 standard?
    a. The standard is explicit about details of the roaming process.
    b. The standard does not address roaming at all.
    c. Only pre-standard roaming is supported.
    d. The standard includes what should happen during roaming, but not how it should be accomplished.

14. What type of roam is in play when a client moves from an access point on Network 1 to an access point on Network 2?
    a. Data Link roam
    b. Layer 3 roam
    c. Layer 2 roam
    d. Out of band roam

15. For proper roaming, cell overlap should be what values, roughly?
    a. 15-30%
    b. 20-40%
    c. 10-25%
    d. 25-35%

16. What special enhancements do WPA-Personal and WPA2-Personal require for fast roaming?
    a. Preauthentication
    b. PMK caching
    c. OKC
    d. None

17. On enterprise secure wireless networks, which of these can add to overall roaming slowness?
    a. Delays between AP and STA
    b. Delays between RADIUS and LDAP servers
    c. RADIUS processing times when server is busy
    d. All of these

18. One of the following is not a requirement for Voice-Personal certification. Which is it?
    a. Zero packet loss
    b. Less than 1% packet loss
    c. Less than 50 ms of latency
    d. Less than 50 ms of jitter

19. Voice-Enterprise certification requires all but one of the following. Select the option not associated with Voice-Enterprise certification.
    a. 802.11r
    b. 802.11e
    c. 802.11d
    d. 802.11k

20. Which client types have the most problems with roaming on Wi-Fi networks?
    a. Smart TVs
    b. VoIP
    c. Digital Signage
    d. Retail scanners

21. The main disadvantage of preauthentication as a roaming enhancement is
    _____.
      a. It is not standardized by the IEEE.
      b. It only works with a single access point.
      c. It is only supported by certain infrastructures.
      d. It does not scale well.

22. Which of the following is not defined by the 802.11 standard, and is therefore
    a proprietary mechanism?
      a. OKC
      b. PMK caching
      c. Preauthentication
      d. FT

23. You are training a junior engineer how to troubleshoot 802.11r. She asks how
    the PMK-R0 and PMK-R1 keys are derived. How do you reply?
      a. PMK-R0 derived from MSK, R1 derived from MSK response.
      b. PMK-R0 derived from PSK, R1 derived from MSK.
      c. PMK-R0 derived from MSK, R1 derived from R0.
      d. PMK-R0 derived by R1, R1 derived from MSK response.

24. The 802.11i solution to the delay caused by establishing a PMKSA is what?
      a. PMK stacking
      b. PMK caching
      c. PMK pre-fetch
      d. PMK-to-self

25. When PMK caching is in use, what frames have PMKID Count and PMKID List fields?
    a. Association
    b. Beacon Probe
    c. Reassociation
    d. Roam

Chapter 8: Review Answers

1. **B** is correct. Though it is not often used, transition and roam are the same thing.

2. **A** is correct. PSK is much friendlier to roaming than enterprise security.

3. **C** is correct. With too much delay during roaming, full client associations need to be re-accomplished.

4. **D** is correct. Roam times should be under 150 ms by established best practices.

5. **B** is correct. In a slow roam, a full association has to occur again, so there is no reassociation.

6. **C** is correct. VoIP protocols are real-time and usually UDP for greatest efficiency.

7. **D** is correct. Security can impact network operations, so knowing the details of roaming on secure networks help in troubleshooting.

8. **C** is correct. In the SCA, the controller decides when clients roam to other APs.

9. **A** is correct. 802.11-2012 is currently the most efficient roaming method.

10. **B** is correct. Preauthentication happens with all nearby APs, not just a single one.

11. **B** is correct. Voice-Enterprise aims for roams under 50 ms, although breaks to 100 ms are allowed.

12. **C** is correct. QoS (Quality of Service) is important in wired and wireless networks.

13. **D** is correct. Roaming is one of those areas in the 802.11 standard where vendors have a lot of freedom to decide their own mechanisms.

14. **B** is correct. When the client leaves one network for another, it has crossed the Layer 3 boundary.

15. **A** is correct. Though it cannot be easily or precisely measured, desired overlap is 15-30%.

16. **D** is correct. WPA/WPA2-Personal require no special enhancements for fast roaming.

17. **D** is correct. It is important to know the various processes that can contribute to delay.

18. **A** is correct. For Voice-Personal, less than 1% of packet loss is required. Zero percent is pretty hard to achieve in wireless.

19. **C** is correct. 802.11d does not apply to Voice-Enterprise.

20. **B** is correct. VoIP clients are both highly mobile and susceptible to many factors that could impact communications while roaming.

21. **D** is correct. Preauthentication does not scale well.

22. **A** is correct. OKC is proprietary and not part of 802.11.

23. **C** is correct. R1 is derived from R0; remember it!

24. **B** is correct. 802.11i includes PMK caching to overcome PMKSA delays.

25. **C** is correct. Reassociation Request frames have PMKID Count and List fields.

Chapter 9:

Network Monitoring

Objectives

3.7   Describe and demonstrate the use of secure infrastructure management protocols, including HTTPS, SNMP, secure FTP protocols, SCP, and SSH.

3.9   Understand additional security features in WLAN infrastructure and access devices, including management frame protection, Role-Based Access Control (RBAC), Fast BSS transition (pre-authentication and OKC), physical security methods, and Network Access Control (NAC).

4.1   Explain the importance of ongoing WLAN monitoring and the necessary tools and processes used as well as the importance of WLAN security audits and compliance reports.

4.2   Understand how to use protocol and spectrum analyzers to effectively evaluate secure wireless networks including 802.1X authentication troubleshooting, location of rogue security devices, and identification of non-compliant devices.

4.3   Understand the command features and components of a Wireless Intrusion Prevention Systems (WIPS) and how they are used in relation to performance, protocol, spectrum, and security analysis.

4.4   Describe the different types of WLAN management systems and their features, including network discovery, configuration management, firmware management, audit management, policy enforcement, rogue detection, network monitoring, user monitoring, event alarms, and event notifications.

4.5   Describe and implement compliance monitoring, enforcement, and reporting. Topics include industry requirements, such as PCI-DSS and HIPAA, and general government regulations.

When it comes to security and enterprise Wi-Fi, designing and installing a well-designed WLAN is just the beginning. Once implemented, the WLAN must be monitored for compliance with policies and regulations. It also needs to be monitor to detect attacks and address them as quickly as possible. Additionally, the WLAN must be managed using secure management protocols. This chapter introduces WLAN network monitoring and management solutions.

Secure Management Protocols

If you administer the individual APs in your wireless LAN, be sure to use secure methods for management. While you are able to connect to many vendors' APs using standard HTTP by default, this is not a recommended practice. All HTTP traffic is transmitted as clear text, which means the configuration settings applied via HTTP are easily eavesdropped on.

The following image demonstrates the vulnerability of using HTTP for systems administration. In this real-world example, we have blocked out identifying information to protect the site owners. You can clearly see the logon is "swettmarden" and the password is "drow1ssap1." This is because the web server does not use HTTPS for the logon process and the credentials are passed in the clear.

Of course, this scenario was created completely for this text, but this scenario occurs every day thousands (if not millions) of times around the world.

Understandably, HTTPS should always be used when a web-based interface is employed to manage your APs. If the AP does not support HTTPS, it is best not to use HTTP to manage the device. (Chances are, you are not dealing with enterprise equipment if only HTTP is available.) HTTPS actually uses SSL and requires that a certificate be made available to the server. APs that support HTTPS have a certificate installed in the AP already. SSL is a Layer 7 encryption technology.

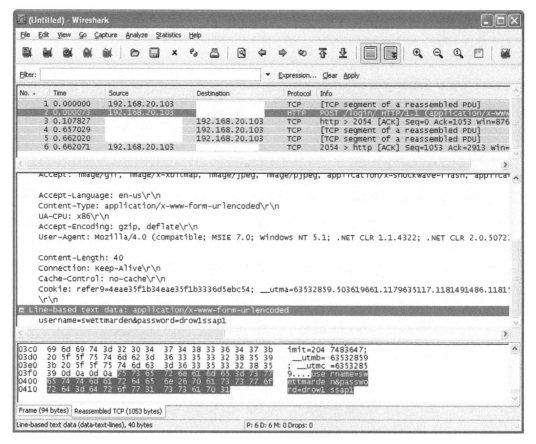

Figure 9-1: Wireshark showing HTTP Logon Credentials

Another Layer 7 encryption solution is SSH. The first version of SSH has known vulnerabilities and should be avoided, but SSH2 is currently considered secure. SSH2 is usually used to provide command line interface (CLI) access to the managed device. SSH2 provides the following benefits in a secure networking application:

- Public and private key authentication, or username and password authentication.
- Data signing through the use of public and private key pairs.
- Private key passphrase association.
- Multiple encryption algorithms are supported such as AES, 3DES, and DES.
- Encryption key rotation.

- Data integrity enforced through hashing algorithms.
- Data compression may be supported.

The *Simple Network Management Protocol* (SNMP) is a standard solution for centrally monitoring and managing network devices. SNMP was plagued by security vulnerabilities early on, and these weaknesses have been addressed in SNMP v3. Version 3 has added authentication and privacy controls to help protect the management information passed on your network. You should ensure that any device you manage with SNMP uses version 3 or higher of this protocol. As is true with any technology, you must be proactive and continually be on the lookout for new vulnerabilities that would impact your network. That which is secure today may be vulnerable tomorrow.

Additionally, if file copy processes are used, secure FTP (which combines FTP with SSH) should be used or the secure copy protocol (SCP), which is common in Linux environments. SFTP is different from FTPS.

- SFTP is FTP combined with SSH.
- FTPS is FTP combined with TLS.

Along with secure management protocols, many security-minded network environments manage their network gear on a private, isolated subnet. This does not negate the need to use secure protocols for management, but does provide a tremendous increase in security.

WLAN Monitoring

One way to verify the functionality and integrity of a WLAN is by using monitoring processes of various types. The monitoring process

- ensures a system maintains the needed performance levels and
- provides the required security based on the design and the corporate security policy.

Monitoring is an on-going process that gathers key system information, and uses that information to validate that a system is operating as intended and designed.

A well thought out and designed monitoring system provides valuable metrics and indicators that allow information technology (IT) professionals the ability to

- conduct security audits and locate vulnerabilities
- maintain regulatory compliance
- maintain proper performance levels, and
- verify network availability.

Both manual and automated methods exist that are used with wireless network monitoring. Determining which process and tools you use really depends on

- the size of the infrastructure, and
- the number of devices that are used on the network.

Also, the staffing structure of a network support organization influences which tools are used, as automated testing can augment staff's capabilities, if implemented properly.

Some of the common tools used for network monitoring include:

- Wireless Intrusion Detection System (WIDS)
- Wireless Intrusion Prevention System (WIPS)
- Wireless Network Management Systems (WNMS)
- Protocol analyzer software and hardware
- Spectrum analyzer software and hardware
- Hardware sensors

These tools are designed to perform specific tasks. The following provides a brief description of each.

Wireless Intrusion Detection System (WIDS)

A WIDS is used to gather information about a computer network. The type of information collected depends on the business model and the requirements of the organization. Hardware sensors distributed around the physical network are used to gather and report information to a physical appliance or a server database. The WIDS only detects and reports anomalies that are determined from a baseline of the network. WIDS is usually "always on" and can be set with various levels of automated reporting and alerting.

Wireless Intrusion Prevention System (WIPS)

The WIPS has many of the same characteristics as the WIDS system; however, in addition to detection of threats, a WIPS system may be able to mitigate the threats (an important distinction). Information that is collected from the sensors is reported to a central server database or network appliance for proper analysis and handling. Alarms trigger and alerts are sent to notify network personnel of the potential intrusion and the severity of the intrusion. Depending on how the system is configured, mitigation may ensue.

Wireless Network Management Systems (WNMS)

The WNMS is a centralized solution that may run on a hardware server in a virtual environment or in the cloud. A WNMS allows a network engineer to manage and control the entire WLAN centrally, including the APs and controllers. These centralized management systems are available from many manufacturers for use with their own infrastructure devices. As WLAN systems get more complex, the number of vendor-neutral WNMS solutions that work well with many different manufacturers' equipment is shrinking, but third-party NMS do exist. A WNMS may also incorporate WIPS technology for a complete wireless network management, monitoring, and security solution. In these systems, each major feature is typically licensed at additional cost.

Protocol Analyzer Software and Hardware

Protocol analysis software is used to capture frames that travel through a network medium. Protocol analyzers are used for both wired and wireless networks. Some analyzers have the capability to function on both types of networks. Protocol analyzers are great troubleshooting tools, and can be used for discovering potential security issues. Protocol analyzers can be stand-alone, or for use with a laptop computer or other mobile devices. They can be integrated with a wireless AP, a dedicated remote infrastructure device, or part of a WIPS system. In some cases, such as with cloud-controlled WLAN systems, you can do remote packet capture on far-away access points but save the capture files locally to your PC for analysis.

Spectrum Analyzer Software and Hardware

Spectrum analyzers are used to monitor the open air and to help identify what type of radio frequency is present. With respect to wireless networks, a spectrum analyzer helps to identify issues and threats that other monitoring tools such as a protocol analyzer cannot. Spectrum analyzers vary in size, complexity, and cost based on the intended use. Some manufacturers build spectrum analyzers to work specifically with standards based IEEE 802.11 wireless networks while others may be used for a variety of other RF monitoring purposes. It is common to see some form of spectrum analyzer utility baked into the access points themselves, but the quality and granularity of spectrum analysis can vary widely across devices.

Hardware Sensors

Sensors are used to gather needed information by constantly monitoring the open air. These devices can be integrated within a wireless AP or a stand-alone dedicated device. Sensors operate in what is known as monitor mode and are passive devices that will not interfere with other wireless devices that occupy the same radio frequency space. Some access points can be configured as full-time sensors as part of their configuration.

Rogue AP and Client Detection

Much emphasis has been placed on rogue APs throughout the years. Since wireless LANs first began to be implemented, rogue devices were recognized as both a security concern and a potential source of RF interference and they still pose a threat to our networks today. A rogue AP can be defined as any AP that is operating in your owned space that has not been authorized by you. The rogue AP may have been placed by

- an intruder seeking to gain access to your wired network, or
- a well-meaning user hoping to make his or her life easier and more mobile while at work.

Either way, the rogue AP is a threat to your security.

There are two primary reasons that motivate an attacker to install a rogue AP in your environment.

- The first is to gain access to your wired or wireless network by extending it into the air.
- The second is to attack your valid wireless client STAs.

In the first case, the attacker usually finds an out-of-the-way spot where a live Ethernet port provides connectivity to the wired LAN. He connects the Ethernet port to the AP using a standard cable and powers the AP with a nearby power outlet. Some APs may even be powered by battery if the attacker only needs access for a short time. Once the attacker has the AP in place, he can begin attacking your wired LAN or other WLANs that may be connected to the wired LAN while not needing to be physically close to the AP itself. Of course, the attacker has to be willing to lose his AP in a scenario like this because he risks not being able to retrieve after the attack. With the physical security being as lax as it is in many organizations, however, the retrieval may not be too difficult.

 Note: **Many rogue APs are placed by intruders for the sole purpose of gaining high-speed Internet connectivity. They often know that companies have very fast connections to the Internet and, since they will be the only user connected to the AP, they can download a tremendous amount of illegal software, movies, music and more in a short window of time. This malicious use of your network can be protected against by using an Internet proxy server that requires authentication.**

Protecting against the placement of such APs is important. The first thing to consider is the disabling of all Ethernet ports that are not actually in use. When those ports are needed, they can be administratively enabled through software, usually by using a wired NMS. In addition to this, you should have good physical security in place that deters such behavior. Even fake surveillance cameras can go a long way here. Install a fake surveillance camera in areas where you think an attacker may attempt to install a rogue AP. The presence of this device—as long as it looks real—frequently deters the attacker.

The second motivation for placement by an attacker is that of direct attack against your WLAN clients. In this case, the attacker may be using the AP to perform a hijacking attack in an attempt to gain access to the data on the wireless LAN computers. She may also be attempting to install backdoors on these WLAN clients that allow her access to the network in the future. In these scenarios, rogue AP detection can be more difficult. The attacker may be a temporary employee who has valid access to the premises and has been granted permission to use her laptop at work. She may be running a software-based rogue AP, or she may be using a USB-power pocket AP like the one shown in the following image. While the shown pocket AP is an older 54 Mbps 802.11g AP, this is still sufficient for performing network attacks and is very inexpensive to acquire through websites like eBay. Newer 802.11n and 802.11ac pocket APs are also available now.

Figure 9-2: D-Link Pocket AP (DWL-G730AP)

Protecting against this type of rogue AP can be challenging. The attacker is not connecting to an Ethernet port and does not likely desire to connect to one.

Therefore, disabling unused ports is not helpful. CWSPs should remember that the best protection against this type of rogue AP attack is to implement a secure 802.1X/EAP authentication type that uses mutual authentication. This will also help protect your clients from other rogue AP type attacks.

 Note: It is not the intention of this book to suggest that a pocket AP is only useful in rogue AP scenarios. They are used quite frequently, with permission, in training centers to provide wireless networks to students, and in other travel scenarios.

Rogue AP detection generally takes place in two ways, through the wired or wireless interface. Remember that a rogue AP is still an access point, and it will therefore transmit Beacon frames at a regular interval. If you use a site survey tool to map the RF coverage in your area and then perform a pass-through on foot with this tool again periodically, you can detect the existence of new APs by comparing RF coverage as it varies from the original survey. This would be one method of rogue AP detection through the wireless interface.

Some vendors allow for the implementation of either uncommon channel widths, such as 5 MHz or 10 MHz channels and even the use of uncommon Wi-Fi modulation methods like TDMA mode. This makes rogue AP detection even more difficult.

Another method of detection through the wireless interface would be to keep up-to-date documentation of the number of APs you have installed that can be detected at a given location. Then you can go to that location—and other locations as well—and use a tool like inSSIDer to see if more APs are now present. When you see a new AP, note its MAC address; you can then monitor the signal strength of the Beacons from that MAC address while moving throughout the area. You should notice the strength weakening and strengthening as you move around. Using this process, you should eventually be able to find the proximity of the AP, and then the AP itself. It may be an innocent neighbor AP or it may be a rogue AP installed within your facility.

You can also detect rogue APs through the wired port. Many APs are installed by users who want the flexibility provided by a WLAN, or who want less wireless security than the business WLAN enforces. These users seldom know how to prevent you from detecting the AP through the wired port. Most APs installed by attackers are not configured in such a way to prevent you from detecting them through the wired port either. The key fact is that these rogue APs are usually cheap SOHO APs or routers that either do not support the disabling of the HTTP management interface on the Ethernet port or, again, the installer does not know how to do so.

Since you know that an HTTP server is running on most APs but not on most desktop PCs or network servers, you can perform a port scan subnet-by-subnet looking for IP addresses with port 80 open. When you discover an IP address with port 80 open that was not there before, it is possible that you have discovered a rogue AP (or some other unauthorized rogue device). Use the following trick to build your own rogue detection system:

1. When you have finished installing your WLAN and you know that there are no rogues at this point
   a. do a port scan of every segment, and
   b. save the output to a text file.
2. Run the same port scan every week or two during off peak hours (if you have them) and save the new scan to a different file.
3. Use any of dozens of file comparison tools to look for differences. Or, even better, write your own script that compares the two files and only tells you of new references to ports 80 (HTTP) and 23 (telnet).

With this process, you can build your own rogue detection system very easily. It will not be as powerful as a commercial WIPS solution, but it certainly is better than no detection system at all. If your network supports it (and you have the ability), you could even write your script in such a way that it disables the Ethernet ports where the new TCP ports 80 or 23 are found, and e-mails a report to you.

You could take action as soon as you receive the e-mail, but at least the script disabled the device on the assumption that it is a rogue. This provides you with a form of automatic containment. This model works well in SOHO implementations and smaller SMBs.

In larger enterprises and larger SMBs, you will need to install more powerful centralized management solutions. For example, Cisco System's Unified Wireless Network solution takes advantage of the fact that all Cisco controllers include a method to automatically detect rogue APs on and off the network. This allows you to spend your time doing more than running scripts and setting up manual solutions.

The old saying reminds us that an ounce of prevention is worth a pound of cure. This saying is certainly true for rogue APs. There are a number of methods you can use to prevent individuals from connecting unauthorized APs to your wired network. These include:

- **Disabling unused Ethernet ports**—This was covered earlier and it is an easy solution, but it should not be relied on by itself because people do make mistakes and leave ports open. It can also be hard to manage in large dynamic Ethernet environments.

- **Using port security on switches**—Many switches support port-based filtering by MAC addresses and other parameters. You can specify that the only MAC addresses that can connect to your switch are those in the specified list. Wired MAC addresses are far more difficult than WLAN MACs for an intruder to find, so it is not easy for an attacker to get an AP's MAC into this list.

- **State clearly in your acceptable use policy that users cannot install APs**— This most certainly does not prevent the installation of all rogue APs, but it does deter many from installing them.

- **Implement Network Access Control technology**—This causes the attacker's computer to go straight to a quarantine area when he or she accesses the network. The NAC device/server would be installed between the switch that provides connectivity to your Ethernet ports and the rest of the network. Any device that connects would require authentication and validation. The operational theory is that this would drive the typical would-be attacker away for fear of being caught by IT staff.

Implement enterprise-capable wireless LAN solutions that automatically detect and report rogue APs and graphically show their locations. Wireless network management systems from a number of market leaders detect and report rogue APs automatically and can display their locations on floorplans in the management solution.

As you can see, there are multiple methods that you can use to prevent the connection of rogue APs to your wired LAN. Some of these methods are psychological and others are technological, but a combination of both types usually works best.

WIPS—Features

Enterprise-class wireless intrusion prevention system (WIPS) solutions are used to compliment an organization's wireless network encryption and authentication solutions. They give you all the rogue detection capabilities referenced earlier in an automated solution. The WIPS can be configured to recognize trusted and known wireless devices installed in a service area and report changes to the administrator's console. Additionally, a WIPS is capable of providing collected data to a server regarding the overall security and potential threats that are recognized. Implemented correctly, WIPS solutions can provide a wealth of information as well as protection for your network infrastructure and wireless devices.

WIPS solutions are software-based, hardware-based or cloud-managed, and are capable of monitoring the unbounded wireless medium through the use of wireless hardware sensors. A WIPS typically reports captured information to software programs to be recorded in a server database. The WIPS solution is able to take the appropriate countermeasures to prevent wireless network intrusions as needed to comply with security policies. These countermeasures are based on identifying the intrusion by comparing the captured information to an intrusion signature database within the WIPS server.

WIPS solutions contain a variety of features which include:

- Use of hardware sensors for monitoring.

- 24x7x365 monitoring.
- Mitigation features (containment, blocking, notifications, etc.).
- Provide notifications of threats through a variety of mechanisms.
- Detection of threats to the wireless infrastructure such as denial of service (DoS) attacks and rogue APs.
- Built-in reporting systems.
- Integrated RF spectrum analysis to monitor and view the RF spectrum.
- Validation of compliance with corporate security policy and legislative compliance.
- Capable of retaining collected data for further forensic investigation.
- Location of RF devices.

Exam Moment: For RF location features to work in most WIPS solutions, the RF environment must be properly sampled with a calibration process during installation and configuration. Proper set-up is critical for WIPS to function as desired.

Enforcing Functional Policy

Earlier you learned about the importance of corporate security policy. CWSPs need to understand that functional policy defines the technical aspects of network security. An enterprise WIPS has the capability to provide the necessary enforcement of functional policy. Functional policy includes the following components, among others:

- Password policy
- Acceptable use policy
- Authentication and encryption policy
- Wireless LAN access policy
- Wireless LAN monitoring policy
- Endpoint device policy
- Personal device policy

In order to provide enterprise-class WLAN security enforcement, the organization should require the use of an unattended WIDS. Here is an important distinction: WIDS that include the ability to perform intrusion containment and mitigation are typically referred to as WIPS. As mentioned earlier, the main difference between WIDS and WIPS solutions is the fact that

- a WIDS system detects threats and reports those threats, and
- a WIPS system has the capability to detect threats and mitigate those threats.

While it is important to write a security policy to document the desired security practices for a network, enforcement of a formal policy is a different challenge. WIPS platforms are designed to complement written policy and to provide monitoring and enforcement of that policy. Monitoring and security auditing are crucial in determining security policy adherence. All companies should perform continuous monitoring—especially those that have a "no WLAN" policy (this can be counterintuitive to some people, but is important to grasp). WIDS platforms stop at the level of intrusion detection and reporting, but WIPS take it a step further by preventing some threats, and assisting in the enforcement of a functional security policy.

Security Monitoring

The initial security audit provides a critical baseline of all active wireless devices (both infrastructure and client), and is used to classify those devices by their roles. The baseline is used to properly identify and categorize devices based on how they fit within the wireless network infrastructure. In all types of network security, a baseline is not a one-time event. To ensure that the security audit baseline remains current, it is necessary to provide on-going monitoring, as most wireless networks have components that are constantly changing and introducing new technology to the monitored environment. The baseline can be done manually or through the use of automated sensing systems like WIPS. Many WIPS systems are equipped with the ability to isolate and nullify the actions of threatening wireless devices. This activity is referred to as "threat mitigation."

WIPS use distributed sensors strategically placed around a facility, campus, or other service area to report performance and security policy violations to a central analysis engine.

Some common enterprise-class WIPS system manufacturers are:

- AirTight (now Mojo Networks)
- Cisco Systems
- Fluke Networks / AirMagnet Enterprise (Netscout)
- Motorola (Zebra) AirDefense Enterprise
- Wildpackets (Savvius) WatchPoint Platform
- Aerohive
- Cisco-Meraki

Reporting and Auditing

Compliance monitoring is essential for many organizations today. Implementation of legislated regulatory constraints of the WLAN is usually the responsibility of the IT department. Compliance with regulatory requirements must be verifiable and auditable by third party inspectors. Technical solutions such as WIPS reporting functions automate these tasks.

Some examples of legislated security requirements include the following:

- Directive 8100.2 (DoD)
- Health Insurance Portability and Accountability Act (HIPAA)
- Sarbanes-Oxley (SOX)
- Gramm-Leach-Bliley Act (GLBA)
- Payment Card Industry (PCI) Data Security Standard (DSS)

Although all of these are very important, two that get a lot of attention are HIPAA and PCI. If a WIPS system is used, it can automate this task to decrease the administrative overhead in maintaining compliance.

The type of business done by an organization will determine if it must comply with one or more of these regulatory requirements. For example, a healthcare organization may also process credit and debit card payments. This scenario requires compliance with both HIPAA and PCI. By contrast, a small restaurant that takes credit card payments would just need to be PCI compliant.

PCI Compliance as an Example

Payment Card Industry (PCI) compliance is a statement of conformity to the PCI Data Security Standard (DSS). PCI DSS is a set of standards that help to ensure that companies processing payment cards (credit cards, debit cards, etc.) do so in a universally agreed upon secure manner. The standards encompass payment card processing, account data storage, and information transfer.

The PCI DSS is a 112 page document (as of version 3.0) that outlines the process of implementing a secure payment card processing environment. The document covers the following components:

- Building and Maintaining a Secure Network
- Protecting Card Holder Data
- Maintaining Vulnerability Management Programs
- Implementing Strong Access Control Measures
- Regularly Monitoring and Testing Networks
- Maintaining an Information Security Policy

If you have been a student of information security, you will immediately recognize most of these components as standard security best practices. Indeed, the only unique component of PCI is that of protecting card holder data, and even that could likely be classified under the normal heading of protecting valuable data. In the end, there is really nothing new in the PCI DSS document; however, more and more states and credit card companies are requiring compliance with it in order to process payment cards. The good news is that if you already implement security best practices, you will have very little to change in order to comply with PCI DSS.

The PCI DSS standard lists both recommended and required practices. In the standard, network segmentation is only recommended while the installation of perimeter firewalls between wireless networks and the payment processing segment is required. In fact, the standard lists many requirements for WLAN implementations including:

Install perimeter firewalls between any wireless networks and the cardholder data environment, and configure these firewalls to deny or control (if such traffic is necessary for business purposes) any traffic from the wireless environment into the cardholder data environment.

For wireless environments connected to the cardholder data environment or transmitting cardholder data, change wireless vendor defaults, including but not limited to default wireless encryption keys, passwords, and SNMP community strings. Ensure wireless device security settings are enabled for strong encryption technology for authentication and transmission.

Ensure wireless networks transmitting cardholder data or connected to the cardholder data environment, use industry best practices (for example, IEEE 802.11i) to implement strong encryption for authentication and transmission.

Implement additional security features for any required services, protocols, or daemons that are considered to be insecure—for example, use secured technologies such as SSH, S-FTP, SSL, or IPSec VPN to protect insecure services such as NetBIOS, file-sharing, Telnet, FTP, etc.

Ensure that security policies and operational procedures for managing vendor defaults and other security parameters are documented, in use, and known to all affected parties.

The following testing procedures apply to modification of default settings for WLANs:

1) Interview responsible personnel and examine supporting documentation to verify that:
   - Encryption keys were changed from default at installation.
   - Encryption keys are changed anytime anyone with knowledge of the keys leaves the company or changes positions.
2) Interview personnel and examine policies and procedures to verify:
   - Default SNMP community strings are required to be changed upon installation.

- Default passwords/phrases on access points are required to be changed upon installation.

3) Examine vendor documentation and login to wireless devices, with system administrator help, to verify:
   - Default SNMP community strings are not used.
   - Default passwords/passphrases on access points are not used.

4) Examine vendor documentation and observe wireless configuration settings to verify firmware on wireless devices is updated to support strong encryption for:
   - Authentication over wireless networks
   - Transmission over wireless networks

5) Examine vendor documentation and observe wireless configuration settings to verify other security-related wireless vendor defaults were changed, if applicable.

The following guidelines apply in relation to the modification of default settings for WLANs:

- If wireless networks are not implemented with sufficient security configurations (including changing default settings), wireless sniffers can eavesdrop on the traffic, easily capture data and passwords, and easily enter and attack the network.
- In addition, the key-exchange protocol for older versions of 802.11 encryption (Wired Equivalent Privacy, or WEP) has been broken and can render the encryption useless. Firmware for devices should be updated to support more secure protocols.

The following testing procedures apply in relation to authentication and encryption on WLANs:

- Identify all wireless networks transmitting cardholder data or connected to the cardholder data environment.
- Examine documented standards and compare to system configuration settings to verify the following for all wireless networks identified:

- Industry best practices (for example, IEEE 802.11i) are used to implement strong encryption for authentication and transmission.
- Weak encryption (for example, WEP, SSL version 2.0 or older) is not used as a security control for authentication or transmission.

Apply the following guidelines in relation to WLAN authentication and encryption:

- Malicious users use free and widely available tools to eavesdrop on wireless communications. Use of strong cryptography can help limit disclosure of sensitive information across wireless networks.
- Strong cryptography for authentication and transmission of cardholder data is required to prevent malicious users from gaining access to the wireless network or utilizing wireless networks to access other internal networks or data.

Again, the entire PCI-DSS document is well over 100 pages, but these excerpts give a sense of what to expect when dealing with PCI as a CWSP. In summary, to comply with PCI DSS, a WLAN that is not involved in payment card processing must be segmented from the payment card processing segment using firewalls, vendor defaults must be changed, and strong encryption based on 802.11i must be implemented. In fact, the standard explicitly states that the use of WEP as a security control is prohibited.

HIPAA Compliance as an Example

The HIPAA regulations require that healthcare organizations (including hospitals, doctor's offices, and any other organization that handles health information) implement policies and procedures to ensure that only authorized individuals may access patient health information in the United States. HIPAA (the name stands for Health Insurance Portability and Accountability Act) was enacted within the U.S. in 2006. Organizations covered by the act include:

- Health plan providers
- Healthcare clearinghouses, and
- Any healthcare provider who transmits health information in electronic form.

The health information protected by HIPAA includes all individually identifiable health information. This information is identified as information that is unique to an individual and related to the health of that individual. Examples include

- Past, present, or future mental or physical health condition
- Healthcare that has been provided to the individual, and
- Healthcare payment information.

Information classified as de-identified does not require compliance with HIPAA regulations. De-identified information is information that neither identifies nor provides a foundational knowledge base on which a patient may be identified.

The HIPAA regulations are nonspecific, allowing organizations of differing sizes to implement appropriate security measures that result in the protection of health information. The general requirements include these stipulations:

- Privacy policies and procedures must be documented.
- A privacy official must be designated to oversee the HIPAA regulation implementation and maintenance.
- All workforce members must be trained to understand and comply with the privacy policies.
- Mitigation efforts must be taken when privacy policies are breached.
- Effective data safeguards must be implemented.
- Complaint processing procedures must be implemented.
- Patients must not be asked to waive privacy rights, and retaliation against complaints is not allowed.
- Privacy policies and incident documentation must be maintained for six years.

With an understanding of the HIPAA regulations, the only remaining question is this: How do these regulations apply to a WLAN? The answer is simple: they apply to WLANs in the same way that they apply to wired LANs. There is no significant difference. Whether wired or wireless, use the following five security solutions to effectively comply with HIPAA regulations:

- Authentication
- Authorization

- Confidentiality
- Integrity
- Nonrepudiation

All of these terms were defined earlier in the book. Wired networks do not provide confidentiality by default, and encryption solutions must be used to comply with HIPAA. This requirement is the same for wireless networks. The same is true for the other four requirements, as well. You must comply with all five of these requirements on both wired and wireless networks under HIPAA directives.

Many vendors attempt to differentiate between wired and wireless networks in order to indicate that their wireless solution is the best when it comes to HIPAA compliance. The truth is that any hardware and software combination that allow the implementation of 802.11i security can be fully and completely HIPAA compliant. Do not fall into the trap of marketing hyperbole when it comes to regulatory compliance.

Auditing and Forensics

In addition to regulatory compliance auditing, WIPS platforms automate internal network security auditing practices. Data collection is performed by the WIPS sensors and is logged by the WIPS server for easy auditing. When security breaches are detected, forensic analysis may be done to determine the impact of a network threat. Some WIPS vendors have added a strong forensic analysis component to their WIPS platforms.

Corporate security policy determines how the organization handles auditing and forensics, such as

- frequency and detail of the audits, and
- how forensics data is logged, stored and archived.

By continuously monitoring, analyzing, and logging wireless traffic signatures, WIPS solutions provide automated forensics and security auditing. This can streamline the process and provide quality, accurate results, and reports. At the same time, effective WIPS does not just happen by purchasing a system, proper setup is crucial to the effectiveness of the WIPS investment.

Audit Methods

During the risk assessment, any legal or legislated requirements that pertain to the organization implementing the WLAN should be recognized and accommodated. These vary depending on the business that the organization is in. Some examples of legislated security requirements include the following:

- Directive 8100.2 (DoD)
- Health Insurance Portability and Accountability Act (HIPAA)
- Sarbanes-Oxley (SOX)
- Gramm-Leach-Bliley Act (GLBA)
- Payment Card Industry (PCI) Data Security Standard

Implementation of the legislated requirements is the responsibility of the IT department. These procedures must be verifiable and auditable in documentation and practice by third party inspectors. Again, some technical solutions such as WIPS reporting functions automate these tasks.

In order to be able to verify security policy compliance, network administrators including CWSPs must be competent with analysis utilities. An understanding of networking concepts is fundamental to this ability. Networking professionals frequently refer to a seven-layer model (the OSI model) when discussing the interactions of the many protocols which are used to allow reliable, distributed data communications. Often the documentation for auditing tools references these layers and the way they communicate.

As you have learned in CWNA, each layer of the networking model communicates only with the layer above and the layer below and this communication is unidirectional. Stated differently, the flow of the communications either goes down the protocol stack on its way to be transmitted or flows up the protocol stack after having been received. As a quick review—each layer either adds its own interpretive information in the form of a header (if preparing to transmit) or interprets the header information that was added by its counterpart on the remote terminal (if receiving). When a layer adds its own unique information to data sent from a higher layer the resulting information field is known as a protocol data unit (PDU). PDUs are distinct for each layer and are only meaningful to the same layer on the remote end of the conversation.

Audit Tools

There are several tools on the market to facilitate the process of audits and reports. Some monitoring tools, like WIPS, help automate the reporting process for compliance.

Other types of audits include security posture auditing, also known as penetration testing. In this more active type of audit, an inside employee and/or outside contractor test the security posture of an organization in an attempt to expose any weaknesses. Purpose-built tools like Immunity's SILICA are designed specifically to automate the process of discovering and exposing network vulnerabilities. This tool includes automated reporting of its findings. The SILICA website (www.immunityinc.com/products/silica) lists some the tasks that can be performed and information that can be collected includes:

- Recover WEP, WPA 1,2 and LEAP keys.
- Passively hijack web application sessions for email, social networking and Intranet sites.
- Map a wireless network and identify its relationships with associated clients and other APs.
- Identify vendors, hidden SSIDs and equipment passively.
- Scan and break into hosts on the network using integrated CANVAS exploit modules and commands to recover screenshots, password hashes and other sensitive information.
- Perform man-in-the-middle attacks to find valuable information exchanged between hosts.
- Generate reports for wireless and network data.
- Hijack wireless client connections via AP impersonation.
- Passively inject custom content into client's web sessions.
- Take full control of wireless clients via CANVAS's client-side exploitation framework (clientD).

- Decrypt and easily view all WEP and WPA/2 traffic.

Note that the list shows some of what look like attacks an intruder would use on a network. It is important to understand that these are auditing tools used specifically for that purpose. Unfortunately, some auditing tools can end up in the wrong hands and can work against you. That is why understanding what can be collected and used on a wireless network benefits the network security professional to be able to better secure their network.

Exam Moment: To ensure that an assessment of network security is exhaustive, the auditor should start with a list of wireless security solutions in use. Each solution should be tested for strength and proper configuration.

Other tools are available as well, including compilations of security auditing tools like the Kali Linux project. This software includes several of the best penetration testing tools available for Linux distributions.

Auditing tools including in Kali Linux 1.1 include:

- AirCrack-NG
- ASLEAP
- Bully
- Cowpatty
- EAP-MD5-Pass
- Fern-WiFi-Cracker
- FreeRADIUS-WPE

- GenKeys
- GenPMK
- GisKismet
- Kismet
- MDK3
- nmap
- WiFiARP

- WiFiDNS
- WiFi-Honey
- WiFiPING
- WiFiTap
- WiFiTE
- WireShark
- zenmap

Enterprise WIPS Topology

Enterprise-class WIPS systems usually consist of a centralized server that runs the main application, a remote console, and a number of remote sensors located at various locations throughout the organization's facilities. The sensors send a constant low-bit rate stream of data to the server application over tunneled LAN or WAN connections. The central server accumulates, logs, and reports on the data from the various sensors. The remote console can connect to the server and review the state and alarm conditions.

Enterprise WIPS may be configured to

- work with some popular WNMS solutions, and
- recognize and work with popular WLAN controller systems.

WIPS sensors are configured as passive—unless they are actively mitigating a threat—devices that quietly listen to all in-band radio traffic in a service area. These readings are forwarded upstream to the WIPS server. Some manufacturers enable autonomous and lightweight APs to be converted to full-time or part-time WIPS sensors, but additional licensing may be required to take advantage of this option.

It is important that the WIPS sensors use the correct radio frequency band that is to be monitored, and that the WIPS system has the same capabilities as the installed network infrastructure wireless APs. If the sensors are not configured correctly or do not parallel the network capabilities of the specific WLAN being monitored, some events may go unnoticed and result in potential security issues.

Integrated vs. Overlay

The two high-level WIPS deployment techniques are known as *integrated* and *overlay*.

In an integrated WIPS solution, WIPS functionality is integrated into AP hardware. The hardware performs dual roles as both a wireless AP and a WIPS sensor. There are different implementations of integrated solutions. Some use dedicated WIPS radios for full-time scanning, while others use part-time scanning with the same radios that are used for client access.

Integrated WIPS solutions often use part-time scanning to make the most of the existing AP's radios. In this setup, the radio rotates between client access and off-channel scanning. While there is often an element of cost-effectiveness with integrated WIPS solutions, the scanning capabilities can sometimes be severely limited compared to dedicated WIPS hardware.

Many AP manufacturers currently offer the option to configure an AP radio as a WIPS sensor. In most cases, this would be a dual-radio AP in which one radio is configured to provide client access and the other provides WIPS functions. Only a few vendors have developed tri-radio APs where dual-radio client access is provided with the third radio configured as a WIPS sensor. This is the most robust integrated solution, but the additional radio adds cost. Some manufacturers build APs that are band unlocked, or software-defined. This means you would have the flexibility to specify which radio frequency band the AP radio would operate in. If the infrastructure consists of dual-radio APs and you were only using the 2.4 GHz band for the wireless infrastructure, the second radio could be configured for 2.4 GHz and used as a WIPS sensor.

In most cases, integrated solutions use part-time scanners. The advantages with this model are cost savings and simplicity. An AP is already cabled for Ethernet connectivity to the network, so there is no need for additional cabling, power, or mounting. (In some environments, the cost of cabling for an AP or sensor can exceed the cost of the device.) This also means that the WIPS solution is integrated with the AP solution, which usually indicates a shorter learning curve for the WIPS infrastructure administrator. The drawback of this solution is that WIPS scanning is only part-time. The same radio must perform both client access and WIPS scanning, thus there is often a tradeoff between frequency/length of scans and availability for associated clients. It is worth noting that in cases where VoWiFi is supported, most part-time scanners cease scanning altogether to accommodate the latency-sensitive client traffic. Further, when a wireless threat is detected during an off-channel scan, the radio has limited time resources to dedicate to threat mitigation. Client access could be compromised if rogue mitigation is prioritized. Pair these drawbacks with the number of available Wi-Fi channels for scanning and it is easy to see why dedicated WIPS radios provide much greater security.

Third-party WIPS vendors are often highly focused on wireless security as their core offering, and so often provide high quality dedicated overlay products. The obvious drawback of this solution is that an overlay means more hardware and wiring to that hardware. Dedicated WIPS appliances and dedicated hardware sensors can add significant cost to a wireless deployment. However, for those customers who are particularly security conscious, an overlay WIPS solution typically provides the greatest protection. Overlay sensors are often dual-radio and dual-band, which is a significant advantage for maximum scanning and threat detection.

When deploying dedicated WIPS sensor hardware, it is important to consider both the security requirements of the network and the features available with the solution in order to know how many sensors to deploy and where to mount them. Since WIPS sensors listen passively to network traffic and collision domains are not an issue, sensor radios are often configured to receive at low signal levels. This allows for an AP-to-sensor ratio that is generally between 1:3 and 1:5, meaning you need less sensors than you have access points. Of course, each deployment is unique, so some situations may call for more sensors and some for less. Customers should always consult with qualified integrators or the WIPS vendor documentation to determine best practices for sensor deployment locations and quantities.

WIPS has a strategic role in location services. When location services are desired, higher quantities of sensors provide greater location accuracy. This may also require sensors at the edge of the desired access area where you generally might not locate APs.

By deploying more sensors, you can ensure that channels are being scanned more frequently or for longer intervals, which will improve the likelihood of detecting an attack. The trade-offs are increased cost and administrative overhead, but some environments warrant both.

Defining WIPS Policies

WIPS allows an organization to define the allowed usage policies for their WLAN within the monitoring capabilities of the WIPS. For example, your organization may have a security policy that only allows WPA2-Enterprise using 802.1X/PEAP with CCMP/AES. If this is the case, the WIPS would alarm and/or report upon seeing WEP, WPA-Personal, etc.

The WIPS can use various methods including manual configuration to determine the identity and intention of the wireless devices which reside in a service area. If the parameters set by the manufacturer do not suit your environment, they can be manually manipulated in many cases. For example, the manufacturer may set a deauthentication frame threshold of 10 frames in 1 minute. Any more than that, and they report a deauthentication frame attack. Perhaps you want to reduce the chance of false positives, so you might set the threshold to 20 frames in 1 minute. WIPS platforms come pre-configured with an extensive catalog of attacks and attack signatures.

The administrator can customize the rules which govern acceptable usage of the organization's WLAN. When conditions are met within the defined rules, automated actions can be taken by the WIPS if configured to do so. For example, if a client station's MAC address starts with anything other than 00:40:96, then the WIPS should alarm and take steps to contain that station as a rogue or intruder. The customer's network needs and security policy will dictate the type of response that accompanies a policy violation or network attack. Policies should specify these actions.

Similarly, you may desire a performance report to analyze network utilization every 2 weeks. A WIPS can automate this report and have it emailed to you as a PDF.

Responses to alarms can also be customized and automated. Alarm filter configurations can be highly granular if so desired by the administrator, although default settings for many of the alarms are usually sufficient to start using the solution.

Enterprise WIPS allows the management of alarms to be centralized. This allows the enterprise security policy to be extended to all of the organization's locations, including branch offices and remote offices. It also allows the organization to view trends in security policy violations and performance issues over an extended period of time.

WIPS should be running on a constant basis in order to track security policy violations. Organizations that have a No Wi-Fi policy should use a WIPS in order to be sure that their policy is followed. Despite the popularity of WLAN, you very well might support environments where Wi-Fi is prohibited. The best way to implement and assure an organization's No Wi-Fi policy is through the use of an enterprise-class WIPS. Sensors can be distributed around a business' premises so that all WLAN conversations in the 2.4 GHz and 5 GHz bands are monitored in real-time.

Classifying Devices

After the WIPS has been configured, it performs its initial discovery of the radio service area. At first all of the devices that are discovered typically are considered unknown and threatening. The administrator must perform a manual identification of all of the known devices.

Although each manufacturer uses their own classification terms to describe the devices discovered within a wireless service area, the following terms can serve as a general hierarchy for these classifications.

Classified	<ul><li>Friendly<ul><li>○ Internal/Trusted—Authorized and supported by this organization</li><li>○ Neighbor/Known/Interfering—Neighboring system that has a right to be in the same air space, but does not fall under the jurisdiction of this organization</li></ul></li><li>Rogue—Demonstrates aggressive activity. Could be attacking the network wirelessly or could be connected to the network's wired backbone</li></ul>
Unclassified	Until a device can be categorized with surety, it should remain unclassified

Classification of devices is an initial and ongoing WIPS configuration measure that must be performed to ensure proper operation and application of WIPS policies.

Exam Moment: Wi-Fi client devices are uniquely identified based on their MAC addresses. If a user inserts a USB Wi-Fi adapter and uses it instead of the built-in adapter of a laptop, for example, he may not be able to access the network without administrative intervention as the WIPS system may not recognize client computers, but rather it may recognize the adapters in those computers.

Establishing a Baseline

In order to properly configure the WIPS, it is important to determine the nature of the existing radio environment surrounding an organization. In some cases, the organization will be isolated from other WLAN users, but in most cases there will be legitimate outside WLAN activity coexisting with the devices supported by the organization. This normal activity should be monitored and trends established before WIPS policies are set. If you rush the WIPS into service before a meaningful baseline has been established, you will more than likely have to start over at some point when the WIPS proves unreliable or too sensitive.

Event Logging and Categorization

Enterprise-class WIPS can monitor all of the radio activity on a given channel in the service areas being scrutinized on a 24x7x365 basis.

The WIPS will track, categorize, and log the wireless activities of APs, client stations, and stations operating in ad hoc (IBSS) mode. Activities which lead to vulnerabilities, and in some cases degraded performance, in the WLAN will be monitored and reported for further action by the administrator. Such a system can detect the energy of a non-802.11 transmitter, but cannot typically identify them.

Activity Reports

The data from the remote sensors can be accumulated, sorted, and compared to the acceptable usage thresholds which were defined during configuration. The WIPS can gauge and predict trends in WLAN usage. All WIPS systems have a dashboard that summarizes what is happening with both security and performance across the entirety of its sensor fleet. The dashboard typically allows the administrator to define areas where sensors are deployed (e.g., City, Building, and Floor). This provides a snapshot of events, and an administrator can drill down to view specific activity details with a geographical frame of reference.

WIPS can often be used to track performance as well as security metrics. While most customers deploy WIPS for their security benefits, they also provide beneficial oversight of network performance. However, vendors like 7Signal are now producing high-end solutions specifically for this use. In this role, the WIPS or WIPS-style overlay can provide extremely granular insights into hundreds of key performance indicators.

Measuring Threats

A well-configured WIPS makes the identification of unknown devices clear. Though unknown devices are not necessarily hostile, they should be monitored for behavior that indicates their intention. Even unknown devices which do not give outward signs of aggression should be viewed suspiciously since they may be eavesdropping on network traffic in an attempt to steal information, or to determine vulnerabilities in the WLAN before engaging in an active attack. We have established early in this text that you certainly cannot detect eavesdropping with a WIPS solution, but you may receive an alert that an unknown wireless device exists in a specific area. Of course, a more skilled attacker would ensure that no wireless signals are transmitted from his or her device so that it could not be detected in by a WIPS.

Despite the usual connotations of the word "rogue," not all rogue devices are hostile. The generally accepted definition of a rouge network device is one that is considered unauthorized for where it is located. In many cases, well-meaning employees, motivated to try and improve efficiency for their department will install an unknown and unsupported AP without following the procedures outlined in the enterprise security policy. In this scenario, the action is not hostile or malicious but it does still impose a threat.

Given that each network vulnerability poses a different network threat, it is helpful for WIPS to categorize threats in accordance with their severity. A rogue client performing deauthentication DoS attacks is a major threat. By contrast, the presence of a new client that is not associated to any APs and is not transmitting frames other than probe requests is not a major threat, assuming that strong authentication and encryption is in use on the WLAN (for example 802.1X/EAP). While the administrator may want to be notified of this new unclassified client, it is not a severe problem and may get considered a minor threat in comparison to active attacks.

These examples illustrate different methods of mitigating threats—one a rogue AP and the other an accidental association. Threat mitigation is a general term that includes all the different types of WIPS response. Rogue containment and port suppression are two specific terms that may be used to identify specific WIPS response actions.

The use of threat mitigation tactics should be performed cautiously, especially automated mechanisms. Some WIPS systems intentionally isolate suspicious APs by continuously deauthenticating all clients that associate with the intruding device. This technique renders the suspicious AP useless as no client devices will be able to maintain an association with it. It may be very tempting to liberally use this sort of mitigation technique because it is part of the WIPS. However, if the suspicious device should turn out to be a legitimate and harmless neighboring AP, there could be serious, civil repercussions.

Because WLANs use unlicensed frequency bands, it is legal for anyone to use the channels allocated for 802.11 WLANs. It is not legal for one WLAN user to disrupt the legal networking activities of another WLAN user. WIPS makes it possible to do just that through intruder mitigation services. If an organization decides to implement these mitigation services to curtail the activities of an unknown wireless device operating within the same radio service area that they occupy, then they must be very sure that the target device is not a legitimate neighbor device. WIPS intruder mitigation services are in themselves aggressive attacks against WLAN systems and their usage could result in prosecution or civil litigation. There have been a number of fines levied by the FCC against companies that have used rogue mitigation tools provided by their WIPS vendors against new "rogues" like MiFi devices. The smart CWSP should follow these events closely as the laws and technology try to figure out how to handle each other in our rapidly evolving WLAN world.

If an unknown WLAN device exhibits aggressive behavior against an organization's infrastructure, the response should be anticipated and defined within the enterprise WLAN security policy addendum. If the organization allows for self-defense mechanisms to be enacted, then the policy should also define the circumstances which would predicate the use of mitigation tactics as well as how to establish a chain of evidence that supports the decision to contain or nullify the attacker.

Intrusion mitigation consists of a targeted attack against either the unauthorized device (client or AP) or an organization's own client stations in an effort to prevent successful, unauthorized associations. In this case, the nearest sensor will issue the targeted commands which are used to isolate the intruding device. Generally, this would be the only time that the sensors operate in anything other than a strictly passive (listening) mode.

Consider the three common phases of rogue management as a summary to this section:

- **Rogue detection**—Rogue devices detected by RRM scanning, their attempts to associate, or with RF spectrum activity. The different WIPS solutions will do this in varied ways.
- **Classification**—Rogues can be classified as wired or unwired by many systems. For example, in Cisco solutions the Rogue Location Discovery Protocol (RLDP) can be used to determine if the device is connected to the wired network or not.
- **Mitigation/Containment**—Switch ports can be shutdown, the location of the rogue can be identified and the rogue can be contained—usually through the use of deauthentication frames.

 Note: **For more detailed information on this process from the Cisco system perspective, see: bit.ly/1BUelaU.**

Compliance Reporting

Recall that the use of a WIPS greatly simplifies the requirement to provide legislated security compliance. Various compliance reports may be pre-formatted and included as part of the WIPS' report manager sub-system. This allows the administrator or security officer to generate a near real-time compliance report which can then be supplied to visiting auditors or inspectors.

Forensics

WIPS can retain continuous logs of all known activity on a 24x7x365 basis. Since this information is automated, it can be used as part of the evidentiary chain during criminal or internal corporate security investigations. Some WIPS even include a forensics analysis component which can be valuable in the event that the organization decides to pursue litigation or prosecution against an apprehended intruder.

Device Location and Tracking

Some WIPS platforms can provide device location identification by using sophisticated radio techniques, including triangulation, RF Fingerprinting, and Time Difference of Arrival (TDoA). Understanding the basic differences of each will serve you well as a CWSP.

Triangulation and RF Fingerprinting are the most common techniques for device tracking. With triangulation (or trilateration), multiple sensors (at least three) that have a view of the intruding device measure signal strength metrics and send this data to the WIPS server. The WIPS server compares these signal strength measurements and performs a calculation based on known path loss formulas that can identify the location of the intruder. The location of the device can then be graphically plotted on a floor plan.

A modern technique known as RF Fingerprinting may also be used by some WIPS as a method to provide a more accurate device location solution. RF Fingerprinting requires that a detailed survey analysis be performed in advance. After a WIPS solution has been installed, a manual walk about is performed with a client device to calibrate the WIPS system. Later the radio signature of a moving target is tracked throughout the premises and the resulting signal strengths are logged to a database. When used in conjunction with the triangulation or TDoA information, this RF

Fingerprint detail can improve the accuracy of the WIPS, allowing it to locate the offending intruder within a relatively precise area.

In TDoA systems, a WIPS platform uses the known speed of radio wave travel to locate a device. As the WIPS server processes frames from the sensors, it uses time stamping to mark the first instance of a specific frame. As subsequent instances of this same frame are recorded by other sensors, the WIPS server can compare the time delay of the same frame as received by different sensors to determine the distance of the transmitting device from the sensors. Again, the goal is for WLAN security staff to rapidly locate the intruder device and remove it from the premises.

Integrated Spectrum Analysis

Another advanced feature which may be found within a limited number of enterprise-class WIPS is an integrated spectrum analysis engine. With this feature, a number of the remote sensors contain an integrated spectrum analyzer chipset which can upload its data to the central WIPS server.

This capability allows the remote administrator to view the exact state of a remote radio environment through the management console. Remember that spectrum analysis is associated with Layer 1, and using a spectrum analyzer allows the accurate diagnosis of spectrum problems, such as Layer 1 denial-of-service attacks, from the remote console.

New 802.11 Challenges

As the 802.11 specification continues to expand, new beneficial features are introduced that also create new problems. 802.11n/ac and 802.11w are developments that may be a hindrance for some older WIPS systems.

With the new PHY frame formats of 802.11n/ac and the 40 MHz, 80 MHz and possibly 160 MHz wide channels, legacy IEEE 802.11a/b/g WIPS systems will not be able to recognize and/or interpret some IEEE 802.11n/ac transmissions. This means that some attacks could be conducted by 802.11n/ac devices that are not identified by dated WIPS systems.

IEEE 802.11w introduces new frame protection features that provide management frame authentication. When these features are enabled, only securely associated stations will be able to terminate the session with a disassociation or deauthentication frame. Before 802.11w, a deauthentication or disassociation frame was a notification and could not be refused. This functional operation made it possible for any WIPS to terminate an active association with a deauthentication or disassociation frame. However, when these management frames require authentication (MIC validation), some rogue containment measures will no longer work. 802.11w is a double-edged sword, so the decision to use it or not should be carefully considered.

Monitoring in the Cloud

Cloud-managed WLAN systems continue to gain popularity. This technology is becoming widely used and popular for many different markets including enterprise wireless network deployments. In addition to the cloud, some manufacturers create on premise solutions so they can have the features of a cloud solution in their own data centers. Cloud-managed infrastructures are sometimes referred to as controller-less solutions because they operate without the need for a hardware controller. Some companies manufacture infrastructure devices that are only cloud-managed and some that previously built controller-only solutions now have some cloud-managed models. These companies provide primarily cloud-managed solutions:

- Adtran—Bluesocket
- Aerohive
- Mojo Networks (AirTight)
- Cisco-Meraki
- Open Mesh

Cloud-managed monitoring and WIPS solutions have many if not all of the same features as hardware and software-based WIPS solutions. The main difference is that there may not be a physical presence on location. Instead, the information collected is accessible from anyplace with an active Internet connection. Many of these solutions offer the following features, and more:

- Alarm management
- Automatic device classification
- Event logging and categorization
- Location tracking features
- Auditing and forensics
- Rogue AP detection
- BYOD policy enforcement
- Traffic analytics
- Security monitoring
- Reporting
- And more

With some of these solutions, the cloud-managed AP can act as a part-time or full-time WIPS sensor based on administrative configurations. The same software that is used to manage the wireless infrastructure is also used for the WIPS functionality, and usually a common interface provides tight integration between the two functions. The main benefit to these solutions is there is no hardware, server or appliance that needs to be purchased or installed. This can be a significant cost savings to many organizations. It also allows for smaller networks such as small office home office (SOHO) and small and medium-sized businesses (SMBs) to be able to easily incorporate a WIPS solution into their infrastructures. Another benefit, as stated above, is that these solutions can be accessed and managed from any place with an active Internet connection, which makes system administration very accessible.

Wireless Network Management Systems (WNMS) Security Features

A WNMS can be used to provide much of the functionality found in some WIPS solutions. For instance, a WNMS can be used to identify trusted, known, and rogue devices. However, a WNMS differs from a WIPS in that they do not have the ability to use dedicated, remote, hardware sensors. Instead, they use APs as sensors. You may have to buy additional licenses for the WNMS to leverage WIPS functionality, and APs in use can function as dedicated full-time sensors or split their operations between WIPS and providing client access.

> **Exam Moment:** WNMS solutions may use SNMPv3 to execute secure configuration commands with APs and other managed devices when supported.

A WNMS can identify and display authentication types in use on a per-association basis. A WNMS can also be configured with graphical floor plans that encompass multiple floors of multiple buildings. The WNMS can then display coverage maps and identify user locations, rogue device locations, information on interferers, and a range of other indications that help show the status of system security and health.

WLAN Controllers

Wireless LAN controller-based WLANs may allow some of their APs to be recommissioned as dedicated, remote, hardware sensors. Some WLAN controller systems also allow their controller-based APs to multitask these duties, switching briefly between sensor and AP operations. However, in this scenario it may be possible for the sensor to miss some crucial information because it is busy acting as an AP.

While controller-based WIPS functions are usually not as robust as dedicated third-party WIPS products, they still offer substantial security benefits and configuration options. The cost savings of integrated WIDS/WIPS functionality may be significant. Beyond smaller WLAN environments, WLAN controllers are typically managed by a WNMS. This includes the WIPS capabilities of both, which are integrated through licensing and the UI of the WNMS.

Distributed Protocol Analysis as a Monitoring Solution

Wireless LAN Protocol Analyzers may have the ability to use distributed sensors to accumulate and report packet/protocol capture detail from remote locations to a desktop application. This can allow the administrator to view live Layer 2 data from different points in the WLAN in a remote console.

Dedicated WIPS platforms are improving traffic analysis functionality in newer implementations by providing remote decodes and frame captures.

Protocol analysis includes frame exchanges and frame decoding.

Protocol analyzers can be important wireless security analysis tools for both network security administrators and intruders. Protocol analyzers can be used to capture and save wireless traffic in formats that can be imported by attack applications such as password crackers. The use of protocol analyzers is a major component of the Certified Wireless Analysis Professional (CWAP) certification, and a routine part of the job for WLAN administrators.

Not all wireless protocol analyzers can decode every OSI layer. Some protocol analyzers only display 802.11 MAC layer networking information while others can capture, filter, decode, and display all network traffic, including user data from layers 2–7. Most protocol analyzers allow the insertion of a pre-shared key so that captured, encrypted traffic can be unencrypted and displayed in real time or saved and decoded later. This feature is a must-have on PSK networks, but is not beneficial when 802.1X/EAP is in use.

Some protocol analyzers can capture and reconstruct TCP sessions into their application layer information (layers 4–7) while others can generate and transmit customized 802.11 frames (Layer 2). Distributed protocol analyzers can be placed throughout an enterprise and be configured to supply constant data captures of wireless frames from each location to a centralized console and database. This capability can be invaluable for forensics work.

Popular Protocol Analyzers used for 802.11

- Wildpackets—Omnipeek (Savvius)
- AirMagnet—WiFi Analyzer (Fluke Networks/Netscout)
- Tamosoft—Commview for WiFi
- Network Instruments—Observer Analyzer
- Wireshark

Exam Moment: When using a WLAN protocol analyzer, special drivers are typically used. These drivers may not offer the full supplicant feature set of the normal use-case drivers. After performing protocol analysis, it is important to revert drivers back to the standard use-case drivers for network access or the computer running the analyzer may not be able to access the WLAN

Working with IEEE 802.11 Frames

Knowledge of the different 802.11 frame types, their formats and usage is crucial to being able to interpret protocol analyzer captures and decodes. Competency in protocol analysis is expected from any network administrator that intends to provide a secure, high-performance, wireless network. For more detailed information on this, see the CWAP Official Study Guide.

Unlike Ethernet, the 802.11 protocol uses many different frame layouts, but all of them are based on a general frame format. 802.11 uses specialized frames for:

- Data
- Control
- Management

IEEE 802.11 Frames vs. 802.3 Frames

Frames used by Project 802, which is the IEEE project that is inclusive of all 802 standards, all have similar structures. They are all defined as fields that are made up of bits, which together form octets and ultimately frames. This similarity in frame structure makes for easier conversion from 802.3 networks to 802.11 networks and vice versa. For example, a frame originating from a wired client and destined for a wireless client will first be transmitted on the wire as an 802.3 frame. Then the access point will strip off the 802.3 headers and reframe the data unit as an 802.11 frame for transmission to the wireless client. The access point bridges 802.11 and 802.3 networks.

The first difference between 802.3 and 802.11 frames is the frame size. 802.3 frames support a maximum MSDU payload size of 1500 bytes or octets (There are "jumbo" frames allowed in 802.3 Ethernet networks that are larger than the standard-defined 1500 bytes, but these are beyond the CWSP course). 802.11 frames support a maximum MSDU payload size of 2304 bytes (or larger in 11n and 11ac). At first, it may seem that extra processing will have to occur in order for 802.3 and 802.11 networks to coexist. It might seem that a certain amount of frame fragmentation will have to occur to convert 802.11 frames to 802.3 frames. However, since TCP/IP is the most commonly used protocol, and since IP packets are usually no larger than 1500 bytes, the vast majority of data units passed to the 802.11 MAC layer will be 1500 bytes or smaller anyways, allowing for easy conversion to the 802.3 format.

Most network engineers are familiar with the IP Maximum Transfer Unit (MTU) of 1500 bytes that exists because of Ethernet networks. Wireless LAN standards were designed to easily bridge with Ethernet. For this reason, the IP MTU on a WLAN is held to 1500 bytes even though it could be as high as 2304, minus 8 for the LLC SNAP header. A 1500 byte IP PDU becomes a 1508 byte LLC PDU with the LLC SNAP header and this, in turn becomes the wireless LAN MSDU. The LLC 8 byte header is often ignored and results in the varied and confusing byte or octet size values you read and hear about.

The second difference between the 802.3 and 802.11 frames is the MAC address fields. Both frame types use the same standard for MAC address structuring based on Clause 5.2 of the IEEE 802-1990 standard. But, 802.3 frames have only two MAC address fields whereas 802.11 frames have one, two, three, or four. These four MAC address fields can contain four of the following five MAC address types and the contents will be dependent on the frame subtype:

- Basic Service Set Identifier (BSSID)
- Destination Address (DA)
- Source Address (SA)
- Receiver Address (RA)
- Transmitter Address (TA)

The 802.11 standard documents the frame types supported by the 802.11 MAC. According to the standard, there are three frame types supported in 802.11 networks: management frames, control frames and data frames.

- The *Type* subfield in the *Frame Control* (FC) field of a general 802.11 frame may be 00 (management), 01 (control), or 10 (data).
- The *Subtype* subfield determines the subtype of frame, within the frame types specified, that is being transmitted.

For example, a *Type* subfield value of 00 with a *Subtype* value of 0000 is an association request frame; however, a *Type* value of 10 with a *Subtype* value of 0000 is a standard data frame. Understanding all of the details about the frame structures and formats is not required of a CWSP; however, it would be of great benefit to you to review the 802.11 standard, which defines each frame and each frame field with diagrams. Should you advance to CWAP, this information is invaluable.

Management frames are used to manage access to wireless networks and to move associations from one access point to another within an Extended Service Set. Control frames are used to assist with the delivery of data frames, and must be able to be interpreted by all stations participating in a Basic Service Set. This means that they must be transmitted using a modulation technique and at a data rate compatible with all clients participating in the Basic Service Set. Finally, data frames are the actual carriers of application-level data. These frames can be either standard data frames or Quality of Service (QoS) data frames for devices supporting the 802.11e amendment. To round out the discussion, you should know that the type value of 11, with any subtype, is a reserved frame type. This simply means that it is not used today, but is reserved for any future needs.

Frame Exchanges

While you will not be required to understand every detail of the frames and frame exchanges that occur on a WLAN in order to become a CWSP, you will need to understand the basics of frame exchange sequences and the flow of creating a WLAN, accessing a WLAN and disconnecting from a WLAN. Though much of this is review at this point in the text, it is important to reiterate. You should be able to define and explain the following basic MAC layer functions:

Scanning—Before a station can participate in a Basic Service Set, it must be able to find the access points that provide access to that service set. Scanning is the process used to discover Basic Service Sets or to discover access points within a known Basic Service Set.

Synchronization—Some 802.11 features require all stations to have the same time. Stations can update their clocks based on the timestamp value in Beacon frames.

Frame Transmission—Stations must abide by the frame transmission rules of the Basic Service Set to which they are associated. These rules are defined for standard operations (DCF) and QoS solutions within the 802.11 standard.

Authentication—Authentication is performed before a station can be associated with a Basic Service Set.

Association—After authentication is complete, the station can become associated with the Basic Service Set. This includes discovery of capability information in both directions—from the station to the access point and from the access point to the station.

Reassociation—When a user roams throughout a service area, they may reach a point where one access point within an Extended Service Set will provide a stronger signal than the currently associated access point. When this occurs, the station will reassociate with the new access point (provided the stations drivers are behaving).

Data Protection—Data encryption may be employed to assist in preventing crackers from accessing the data that is transmitted on the wireless medium.

Power Management—Since the transmitters/receivers (transceivers) in wireless client devices consume a noteworthy amount of power, power management features are provided that assist in extending battery life by causing the transceiver to sleep for specified intervals.

Fragmentation—In certain scenarios, it is beneficial to fragment frames before they are transmitted onto the wireless medium. This type of scenario most often occurs due to intermittent interference.

RTS/CTS—Request to Send/Clear to Send is a feature of 802.11 that will help prevent hidden node problems and allow for more centralized control of access to the wireless medium.

Spectrum Analysis

Spectrum analyzers capture raw RF signals (Layer 1) and display visual representations of ambient signals. Spectrum analyzers are the most useful tool for performing RF-specific security audits (e.g., locating RF DoS attacks) and finding RF interference types and sources. These analyzers give the wireless network professional a unique monitoring visibility that can be leveraged to accomplish many performance and security related tasks.

Some spectrum analyzers have the ability to identify suspicious activities and devices, and to home-in on the trespassing devices based on signal strength comparisons and known device RF signatures. Hardware and software combinations can also automatically classify many common types of RF sources such as Bluetooth devices, wireless video cameras, microwave ovens, and cordless phones.

Spectrum analyzers may have distributed sensors and be configured to send their reports to a centralized console. This information can be used for forensics purposes if an attack should occur. The spectrum analysis information can be searched and analyzed to provide clues and evidence as to the time, location, and possible identity of the perpetrator. Careful handling of this information is important if the analysis is intended to be used as legal evidence in court. For more information on this aspect, the corporate legal department should be consulted and have input into the security policy formation.

Spectrum analysis will facilitate the discovery of intentional and unintentional DoS attacks by RF interferers. As an added benefit, being able to effectively use a spectrum analyzer will make you better at general wireless network support, too.

Physical Layer Defenses

The only defenses against a Physical Layer Denial-of-Service (DoS) attack are great distances between the WLAN and potential attackers, or to RF-harden the building or room where wireless communications are in use. Likewise, the way to keep RF signals from propagating outward is to RF-harden the coverage areas.

Some methods used to RF-harden an area against RF DoS attacks include:

- TEMPEST protection—Government/Military strength RF leakage protection.
- Anti-RF paint / wallpaper
  http://informationweek.com/story/showArticle.jhtml?articleID=56200676
- Faraday Cage / Faraday Shielding
  Wikipedia— "A Faraday cage or Faraday shield is an enclosure formed by conducting material, or by a mesh of such material. Such an enclosure blocks out external static electrical fields. Faraday cages are named after physicist Michael Faraday, who built one in 1836 and explained its operation."
  - Faraday shielding in which the metal mesh spacing is less than one-half the wavelength being used can effectively restrict that radio wave.

Due to the expenses involved, installation of anti-RF paint or Faraday shielding is not typically a practical solution to wireless security vulnerabilities for most organizations.

Laptop-based Intrusion Analysis

It is possible to combine protocol and spectrum analysis with expert security knowledge to manually perform WLAN monitoring with a single laptop. In many smaller networks, administrators will choose to perform manual analysis. This decision is often based on smaller budgets. At the same time, larger networks may also do spot checks with "boots on the ground" in addition to running enterprise-class IDS or IPS solutions. Manual analysis is performed with spectrum and protocol analyzers.

Examples of protocol analyzers include Wireshark, AirMagnet Wi-Fi Analyzer Pro, OmniPeek and Commview for Wi-Fi. When selecting a protocol analysis laptop-based solution, the engineer must consider the following:

- Protocol analysis software does not work with every wireless adapter or chipset, and an adapter must be selected that works with the software (usually specified by the software vendor).
- Protocol analysis software has a wide range of features that varies between vendors, and the engineer must carefully analyze available options to choose the right solution.
- All of the mentioned protocol analyzers can import PCAP file formats so captures can be performed using external tools/software and then analyzed using the specific wireless protocol analyzer software of choice.

Exam Moment: The right adapter must be chosen to perform protocol analysis with a given software solution. The majority of internal adapters do not work with most protocol analyzers for Wi-Fi frame captures, and USB adapters are often used for this reason.

Examples of spectrum analyzers include the AirMagnet Spectrum XT device (and software) and the MetaGeek Wi-Spy dBx (and software, which includes the MetaGeek software or CommView for WiFi, which can include spectrum analysis from a Wi-Spy dBx device). Oscium's WiPry uses the lightning connector on Apple mobile devices, with a compatible app, to provide a unique spectrum analysis option. AirMagnet Spectrum XT is a USB form factor protocol analyzer for use with laptops (or desktops, if you have a need for stationary analysis). The features of the AirMagnet Spectrum XT include:

- USB form factor for use with practically any modern computer
- Combining spectrum analysis with traffic analysis (traffic analysis required a compatible Wi-Fi adapter)

- Automatically identify WLAN and non-WLAN interference sources.
- Real-time RF spectrum and WLAN graphs
- Integration capabilities with other AirMagnet solutions such as Survey PRO and Wi-Fi Analyzer PRO
- Recording and playback of spectrum analysis sessions
- Support for both the 2.4 GHz and 5 GHz bands

The following types of intrusions can be located with a laptop analyzer:

- Rogue APs
- Unauthorized clients
- Denial of Service attacks
- MAC layer wireless attacks

To locate a physical DoS attack source, you can use the laptop analysis software to find the location where the signal is strongest. Then, you can simply look around until you find the RF generating source. Tools like AirMagnet Spectrum XT often include device locator tools with graphical elements like that represented in the following image:

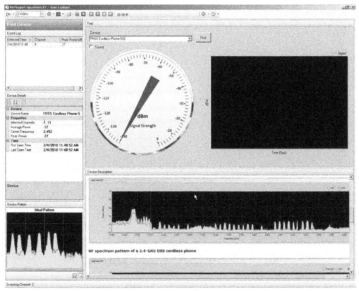

Figure 9-3: AirMagnet Spectrum XT Device Locator

In most cases, laptop-based spectrum analysis products are used for auditing purposes. Audits can expose security risks and accidental interference sources. Devices like AirMagnet Spectrum XT can locate and identify non-WLAN interference sources such as:

- Baby monitors
- Cordless phones
- Microwave ovens
- Bluetooth devices
- Wireless cameras
- Game controllers
- Digital video devices

Intentional security attacks can also be detected during an audit. You can locate RF jammers using Spectrum XT and you can locate laptops being used to flood WLANs with "junk" frames (frames that do not contain meaningful data), thanks to the ability to perform parallel protocol analysis as well as the spectrum analysis. When AirMagnet Spectrum XT locates an interference source, it can provide detailed information about the source including:

- Peak and average output power
- Center channel frequency
- Channels impacted by the interference
- First and last times the source was detected
- Number of times the source was detected

When used with a directional antenna, spectrum analyzers can often pinpoint the location of the interference source down to a few meters.

The following figure shows the AirMagnet Spectrum XT application running a standard spectrum analysis view with the ability to select different frequencies. The tool can be used for 802.11n and 11ac analysis since it supports both 2.4 GHz and 5 GHz bands.

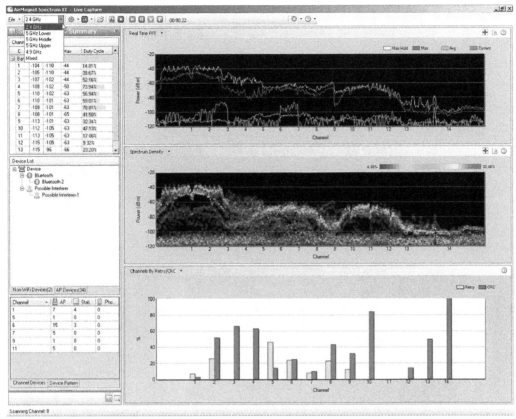

Figure 9-4: AirMagnet Spectrum XT Spectrum Analysis

The following image shows AirMagnet Spectrum XT displaying non-Wi-Fi devices. In this image, a Bluetooth device and a potential interference device is shown.

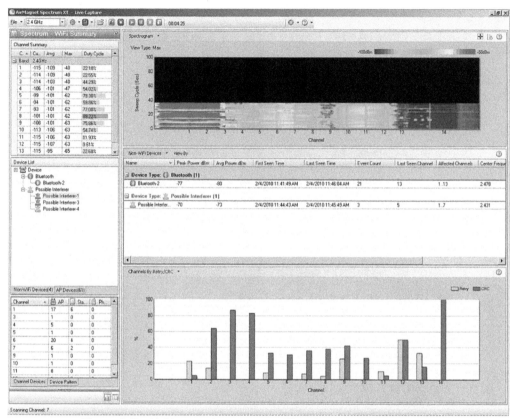

Figure 9-5: AirMagnet Spectrum XT Showing non-Wi-Fi Devices

🗨 From the Blogs

The Need for Continual Monitoring

URL: divdyn.net/need-continual-monitoring
Author: Devin Akin
Blog: Divergent Dynamics Blog—divdyn.net/blog

2.4GHz interference advances with the determination of General George S. Patton, perhaps with General "Chesty" Puller as a teammate. BYOD, IoT, and STUFF fuels the onslaught. Because of so many devices (Wi-Fi, other types of communication devices, and unintentional interference sources) being haphazardly thrown into the 2.4GHz band both now and in the immediate future, average utilization on 2.4GHz ISM channels continues to rise very quickly. The rise in 2.4GHz "noise" requires higher signal levels from Wi-Fi devices in order to achieve usable Signal-to-Noise (SNR) ratios, which in-turn greatly exacerbates co-channel contention (CCC) and adjacent channel interference (ACI). To make matters worse, there are only 3 non-overlapping channels in the 2.4GHz ISM band, with no more on the way. It's a death spiral with no hope of recovery when it comes to using it for Wi-Fi.

Interference Hinders Performance

This ever-growing tidal wave of interference impedes performance and reliable connectivity in so many ways that the only way to reasonably understand your RF environment, and the problems your Wi-Fi is experiencing in real-time and over time, is to continually monitor the Layer 1 and Layer 2 environments and reference the data against baselines. I foresee cloud-managed infrastructure being an avenue to collect, store, and analyze such data in the very near future.

Most analyst firms agree that by CY2020, we'll have 30+ billion always-connected devices with 200+ billion intermittently-connected devices on the Internet. Wi-Fi has now surpassed Ethernet for how devices connect to networks. With IoT and BYOD both causing a sharp increase in Wi-Fi and Bluetooth connectivity, many (or most) of these devices supporting 2.4GHz, we're bound to see a continually and sharply rising trend of increased support costs for networks supporting 2.4GHz. It's a losing outcome that we can absolutely avoid if we start now.

What Do We Need To Monitor?

There are a large variety of useful statistics gathered by performance diagnostic system vendors like 7signal Solutions and AirMagnet Enterprise (from Fluke Networks), and while you may say to yourself, "Dude, my infrastructure vendor has this covered!", I challenge you to consider:

- APs can only hear half of a Wi-Fi conversation.
- Non-dedicated APs performing background scanning capture very little useful performance-related information.
- Due to limited development resources, infrastructure vendors do not focus much time on performance measurement, metrics, alerting, and reporting.

Some of the useful Key Performance Indicators (KPIs) and statistics available from these systems include:

- Layer 2-Layer 7 infrastructure connectivity validation
  - This is useful when "sensors" simulate client behavior, connecting to APs and running Layer 2-Layer 7 operational tests.
- Spectrum analysis with source identification & effect determination
- The number and type of frames (total, per-AP, per-STA, and per connection)
- Protection mechanism use (RTS/CTS and CTS-to-Self)
  - Use of protection mechanisms for backwards compatibility can quickly lose you 40%+ of a cell's capacity.
- Frame capture and protocol analysis
- Channel utilization by media type, noise, and throughput
  - This is very important to understanding how much usable airtime is available.
- TCP Throughput (uplink & downlink)

- SNR for particular APs & STAs
  - SNR is a very important factor to drivers (in both APs and Clients) in deciding which data rates to use.
- Ping Round Trip Time (RTT)
  - This shows this general latency of the network.
- VoIP MOS scoring (bi-directionally), including delay, jitter, & packet loss.
  - Even when the network isn't used for VoIP, these can be a good performance and user experience indicator.
- Layer 2 Retransmissions (per-AP, per-STA, and aggregate)
  - Rules of thumb are generally <10% is Good. 10-50% is acceptable. >50% is Bad. It's worth noting that when Auto RRM powers APs down too far, it can cause high AP retries while client device retries remain OK.
- Beacon Availability (beacons received/expected).
  - As my friend Mike Graham at 7signal puts it, "APs were born to beacon." If an AP radio stops beaconing or if enough beacons aren't received by client devices (because of a saturated channel or interference sources), clients will be disconnected.
- Attach Success Rate
  - "Attach" is often defined as "Authentication + Association", and if this parameter is low, then you may need to dig into whether Authentication or Association is the problem.
- Authentication Time
  - If your Wi-Fi network doesn't support a fast/secure roaming algorithm (e.g., Voice-Enterprise, OKC, PreAuthentication, etc.), then authentication time becomes critical to both user experience and application performance. This is an important metric to watch when running 802.1X/EAP over a WAN.
- IP Address Retrieval Success Rate and Time
  - These metrics will show you if your DHCP server is responding properly and how fast. While DHCP servers are usually fast enough (there are some exceptions), sometimes client devices

don't get a response at all. Clients then must re-request an IP address, and this makes the overall process very slow. A broken Layer-3 process is a performance equivalent to a broken Layer-2 process because you must have both Layer 2 and Layer 3 connectivity in order to communicate.

- AP Signal Level
  - This metric should be fairly steady on most APs, even if Auto RRM is enabled. With most RRM based deployments, there should be high and low boundaries placed on AP power output, and AP signal level changes shouldn't be constant (flapping).
- Channel Changes
  - This metric can indicate a misconfigured or malfunctioning RRM algorithm, where changes are rippling back and forth across the network. This can wreck both performance and user experience.
- Airtime Utilization
  - This metric is vital to understanding how much airtime is consumed by particular APs or client devices and what types of transmissions (e.g., frame types) are consuming the airtime. It is useful to validating an infrastructure manufacturer's Airtime Fairness algorithm or misconfigured Wi-Fi infrastructure.
- Number of Client Devices
  - This metric can be per-BSSID and per-AP and will help you understand when load-balancing or power output are misconfigured (or broken) or when APs are not optimally located.
- Data Rates (in use between Clients and APs)
  - This is one of the most important performance-related metrics. Selective data rate configuration can be used to optimize performance in a big way, but can also cause connectivity problems with some clients. Data Rate configuration goes hand-in-hand with optimal AP placement, so drastic configuration changes without APs being moved can be problematic.

- It's very common, even after optimal data rate configuration, to see strange data rate behavior—especially from client devices.
  - 5 GHz-capable clients using 2.4 GHz
    - It's strongly recommended to get as many clients onto 5 GHz as possible, and some dual-band client devices will resist moving to 5 GHz.

Summary

If you can't see it, you can't measure it, adequately understand its effects, or plan for the future. Being able to monitor both Layer 1 and Layer 2, you can see cause and effect, trends, and solutions for interference and malfunctioning networks. When feasible, decisions should be made based on collected data, not the wet-finger-in-air tests. Wi-Fi is now mission-critical or life-critical in many organizations and vertical markets. Why "not know" when you can "know you know"? Stop spending time and money groping around in the dark (blind troubleshooting) and trying to fix problems that you should've never had. Spend the money to proactively implement a performance monitoring solution that shows you the real deal 24/7. #JustSayin

Chapter 9 Summary

In this chapter you learned about intrusion monitoring solutions. Wireless intrusion detection systems (WIDS) detect potential intrusions and may log or report the intrusion. Wireless intrusion prevention systems (WIPS) detect potential intrusions and react to the attempted intrusion in order to prevent further damage. Common features of WIPS solutions include rogue AP and unauthorized client detection as well as detection of DoS and MAC layer wireless network attacks. You also learned about using a laptop-based spectrum or protocol analyzer to monitor environments that are smaller, or to locate and detect specific kinds of attacks in environments of any size.

Facts to Remember

Be sure to remember the following facts as you prepare for the CWSP certification and be sure that you can explain the details related to them:

- If you want to troubleshoot roaming issues, some modern WIPS will help, but you can also do it with a laptop-based protocol analyzer that has multiple 802.11 adapters.
- WIPS can be used for performance monitoring as well as security monitoring/notification and enforcing wireless policies.
- In order for RF fingerprinting to work properly, the RF environment must be sampled using an RF calibration process in most WIPS.
- WIPS solutions cannot detect every attack. For example, they cannot detect eavesdropping or social engineering, which cause no direct network activity to detect.
- In order for a WIPS to properly classify devices, it must be configured properly and this is usually part of the staging, change management and/or installation procedures.

- A WIPS solution may take action to prevent an attack. For example, it could use SNMP to disable a switch port that has a rogue AP connected, if the environment is configured to allow it.
- Most WIPS solutions provide a policy framework that helps in the classification of new authorized devices added to the WLAN.
- Remember that location systems can use TDoA, trilateration of RSSI, and RF fingerprinting.
- Older WIPS solutions cannot properly detect and identify newer 802.11 PHYs. They must be upgraded with new software and sensors.
- Some integrated WIPS systems, when detecting voice traffic, will stop scanning entirely to service the voice traffic with its priority demands.

Chapter 9: Review Questions

1. As you talk with a client about wireless security, she asks you the difference between WIPS and WIDS. You tell her which of the following?
   a. Both can detect threats, but WIDS can also do threat mitigation
   b. Both can detect threats, but WIPS can also do threat mitigation
   c. WIDS can only detect, WIPS can only mitigate
   d. WIPS is only used in PCI environments

2. You are auditing the WLAN security practices of a stadium that uses wireless Point of Sale terminals. Which regulation are you most concerned with regarding credit card operations?
   a. FERPA
   b. HIPPA
   c. Sarbanes-Oxley
   d. PCI

3. You are troubleshooting a WIPS system used to secure an 802.11ac WLAN that does not seem to be working as expected. Which of these is not a potential reason for the trouble?
   a. The WIPS system was not staged right
   b. The WIPS system uses 802.11a/g sensors
   c. The WIPS system has one sensor for every 3 access points
   d. The WIPS sensor is not part of the IT change control process

4. A fellow CWSP is seen doing wireless protocol analysis with a laptop that has three wireless USB adapters in use. What might she be doing, specifically?

    a. Troubleshooting VoIP roaming

    b. Calibrating a PCI system

    c. Setting up mobile WIDS

    d. Tuning the WIPS for voice traffic

5. What type of WIPS might stop scanning in the presence of voice traffic?

    a. Dedicated WIPS

    b. Full-time WIPS

    c. Integrated WIPS

    d. Distributed WIPS

6. You have been asked to provide a customer site with the ability to detect passive eavesdroppers. Which tool do you recommend?

    a. WIDS

    b. Protocol Analyzer

    c. IoT Sensors

    d. None, as passive eavesdropping cannot be detected

7. You have been hired to conduct clandestine "security posture auditing" at a corporate site. What is another description for what you have been hired to do?

    a. Penetration testing

    b. Installing NAC agents on each host

    c. Network scanning

    d. Social engineering

8. Which of the following can enterprise WIPS be configured to work with?
   a. WNMS
   b. WLAN controllers
   c. Sensors
   d. All of these

9. A WLAN that employs which type of security should be able to meet HIPAA requirements?
   a. 802.11ac
   b. 802.11i
   c. 802.11dss
   d. 802.11avc

10. When it comes to WLAN security, Sarbanes-Oxley, PCI, and GLBA are all examples of what?
    a. Security best practices
    b. Optional enhancements
    c. Legislated security requirements
    d. Security overlays

11. One important outcome of an initial security audit is the ____.
    a. Baseline
    b. Security Policy
    c. Inventory
    d. Executive summary

12. How can you protect against rogue access points being installed from the wired network perspective?
    a. Keep doors to common spaces locked.
    b. Power down network switches until needed.
    c. Disable individual network ports not in use.
    d. Do not make patch cables easily available.

13. Which of the following will best help the CWSP to identify security threats at Layer 1?
    a. Spectrum analyzer
    b. Protocol analyzer
    c. Integrated analyzer
    d. WNMS

14. WLAN monitoring tools include all of the following except which of these?
    a. WIPS
    b. WNMS
    c. Client utilities
    d. Protocol Analyzer

15. You have been asked to advise on the purchase of a WIPS system. Your customer has a modern, robust WLAN, but budget is a significant concern for a potential WIPS project. Knowing this, what do you recommend?
    a. Dedicated WIPS
    b. Stand-alone WIPS
    c. No WIPS because of expense
    d. Integrated WIPS

16. Locating a device with a system that uses knowledge of the rate of travel of RF systems is a capability of which type of system?
    a. Doppler
    b. Echo-location
    c. TDoA
    d. Telemetry

17. A system that can manage and monitor access points and controllers, and optionally integrate with a WIPS system, is which of these?
    a. WNMS
    b. SNMP
    c. WIDS
    d. Automated Audit

18. Which of these is not a valid defense against RF DOS attacks?
    a. RF Paint
    b. Distance
    c. Faraday cage
    d. Management frame protection

19. The two primary reasons rogue APs are typically installed are for an attacker to ____ and ____.
    a. Gain network access, attack switches
    b. Gain network access, attack stations
    c. Deny network access, attack stations
    d. Deny network access, gain switch access

20. Monitoring systems used in wireless network security operations will provide which of these functions?
    a. Reporting
    b. Auditing
    c. Detection
    d. All of these

21. Which form factor is not a valid example of protocol analyzer form factor?
    a. Mobile device
    b. Laptop
    c. Overhead
    d. Stand-alone

22. What will determine how an organization handles security auditing and forensics?
    a. The mandate of hired pen testers
    b. Organizational security policy
    c. Capabilities of the WIPS
    d. The WLAN technology in use

23. During a security audit, you find that port 80 on a number of access points is open. What best practice has been violated?
    a. Only manage network devices with secure protocols.
    b. All access points should be behind firewalls.
    c. Once put into service, access points should not be managed.
    d. Port 80 can only be used for management if it is closed.

24. Which of these statements about security baselining is correct?
    a. Baselining is only done before a monitoring system is installed.
    b. Baselining is not a one-time exercise.
    c. Baselining is optional.
    d. Baselining is irrelevant if WIDS is in use.

25. Your company has a strict "No Wi-Fi" policy. Which of these has no benefit in enforcing that policy?
    a. Distributed spectrum analyzer
    b. Stand-alone spectrum analyzer
    c. WIPS
    d. Enterprise firewall

Chapter 9: Review Answers

1. **B** is correct. Knowing this fundamental difference between WIPS and WIDS is important.

2. **D** is correct. PCI is all about retail environments that process credit cards.

3. **C** is correct. A ratio of 1:3 to 1:5 WIPS sensors to APs is generally accepted design.

4. **A** is correct. Troubleshooting roaming uses multiple adapters to listen to different channels as a client moves between cells.

5. **C** is correct. Integrated WIPS often defers to voice traffic above all other functionality.

6. **D** is correct. No system will detect passive eavesdropping.

7. **A** is correct. Many wireless security professionals work in the pen-testing realm.

8. **D** is correct. Some WIPS systems can integrate with a variety of other systems.

9. **B** is correct. 802.11i-compliant networks should have all of the ingredients to be HIPAA compliant.

10. **C** is correct. Many aspects of wireless security are based in legislated requirements.

11. **A** is correct. A security baseline is an important outcome of the initial security audit.

12. **C** is correct. Disabled network ports will not support rogue APs.

13. **A** is correct. Spectrum analyzers work in the physical layer domain.

14. **C** is correct. WIPS, WNMS, and protocol analyzers are all WLAN monitoring tools, whereas client utilities are single-device views and configuration tools.

15. **D** is correct. In this case, integrated WIPS will provide benefit while saving money versus stand-alone/dedicated WIPS.

16. **C** is correct. TDoA systems use RF rate of travel values to locate devices.

17. **A** is correct. The Wireless Network Management System configures and monitors APs and controllers.

18. **D** is correct. RF DOS attacks are nearly impossible to defend against, and in typical WLAN scenarios have no real defense. But technically RF Paint, distance, and Faraday cages all can help against RF DOS attacks.

19. **B** is correct. Rogue APs are used to gain an attacker network access on the victim LAN, or to attack wireless clients lured to the rogue.

20. **D** is correct. Monitoring systems in enterprise WLAN environments tend to be feature-rich.

21. **C** is correct. Protocol analyzers are available in mobile device, laptop, and stand-alone form factors.

22. **B** is correct. Organizational security policy should guide auditing and forensics along with monitoring and usage.

23. **A** is correct. Port 80 is non-secured web access.

24. **B** is correct. Baselining is not a one-time exercise, and needs to be done as frequently as required to keep up with system, organizational, and policy changes.

25. **D** is correct. An enterprise firewall will not monitor RF or for 802.11 activity.

Appendix A:

About Real-World WLAN Security Testing/Experimenting

Creating a Kali Linux Virtual Machine for Security Testing and Lab Utilization

About Real-World WLAN Security Testing and Experimentation

Beyond simply reading about wireless network security, there are a number of ways where you can get real-world experience with a range of tools used by professional penetration testers and wireless intruders alike. By getting hands-on familiarization with auditing tools, you will sharpen your knowledge and abilities as a CWSP.

Among the many options available for penetration testing and self-guided education is the Wireless Pineapple, available from Hak5.org. Based on the OpenWRT operating system (read more at OpenWrt.org), the Pineapple is a pre-packaged router and software combination with a number of utilities that either work individually or in combination to deceive and frustrate victim clients by manipulating wireless frames, or to get information from the clients. This information might include just SSIDs of networks the victim connects to, or it may be more sinister as user logins and passwords are harvested. Real hackers practice their craft, and so should wireless security professionals. The Pineapple framework supports dozens of attacks or eavesdropping utilities, and an active user community is very generous in helping new users get started in using this fascinating device.

Do not forget about "wardriving." It is an easy activity to do, and simply seeing what wireless networks are "out there," along with their signal strengths and security characteristic keeps you thinking about the basics of Wi-Fi. Most of us can do this activity on our lunch breaks or on the way home from work.

If you are Linux-minded, you likely have a head start in wireless auditing even if you do not realize it. Many of the better tools a CWSP should be familiar with are built on Linux. If you have been interested in getting started with Linux to bolster your knowledge and capabilities as a CWSP but need a little encouragement, the next section will provide some motivation to take the first step. However, you get busy in your own time learning and experimenting, know that doing so will absolutely make you better at wireless networking and security.

Creating a Kali Linux Virtual Machine for Security Testing and Lab Utilization

Kali Linux is an open source distribution based on Debian that includes many security testing and learning tools. Included in the toolset is everything you need to test wireless security from an authentication and encryption cracking perspective. Additionally, it includes phenomenal utilities providing insight into WLAN operations and adapter features. This Appendix

- provides you with step-by-step instructions for installing Kali Linux in a VirtualBox virtual machine (VM), and
- explains how to insert and use a USB 802.11 NIC to perform penetration tests, wireless captures, and so on.

 Note: **This lab is based on Kali Linux 1.1.0 and alterations may be required to make it work with later versions. Additionally, VirtualBox 4.3.24 was utilized and changes may also be required in that area. However, the overall process should remain relatively the same for the near future. Finally, Kali Linux works just fine in VMware and Hyper-V should you desire to run it in those virtualization environments instead.**

Installing VirtualBox

You can acquire VirtualBox from www.VirtualBox.org. While the following instructions are based on version 4.3.24 build 98716, it is possible that the entire lab here presented will work with future versions. Additionally, using the "VirtualBox Older Builds" section of the website, you can download the same version used in these labs.

1. Download the VirtualBox installer.
2. Launch the VirtualBox installer according to the normal procedures of your operating system. This lab assumes you are installing on the Windows

operating system; however, versions are available for Mac OS X and Linux distributions. The steps may vary for different operating systems.

3. On the **Welcome to the Oracle VM VirtualBox Setup Wizard** screen, click **Next**.

4. On the **Custom Setup** screen,

   a. choose the defaults for installation unless you require installation on a different hard drive, and

   b. click **Next**.

5. Choose the shortcuts you desire to create.

6. For simpler use, be sure to select "**Register File Associations**".

7. Click **Next**.

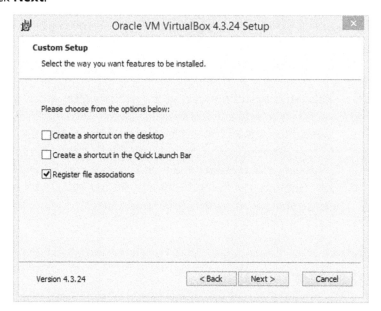

Figure A-1: Oracle VM VirtualBox 4.3.24 Setup

8. Click **Yes** on the **Warning: Network Interfaces** screen to acknowledge that the installation will reset the networking. This does not reconfigure the network—it means that it will stop and restart.

9. On the **Ready to Install** screen, click **Install**. You may be required to grant User Account Control status during the installation.

10. On the **Installation Is Complete** screen, check the box "**Start Oracle VM VirtualBox 4.3.24 After Installation**", click **Finish**.

11. In the **Oracle VM VirtualBox Manager** application, click **File > Preferences**.

12. Browse through the preferences and configure them according to your liking. Particularly take note of the Network settings and consider creating a NAT Network on which the Kali Linux distribution can run.

Creating a Kali Linux VM

1. Download the **Kali Linux 64-bit ISO**. Do not choose the mini version as you want all features. It can be acquired from www.Kali.org/downloads.

2. When the download completes, in **Oracle VM VirtualBox Manager**, select **Machine > New**.

3. On the **Name and Operating System** screen,
   a. enter the name you desire
   b. choose **Type:** *Linux and Version: Other Linux 64-bit*, and
   c. click **Next**.

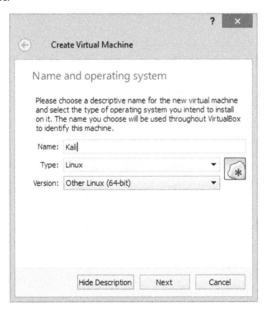

Figure A-2: Create Virtual Machine

4. On the **Memory Size** screen, provide at least 512 MB RAM, the suggested amount is 2048 MB or more, and click **Next**.

5. On the **Hard Drive** screen, choose to **Create A Virtual Hard Drive Now,** and click **Create**.

6. On the **Hard Drive File Type** screen, choose **VHD** for compatibility with other virtualization engines, unless you know that you will only use this virtual machine in VirtualBox, and click **Next**.

Figure A-3: Create Virtual Hard Drive

7. On the **Storage On Physical Hard Drive** screen, choose either **Dynamically Allocated** or **Fixed** size(after reading the description), and click **Next**.

8. On the **File Location and Size** screen, unless you desire to allocate more than 8 GB space, click **Create**.

9. Back in the **Main** screen, ensure the Kali VM is selected on the left by double-clicking it, and click **Machine > Settings**.

10. On the **Display** page, select **Enable 3D Acceleration**.

11. On the **Network** page, unless you wish to use a NAT network, choose **Enable Network Adapter > Attached To: Bridged Adapter,** and select the physical

Ethernet adapter you wish to use. This allows you to get updates across the Internet before configuring Wi-Fi.

12. If you want to perform wired promiscuous scanning, set **Promiscuous Mode to Allow All,** and click **OK**.

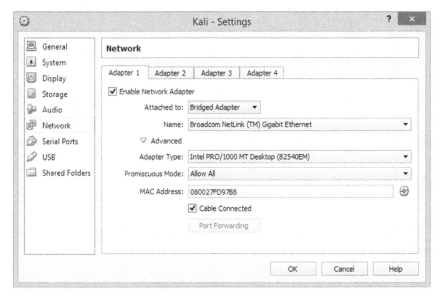

Figure A-4: Kali—Settings

13. On the **Storage** page
    a. choose the **CD-ROM** icon
    b. click the **CD-ROM** icon to the right of the **IDE Secondary Master** field, and
    c. click **Choose a Virtual CD/DVD Disk File**.
14. In the **Please Choose A Virtual Optical disk File** dialog, **navigate** to and **select** the Kali Linux ISO that you previously downloaded, and click **Open**.
15. With the **CD/DVD configured**, click **OK**.

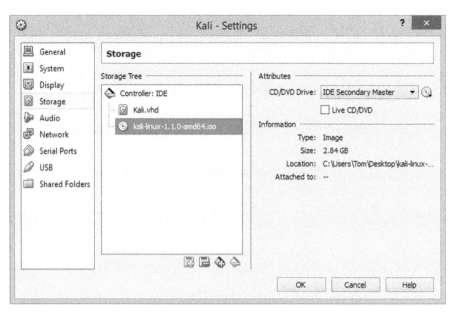

Figure A-5: Kali Settings

16. Click **Machine > Start** to start the VM.
17. When the Kali Linux DVD boots
    a. click in the **Windows** and note that the Right CTRL key releases the mouse from the window and click **Capture**, and
    b. click **Do Not Show This Message Again** when you think you have learned that Right CTRL releases the mouse.
18. Use the **Down Arrow** key to select **Install,** and press **ENTER**.

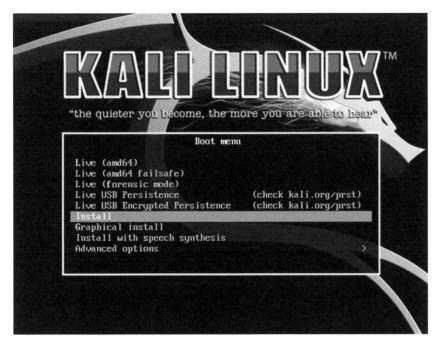

Figure A-6: Kali Linux Screen Print

19. Choose the desired **language** (English for this lab), and press **ENTER**.

20. Choose the **country** of your location, and press **ENTER**.

21. Choose the **keymap** for your language, and press **ENTER**.

22. Enter a **hostname** (this is the same as the Computer Name in Windows—for this lab, consider using simply KALI), and press **ENTER**.

23. In the **Domain Name** field, enter TestWifiSecurityOffline.net or some other domain that you desire, and press **ENTER**.

24. Enter a **Root password** (toor is suggested for this lab), and press **ENTER**.

25. Enter **toor again,** and press **ENTER**.

26. Select your **time zone,** and press **ENTER**.

27. On the **Partition Disks** screen, choose **Guided—Use Entire Disk,** and press **ENTER**.

28. Press **ENTER** to choose the only available disk.

29. Accept the default of **All Files In One Partition,** and press **ENTER**.

30. Press **ENTER** again to commit the disk changes.

31. Press **TAB,** and **ENTER** to commit the changes.

    Wait for the copying process to complete. It can take several minutes to complete the **Installing The System** phase of setup.

32. On the **Configure The Package Manager** screen, choose **Yes** (by pressing ENTER) to use the network mirror, which means you will download the packages from the Internet for installations and updates. Assuming you do not need to enter proxy information, press **TAB** and **ENTER**.

    The installation process now downloads any needed packages from the network mirror. This can take from a few minutes to more than 30 minutes if you have a slower Internet connection or if you are using a very old ISO image.

33. Press **ENTER** to install the GRUB boot loader.

34. On the **Finish The Installation** screen, press **ENTER**.

    The installation is not complete. It removes the live packages and the machine reboots. **The installation is now complete.**

Updating the Kali Linux VM

1. If the KALI VM is not running, start it.
2. When the boot up completes, on the **Kali Logon** screen, click **Other** and logon with the username Root.
3. Use the password of toor that you created during installation.
   You will be taken to the desktop.
4. Click the **Terminal** icon to access a terminal or command prompt.

5. At the prompt, run apt-get update.
   This downloads the most current package list.
6. Now run **apt-get upgrade**.
   This installs updates for all currently installed packages.
7. Press **Y** to begin the download.
   When the process completes, the default Kali Linux installation set is updated to all the latest versions available from the source servers.

```
                          root@KALI: ~                    _ □ ×

File  Edit  View  Search  Terminal  Help
Get:35 http://security.kali.org/kali-security/ kali/updates/main libxml2-dev amd
64 2.8.0+dfsgl-7+wheezy3 [902 kB]
Get:36 http://http.kali.org/kali/ kali/main set all 6.2.0+git20150310-0kali0 [43
.9 MB]
Get:37 http://security.kali.org/kali-security/ kali/updates/main xdg-utils all 1
.1.0~rc1+git20111210-6+deb7u3 [82.5 kB]
Get:38 http://security.kali.org/kali-security/ kali/updates/main ruby1.8-dev amd
64 1.8.7.358-7.1+deb7u2 [910 kB]
Get:39 http://security.kali.org/kali-security/ kali/updates/main ruby1.8 amd64 1
.8.7.358-7.1+deb7u2 [320 kB]
Get:40 http://security.kali.org/kali-security/ kali/updates/main libruby1.8 amd6
4 1.8.7.358-7.1+deb7u2 [2,088 kB]
Get:41 http://security.kali.org/kali-security/ kali/updates/main libruby1.9.1 am
d64 1.9.3.194-8.1+deb7u3 [4,420 kB]
Get:42 http://security.kali.org/kali-security/ kali/updates/main postgresql-9.1
amd64 9.1.15-0+deb7u1 [3,310 kB]
Get:43 http://security.kali.org/kali-security/ kali/updates/main postgresql-clie
nt-9.1 amd64 9.1.15-0+deb7u1 [996 kB]
Get:44 http://security.kali.org/kali-security/ kali/updates/main xserver-xorg-co
re amd64 2:1.12.4-6+deb7u6 [1,766 kB]
Get:45 http://security.kali.org/kali-security/ kali/updates/main libxml2 amd64 2
.8.0+dfsgl-7+wheezy3 [904 kB]
Get:46 http://http.kali.org/kali/ kali/main zaproxy all 2.3.1-0kali2 [71.9 MB]
88% [46 zaproxy 57.1 MB/71.9 MB 80%]                    999 kB/s 30s
```

Figure A-7: root@KALI Screen Print

Connecting a Wireless Adapter to the Kali VM

Not all wireless adapters work with Kali Linux. The Kernel must support the adapter PHYs and the drivers must be available for the chipset. However, many 802.11n adapters work with Kali 1.1 as of late 2016 and more 802.11ac adapters are likely to be supported in the coming months and years. You can search for Kali Linux supported wireless adapter to find many lists of such adapters.

Before you can effectively add USB Wi-Fi adapters to VirtualBox VMs, you need to download and install the VirtualBox 4.3.24 Oracle VM Virtual Box Extension Pack. Download and install this before proceeding into this lab.

1. Start the KALI VM if it is not running.
2. Logon as `root`.
3. Insert the desired and known compatible USB adapter.
4. Wait a moment and
   a. right-click on the USB icon in the VirtualBox status bar, and
   b. select the connected USB adapter.
5. Start a Terminal.
6. Execute `iw phy`. If the adapter is working, you should see output defining the specifications of the chosen adapter.
7. Execute `iwconfig` to see information in summary form.

After the adapter is successfully loaded, you can use airmon-ng and airodump-ng to prepare for captures with Wireshark or to perform various WLAN attacks.

Using VMware Player

As an alternative to VirtualBox, you can use VMware Player, a free virtualization solution from VMware.com, and run one virtual machine at a time. The advantage of VirtualBox is that you can run more than one VM at a time. However, Kali Linux seems to work better in VMware player. Additionally, you can download prepared VMware VMs already loaded with Kali Linux at the Offensive Security website at:

www.offensive-security.com/kali-linux-vmware-arm-image-download

Glossary

A CWNP Universal Glossary

40 MHz Intolerant: A bit potentially set in the 802.11 frame allowing STAs to indicate that 40 MHz channels should not be used in their BSS or in surrounding networks. The bit is processed only in the 2.4GHz band.

4-Way Handshake: The process used to generate encryption keys for unicast frames (Pairwise Transient Key (PTK)) and transmit encryption keys for group (broadcast, multicast) (Group Temporal Key (GTK)) frames using material from the 802.1X/EAP authentication or the pre-shared key (PSK). The PTK and GTK are derived from the Pairwise Master Key (PMK) and Group Master Key (GMK) respectively.

802.11: A standard maintained by the IEEE for implementing and communicating with wireless local area networks (WLANs). Regularly amended, the standard continues to evolve to meet new demands. Several Physical Layer (PHY) methods are specified and the Medium Access Control (MAC) sublayer is also specified.

802.11a: An 802.11 amendment that operates in the 5GHz band. It uses OFDM modulation and is called the OFDM PHY. It can support data rates of up to 54Mbps.

802.11aa: An 802.11 amendment that added support for robust audio and video streaming through MAC enhancements. It specifies a new category of station called a Stream Classification Service (SCS) station. The SCS implementation is optional for a WMM QoS station.

802.11ac: An 802.11 amendment that operates in the 5GHz band. It uses MU-MIMO, beamforming, and 256 QAM technology, up to 8 spatial streams, wider 80 and 160 MHz channels, and OFDM modulation. Support is included for data rates up to 6933.3Mbps.

802.11ae: An 802.11 amendment that provides prioritization of management frames. It defines a new Quality of Service Management Frame (QMF). When the QMF service is used, some management frames may be transmitted using an access category other than the one used for voice (AC_VO). When communicating with stations that do not support the QMF service, the station uses access category AC_VO to transmit management frames. When QMF is supported, the beacon frame includes a QMF Policy element.

802.11ah: An 802.11 draft that specifies operations in the sub-1 GHz range. Frequencies used vary by regulatory domain. The draft supports 1, 2, 4, 8 and 16MHz channels with OFDM modulation.

802.11ax: An 802.11 draft that will support bi-directional MU-MIMO, higher modulation rates and sub-channelization. It is too early to know the final details of this amendment at the time of writing; however, it is planned to operate in the 2.4GHz and 5GHz band.

802.11b: An IEEE 802.11 amendment that operates in the 2.4GHz ISM band. It uses HR/DSSS and earlier technology. It can support data rates of up to 11Mbps.

802.11e: An 802.11 amendment, now incorporated into the most recent rollup, that provided quality of service extensions to the wireless link through probabilistic prioritization based on the contention window. The Wi-Fi Multimedia (WMM) certification is based on this amendment.

802.11g: An IEEE 802.11 amendment that operates in the 2.4GHz ISM band. It uses ERP-OFDM and earlier technology. It can support data rates of up to 54Mbps.

802.11i: An 802.11 amendment, now incorporated into the most recent rollup, which provided security enhancements to the standard and resolved weaknesses in the original WEP encryption solution. It provided for TKIP/RC4 (now deprecated) and CCMP/AES cipher suites and encryption algorithms.

802.11n: An IEEE 802.11 amendment that operates in the 2.4GHz ISM and 5GHz UNII/ISM bands. It uses MIMO, HT-OFDM and earlier technology. It can support data rates of up to 600Mbps.

802.11k: An IEEE 802.11 amendment that specifies and defines WLAN characteristics and mechanisms.

802.11r: An IEEE 802.11 amendment that enables fast-secure roaming between access points using a standardized method.

802.11u: An IEEE 802.11 amendment that adds features for mobile communication devices such as phones and tablets.

802.11w: An IEEE 802.11 amendment to increase security for the management frames.

802.11y: An IEEE 802.11 amendment that allows registered stations to operate at a higher power output in the 3650-3700MHz band.

802.1X: 802.1X is an IEEE standard that uses the Extensible Authentication Protocol (EAP) framework to authenticate devices attempting to connect to the LAN or WLAN. The process involves the use of a supplicant to be authenticated, authenticator, and authentication server.

802.11 State Machine: The 802.11 state machine defines the condition of the connection of a client STA to another STA and can be in one of three states: Unauthenticated/Unassociated, Authenticated/Unassociated, or Authenticated/Associated.

802.3: A set of standards maintained by the IEEE for implementing and communicating with wired Ethernet networks and including Power over Ethernet (PoE) specifications.

AAA Framework: Authentication, Authorization, and Accounting is a framework for monitoring usage, enforcing policies, controlling access to computer resources, and providing the correct billing amount for services.

AAA Server Credential: The AAA server credential is the validation materials used for the server. When mutual authentication is required, a server certificate is typically used as the AAA server credential.

Absorption: Occurs when an obstacle absorbs some or all of a radio wave's energy.

Access Category (AC): An access category is a priority class. 802.11 specifies four different priority classes—voice (AC_VO), video (AC_VI), best effort (AC_BE), and background (AC_BK).

Access Layer Forwarding: Data forwarding that occurs at the access layer, also called *distributed data forwarding*. The data is distributed from the access layer directly to the destination without passing through a centralized controller.

Access Point: An access point (AP) is a device containing a radio that is used to create an access network, bridge network or mesh network. The AP contains the Distribution System Service.

Access Port: An AP used for mesh networks and that connects to the wired or wireless network at the edge of the mesh.

Acknowledgement Frame: A frame sent by the receiving 802.11 station confirming the received data.

Access Control List (ACL): ACLs are lists that inform a STA or user what permissions are available to access files and other resources. ACLs are also used in routers and switches to control packets allowed through to other networks.

Active Mode: A power-save mode in which the station never turns the radio off.

Active Scanning: A scanning (network location) method in which the client broadcasts probe requests and records the probe responses in order to determine the network with which it will establish an association.

Active Survey: A wireless survey conducted on location that involves measuring throughput rates, round trip time, and packet loss by connecting devices to an AP and transmitting data during the survey.

Ad-Hoc Mode: The colloquial name for an Independent Basic Service Set (IBSS). STAs connect directly with each other and an AP is not used.

Adjacent Overlapping Channels: Adjacent overlapping channels are channels whose bands interfere with their neighboring channels on the primary carrier frequencies. Non-overlapping channels are channels whose bands do not interfere with neighboring channels on the primary carrier frequencies.

Adjacent Channel Interference (ACI): ACI occurs when channels near each other (in the frequency domain) interfere with one another due to either partial frequency overlap on primary carrier frequencies or excessive output power.

AES (Advanced Encryption Standard): The encryption cipher used with CCMP and WPA2 providing improved security over WEP/RC4 or TKIP/RC4.

AID: Association ID (AID) is an identification assigned by a wireless STA (AP) to another STA (client) in order to transmit the correct data to that device in an Infrastructure Basic Service Set.

AirTime Fairness: Transmits more frames to client STAs with higher data rates than those with lower data rates so that the STAs get fair access to the air (medium) instead of having to wait for slower data rate STAs.

Aggregated MAC Protocol Data Units (A-MPDU): A-MPDU transmissions are created by transmitting multiple MPDUs as one PHY frame as opposed to A-MSDU transmissions, which are created by passing multiple MSDUs down to the PHY layer as a single MPDU.

Aggregated MAC Service Data Unit (A-MSDU): See *Aggregated MAC Protocol Data Unit.*

Amplification: The process of increasing a signal's power level.

Amplifier: A device intended to increase the power level of a signal.

Amplitude: The power level of a signal.

Antenna: A device that converts electric power into radio waves and radio waves into electric power.

Association: The condition wherein a client STA is linked with an AP for frame transmission through the AP to the network.

Announcement Traffic Indication Message (ATIM): A traffic indication map (sent in a management frame) in an Ad-Hoc (IBSS) network to notify other clients of pending data transfers for power saving purposes.

Attenuation: The loss of signal strength as an RF wave passes through a medium.

Attenuator: A device that intentionally reduces the strength of an RF signal.

Authentication: The process of user or device identity validation.

Authentication and Key Management (AKM): The protocols used to authenticate a client STA on a WLAN and generate encryption key for use in frame encryption.

Authentication Server: The authentication server validates the client before allowing access to the network. In an 802.1X/EAP implementation for WLANs, the authentication server is often a RADIUS server.

Authenticator: The device that provides access to authentication services in order to allow connected devices to access network resources. In an 802.1X/EAP implementation for WLANs, the authenticator is typically the AP or controller.

Automatic Power Save Delivery (APSD): APSD is a power saving method which uses both scheduled (S-APSD) and unscheduled (U-APSD) frame delivery methods. S-APSD sends frames to a power save STA from the AP at a planned time. U-APSD sends frames to a power save STA from the AP when the STA sends a frame to the AP. The frame from the STA is considered a trigger frame.

Autonomous AP: An AP that can perform security functions, RF management, and configuration without the need for a centralized WLAN controller or any other control platform.

Azimuth Chart: A chart showing the radiation pattern of an antenna as viewed from the top of the antenna. Also called an H-Plane Chart or H-Chart.

Backoff timer: The timer used during CSMA/CA to wait for access to the medium, which is selected from the contention window.

Band Steering: A method used by vendors to encourage STAs to connect to the 5GHz band instead of the 2.4GHz band, which is more congested. Typically implemented by ignoring probe requests for some period of time before allowing connection to the 2.4GHz radio by clients known to have a 5GHz radio based on previous connections to the AP or controller.

Bandwidth: The frequencies used for transmission of data. For example, a 20MHz wide channel has 20MHz of bandwidth.

Basic Service Area (BSA): The coverage area provided by an AP wherein client STAs may connect to the AP to transmit data on the WLAN or through the AP to the network.

Basic Service Set (BSS): An AP and its associated STAs. Identified by the BSSID.

Basic Service Set Identification (BSSID): The ID for the BSS. Often the MAC address of the AP STA. When multiple SSIDs are used, another MAC address-like BSSID is generated.

Beacon Frame: A frame transmitted periodically from an AP that indicates the presence of a BSS network and contains capabilities and requirements of the BSS. Also colloquially called a beacon instead of the full phrase, beacon frame.

Beamforming: Directing radio waves to a specific area or device by manipulating the RF waveforms within the different radio chains.

Beamwidth: The width of the radiated signal lobe from the antenna in the intended direction of propagation. It is usually measured at the point where 3dB of loss is experienced.

Bill of materials (BOM): A list of the materials and licenses required to assemble a system, in the case of WLANs, including APs, controllers, PoE injectors, licenses, etc.

Bit: A basic unit of information for computer systems. A bit can have a value of 1 or 0. Used in binary math.

Block Acknowledgement: An acknowledgement frame that groups together multiple ACKs instead of transmitting each individual ACK when a block transmission has been received.

Bridge: A device used to connect two networks. Wireless bridges create the connection across the wireless medium.

BSS Transition: Roaming that occurs between two BSSs that are part of the same ESS.

Byte: A basic unit of information that typically consists of 8 bits. Also called an octet.

Capacity: The number of clients and applications a network or AP can handle.

Captive Portal: Authentication technique that re-routes a user to a special webpage to verify their credentials before allowing access to the network. Commonly used in hotel and guest networks.

Guest Networks: A segregated network that is designed for use by temporary visitors.

CardBus: A PCMCIA PC Card standard interface that supports 32-bits and operates at speeds of up to 33 MHz. It is primarily used in laptops.

Carrier Frequencies: The frequency of a carrier signal or the frequencies used to modulate information.

Carrier Sense Multiple Access (CSMA): CSMA is a protocol that allows a node to detect the presence of traffic before sending data on a shared network. It is used in CSMA/CA.

Carrier Sense Multiple Access with Collision Avoidance (CSMA/CA): CSMA/CA is the method in 802.11 networks in which a node only sends data if the shared network is idle in order to avoid collisions.

CCMP: Counter Cipher Mode with Block Chaining Message Authentication Code Protocol (CCMP) is a key management solution that provides for improved security over WEP.

CCMP/AES: CCMP used with AES, as it is in 802.11 networks, is a key management and encryption protocol that provides more security than WEP. It is based on the AES standard and uses a 128 bit key and 128 bit block size.

Centralized Forwarding: Every forwarding decision is made by a centralized forwarding engine, such as the WLAN controller.

Certificate Authority (CA): A server that validates the authenticity of a certificate used in authentication and encryption systems. The CA may issue certificates or it may authorize other servers to do the same.

CompactFlash (CF): Originally produced in 1994 by SanDisk, CF is a flash memory mass storage device format that can support up to 256 GB. CF devices can also function as 802.11 WLAN adapters.

Channel: A specified range of frequencies used in the 802.11 standard used by devices to communicate on the network. Channels are commonly 20, 40, 80 and 160MHz in width in WLANs. Newer standards will support 1, 2, 4, 8 and 16MHz channels in sub-1 GHz networks.

Channel Width: The range of frequencies a single channel encompasses.

Clear Channel Assessment (CCA): CCA is a feature defined in the IEEE 802.11 standard that allows a client to determine idle or busy state of the medium based on energy levels of a frame or raw energy levels as specified in each PHY.

Client Utilities: Software installed on devices that allows the device to connect to, authenticate with and participate in a WLAN.

Co-Channel Interference (CCI): Congestion cause by the normal operations of CSMA/CA when multiple BSSs exist on the same channel. Commonly called co-channel congestion (CCC) today as well.

Collision Avoidance (CA): A method in which devices attempt to avoid simultaneous data transmissions in order to prevent frame collisions. Used in CSMA/CA.

Coding: A process used to encode bits to be transmitted on the wireless medium such that error recovery can be achieved. Part of forward error correction (FEC) and defined in the modulation and coding schemes (MCSs) from 802.11n forward.

Containment: A process used against a detected rogue AP to prevent any connected clients from accessing the network.

Contention Window: A number range defined in the 802.11 standard and varying by QoS category from which a number is selected at random for the backoff timer in the CSMA/CA process.

Control Frame: An 802.11 frame that is used to control the communications process on the wireless medium. Control frames include, RTS frames, CTS frames, PS-Poll frames, and ACK frames.

Controlled Port: In an 802.1X authentication system, the virtual port that allows all frames through to the network, but only after authentication is completed.

Controller-Based AP: An AP managed by a centralized controller device. Also called a lightweight AP or thin AP.

Coverage: 1) The colloquial term used for the BSA of an AP. 2) The requirement of available WLAN connectivity throughout a facility, campus or area. Often specified in minimum signal strength as dBm; for example, -67 dBm.

Clear-to-Send (CTS) Frame: A CTS frame sent from one STA to another to indicate that the other STA can transmit on the medium. The duration value in the CTS frame is used to silence all other STAs by setting their NAV timers.

Data Frame: An 802.11 frame specified for use in carrying data based on the general frame format. Also used for some signaling purposes as null data frames.

Data Rate: The rate at which data is sent across the wireless medium. Typically represented as megabits per second (Mbps) or gigabits per second (Gbps). The data rate should not be confused with throughput rate, which is a measurement of Layer 4 throughput or useful user data.

dBd (decibel to dipole): A relative measurement of antenna gain compared to a dipole antenna. Calculated as 2.14 dB greater than dBi because a dipole antenna already has 2.14 dBi gain. For example, an antenna with 0dBd gain has 2.14dBi gain.

dBi (decibel to isotropic): A relative measurement of antenna gain compared to a theoretical isotropic radiator. When necessary, calculated as 2.14 dB less than dBd.

dBm (decibel to milliwatt): An absolute measurement of the power of an RF signal based on the definition of 0 dBm = 1 milliwatt (mW).

Distributed Coordination Function (DCF): A protocol defined in 802.11 that uses carrier sensing, backoff timers, interframe spaces and frame duration values to diminish collisions on the wireless medium.

Elevation Chart: A chart showing the radiation pattern of an antenna as viewed from the side antenna. Also called an E-Plane Chart or E-Chart.

Deauthentication Frame: A notification frame sent from an 802.11 STA to another STA in order to terminate a connection between them.

Decibel (dB): A logarithmic, relative unit used when measuring antenna gain, signal attenuation, and signal-to-noise ratios. Strictly defined as 1/10 of a bel.

Delay: The time it takes for a bit of data to travel from one node to another. Also called latency.

Delivery Traffic Indication Message (DTIM): A message sent from an AP to clients in the Beacon frame indicating that it has data to transmit to the clients specified by the AIDs.

Differentiated Services Code Point (DSCP): A Layer 3 QoS marking system. IP packets can include DSCP markings in the headers. Eight precedence levels, 0-7, are defined.

Diffraction: The bending of waves around a very large object in relation to the wave.

Direct-Sequence Spread Spectrum (DSSS): A modulation technique where data is coupled with coding that spreads the data across a wide frequency range. Provides 1 or 2 Mbps data rates in 802.11 networks.

Disassociation Frame: A frame sent from one STA to another in order to terminate the association.

Distributed Forwarding: See *Access Layer Forwarding*. Also called, *distributed data forwarding*.

Distribution System (DS): The system that connects a set of BSSs and LANs such that an ESS is possible.

Distribution System Medium (DSM): The medium used to interconnect APs through the DS such that they can communicate with each other for ESS operations using either wired or wireless for the DS connection.

Domain Name System (DNS): A protocol and service that provides host name resolution (looking up the IP address of a given host name) and recursive IP address lookups (finding the host name of a known IP address). Also, colloquially used to reference the server that provides DNS lookups.

Driver: Software that allows a computer to interact with a hardware device such as a WLAN adapter.

Duty Cycle: A measure of the time a radio is transmitting or a channel is consumed by a transmitting device.

Dynamic Frequency Selection (DFS): A setting on radios that dynamically changes the channel selection based on detected interference from radar systems. Many 5 GHz channels require DFS operations.

Dynamic Rate Switching (DRS): The process of reducing a client's data rate as frame transmission failures occur or signal strength decreases. DRS results in lower data rates but fewer transmissions required to successfully transmit a frame.

Encryption: The process of converting data into a form that unauthorized users cannot understand by encoding the data with an algorithm and a key or keys.

Enhanced Distributed Channel Access (EDCA): An enhancement to DCF introduced in 802.11e that implements priority based queuing for transmissions in 802.11 networks based on access categories.

Equivalent Isotropically Radiated Power (EIRP): The output power required of an isotropic radiator to equal the measured power output from an antenna in the intended direction of propagation.

Extended Rate Physical (ERP): A physical layer technology introduced in 802.11g that uses OFDM (from 802.11a) in the 2.4GHz band and offers data rates up to 54Mbps.

Extended Service Set (ESS): A group of one or more BSSs that are interconnected by a DS.

Extensible Authentication Protocol (EAP): An authentication framework that defines message formats for authentication exchanges used by 802.1X WLAN authentication solutions.

Fade Margin: An amount of signal strength, in dB, added to a link budget to ensure proper operations.

Fast Fourier Transform (FFT): A mathematical algorithm that takes in a waveform as represented in the time or space domain and shows it in the frequency domain. Used in spectrum analyzers to show real-time views in the frequency domain (Real-time FFT).

Fragmentation: The process of fragmenting 802.11 frames based on the fragmentation threshold configured. Fragmented frames have a greater likelihood of successful delivery in the presence of sporadic interference.

Frame Aggregation: A feature in the IEEE 802.11n PHY and later PHYs that increases throughput by sending more than one frame in a single transmission. Aggregated MSDUs or aggregated MPDUs may be supported.

Frame: A well-defined, meaningful set of bits used to communicate management and control information on a network or transfer payloads from higher layers. Frames are defined at the MAC and PHY layer.

Free Space Path Loss: The natural loss of amplitude that occurs in an RF signal as it propagates through space and the wave front spreads.

Fresnel Zones: Ellipsoid shaped zones around the visual LoS in a wireless link. The first Fresnel zone should be 60% clear and would preferably be 80% clear to allow for environmental changes.

Frequency: The speed at which a waveform cycles in a second.

Full Duplex: A communication system that allows an endpoint to send data to the network at the same time as it receives data from the network.

Gain: The increase in signal strength in a particular direction. Can be accomplished passively by directing energy into a smaller area or actively by increasing the strength of the broadcasted signal before it is sent to the antenna.

Group Key Handshake: Used to transfer the GTK among STAs in an 802.11 network if the GTK requires updating. Initiated by the AP/controller in a BSS.

Group Master Key (GMK): Used to generate the GTK for encryption of broadcast and multicast frames and is unique to each BSS.

Group Temporal Key (GTK): Used to encryption broadcast and multicast frames and is unique to each BSS.

Guard Interval (GI): A period of time between symbols within a frame used to avoid intersymbol interference.

Half Duplex: A communication system that allows only sending or receiving data by an endpoint at any given time.

Hidden Node: The problem that arises when nodes cannot receive each other's frames, which can lead to packet collisions and retransmissions.

High Density: A phrase referencing a WLAN network type that is characterized by large numbers of devices requiring access.

Highly-Directional Antenna: An antenna, such as a parabolic dish or grid antenna, that has a high gain in a specified direction and a low beamwidth measurement as compared to semi-directional and omni-directional antennas.

High Rate Direct Sequence Spread Spectrum (HR/DSSS): An amendment-based PHY (802.11b) that increase the data rate in 2.4 GHz from the original 1 or 2Mbps to 5.5 and 11Mbps while maintaining backward compatibility with 1 and 2Mbps.

High Throughput (HT): An amendment-based PHY (802.11n) that increased the data rate up to 600Mbps and added support for transmit beamforming and MIMO.

Hotspot: A term referencing a wireless network connection point that is typically open to the public or to paid subscribers.

Independent Basic Service Set (IBSS): A set of 802.11 devices operating in ad-hoc (peer-to-peer) mode without the use of an AP.

Institute of Electrical and Electronics Engineers (IEEE): A standardization organization that develops standard for multiple industries including the networking industry with standard such as 802.3, 802.11 and 802.16.

Intentional Radiator: Any device that is purposefully sending radio waves. Signal strength of the intentional radiator is measured at the point where energy enters the radiating antennas.

Interference: In WLANs, an RF signal or incidental RF energy that is radiated in the same frequencies as the WLAN and that has sufficient amplitude and duty cycle to prevent 802.11 frames from successful delivery.

Interframe Space (IFS): A time interval that must exist between frames. Varying lengths are used in 802.11 and a references as DIFS, SIFS, EIFS, and AIFS in common use.

Internet Engineering Task Force (IETF): An open group of volunteers develops Internetworking standards through request for comments (RFC) documents. Examples include RADIUS, EAP, and DNS.

Isotropic Radiator: A theoretical antenna that spreads the radiation equally in every direction as a sphere. None exist in reality, but the concept is used to measure relative antenna gain in dBi.

Jitter: The variance in delay between packets sent on a network. Excessive jitter can result in poor quality for real-time applications such as voice and video.

Jumbo Frame: An Ethernet frame that contains more than 1500 bytes of payload and up to 9000 to 9216 bytes.

Latency: The time taken data to move between places. Typically synonymous with delay in computer networking.

Layer 1: The physical layer (PHY) that is responsible for framing and transmitting bits on the medium. In 802.3 and 802.11 the entirety of Layer 1 is defined.

Layer 2: The data-link layer that deals with data frames moving within a local area network (LAN). In 802.3 and 802.11, the MAC sublayer of Layer 2 is defined.

Layer 3: The network layer where packets of data are routed between sender and receiver. Most modern networks use Internet Protocol (IP) at Layer 3.

Layer 4: The transport layer where segmentation occurs for upper layer data and TCP (connection oriented) and UDP (connectionless) are the most commonly used protocols.

Lightning Arrestor: A device that can redirect ambient energy from a lightning strike away from attached equipment.

Line of sight (LoS): When existing, the visual path between to ends. RF LoS is different from visual LoS. RF LoS does not require the same clear path for the remote receiver to hear the signal. When creating bridge links, visual LoS is often the starting point.

Link Budget: The measurement of gains and losses through an intentional radiator, antenna and over a transmission medium.

Loss: The reduction in the amplitude of a signal.

MAC filtering: A common setting that only allows specific MAC addresses onto a network. Ineffective against knowledgeable attackers because the MAC address can be spoofed to impersonate authorized devices.

Management Frame: A frame type defined in the 802.11 standard that encompasses frames used to manage access to the network including beacon, probe request, prober response, authentication, association, reassociation, deauthentication, and disassociation frames.

Master Session Key (MSK): A key derived between an EAP client and EAP server and exported by the EAP method. Used to derive the PMK, which is used to derive the PTK. The MSK is used in 802.1X/EAP authentication implementations. In personal authentication implementations, the PMK is derived from the preshared key.

Maximal Ratio Combining (MRC): A method of increasing the signal-to-noise ratio (SNR) by combining signals received on multiple radio chains (multiple antennas and radios).

Mesh: A network that uses interconnecting devices to form a redundant set of connections offering multiple paths through the network. 802.11s defined mesh for 802.11 networks.

Mesh BSS: A basic service set that forms a self-contained network of mesh stations.

milliwatt (mW): A unit of electrical energy used in measuring output power of RF signals in WLANs. A mW is equal to 1/1000 of a watt (W).

Mobile User: A user that physically moves while connected to the network. The opposite of a stationary user.

Modulation: The process of changing a wave by changing its amplitude, frequency, and/or phase such that the changes represent data bits.

Modulation and Coding Scheme (MCS): Term used to describe the combination of the radio modulation scheme and the coding scheme used when transmitting data, first introduced in 802.11n.

MPDU: A MAC protocol data unit (MPDU) is a portion of data to be delivered to a MAC layer peer on a network and it is data prepared for the PHY layer by the MAC sublayer. The MAC sublayer receives the MSDU from upper layers on transmission and creates the MPDU. It receives the MPDU from the lower layer on receiving instantiation and removes the MAC header and footer to create the MSDU for the upper layers.

MSDU: A MAC service data unit is a portion of transmitted data to be handled by the MAC sublayer that has yet to be encapsulated into a MAC Layer frame.

Maximum Transmission Unit (MTU): The largest amount of data that can be sent at a particular layer of the OSI model. Typically set at layer 4 for TCP.

Multi-User MIMO (MU-MIMO): An enhancement to MIMO that allows the AP STA to transmit to multiple client STAs simultaneously.

Multipath: The phenomenon that occurs when multiple copies of the same signal reach a receiver based on RF behaviors in the environment.

Multiple Channel Architecture (MCA): A wireless network design using multiple channels strategically designed so that the implemented BSSs have minimal interference with one another.

Multiple Input/Multiple Output (MIMO): A technology used to spread a stream of data bits across multiple radio chains using spatial multiplexing at the transmitter and to recombine these streams at the receiver.

Narrowband Interference: Interference that covers a very narrow band of frequencies and typically not the full with of an 802.11 channel when used in reference to WLAN interferers.

Near-Far: A problem that occurs when a high powered device is very close to the AP in a BSS and a low powered device is very far from the AP, thus causing the AP to not hear the far station that otherwise would be heard. Most near-far problems are addressed with standard CSMA/CA operations in 802.11 networks.

Network Allocation Vector (NAV): The NAV is a virtual carrier sense mechanism used in CSMA/CA to avoid collisions and is a timer set based on the duration values in frames transmitted on the medium.

Network Segmentation: The process used to separate a larger network into smaller networks often utilizing Layer 3 routers or multi-layer switches.

Noise: RF energy in the environment that is not part of the intentional signal of your WLAN.

Noise Floor: The amount of noise that is consistently present in the environment, which is typically measured in dBm.

Network Time Protocol (NTP): A protocol used to synchronize clocks in devices using centralized time servers.

Octet: A group of eight ones and zeros. An 8-bit byte. Sometimes simply called a byte.

Orthogonal Frequency Division Multiplexing (OFDM): A modulation technique and a named physical layer in 802.11 that provides data rates up to 54Mbps and operates in the 5GHz band. The modulation is used in all bands, but the named PHY operates only in the 5GHz band.

Omni-Directional Antenna: An antenna that propagates in all directions (360 degrees) horizontally. Creates a coverage area similar to a donut shape (toroidal).

Dipole Antenna: An antenna that propagates in all directions (360 degrees) horizontally. Creates a coverage area similar to a donut (toroidal) shape. It is an omni-directional type antenna.

Open System Authentication: A simple frame exchange, providing no real authentication, used to move through the state machine in relation to the connection between two 802.11 STAs.

Opportunistic Key Caching (OKC): A roaming solution for WLANs wherein the keys derived from the 802.1X/EAP authentication are cached on the AP or controller such that only the 4-way handshake is required at the time of roaming.

OSI (Open Systems Interconnection) Model: A theoretical model for communication systems that works by separating the communications process into seven, well-defined layers. The seven layers are Application, Presentation, Session, Transport, Network, Data Link and Physical.

Packet: Data as represented at the network layer (Layer 4) for TCP communications.

Passive Gain: An increase in strength of a signal by focusing the signal's energy rather than increasing the actual energy available, such as with an amplifier.

Passive scanning: A scanning (network location) method wherein a STA waits to receive beacon frames from an AP which contain information about the WLAN.

Passive survey: A survey conducted on location that gathers information about RF interference, signal strength and coverage areas by monitoring RF activity without active communications.

Passphrase Authentication: A type of access control that uses a phrase as the pass key. Also called personal in WPA and WPA2.

Phase: A measurement of the variance in arrival state between to copies of a wave form. Waves are said to be in phase or out of phase by some degree. The phase can be manipulated for modulation.

PHY: A shorthand notation for physical layer which is the physical means of communication on a network to transmit bits.

Physical (PHY) Layer: The physical (PHY) layer refers to the physical means by which a message is communicated. Layer one of the OSI model.

PLCP: Physical Layer Convergence Protocol (PLCP) is the name of the service within the PHY that receives data from the upper layers and sends data to the upper layers. It is the interaction point with the MAC sublayer.

PMD: Physical Medium Dependent (PMD) is the service within the PHY responsible for sending and receiving bits on the RF medium.

PMK Caching: Stores the PMK so a device only has to perform the 4 way handshake when connecting to an AP to which it has already connected.

Pairwise master Key (PMK): The key derived from the MSK, which is generated during 802.1X/EAP authentication. Used to derive the PTK. Used in unidirectional communications with a single peer.

PoE Injector: Any device that adds Power over Ethernet (PoE) to Ethernet cables. Come in two variants, endpoint (such as switches) and midspan (such as inline injectors).

Point-to-Multipoint (PtMP): A connection between a single point and multiple other points for wireless bridging or WLAN access.

Point-to-Point (PtP): A connection between two points often used to connect two networks via bridging.

Polarization: The technical term used to reference the orientation of antennas related to the electric field in the electromagnetic wave.

Power over Ethernet (PoE): A method of providing power to certain hardware devices that can be powered across the Ethernet cables. Specified in 802.3 as a standard. Various classes are defined based on power requirements.

PPDU: PLCP Protocol Data Unit (PPDU) is the prepared bits for transmission on the wired or wireless medium. Sometimes also called a PHY Layer frame.

Preauthentication: Authenticating with an AP to which the STA is not intending to immediately connect so that roaming delays are reduced.

Pre-shared Key (PSK): Refers to any security protocol that uses a password or passphrase or string as the key from which encryption materials are derived.

Primary Channel: When implementing channels wider than 20MHz in 802.11n and 802.11ac, the 20MHz channel on which management and control frames are sent and the channel used by STAs not supporting the wider channel.

Probe Request: A type of frame sent when a client device wants information about APs in the area or is seeking a specific SSID to which it desires to connect.

Probe Response: A type frame sent in response to a probe request that contains information about the AP and the requirements of BSSs it provides.

Protected Management Frame (PMF): Frames used for managing a wireless network that are protected from spoofing using encryption. Protocol defined in the 802.11w amendment.

Protocol Analyzer: Hardware or software used to capture and analyze networking communications. WLAN protocol analyzers have the ability to capture 802.11 frames from the RF medium and decode them for display and analysis.

Protocol Decodes: The way information in captured packets or frames is interpreted for display and analysis.

PSDU: PLCP Service Data Unit (PSDU) is the name for the contents that are contained within the PPDU, the PLCP Protocol Data Unit. It is the same as the MPDU as perceived and received by the PHY.

PTK (Pairwise Transient Key): A key derived during the 4-way handshake and used for encryption only between two specific endpoints, such as an AP and a single client.

Quality of Service (QoS): Traffic prioritization and other techniques used to improve the end-user experience. IEEE 802.11e includes QoS protocols for wireless networks based on access categories.

QoS BSS: A BSS supporting 802.11e QoS features.

Radio Chains: A reference to the radio and antenna used together to transmit in a given frequency range. Multi-stream devices have multiple radio chains as one radio chain is required for each stream.

Radio Frequency (RF): The electromagnetic wave frequency range used in WLANs and many other wireless communication systems.

Radio Resource Management (RRM): Automatic management of various RF characteristics like channel selection and output power. Known by different terms among the many WLAN vendors, but referencing the same basic capabilities.

RADIUS: Remote Authentication Dial-In User Service (RADIUS) refers to a network protocol that handles AAA management which allows for authentication, authorization and accounting (auditing). Used in 802.11 WLANs as the authentication server in an 802.1X/EAP implementation.

RC4 (Rivest Cipher 4): An encryption cipher used in WEP and with TKIP. A stream cipher.

Real-Time Location Service (RTLS): A function provided by many WLAN infrastructure and overlay solutions allowing for device location based on triangulation and other algorithms.

Reassociation: The process used to associate with another AP in the same ESS. May also be used when a STA desires to reconnect to an AP to which it was formerly connected.

Received Channel Power Indicator (RCPI): Introduced in 802.11k, a power measurement calculated as INT((dBm + 110) * 2). Expected accuracy is +/- 5 dB. Ranges from 0-220 are available with 0 equaling or less than -110 dBm and 220 equaling or greater than 0 dBm. The value is calculated as an average of all received chains during the reception of the data portion of the transmission. All PHYs support RCPI and, though 802.11ac does not explicitly list its formulation, it references the 802.11n specification for calculation procedures.

Received Signal Strength Indicator (RSSI): A relative measure of signal strength for a wireless network. The method to measure RSSI is not standardized though it is constrained to a limited number of values in the 802.11 standard. Many use the term RSSI to reference dBm, and the 802.11 standard uses terms like DataFrameRSSI and BeaconRSSI and defines them as the signal strength in dBm of the specified frames, so the common vernacular is understandable. However, according to the standard, "absolute accuracy of the RSSI reading is not specified" (802.11-2012, Clause 14.3.3.3).

Reflection: An RF behavior that occurs when a wave meets a reflective obstacle larger than the wavelength, similar to light waves in a mirror.

Refraction: An RF behavior that occurs as an RF wave passes through material causing a bending of the wave and possible redirection of the wave front.

Regulatory Domain: A reference to geographic regions management by organizations like the FCC and ETSI that determine the allowed frequencies, output power levels and systems to be used in RF communications.

Remote AP: An AP designed to be implemented at a remote location and managed across a WAN link using special protocols.

Resolution Bandwidth (RBW): The smallest frequency that can be extracted from a received signal by a spectrum analyzer or the configuration of that frequency. Many spectrum analyzers allow for the adjustment of the RBW within the supported range of the analyzer.

Retry: That which occurs when a frame fails to be delivered successfully. A bit set in the frame to specify that it is a repeated attempt at delivery.

Return Loss: A measure of how much power is lost in delivery from a transmission line to an antenna.

RF Cables: A cable, typically coaxial, that allows for the transmission of electromagnetic waves between a transceiver and an antenna.

RF Calculator: A software application used to perform calculations related to RF signal strength values.

RF Connector: A component used to connect RF cables, antennas and transmitters. RF connectors come in many standardized forms and should match in type and resistance.

RF Coverage: Synonymous with coverage in WLAN vernacular. Reference to the BSA provided by an AP.

RF Link: An established connection between two radios.

RF Line of Sight (LoS): The existence of a path, possibly including reflections, refractions and pass-through of materials, between two RF transceivers.

RF Propagation: The process by which RF waves move throughout an area including reflection, refraction, scattering, diffraction, absorption, and free space path loss.

RF Signal Splitter: An RF component that splits the RF signal with a single input and multiple outputs. Historically used with some antenna arrays, but less common today in WLAN implementations.

RF Site Survey: The process of physically measuring the RF signals within an area to determine resulting RF behavior and signal strength. Often performed as a validation procedure after implementation based on a predictive model.

Roaming: That which occurs when a wireless STA moves from one AP to another either because of end user mobility or changes in the RF coverage.

Robust Security Network (RSN): A network that supports CCMP/AES or WPA2 and optionally TKIP/RC4 or WPA. To be an RSN, the network must support only RSN Associations (RSNAs), which are only those associations that use the 4-way handshake. WEP is not supported in an RSN.

Robust Security Network Association (RSNA): An association between a client STA and an AP that was established through authentication resulting in a 4-way handshake to derive unicast keys and transfer group keys. WEP is not supported in an RSNA.

Rogue Access Point: An access point that is connected to a network without permission from a network administrator or other official.

Rogue Containment: Procedures used to prevent clients from associating with a rogue AP or to prevent the rogue AP from communicating with the wired network.

Rogue Detection: Procedures used to identify rogue devices. May include simple identification of unclassified APs or algorithmic processes that identify likely rogues.

Role-Based Access Control (RBAC): An authorization system that assigns permissions and rights based on user roles. Similar to group management of authorization policies.

RSN Information Element: A portion of the beacon frame that specifies the security used on the WLAN.

Request to Send/Clear to Send (RTS/CTS): A frame exchange used to clear the channel before transmitting a frame in order to assist in the reduction of collisions on the medium. Also used as a backward compatible protection mechanism.

RTS Threshold: The minimum size of a frame required to use RTS/CTS exchanges before transmission of the frame.

S-APSD: See *Automatic Power Save Delivery*.

Scattering: An RF behavior that occurs when an RF wave encounters reflective obstacles that are smaller than the wavelength. The result is multiple reflections or scattering of the wave front.

Secondary Channel: When implementing channels wider than 20MHz in 802.11n and 802.11ac, the second channel used to form a 40MHz channel for data frame transmissions to and from supporting client STAs.

Semi-Directional Antenna: An antenna such as a yagi or a patch that has a propagation pattern which maximizes gain in a given direction rather than an omni-directional pattern, having a larger beamwidth than highly directional antennas.

Service Set Identifier (SSID): The BSS and ESS name used to identify WLAN. Conventionally made to be readable by humans. Maximum of 32 bytes long.

Signal Strength: A measure of the amount of RF energy being received by a radio. Often specified as the RSSI, but referenced in dBm, which is not the proper definition of RSSI from the 802.11 standard.

Single Channel Architecture (SCA): A WLAN architecture that places all APs on the same channel and uses a centralized controller to determine when each AP can transmit a frame. No control of client transmissions to the network is provided.

Single Input Single Output (SISO): A radio transmitter that supports one radio chain and can send and receive only a single stream of bits.

Signal to Noise Ratio (SNR): A comparison between the received signal strength and the noise floor. Typically presented in dB. For example, given a noise floor of -95 dBm and a signal strength of -70 dBm, the SNR is 25 dB.

Space-Time Block Coding (STBC): The use of multiple streams of the same data across multiple radio chains to improve reliability of data transfer through redundancy.

Spatial Multiplexing (SM): Used with MIMO technology to send multiple spatial streams of data across the channel using multiple radio chains (radios coupled with antennas).

Spatial Multiplexing Power Save (SMPS): A power saving feature from 802.11n that allows a station to use only one radio (or spatial stream).

Spatial Streams: The partitioning of a stream of data bits into multiple streams transmitted simultaneously by multiple radio chains in an AP or client STA.

Spectrum Analysis: The inspection of raw RF energy to determine activity in an area on monitored frequencies. Useful in troubleshooting and design planning.

Spectrum Analyzer: A hardware and software solution that allows the inspection of raw RF energy.

Station (STA): Any device that can use IEEE 802.11 protocol. Includes both APs and clients.

Supplicant: In 802.1X, the device attempting to be authenticated. Also the term used for the client software on a device that is capable of connecting to a WLAN.

Sweep Cycle: The time it takes a spectrum analyzer to sweep across the frequencies monitored. Often a factor of the number of frequencies scanned and the RBW.

System Operating Margin (SOM): The actual positive difference in the required link budget for a bridge link to operate properly and the received signal strength in the link.

Temporal Key Integrity Protocol (TKIP): The authentication and key management protocol supported by WPA systems and implemented as an interim solution between WEP and CCMP.

Transition Security Network (TSN): A network that allows WEP connections during the transition period over to more secure protocols and an eventual RSN. An RSN does not allow WEP connections.

Transmit Beamforming (TxBF): The use of multiple antennas to transmit a signal strategically with varying phases so that the communication arrives at the receiver such that the signal strength is increased.

Transmit Power Control (TPC): A process implemented in WLAN devices allowing for the output power to be adjusted according to local regulations or by an automated management system.

U-APSD: See *Automatic Power Save Delivery*.

Uncontrolled Port: In an 802.1X authentication system, the virtual port that allows only authentication frames/packets through to the network and, when authentication is successfully completed, provides the 802.1X service with the needed information to open the controlled port.

User Priority (UP): A value (from 0-7) assigned to prioritize traffic that correspond to different access categories for WMM QoS.

Virtual Carrier Sense: The 802.11 standard currently defines the Network Allocation Vector (NAV) for use in virtual carrier sensing. The NAV is set based on the duration value in perceived frames within the channel.

Voltage Standing Wave Ratio (VSWR): The Voltage Standing Wave Ratio is the ratio between the voltage at the maximum and minimum points of a standing wave.

Milliwatt: One thousandth of a watt. A common measurement for output power in WLAN devices.

Watt: A unit of power. Strictly defined as the energy consumption rate of one joule per second such that 1 W is equal to 1 joule per 1 second.

Wavelength: The distance between two repeating points on a wave. Wavelength is a factor of the frequency and the constant of the speed of light.

Wired Equivalent Privacy (WEP): A legacy method of security defined in the original IEEE 802.11 standard in 1997. Used the RC4 cipher like TKIP (WPA), but implemented it poorly. WEP is deprecated and should no longer be used.

Wi-Fi Alliance: An association that certifies WLAN equipment to interoperate based on selected portions of the 802.11 standard and other standards. Certifications include those based on each PHY as well as QoS and security.

Wi-Fi Multimedia (WMM): A QoS certification created and tested by the Wi-Fi Alliance using traffic prioritizing methods defined in the IEEE 802.11e.

Wi-Fi Multimedia Power Save (WMM-PS): A power saving certification designed by the Wi-Fi Alliance and optimized for mobile devices and implementing methods designated in the IEEE 802.11e amendment.

Wireless Intrusion Prevention System (WIPS): A system used to detect and prevent unwanted intrusions in a WLAN by detecting and preventing rogue APs and other WLAN threats.

Wireless Local Area Network (WLAN): A local area network that connects devices using wireless signals based on the 802.11 protocol rather than wires and the common 802.3 protocol.

WPA-Enterprise: A security protocol designed by the Wi-Fi Alliance. Requires an 802.1X authentication server. Uses the TKIP encryption protocol with the RC4 cipher. Implements a portion of 802.11i and the older, non-deprecated TKIP/RC4 solution.

WPA-Personal: A security protocol designed by the Wi-Fi Alliance. Does not require an authentication server. Uses the TKIP encryption protocol with the RC4 cipher. Also known as WPA-PSK (Pre-Shared Key).

WPA2-Enterprise: A security protocol designed by the Wi-Fi Alliance. Requires an 802.1X authentication server. Uses the CCMP key management protocol with the AES cipher. Also known as WPA2-802.1X. Implements the non-deprecated portion of 802.11i.

WPA2-Personal: A security protocol designed by the Wi-Fi Alliance. Does not require an authentication server. Uses the CCMP key management protocol with the AES cipher. Also known as WPA2-PSK (Pre-Shared Key).

Wi-Fi Protected Setup (WPS): A standard designed by the Wi-Fi Alliance to secure a network without requiring much user knowledge. Users connect either by entering a

PIN associated with the device or by Push-Button which allows users to connect when a real or virtual button is pushed.

Index

CPSIA information can be obtained
at www.ICGtesting.com
Printed in the USA
BVHW02s1647310518
517845BV00008B/59/P